THEORETICAL AND PRACTICAL

INTRODUCTION TO FORENSIC MEDICINE

BEAR & BEE

BLUEROSE PUBLISHERS
India | U.K.

Copyright © Bear and Bee (Abinath.A.G) 2024

All rights reserved by author. No part of this publication may be reproduced, stored in a retrieval system, or transmitted in any form or by any means, electronic, mechanical, photocopying, recording or otherwise, without the prior permission of the author. Although every precaution has been taken to verify the accuracy of the information contained herein, the publisher assumes no responsibility for any errors or omissions. No liability is assumed for damages that may result from the use of information contained within.

BlueRose Publishers takes no responsibility for any damages, losses, or liabilities that may arise from the use or misuse of the information, products, or services provided in this publication.

For permissions requests or inquiries regarding this publication, please contact:

BLUEROSE PUBLISHERS
www.BlueRoseONE.com
info@bluerosepublishers.com
+91 8882 898 898
+4407342408967

ISBN: 978-93-6452-798-9

Cover design: Shivani
Typesetting: Sagar

First Edition: September 2024

Acknowledgement:

Thank you, divine spirit my story of the universe

I am grateful for a member of friends and well wishers in encouraging me to start the work and finally to publish it

Our Thannking hearts also goes to **Prof. Dr.Chandrasekar**[DA., MD.,] and Associate professor **Dr. Sadhasivam** [DV.,MD.,] from Madurai medical college for Pictures and guidance.

Co - authors:

A Special word of gratitude who has written on several chapters and helping me develop my ideas for showing confidence in my work.

1) Arun kishor.K from KAPV govt medical college trichy belongs to batch Wyvernz'21 helps in writing the chapter named Identification.

2) Jai pradeep.J from KAPV govt medical college belongs to batch Wyvernz'21 wrote chapter named Forensic science laboratory and Medicolegal Aspects of wounds.

3) Dhinesh.I from Madurai medical college belongs to batch Adhveeraz'21 wrote chapters named Mechanical injuries and Death and it's causes

4) Vaitheeswaran.B From Dindigul govt medical college belongs to batch Cardeanz'21 wrote chapters named Postmortem changes and Thermal deaths

5) Dhanasekar from Kanyakumari govt medical college wrote Chapter named Regional injuries.

I am extremely grateful to **Mrs.E.Pushpalakshmi,** [M.A, B.Ed] & **Mr.S.Baskaran** [M.A] for rectifying Grammatical errors .

I would also like to express my genuine gratitude to our Bear and Bee committee members for their help and good wishes for the completion of this book.

President: Arun kishor.k

Vice president: Dhinesh.I

Dir of publishing organisation: Gopika.B

Dir.of. implementation: Samrish sivaram.J.R

Dir.of. cultural events: Yohalakshmi.V

Dir.of.financial ministry:

Jaipradeep.J

Finally, I would like to acknowledge with gratitude the support of my mother and the support of my love who died accidentally in my past, and my writing works which I'm going leave in this world denotes the quote that 'love can create and it never destroys'.

They kept me going, and this book would not have been possible without them.

      This book is a simple and concise presentation of THEORY AND PRACTICAL ASPECTS OF FORENSIC MEDICINE. I appreciate the sincere and hard works behind this presentation, all the more from a student. This presentation will be helpful for quick review for undergraduate students. I am glad the younger generation takes a keen interest in medico legal works which I am sure will play a crucial role in the near future. I wish a successful and bright future for the author in his future endeavors.

PROFESSOR AND HEAD,
DEPARTMENT OF FORENSIC MEDICINE,
MADURAI MEDICAL COLLEGE, MADURAI.
Professor & HOD
District Police Surgeon
Dept. of Forensic Medicine
Madurai Medical College

To

S.NO	TITLE	PAGE.NO
01	AN INTRODUCTION TO FORENSIC MEDICINE	04
02	INDIAN LEGAL SYSTEM AND LEGAL PROCEDURES	06
03	MEDICAL NEGLIGENCE	14
04	IDENTIFICATION	21
05	MEDICOLEGAL AUTOPSY	74
06	DEATH AND ITS CAUSES	113
07	POST-MORTEM CHANGES	145
08	MECHANICAL INJURIES	169
09	FORENSIC BALLISTICS	205
10	REGIONAL INJURIES	234
11	MEDICOLEGAL ASPECTS OF WOUNDS	252
12	THERMAL DEATHS	271
13	STARVATION	288
14	MECHANICAL ASPHYXIA	291
15	DROWNING	302
16	IMPOTENCE AND STERILITY	307
17	VIRGINITY ,PREGNANCY AND DELIVERY	313
18	ABORTION	322
19	SEXUAL OFFENCES	328
20	INFANT DEATHS	340
21	BLOOD STAINS	345
22	FORENSIC SCIENCE LABORATORY	349
23	FORENSIC PSYCHIATRY	354

CHAPTER - 01
AN INTRODUCTION TO FORENSIC MEDICINE

Introduction:
Forensic medicine and medical jurisprudence are the two distinct aspects by which law and medicine get connected.

Forensic medicine:
- it is the application of medical and paramedical knowledge to aid in administration of justice.
- it is used by legal authorities for finding solutions for legal issues.
- it is also called as **'legal medicine'**.

Branches of Forensic medicine:
1) **Clinical forensic medicine:**
- Medicolegal examination of living being involved in or succumbed to any violence (or) any legal issues.

2) **Forensic pathology:**
- Determination of cause and manner of death by applying the knowledge of various reactions on human body due to any unnatural effects such as disease & violence.
- In court of law forensic pathologists testify about the cause & manner of death rather than **"ultimate issue"** of guilt (or) innocence.
- In such cases, the opinion of a physician is required for taking legal decisions by the court of law.

Medical jurisprudence:
Deals with physicians legal responsibilities arising from the
- Doctor - patient relationship
- Doctor - doctor relationship
- Doctor - state relationship

Ex: Medicolegal negligence, ethics.

Medical ethics and medical etiquettes:
With some moral principles, the members of medical profession are guided as to how they should behave with their colleagues, patients and state. These principles are called 'medical ethics'.

The set of conventional laws and customs of courtesy which governs the relationship among the physician is called medical etiquettes.

A physician should behave with his/her colleagues the way he/she wants them to behave with him/her.

He/she should not criticize his/her colleague while dealing with a patient.

Forensic medicine and its scopes:
- FM deals with the application of experience, intelligence and exact knowledge in various branches of medicine in finding out the truth.
- The duty of a physician is to present the truth within the limits of science.
- Assumption, presumption and conjecture must be avoided during investigation and interpretation in the court of law.

A Doctor may be called to the court under 3 circumstances:
1. As an ordinary witness who saw an incident.
2. As medical practitioner who treated the patient.
3. An expert to give his opinion as a matter of science.
   - In first two scenarios, it is his duty to testify and he can't refuse.
   - In 3rd scenario he can refuse the request by the court.
   - Detailed observation, proper reporting and clear presentation are necessary for the success of a medical witness.
   - After thorough observation, the physician must apply his wide range of exact knowledge and final conclusion.
   - Apart from his/her clinical knowledge, the physician who is going to appear as a witness must apply his experience, common sense and must consider other possibilities.

It is because the failure of the physician producing the evidence may cause harm to those who have no connection with the crime. Innocent people may get punished due to this negligence. Hence, proper investigations must be done by medical witnesses to ensure a dogmatic statement. Opinions must not be converted into dogmatic statements without proper supporting points. The physician must be ready to defend his each findings and conclusion on the report based on both clinical and scientific knowledge.

1. Applying clinical skills on history taking, examination of injuries and investigation.
2. Recording the findings precisely.
3. Clear presentation of findings

Is important in medicolegal practice to provide a proper evidence and to prevent a physician by himself from wrong interpretations.

Objectivity must always be maintained in recording the findings and avoiding conjecture and presumption plays important role in medicolegal practice of medicine.

During testification and interpretation a physician must be guarded on what & how he says.

Because:
1. In some cases, a physician acts as the only witness and based on his/her witness the legal decisions are taken.
2. In some cases, his interpretation may become irreversible if the records of clinical examination are not properly maintained.
- Hence, it is important to maintain proper records about all the facts observed.

Duty of a physician during testification:
- Should not be a partisan.
- Must present the truth within the limits of science.
- Mustn't be influenced by emotional considerations.
- Must avoid prejudicial and sensational statements.

Examination of accused:
- Must be aware of medicolegal issues while examining and investigating an accused one and also while treating a case.
- Avoid reporting and recording the statements given by the accused about the events that led to his arrest.

CHAPTER - 02
INDIAN LEGAL SYSTEM AND LEGAL PROCEDURES

The legal system of India is governed by:

Indian Legal System

Bharathiya Nyaya Sanhita (BNS)
- It is the replacement of Indian Penal Code(IPC).
- Enacted on December 25,2023.
- came into effect on July 1,2024

Bharatiya Nagarik Suraksha Sanhita(BNSS)
- Enacted on 20 Dec,2023
- replacement of Criminal Procedure Code (CrPC).

Bharatiya Sakshya Adhinyam (BSA)
- Replacement of Indian Evidence Act(IEA).
- enacted on December 20,2023

Criminal and Civil law:
Criminal laws deals with disputes/offences comitted against public interest.
- It includes offences against person, property, public safety etc...
- Public prosecutor - represents State (Government & Parliament of India).

Civil law:
- Also called state law.
- Deals with disputes between two parties.

Two parties
- Plaintiff is a Party which brings action in civil case.
- Defendant is a party which is accused in both civil and criminal case.

```
                                    Courts of Law
                                         │
        ┌────────────────────┬───────────┴────────────┬────────────────────┐
        ▼                    ▼                        ▼                    ▼
   Supreme court         High court              Sessions court       Magistrate court
        │                    │                        │                    │
        ▼                    ▼                        ▼                    ▼
```

- Highest judicial tribunal.
- New Delhi
- Can superwise all courts of india purely deals with appeals of criminal cases.
- Have control of all other courts.

- Highest tribunal for state.
- Usually located in capital of state.
- Judges appointed by president of india.
- Deals with appeals of criminal cases.

- Established by state government.
- Usually locaed at district headquarters.
- Only deals with cases committed to it by magistrate and can pass any sentence.

- 3 types of magistrates in district level.
- 2 types in metropolitan cities.

Both do not deals with trial prima facie.

In metropolitan cities.
1. Chief metropoltan magistrate.
2. metropolitan magistrate.

In district level
1. chief judicial magistrate.
2. 1st class judicia magistrate.
3. 2nd class judicial magistrate.

Common law: is made by judges while making and delivering decisions in each cases.

- Chief Judicial magistrate can sentence imprisonment of 7 years & unlimited fine.
- 1st class Judicial magistrate can sentence upto 3 years & 10000 rupees fine.
- 2nd class Judicial magistrate can sentence imprisonment upto a year & 5000 rupee fine.

- District sessions court deals with civil cases.
- Assistant sessions court have rights to pass imprisonment of 10 years unlimited fine.

Juvenile courts and Juvenile Justice board:
Principle:
- Children differ mentally from adults. Juvenile courts deal with offences commited by human beings below 18 years of age.
- It consists of First class woman magistrate and 2 social workers.
- Out of these 2 social workers at least one shall be a woman.

Labour courts:
- Deals with industrial disputes arising from scope of employment.

Family courts:
- Deals with disputes related to marriage and family affairs.
- Promotes speedy settlement of those disputes.

Inquest:

Inquiry (or) investigation related with cause of death.
- It can be conducted
    - in a case of suspicious death
    - If death is suspected to be a murder.

Types:

In India Police inquest and magistrate inquest are 2 types followed yet.

Coroners, inquest, Medical examiner system and Jury are some other types of inquest followed in United states of America.

Police inquest	Magistrate inquest
Officer incharge of a police station conducts inquest.	Conducted by District Magistrate (Collector/Deputy commissioner), Sub divisional magistrate (RDO). Tahsildar (or) Executive magistrate.
The rank of officer conducting inquest must not be below head constable when the investigation officer recieves information about a death that is suspicious and some other person conducts offence the he arrive and conducts inquest.	Conducts in cases such as. <ul><li>Dowry Death.</li><li>Exhumation.</li><li>Rape cases of woman while she is under police custody.</li><li>Death of women within 7 years of marriage.</li></ul>
Procedure: I.O recieves information of suspicious Death. ↓	
In any case of death a magistrate can conduct inquest in addition to police inquest. ↓	
Inform to nearby executive magistrate. ↓	
Arrive to the site. ↓	
Investigation in the presence of two (or) more respectable persons (Panchas). ↓	
Preparing report (Panchanamas)[inquest report prepared by the police in the prence of panchas called panchanamas]. ↓	
Report includes information describing wounds, bruises, fractures, injuries, weapon (or) instrument etc... and signed by I.O. and panchas ↓	
Send body for autopsy to nearby Government doctor, without removing clothes and with a requesition and copy of inquest ↓	
Forward the report to magistrate ↓	
If the death is purely natural (or) Due to disease then handover body to relatives to bury.	

Points to remember:
If a person is accused for more than one offence at a single trial then twice the amount of punishment can be passed by magistrate.
- Appropriate government has the power to decrease, enhance (or) to suspend any sentence passed by court of law.
- It can also decrease (commute) life time imprisonment ≥ 20 years to 14 years.
- Executive magistrate is an officer of executive branch (ex. government department, typically revenue department) rather than Judicial branch.
- Section 195 BNSS and Section 196 BNSS deals with Police inquest.
- Section 196 BNSS deals with magistrate inquest.
- Private doctor can examine a living in medicolegal cases but for autopsy, permission should be got from State government.

Offence:
Act (or) omission which is punishable under law is considered as offence.

Example:
1. Murder is a Punishable act.
2. Omission of Subpoena without any considerable reason.

Types of offence:
- Bailable
- Non Bailable

In Bailable offence:-
Court cannot refuse bail and police cannot continue the person in custody.

Non Bailable offence:-
Court can refuse bail and police can continue the person in custody.

Cognisable offence	Non Cognisable offence
The police can arrest the accused without a warrant.	The accused can be arrested only following the warrant from magistrate.
May be bailable or non bailable depends on nature of offence.	Generally bailable due to less severity.
Example: Rape, murder, Dowry death, robbery, ragging, etc.....	The suffered person go direct to doctor or may file affidavit in court.
The individual is sent to medical examination by police.	The magistrate sent the person to hospital after received the affidavit from suffered person.

Subpoena / Summons:
It is a document which compelling the attendance of the witness in court of law on a particular day, time and place for giving evidence.

These summons should be obeyed and if asked for any documents by the court then the witness must submit it.

Punishment for disobedience of summons:
1. In case of civil case if the witness fails to attend court he will be liable to pay damages
2. In criminal cases if the witness neglect the summon he may be sentenced with
    - Imprisonment for one month
    - Fine
    - Both under Section 174 BNS.
    - In case of valid or urgent reason the witness can be excused by court of law.

Points to remember:
- Criminal courts have priority over civil courts.
1. If the witness is called to testify on civil and criminal courts on same day, he must attend criminal court & inform about it to the civil court.
- Higher courts have priority over lower courts.
2. If he is summoned from two courts of same status, he must attend the court from which he recieved the Summon first & he must inform about it to other court.
3. The fee offered or paid to a witness in civil cases along with Summon in order to meet the expenses for attending court is called Conduct money.
- In case of insufficient fee the witness can inform about it to the judge and the judge till decide the amount to be paid.
4. In criminal cases the witness won't be paid during Summon.
- But conveyance charges and daily allowance can be daimed under government rules.
5. Regular witness do not get paid, expert proffesionals hired for witness alone get paid.

Evidence:
It includes :
- All the statements permitted by court of law related to the fact.
- All the statements requires to be made before it by the witness related to the fact.

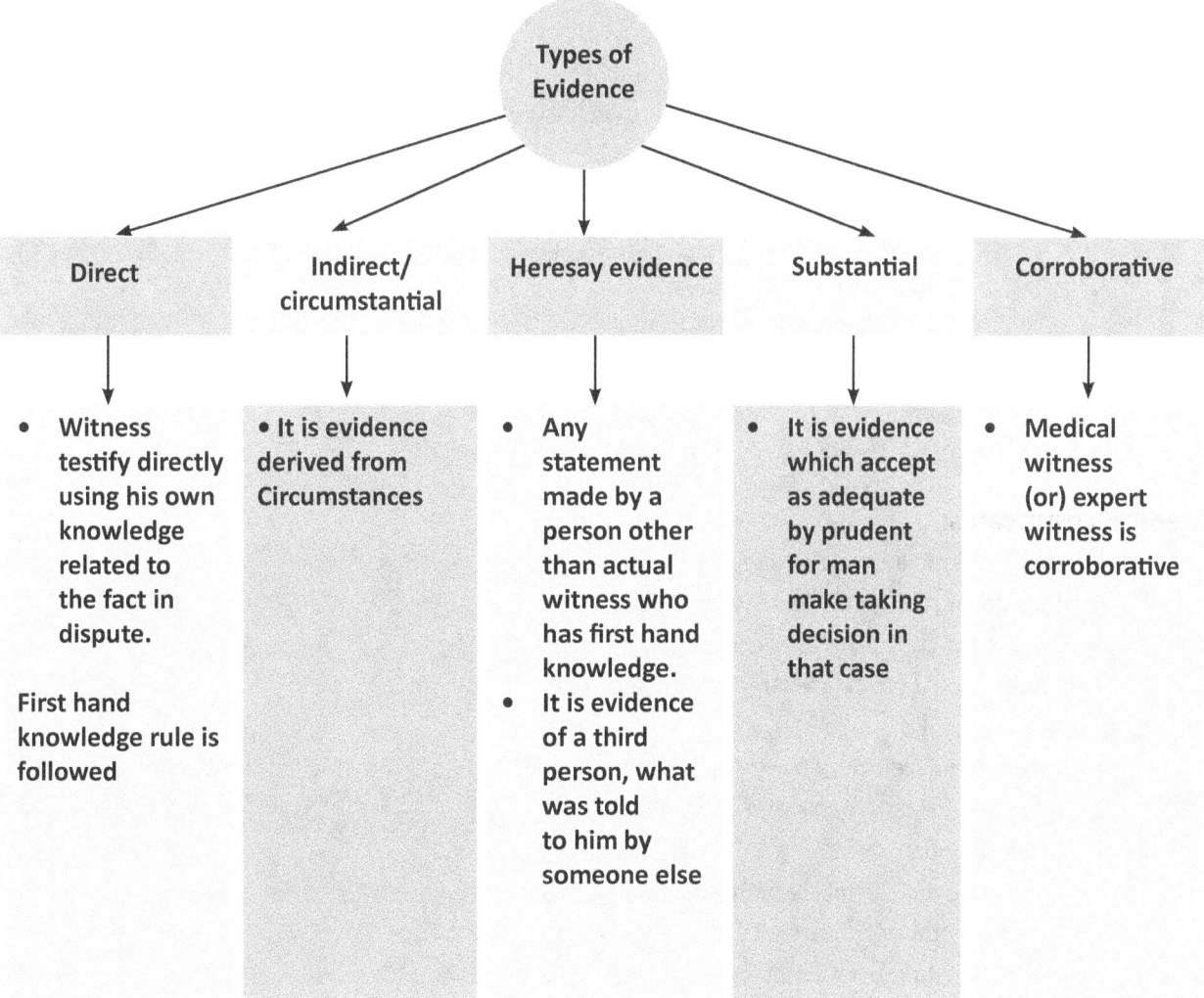

Types of Evidence

Direct
- Witness testify directly using his own knowledge related to the fact in dispute.

First hand knowledge rule is followed

Indirect/circumstantial
- It is evidence derived from Circumstances

Heresay evidence
- Any statement made by a person other than actual witness who has first hand knowledge.
- It is evidence of a third person, what was told to him by someone else

Substantial
- It is evidence which accept as adequate by prudent for man make taking decision in that case

Corroborative
- Medical witness (or) expert witness is corroborative

Based on the ways in which evidence can be presented in the court, evidence can be classified into
1. Documentary evidence
2. Oral evidence.

Evidence

Documentary Evidence
Includes all documents produced in the court for inspection.

Oral Evidence
- Must be direct in all cases.
- Given more preference in court of law.
- It is best type of evidence because of allowing cross examination.

Medical certificate
- Accepted in court of law only when issued by qualified registered medical practitioner.

Medical reports
- Reports prepared.
- By doctor following the request from I.O from magistrate.
- Usually consider in criminal cases.

Parts of medicolegal reports.
1. Facts observe during examination.
2. Opinions drawn from facts observed.
- The opinion should not be based on information from other sources.
- Physician should keep copy of report for future reference.
- If the reports exceeds one page then physician must sign his initial at end of each page.
- Name & designation of physician noted in last page.

Dying declaration
- it is written (or) oral form of statement given by a person dying as a result of any offence (or) unlawful act

Medical certificates:
→ Certificate of illness won't be provided without proper examination.
→ Issue certificate for not more than 15 days.
→ Reissue the certificate after 15 days following examination.
→ Fitness should not be declared on advance.

Points to remember by a physician:
1. Signature (or) left thumb impression of patient should be taken at top or bottom of certificate.
2. Two identification marks should be noted.
3. Physician must
   - Issue the certificate without charging fee.
   - Issue the certificate after complete inspection of body.
   - Shouldn't delay eventhough doctor fees is not paid.
   - In case of suspected foul play, certificate should not be provided and inform to police.
   - Physician should keep the duplicate copy of certificate provided for 2 years.

Dying Declaration (leterm mortem- words said before death):

It is written (or) oral form of statement given by a person dying as a result of any offence (or) unlawful act.

- If there is possibility on the basis of time available, executive magistrate should be called to record the declaration.
- If the patient is too critical in condition, in doctor should record declaration in presence of 2 witness.
- Before recording the doctor should certify that the person is conscious and his mental faculties are normal (compos mentis).
- The physician who declare the victim as compos mentis and one who record the declaration must not be same.
- Oath is not administered becaues of the belief that the dying person tells the truth.

Remember:
- Statement must be in patient own words.
- Leading questions should not be asked.
- If point is not clear, ask question to make it clear but actual question & answer must be recorded.
- If the person, becomes unconscious while recording the physician must Verify upto the collected statement & sign it.
- Sign language is acceptable if the person not able to speak.

Dying deposition:
- Superior to dying declaration.
- Not followed in India.
- recorded by magistrate in presence of accused (or) his lawyer following oath.
- Cross questioning is allowed.

Oral evidence:

Documentary evidence is accepted by court of law if and only if the person concerned is gives the Oral testimony.

Exceptions:
1. Dying declaration, If the person died after declaration.
2. Evidence of doctor recorded in lower court.
3. Evidence of witness recorded in previous hiering.
4. Evidence of Mint officers and officer of india security press.
5. Reports of some scientific experts such as.
- Chemical examiner & assistant chemical examiner.
- Chief inspector of explosives.
6. Public records.
7. Hospital records.

But in any of above case the appropriate person can be hired for testimony by court if possible.

Oral evidence:
- Witness is a person who testifies in the court of law regarding facts.
- All persons are competent to testify unless they are prevented from doing so.
- No age limit to be a witness but the individual Should have enough mental maturity.
1. To understand the court questions.
2. To answer them logically.
- Preferably the age of witness must be more than 12.

Witness

Common witness	Expert witness	Hostile witness
Any individual who was present near by (or) comes to know about the crime (or) perceived any information about it. • The common witness must possess first hand information regarding matter under dispute. • Common witness is not permitted to volunteer any statement card is bound to answer only what is being asked to him.	A person who is trained or skilled in technical (or) scientific subject and is capable of drawing conclusions (or) opinion from facts observed. Expert witness help the court to arrive near the truth by his special knowledge & skill. He is called to court to clarify certain doubts logically and scientifically. His answer must be direct wherever possible. As far as possible he should not volunteer any statement and at the same time never hesitate to volunteer a statement if he feels there is chance of miscarriage of justice.	After making a particular statement the witness contradicts his own statement and try to conceal part of truth or gives completely false evidence. The court declare him hostile. • Then he can be cross examined by the side by which he was called. • Both common and expert witness can be hostile.

CHAPTER - 03
MEDICAL NEGLIGENCE

Negligence
- Diligence means due care and skill; Negligence is the opposite of diligence.
- In negligence, the degree of skill and care exhibited by a doctor while performing the procedure was below the prescribed standard.
- Negligence is defined as "omission to do something which a reasonable man would do or doing something which a prudent reasonable man would not do.

Consent
- Consent is defined as **"voluntary agreement, compliance, permission or accepting for the act proposed by another"** and is valid only for that specified act or purpose.
- Indian Contracts Act, Section 13 states that **"two or more persons are said to consent when they agree upon the same thing in the same sense."**
- To be legally valid, the consent given must be intelligent and informed.
- The doctor examining or treating a patient without the consent amounts to the offence of assault.

Types of consent

There are two types of consent

Implied consent:
The behavior or the act of patient or the individual, itself indicates that he has consented for the act; you can take it for granted that he/she has given the consent. This is applicable only for minor procedure of medical practice like general physical examination, checking the pulse, blood pressure or giving injection, etc.

Expressed consent:
The doctor has to ask for the consent and obtain it before any procedure or treatment.
- **Oral consent**
- **Written consent**

– **Oral consent:** It is of equal value as that of written consent, but when a dispute arises between the two parties then it becomes difficult for the doctor to prove that he has obtained a proper consent. Hence, oral consent holds good only for simpl procedures like per abdominal examination, giving IV fluids or testing the blood, etc.

– **Written consent:** It is always better to go for written consent whenever the procedure is a slightly complicated or prolonged procedure like a suturing for an injury, an incision and drainage for an abscess, etc.

Informed written consent (The cornerstone of medical practice):
This is the most superior form of consent in medical practice. Informed consent is called as the **"doctrine of full disclosure."** The law believes that the patient alone is the best person to care for himself and he has the right to choose what is good or bad for him and what is needed to be done on him to get cured of his disease or the problem he is suffering from.

Informed written consent in medical practice

A doctor after examining the patient must explain to the patient and/or the relatives:
i. What's the disease or problem he is suffering from?
ii. What is his proposed treatment plan for that disease or condition?
iii. What are the other standard alternate treatments /procedures available for that particular disease or condition?
iv. What are the advantages and disadvantages of his proposed treatment; and why he prefers to follow that particular treatment option?
v. What are the advantages and disadvantages of the alternative line of treatment?

- The information provided to the patient should be in writing in simple language and in the language in which the patient is familiar. Then allow the patient to choose what type of treatment he needs and to be done for him.
- In important situations like surgery, it is always better to explain all these to the patient and to the close relatives of the patient and get it signed by the patient as well as the legal guardian. Since, if suppose the patient dies, the relatives are the people who are going to file the case if any and hence they should be convinced that the doctor did everything which is good for the patient and death was unavoidable.
- **Informed refusal:** When the doctor feels that a particular type of treatment will be the best for the patient and if the patient does not accept for the proposed treatment plan, there are many chances that it could result in some complications at later time; in spite of explaining all these in detail, the patient still refuses for the doctor's proposed treatment plan, then the doctor has to bring all in writing and get it signed by the patient; this is called as "informed refusal".

Consent in medicolegal cases

- Informed written consent should be obtained in all medicolegal examinations. It should be informed to the individual that, the opinion you are going to arrive after the examination, will be issued in the form of a certificate; which may go in favor of him or against him in the court of law; but, if he refuses to give consent for examination then it will definitely (100%) go against him in the court.

Rules of obtaining consent

- Consent is a mandatory for every medical examination and treatment.
- Oral consent should be obtained in the presence of disinterested third party.
- Written consent is not necessary in all situations, but when a dispute arises it becomes difficult for the doctor to prove that he obtained a valid consent. Hence, any procedure beyond routine physical examination
- Such as blood transfusion,collection of blood, etc. expressed consent, preferably written consent is necessary.
- In major procedures such as surgery, written informed consent is necessary and is mandatory.
- The doctor should explain the objective of his examination and also inform the patient that he has the right to refuse consent.
- When the person subjects himself voluntarily for examination, such as insurance or for issuing driving license, no consent is necessary and also there exists no professional secrecy.
- In criminal cases, the victim cannot be examined without informed consent; but the accused of a crime can be examined using reasonable amount of force without consent, under the request of police not below the rank of sub-inspector(Section 51 BNSS).
- As per Section 53 BNSS, an accused person can request for medical examination to prove his innocence.

- In cases of drunkenness or under the influence of any drug, the individual may be unconscious or not in a state to understand and give consent. In such situations, the doctor can examine the patient without consent if requested by the investigating officer, withhold the results of examination and hand it over to the authorities after the individual becomes fit to give consent. But if he refuses to handover the report at this stage, it has to be obliged; but not in criminal cases (Section 51 BNSS: If he is accused of a crime), the doctor can handover the results without the consent.
- A prisoner can be treated forcefully in the interest of the society. Same way an individual starving himself to death can be treated forcefully without consent, since no individual has the right to die.
- Consent given for committing a crime or illegal act such as criminal abortion is not valid.

Note:
- *An individual under 18 years cannot give consent to suffer any harm (Section 25 BNS). Section 26 BNS*
- *An individual above 18 years can give valid consent to suffer any harm which may result from an act, done in good faith, not known or intended to cause death.*
- *An individual less than 12 years of age cannot give consent to suffer any harm, done in good faith and for his benefit. The consent has to be obtained from the parents or guardian, if they refuse to give consent, the doctor cannot treat the patient even to save the life (Section 27 BNS).*
- *Consent given by an individual under fear or in toxication or by an insane is invalid.*
- *In case of emergency, when no relatives are available or no time to wait for their arrival, the doctor can proceed on with the treatment even without consent.*
- *When a treatment is made compulsory by the law, then no consent is necessary (Example: Vaccination, where the government gives the consent)*
- *In treatment or surgery, which is expected to involve his sexual capacity or fertility, the consent of both the husband and the wife are necessary.*
- *An adult individual cannot be detained inside the hospital without his consent, he has to be discharged under 'Against Medical Advice'.*
- *If any person has consented or given willingness for donation of any organ or body after his death; the consent of the legal heirs is mandatory to harvest the organs, after death of the individual (no individual has any right over his body after his death).*

Loco Parentis: (Local parent)
- In an emergency involving children when the parents or guardian is not available, the person in-charge can give consent (e.g. teacher in a school).

Professional Negligence (Medical Malpractice)
- Professional negligence is defined as **"omission to do something which a reasonable competent man would do or doing something which a prudent reasonable man would not do, either of these results in direct damage or death of the patient."**
- Medical negligence arises when the standard of care exhibited by the doctor while doing a procedure or treatment was below the prescribed standard.
- Negligence results either from the doctor's lack of knowledge and skill or failure to excise reasonable degree of care and skills while performing the procedure/act.
- When a patient dies during the treatment due to alleged medical negligence, the doctor is booked under Section 106 (1) BNS

Note:
- *Section 106 (1) BNS*
- *Whoever causes death of any person by rash and negligent act, not amounting to culpable homicide, shall be punished with imprisonment for a term which may extent to 2 years, with or without fine.*

Components of a negligence suit:
- For the charge of negligence to be established against a doctor, the following components have to be proved beyond any reasonable doubt.
  i. Existence of a duty of care
  ii. Dereliction of such duty
  iii. Damage
  iv. Direct cause: The resultant damage should be a direct effect of such dereliction. Also, it has to be proved that the resultant damage was reasonably foreseeable (commonly expected).
- Even if it is proved that the doctor was negligent but such an act did not cause any damage to the patient, then the doctor cannot be held liable for any compensation.

Ordinary degree of professional skill is a must:
- The doctor is not expected to give the best available treatment; he is only expected to give the reasonable degree of care. Hence, average degree of professional skill is the minimum requirement from any doctor.
- His act will be compared with that of another doctor possessing the same qualification and practicing medicine under the same circumstances. The care given by a doctor in a rural set up cannot be compared with that of a doctor practicing medicine at a corporate hospital in a city.

Error in judgment either in diagnosis or treatment is not negligence:
- The doctor cannot be held liable for the error in investigations and if his treatment was based on the results.
- If he has treated the patient presuming a diagnosis and later found by investigations that his diagnosis was wrong, even then the doctor cannot be held liable but he has to clarify clearly what was the basis on which he arrived at that diagnosis.

Novus actus interveniens:
- An unrelated act intervening: This arises rarely when some new unrelated act interferes; Example: Some accidental injuries sustained in the course of the treatment by a doctor which added to the damage/precipitated death. In these circumstances, the doctor can prove that death was due to unrelated act which happened in between.
- Res ipsa loquitur means "the evidence speaks for itself".
- In any case of negligence, the burden of proof rests on the patient and he has to prove by evidence and witnesses that the doctor was
- negligent and the damage has been caused directly by his negligent act.
- In **'res ipsa loquitur',** it is clearly evident that the doctor has committed some negligent act and hence the burden of proof is shifted to the doctor's side and he has to prove his innocence and that the resulted damage was not due to his act.

- **Examples:**
  Leaving surgical instruments or any foreign body like gauze or blade inside the abdomen during an abdominal surgery; operating on the wrong limb or operating on a wrong patient, etc. In these circumstances, it is proved that the doctor was negligent; hence, the burden of proof shifts to the doctor's side.

Defenses available for a doctor in cases of medical negligence:

i. Consent
- It is a very good defence in any charge of negligence, provided it has been obtained following the rules of consent in a proper format.

- Most of the charges of negligence against a doctor are due to failure in obtaining a proper informed written consent. A proper consent saves the doctor in almost 99 % cases of negligence. Since, most of the treating doctors are not much aware of the legal provisions and anyone cannot judge the outcome of the case at that moment of time, and no one can guess which case will go wrong and which patient may file a case at a later time. But doctors should note that consent is a defence only in civil cases.

ii. Contributory negligence
- The doctor was already negligent and the patient also has added to the resultant damage; the doctor has to prove that the patient by his negligent actions has added to the damages caused. Then the amount of compensation may be reduced.

• **Examples**
  i. A doctor has advised the patient to keep the wound clean; come and change the dressing everyday in his clinic; the patient fails to follow the instructions and advice, which resulted in severe infection and in some damage.
  ii. Failure of the patient to take medicines as advised by the doctor can all be brought forward as a defence, but the doctor has to prove it.

iii. Corporate negligence
- In corporate hospitals, the management is responsible for the negligent act of any individual doctor or paramedical staffs. The case is filed against the hospital in most cases and the hospital has to give the compensation. May be the hospital authorities can recover the amount from the doctor or may terminate his service as they feel correct.

iv. Products liability
- The burden of proof rests on the doctor; he has to prove that the resultant damage was due to faulty machine, instrument or drug.
- Here again, the instrument has to be maintained as per the norms of the manufacturer; faulty handling of the instruments, not servicing the instrument at the proper interval of time or not checking the functional status of the instrument before commencing the procedure are duties of the doctor. If the damage is due to faulty usage of the machine, then the manufacturer will not be held liable for the resultant damage.

v. Therapeutic misadventure
(Medical maloccurance)
- This is a very good defence for the doctor, if he has excised reasonable degree of skill and care while doing that procedure or a line of treatment.
- This is applicable in situations where the treatment procedure carries inherent risk of complications. The doctor was reasonably good and has taken proper care and precautions while giving treatment, and in spite of
- doing everything correctly, unfortunately the patient suffers some damage or dies.
- This is mainly due to individual variation in response of different patients to different procedures or drugs, which is totally unexpected.
- Here again, the burden of proof rests on the doctor and he has to prove that he had followed standard guidelines and taken enough precautions to avoid the expected adverse effects, and in spite of this the death or damage had resulted.

• **Examples**
  - Breaking of a needle while giving intramuscular injection.
  - Damage to recurrent laryngeal nerve during thyroidectomy.
  - When a seriously ill patient is under treatment of a doctor and later the patient dies, it is enough if the doctor brings forth evidences to prove that he had taken all necessary measures to save the life of the patient, but death was inevitable.

vi. Calculated risk doctrine
- Every medical procedure, how small it may be has got some inherent risk, hence the percentage of the expected risk is important in any case of negligence and again the same has to be well-informed to the patient at the time of obtaining the consent. If the risk percentage/the expected mortality rate is high, then the doctor can defend himself that death was inevitable.

vii. Vicarious liability: (Respondent Superior)
"let the master answer."
- For any act done by the employee, the employer is responsible. The chief doctor is responsible for the entire negligence act done by his assistants and paramedical staffs.
- This doctrine can be enforced only in cases of civil negligence involving monitory compensations.

Steps to be taken by a doctor to prevent medical negligence:
- Always take valid consent, how small the procedure may be.
- Employ fully qualified staffs and associates.
- Attend the patient in time; in cases of emergencies, treatment has to be done even if the patient does not pay the fees at that moment.
- Update your knowledge as far as possible, especially on the commonest issues and on those types of cases which you are seeing
- frequently.
- Maintain accurate and complete medical records about all the patients, for a minimum period of three years; general practitioners at the periphery can atleast make a note of all the patients in the diary, which is difficult to be manipulated at a later date and hence the court will have better belief on the doctor.
- Reasonable degree of care and skill is a must, atleast be thorough in what you do.
- Do not criticize another doctor, even though the other doctor may be wrong or may not have been right.
- Guard against therapeutic hazards: Even if you don't do good to the patient, be sure you don't harm him and cause any damage due to improper treatment procedures.

Consumer Protection Act 1986: CPA /COPRA and the Three tiers of consumer forum;
- The aim of the act is to provide better protection of the interests of the consumer and speedy justice to the consumers.
- Doctors are also covered under the Act (Supreme court judgment, 13th November 1995) as the doctor provides a service to the patient and for which he is being paid. Government hospitals and those who provide free treatment to all the patients at all times, are not covered under this act.
- **Consumer Dispute Redressal Forums are established at 3 levels (tiers):**
1. **District Consumer Disputes Redressal Forum:** Compensations upto ` 20 lakhs.
2. **State Consumer Disputes Redressal Forum:** ` 20 lakhs to 1 crore.
3. **National Consumer Disputes Redressal Forum:** More than ` 1 crore.
- The complaint can be lodged in the consumer court, in a white paper, with relevant documents to support the allegation and the amount of
- compensation he is claiming.
- No court fee is charged in such cases and once the cases are taken up compensations if any are awarded within a reasonable period of time.
- Either of the parties can go for an appeal to the next level forum, if they are not convinced.

Professional indemnity policy:
- The doctors can insure their professional practice by way of taking professional indemnity policy. In the event of compensation if any to be paid in medical negligence cases, the insurance company which provides the service will pay the compensations to the patient.
- The professional indemnity service is also provided by the respective Indian Medical Association at the state level branches.
- Depending on their clinical setup and the types of patients they handle, the doctors can take policies upto their convenience and necessity, and make their own options in payment of premium money.
- In such cases, the case itself is taken over by the insurance company and the compensation is also paid by them directly to the patient, within the limits of their insurance amount.
- Hence, it is advisable that every doctor should protect his practice by taking a professional insurance cover before they start up their medical practice, since no one can say when things may go wrong and at what moment of time litigations may arise during their professional practice

IMPORTANT POINTS:
Workmen compensation act (1923):
- This act provides for the payment of compensation to the employee for the injuries sustained by accident, in the course of his work or employment at his work place.
- If the workman dies, then the entitled dependents are to receive the compensation.
- If he contracts any diseases, as an occupational disease related to that particular employment, it is deemed to be an injury by accident for the purpose of compensation.
- The amount of whether compensation depends upon the injury has caused death, permanent total disablement or permanent part disablement.
- Any medical sequence which connects the disability or death with the event at work is legally adequate for awarding compensation.
- The workman is not eligible for compensation if at the time of sustaining the injuries he was under the influence of alcohol or
- drugs.
- In all industrial diseases and injuries, medical evidence is mandatory; hence the doctor must keep all relevant treatment records and is also bound to opine the relationship between the injury and death or acceleration of a pre-existing natural disease by the injury.
- The medical certificate issued in all such cases must be accurate and without any influence or ambiguity.

CHAPTER - 04
IDENTIFICATION

Identification:
Identification is the determination of the individuality of a person based on certain physical characteristics.
Example: exact fixation of personality

Types of identification:

Types of identification

Complete identification
1. Finger printing
2. DNA finger printing
3. Tattoo marks
4. Super impaction
5. Lip, palate printing

Incomplete identification
1. Race
2. Age
3. Sex
4. Stature (height)

Necessities of Identification

Criminal cases	Civil cases	Others
Persons accused of assault	Marriage	Living persons
Murder	Passport	Recently dead person
Rape	Insurance claims	Decomposed bodies
Interchange of newborn baby in hospital	Disputed sex	Mutilated and burst bodies
Impersonation etc	Missing person etc	Skeleton

Note:
- *At least two identification marks should be noted by the doctor in all medicolegal cases.*
- *Before identifying the accused person in the court, the doctor should verify identification marks noted by him.*

Corpus delicti (body of crime/essence of crime):
- The corpus delicti of murder is the fact that a person died from unlawful violence
- In includes the body of the victim and other facts which are conclusive of death by foul play, such as a bullet or a broken knife blade found in the body and responsible for death
- Clothing showing marks of the weapon, drawing and photographs of the deceased showing fatal injuries are also included in this term

Motive of corpus delicti:
- Establishment of identity of the dead body
- Infliction of violence in a particular way, particular time, particular place.

Note:
The case against the accused cannot be established unless there is convincing proof of these points
Identification data
* *Race and religion* • *Sex* • *Age* • *General development* • *Stature* • *Complexion and features*
* *External peculiarities - moles, birthmarks, malformation, scars, tattoo marks occupational marks*
* *Anthropometric measurements* • *Finger prints and fact prints* • *Teeth* • *Personal effects* • *Speech* •
Voice • *Gait and habit*

As no single feature is reliable for identification combination of features is taken
Primary characteristic of identification:
* *Race* • *Sex* • *Age* • *Stature*

RACE:

Race is a categorization of humans based on shared physical or social qualities into groups
Race categorized by:
* Skin • Hair • Eyes • Skeleton

Skin:
- Brown colour in Indians
- Fair in Europeans
- Black in negroes
» Skin colour is changed by decomposition, burning etc.

Eyes:
- Dark eyes in Indians (few brown eyes also seen)
- Blue or grey eyes in Europeans

Hair:

characteristics	Indian	Europeans	Mongolian	Negros
Colour	Black	Fair, k=light brown, reddish	Dark and dense uniform pigmentation	Dense pigmented with irregular distribution
arrangement	straight or navy	straight or navy	straight or navy	arranged in tight spirals

Skeleton:

The important indices for race determination is cephalic index which is measured by Vernier calipers

$$\text{Cephalic index} = \frac{\text{max breath of skull}}{\text{max length of skull}}$$

Cephalic index	Types of skull	Race
70-74.9	Dolichocephalic	Aryans/negroes
75-79.9	Mesaticephalic	Europeans, Chinese and Indians
80-85	brachycephalic	Mongolians

Characteristics based on groups:

	Caucasian	Mongolian	Negro
Country	Europeans, West Asian, Indians and some Americans	Natouramericans, Koreans, Japanese, Chinese and South Asians	West Africa
Colour	White	Yellow	black
Position and shape of skull	Skull tends to be high with almost completely straight lower fare, and rounded skull	Flatter facial skeleton than Caucasian and square shaped skull	The lower face project forced
Shape of orbit	triangular	rounded	square
Nasal aperture	elongated	rounded	Broad
Size of upper and lower limbs	Normal in proportion to body	Smaller upper and lower limbs	Lower upper and lower limbs

Race based on religion:

Hindu males	Hindu females	Muslim males	Muslim females
Sacred thread	Cinnabar on head	Marks of corns and callosities on lateral aspects of knee and feet	Nose ring aperture septum curly
Necklace of wooden beads	Silver toe ornaments		Sevord openings in the ear celronhelir
Caste marks on forehead	Thali		
Types of hair on back of head	Nose ring aperture in left nostrils		
Piercing of ear lobes	Few openings for ear rings along the helix		Usually no tattoo marks

Age:

The age of an individual especially in earlier years can be determined from
1. Teeth
2. Ossification of bones
3. Secondary sex characters
4. General development in case of children

Teeth:

Teeth are useful for age determination:
- By the state of development
- By secondary changes

Types of Teeth

Based on age
Temporary teeth
Permanent teeth
5 superadded permanent teeth
successional permanent teeth

based on morphology
incisor
Canines
premolars
molars

Temporary teeth:
- Temporary or milk teeth or deciduous teeth are 20 in number.
  » Incisor - 4
  » Canines- 2
  » Molars-4 in each jaw

Conditions for delayed dentition:
- Malnutrition
- Hypothyroidism
- Rickets

Conditions for premature dentition
- Congenital syphilis

Note:
If there is doubt whether a particular tooth is temporary, take an x ray. If it is a temporary tooth, the germ of the permanent tooth can be seen underneath.

Permanent teeth or adult teeth:
Teeth which appear after the fall off of temporary teeth are called permanent teeth.
- Permanent teeth are 32 in number they are
  » 4 incisors
  » 2 canines
  » 4 premolars
  » 6 molars in each jaw

Superadded permanent teeth
- These teeth do not have deciduous predecessor
- They erupt behind the temporary teeth
- All permanent molar are superadded permanent teeth
- The first permanent molar tooth of each side erupts 1 white all other deciduous are present in the jaw
- Superadded permanent teeth are six in each jaw

Successional permanent teeth:
- These are the teeth which erupt in place of deciduous teeth
- Permanent premolars erupt in place of deciduous molars
- Successional teeth are ten in each jaw

Morphology of permanent teeth:
- Parts of tooth
  » Crown
  » neck
  » root which is embedded in jaw bone
  » teeth are composed of dentin
  » crown parts of teeth covered by enamel and root part covered by cementum
  » root is attached to the alveolar bone by periodontal membrane

Characteristics of teeth with different morphology.

Characteristics	Incisor	canines	premolar	Molars
Crown shape	Chisel	Long painted	Maxillary premolars	Flat with four five cusps
Labial surface	Convex	concave	-	Convex
No. of roots	One	one	One may be two	Upper molar3
uses	To cut food	Help to cut and large foods into small sized pieces	Crush and grint food into smaller pieces	Grinding food into easily smaller pieces
Lingual surface	concave	concave	-	convex

Difference between temporary and permanent teeth

Trait	Temporary teeh	Permanent
Size	Smaller, lighter, narrower, except temporary molars which are longer than permanent premolars replacing them	Heavier, stronger, premolars replacing temporary molars which are smaller
Direction	Anterior teeth are vertical.	Anterior teeth are usually inclined a little forward
Crown	China – white colour.	Ivory – white colour
Neck	More constricted	Less constricted
Root	Roots of molar are smaller and more divergent	Roots of molars are larger and less divergent
Ridge	A ridge or thick edge at the junction of the crown with	No ridge

Eruption of teeth:

Eruption is defined as the superior part of the crown of the tooth appearing level with the surface of the alveolar bone

- In both deciduous and permanent teeth dentition occurs earlier in lower jaw except for the lateral incisors which erupt earlier in upper jaw
- The lower permanent incision, premolars and molars erupt about one year earlier than do the corresponding teeth in the upper jaw
- Wisdom tooth first erupts in the lower and on left side and them on the right side
- The number and eruption of deciduous teeth is more regular than the permanent dentition.
- Eruption is not always bilaterally symmetrical
- Tooth eruption in female may be one year before that of males

---

Note:
- *The dental and skeletal age, correspond closely in the male but in the female the skeletal age is generally one year ahead of the dental age*
- *Orthopantogram - is a dental panoramic tomography in which all the teeth can be visualised by single x ray.*
- *Gustafson's method plays a role of age estimation only in the dead people, multiple tooth needed.*

Estimation of age using dentition

Age	Factors for age estimation
Birth to 14 yrs.	The degree of formation of root and crown structures The stage of eruption Intermixture of temporary and permanent teeth
14 to 20 yrs.	Stage of development of third molar Accuracy may vary from plus or minus three years
Above 17yrs	Fully erupted

Gustafson's method:

The age estimation of adult over 21 years depends on the physiologic age changes in each of the dental tissue.

Gustafson's criteria :

1. Attrition   2. Periodontosis   3. Secondary dentin
4. Cementum apposition   5. Root resorption   6. Transparency of the root

1. **Attrition:**

    Due to tear and wear from mastication, upper surface of the teeth is destroyed gradually first involving the enamel, then dentin and at last pulp is exposed in old age .It depends on the functional use of teeth and also upon the hardness of the enamel.

2. **Periodontosis:**
    - Regression of the gums and periodontal tissues surrounding the teeth takes place in advancing age, gradually exposing the necks and the adjacent part of roots, due to which the teeth become loose and fall off
    - There may be deposition of hardened debris which occurs gradually over a long period

3. **Secondary dentin:**
    - It may develop from the walls within the pulp cavity and decrease the size of the cavity. First it is deposited at the pulp chamber and gradually. extends downwards to the apex and may completely fill the pulp cavity
    - This is truly due to ageing and partly due to pathological conditions like caries, periodontosis.

4. **Cementum apposition:**

    The cementum increases in thickness particularly due to changes in the tooth position especially near the end of the root
    - Secondary cementum is slowly and continuously deposited throughout life and forms incremental lines
    - Incremental lines appear ad cross striations on the enamel of teeth due to cementum apposition and are thought to represent daily increment of growth
    - They can be seen on histological section.
    - The age can be calculated by counting the number of lines from the neonatal line rewards
    - This is mainly applicable for infants

Root resorption:
- It involves both cementum and dentin which show characteristically sharp groves
- Absorption of the root starts first at the apex and extends upwards
- Transparency of the root
- It is not seen until about 30 yrs. of age
- The canals in the dentin are at first wide
- With the age they are filled by mineral so that they become translucent gradually and the dentine becomes transparent to rarefaction
- Transparency of root occurs from below upwards in lower jaw and from above downwards in upper jaw
- It is the most reliable of all criteria

Note:
Before one tooth is extracted from a body the degree of periodontitis is estimated
The tooth is ground down on glass slabs from both sides of the tooth to about one mm which allows the estimation of transparency.

Calcification and eruption of deciduos teeth

Tooth	Calcification begins	Eruption	Calcification of root completed	Resorption of root begins
Central incisor				
Lower	5 to 6 months	6 to 8 months	1 ½ to 2 years	4 th year
Upper	5 to 6 months	7 to 9 months	1 ½ to 2 years	5 th year
Lateral incisor	5 to 6 months			
Upper	5 to 6 months	7 to 9 months	1 ½ to 2 years	5 th year
Lower	5 to 6 months	10 to 12 months	1 ½ to 2 years	5 th year
First molar	5 to 6 months	12 to 14 months	2 to 2 ½ years	6 th year
Canine	5 to 6 months	17 to 18 months	2 to 3 years	8 th year
Second molar	5 to 6 months	20 to 30 months	3 years	7 th year

Calcification and eruption of permanent teeth

Tooth	Calcification begins	Eruption	Calcification complete
First molar	At birth	6 to 7 years	9 to 10 years
Central incisor	3 to 4 months	6 to 8 years	10 years
Lateral incisor	1 year	7 to 9 years	11 years
First bicuspid	1 ½ years	9 to 11 years	12 to 13 years
Second bicuspid	2 years	10 to 12 years	12 to 14 years
Canine	4 to 5 months	11 to 12 years	12 to 13 years
Second molar	2 ½ to 3 years	12 to 14 years	14 to 16 years
Third molar	8 to 10 years	17 to 25 years	18 to 25 years

Calculation of age based on criteria:
- Anterior teeth are more suitable than the posterior teeth and the merit decreases from incisors to premolars, while third molar is quite unsuitable
- All changes are absent at 15 yrs.
- 0 to 3 points are allotted to indicate the degree of any of these changes that occurs in dental tissues

stages	Changes
0	No change
1	Beginning of change
2	Obvious change
3	Maximum change

- The result corrected for standard deviation, gives an estimate age of the person
- The error is said to be +/- 4 to 7 yrs.
- The Limit of error increases above 50 years of age

Boyde's method:
- Cross striations develop in the enamel of teeth, till the complete formation of enamel
- They represent daily incremental lines
- The age of an individual can be calculated in terms of days by counting the number of lines from the neonatal line onwards
- Neonatal line is formed very soon after birth and can be seen in absent necks or by electron microscopy within one to two days after birth
- It is useful to estimate the age of dead infant

Stack's method:
- Stack evolved a method to know the age of infants from the weight and height of the erupting teeth of child
- This method can be used in both deciduous and permanent teeth during their erupting phase

Age estimation from ossification:

Basic rules of ossification:
- Long bones have primary & secondary ossification center
- Secondary centers grow to fuse with the primary center
- Fusion of epiphysis in females in 1 year earlier than in males
- Fusion starts in the center and progress to periphery

Note:
- *The bones of the human skeleton are performed in hyaline cartilage*
- *The earliest centers of ossification appear at the end of second month of pregnancy*
- *At eleventh intrauterine week there are 806 centre of bone growth, at birth about 450, while the adult skeleton has 206 bones centres to form the adult bone*
- *This shows that 600 centres of bone growth have disappeared they have united with the adjacent centres to form the adult bone.*

Epiphyseal plate:
- The long bone such as the tibia has become adjust throughout its shaft (diaphysis) at birth; whereas its two ends (epiphyses) are later by secondary centres
- A layer of hyaline cartilage which is known as epiphyseal plate persists between the diaphysis and epiphysis
- The bone increases in length at this epiphyseal plate or disc until its final dimensions are attained

Fusion:
- The process of union of epiphysis and diaphysis is called fusion
- Union is a process not an event
- Union of bone can be divided into various stage
1. 0th – stage – no union
2. 1st stage – starting union
3. Vth –stage – completely united

Epiphyseal arrangements	bones
At both ends	Long limb bones
At one end	Metacarpals, metatarsals, phalanges, clavicle and ribs
One or both ends	Proximal end of the humerus

Note:
- *Growth cartilages do not grow at the same rate at all points throughout their substance*
- *There may be maturity imbalance between bones from different parts of the same individual*
- *For determining the age, skiagrams of the shoulder, elbow, wrist, hip, knee, ankle pelvis and skull should be taken in anteroposterior direction.*

Variability:
- In biology, stability is the exception variability is the rule there really is no average.
- The variability increases with age
- As a general rule, the ageing of bones is more accurate with respect to the appearance of centres of ossification than it is with respect to the union of epiphysis
- A study of various anatomical authorities shows that there is a considerable variation regarding the ages at which the various centres of ossification in the epiphysis fuse with their respective diaphysis
- As a general rule, the secondary centres of the limb bones that appear first are the last to fuse, whereas the late-forming `epiphyses reach union with their primary centres in a shorter time period

Order of union in upper limbs

Elbow joint
↓
Wrist
↓
Head of humerus

Order of union in lower limbs

Hip joint
↓
Ankle joint
↓
Knee joint

Factors determining variation:

● Health ● Hereditary ● Nutritional ● Infections disease
● Metabolic disorder ● Physical activity ● Race ● Sex ● Endocrine and environmental factors

Note:
Multiple criteria of skeletal age should be employed whenever possible
- An estimated skeletal age can be expressed as one year plus or minus
- **E.g.=10 +/- 1**
- Skeletal development in the female can be in advance of the male up to one year, while dental development may differ only from one to four months
- In males, dental and osseous ages are almost similar but in females osseous age is in advance of the dental age
- In tropical climates, ossification centres appear and epiphyseal union takes place about 2 years earlier than in temperature zones
- Union of epiphysis in cartilaginous one occurs slightly earlier (by about the year) in the female than in the male but the reverse is seen in the closure of the sutures of the skull

Radiography:
- Forensic radiography uses medical imaging techniques like x rays, CT scans, MRI and fluoroscopy to assist with legal investigations and identification of remains
- The epiphyseal lines on the long bones of a young individual appear as circular grooves around the ends of the bones and on radiographs as irregular lines resembling a fracture
- The union of epiphyses as seen in radiographs appear earlier approximately about plus or minus six months than the period of fusion indicated by anatomical evidence
- This is due to the fact, that towards the end of the growth period, the epiphyseal plate of the cartilages becomes very thin and irregular in outline and may not show on radiograph
- In an individual bone, once union has begun it will be completed in about 12 to 18 months

---

Note:
- *In skeletal remains of a young person where the bones have become completely dry, the epiphyses often separate from the shaft, which should not be mistaken for fractures*
- *In radiography of growing long bones, one or more transverse lines are often observed at the diaphysial ends, this is thought to be evidence of growth disturbance and are called scars of arrested growth disturbance and one called scars of arrested growth. Public symphysis*
- *The public symphysis is probably the best single criterion for determining age from third to fifth decade*

Age	Structure of bone
Before 20 yrs.	Has a layer of impact bone near its surface
About 20 yrs.	Markedly irregular or uneven, the ridges run transversely across
Between 24 and 36 yrs.	The ridges gradually disappear and the surface has a granular appearance ventral (outer) And dorsal (inner) margins are completely defined
Early in fifth decade	The symphyseal face has an oval smooth surface with raised upper and lower ends
End of the fifth decade	A narrow-beadedrim develops on the margins
Seventh decade	The surface becomes irregularly eroded
Sixth decade	Erosion of surface and breakdown of ventral margin begins

---

Note,
If the male criteria are used for females, the age would be under estimated by about ten years as the female pubis reaches full maturity about 10 yrs later than the male.

Sternum

Age	Fusion of bones
14 to 25	Four pieces of the body of sternum fuse with one another from below upwards between 14 to 25 yrs.
40	The xiphoid unites with the body
60	The manubrium fuses with the body

Ribs.
Progressive ossification of sternal rub ends of the costal cartilages correlate with increasing age within 5 to 8 years of real age

Hyoid bone:
The greater cornu of the hyoid bone unites with the bodies between 40 to 60 years

Skull:

Bones of the calvaria are 8 in number

Bones.	Number
Parietal.	2
Frontal.	1
Temporal.	2
Occipital.	1
Sphenoid.	1
Ethmoid.	1

Bones of the face and jaws are 14 in number

Bones.	Number
Maxillary.	2
Zygomatic.	2
Nasal.	2
Lacrimal	2
Palatine	2
Inferior nasal concha.	2
Mandible	1

The flexible cartilaginous joints of early life are replaced with interlocking connection between bones in maturely

Fontanelles
- Lateral and occipital fontanelles usually close within the first two months
- Posterior fontanelle closes in 6 to 8 months
- The anterior fontanelle closes between 1-5 to 2 years
- Suture closure:
- Beginning union in the vault sutures may be identified by irregular radio - opacity on each side of the suture
- In the vault of the skull, closure of the sutures begins on the inner side 5 to 10 years earlier than on the outer side

Age	Name of sature closed
3	The condylar portions of occipital bone fuse with the squama
5	The conductor portions of occipital bone fuse with basioccipital
18 to 21	Basio occipital fuses with the basisphenoid
25 yrs.	The coronal sagitta and lambdoid sutures start to close on their inner side
30 to 40 yrs.	Fusion of posterior one third of the sagittal suture
40 to 50 yrs.	Anterior one third of the sagittal and lower half of the coronal
50 to 60 yrs.	Middle sagittal and upper half of the coronal

Notes:
- *Suture closure in skull occurs later in females than in males*
- *The most successful estimate is done in the preference of*
1. *Sagittal*
2. *Lambdoid*
3. *Coronal*
- *Ossification centre in the mandible appears at second months of intrauterine life and the two halves of the mandible unite at the second years*

Sacrum
- Centres appear in upper segments in third month
- The five sacral vertebrae are separated by cartilage until puberty where the lateral portions grow togetherAfter this fusion of epiphyses takes place and ossification of intervertebral discs extends from before upwards
- The sacrum becomes a single bone between 21 and 25 years
- A gap may persist between 51 and 52 until 32 yrs. due to 'lapsed union'

Vertebrae:
- There is a close relationship between the developments of cervical vertebral and age
- The immature vertebral body has a series of deep radial furrows both on the upper and lower surface
- This feature increases in prominence up to the age of ten and them gradually facts at from 21 to 25 years
- After 45 years, osteoarthritic changes in the joints seen in the form of lipping of the vertebrae

Scapula

age	Changes in scapula
30 to 35	Lipping starts on the ventral margin of the glenoid cavity
35 to 40	Irregular lipping occurs around the clavicular facet and inferior surface of the acromion process
45	Localised bony atrophy cab be seen
50	Cristae scapulae occurs

Secondary sex characters In males

age	Character
13 to 14	Fine hair begins to appear on pubis The testes become larger and firmer and penis begins to enlarge
15 yrs above	Hair is moderately grown on pubis Hair begins to grow on axilla
About 16 yrs	Hair on pubis is well grown The external genitals have an adult appearance
16 to 18 yrs	Voice becomes hoarse

Secondary sex characters In females

Age	Characters
12 to 13	The breasts begin to develop
	The vulva becomes more horizontal due to forward tilting of the pelvis
	The labia minora develop and some fine, pale, downy hair appears on mons veneris
	The labia develop and menstrual starts
14 to 15 yrs	The public hair is well grown and hair appeared in the axilla

Sex Characteristics

Trait	Male	Female
1) Gonads	A functioning tests. The peals, prostale etc. are only appendages	A functioning ovary. the uterus, vagina, etc. are only appendages.
2) Build	Larger with greater muscular development.	Smaller with less muscular development
3) Shoulders	Broader than hips	Narrower than hips
4) Waist	Ill – defined	Well defined
5) Trunk	Abdominal segment smaller	Abdominal segment longer
6) Thorax	Dimensions more.	Shorter and rounded.
7) Limps	Longer	Shorter.
8) Arms	Flat on section	Cylindrical on section
9) Thighs	Cylindrical.	Conical, due to shorter femur and greater deposition of fat
10) Gluteal region	Flatter	Full and rounded
11) Wrists and ankles	Not delicate	Delicate
12) Breasts	Not developed.	Developed
13) Pubic hair	Thick and extends upward to the umbilicus (rhomboidal).	Thin, horizontal and covers mons veneris only (triangular).
14) Body hair	Present on face and chest	Absent on face and chest
15) Head hair	Shorter, thicker and coarser.	Longer, thinner and finer.
16) Larynx	Prominent. Length 4.8 cm	Not prominent. length 3.8 cm

Sex

Sex has to be determined in cases of
- Heirship ● Marriage ● Divorce ● Legitimacy ● Impotence ● Rape

» In normal cases, sex determination is easy from external examination only, but it is difficult in cases of
- Hermaphroditism ● Concealed sex ● Advanced decomposition ● Skeleton

» A normal person has 46 chromosomes. The chromatin pattern in male is xy and in female xx – masculine and feminine characteristics most directly depend on the level of circulating sex hormones

Sex chromatin

Barr body	Davidson body
It is a small plano convex mass	In females, neutrophil leukocytes contain a small nuclear attachment of drumstick in about 3% of cells
In the buccal smear the percentage of nuclei containing chromatin body ranges from zero to four in males and 20 to 80 in females	This is absent in males

Specimen for sex determination
- Buccal smear ● Saliva ● Hair follicle
- Bone marrow ● Dental pulp ● Amniotic fluid

Tests for sex determination
- Combined treatment of quinacrine dihydrochloride staining for y chromosome which is seen as bright fluorescent body in the nuclei of male cells and fluorescent Feulgen reaction using acriflavine schiff reagent for x- chromosomes which is seen as bright yellow spot in the nuclei
- The percentage of quinacrine position bodies ranges from 45 to 80 % in males and o to 4 % in females
- With Feulgen reaction technique, fluorescent bodies are found in 50 to 70 % of cells in females and 0 to 2 % in males
- By using fluorescent dyes y chromosome can be demonstrated in dental pulp tissue up to one-year F – bodies are seen in 30 to 70 % of cells in males and 0 to 4 % in females

Notes:
In decomposed bodies sex chromatin cannot be made out

Intersex

It is an intermingling in one individual of characters of both sexes in varying degrees including physical form, reproductive organs and sexual behaviour

Intersex
- Gonadal agenesis
- gonadal dysgenesis
  1. Klinefelter syndrome
  2. turner's syndrome
- true hermaphrodites
  1. Male pesudohermaphroditism
  2. Female pesudohermaphroditism

gonadal agenesis
- In this condition the testes or ovaries have never developed
- The nuclear sex is negative

Gonadal dysgenesis:
The external sexual structures are present but at puberty the tests or the ovaries fail to develop

1. Klinefelter's syndrome
In this condition the anatomical structures are male but the nuclear sexing is female the sex chromosome pattern is xxy (47 chromosomes)

Characteristics features
- » Delay in onset of puberty
- » Behavioural disorder
- » Mental retardation
- » Axillary and public hair are absent
- » Hair on chest and chin are reduced
- » Gynecomastia, azoospermia low levels of testosterone
- » Sterility
- » Increases urinary gonadotrophins
- » Signs of eunachoidism
- » Increased height

Note:
- Testicular atrophy with hyalinization of seminiferous is seen histologically
- Hypogonadotropic hypogonadism is seen

2. Turner's syndrome
- It is the most common sex chromosome abnormality of human females
- Its incident in newborn is about 1 in 2500
- In this condition the anatencial structure is female but the nuclear sexing is male
- The orories do not certain premoridalfeelindes
- The sex chromosome pattern is xo (45 chromosome)

Characteristic features
- Oedema of the dorsum of the hands and feet
- Loose skin folds in the nape of the neck
- Low binter weight
- Shout stature
- Primary amenorrhoea
- Sterility
- Lack of development of primary and secondary
- Sexual characteristic
- Increased urenallgenaddtrophinexcretia
- Pigmented naevi
- A short fourth metatarsal
- Webbed neck
- Shildchut
- Wide set nipply
- High arched pahlate
- Low set ears
- Slow growth
- Learning problems

True hermaphrodite:
- This is a very rare condition of bisexuality in which an ovary and a testicle or two ovotestis are present with the external genitalia of both sexes
- The gonoad may be abdominal inguinal or labio – scrotal in position
- There may be uterus
- Phallus may be penile or clitoral
- The labia may be bifid as in female or fused resembling the scrotum of the male
- The somatic sex chromatin may be male or female

Pseudo – hermaphroditism:
In this condition gonadal tissue of only one sex is seen internally but external appearance is of the opposite sex

	Male pseudohermaphroditism	Female pseudohermaphroditism
Nuclear sex	Xy but sex organs and sexual characteristic denote to female form ,because of testicular feminisation	Xx but deviation of sex organs and sexual character towards male are seen due to adrenal hyperplasia
Enzyme degrees	5 – a reductase	21 hydroxylase

Concealed sex
Criminals may conceal their sex to arid detection by changing dress or by other methods
This can be detected by physical examinations

Note:
In advanced putrefaction, sex can be determined by identifying uterus or prostate which resist putrefaction for a long time

Skeleton
- Human skeleton is both exo and endoskeleton
- Recognisable sex difference does appear until after puberty except in the pelvis and the accuracy from this bone is about 75 to 80 % and without pelvis only 50%
- Sex determination is rarely based on any one skeletal feature alone
- The determination of sex is based namely upon the appearance of the
- Pelvis
- Skull
- Sternum
- Long bones
- In the skull, several features are modified by senility
- In the pelvis sex features are independent of each other and ay even contradict the other in the same pelvis

characteristic	male	female
pelvis	Stands higher and more erect when compared with female pelvis	Stands lower and less erect when composed with male pelvis
Subpubic angle	less	more
Greater sciatic notch	Less	More
Pelvic inlet	less	More
Pelvic outlet	Less	More
Obturator foramen	More	less
Curve of illum	more	less

Note:
Greater sciatic notch is the ideal feature determines the sex of a female child

Chilotic line
It is an anthropometric line in pelvis the index of which is used in identifying the sex

Medullary index of bones
The sex of the long bones can be determined on the basis of their medullary index from tibia, humerus, ulna and radius

$$\text{Medullary index} = \frac{\text{diameter of cortex}}{\text{Diameter by whole}} * 100$$

Note:
In general adult female skeletal measurements are about 94% that of the male of the same race, but different measurements may vary from 91 to 98

Krogman degree of accuracy in sexing adult skeletal remaining:
- Entire skeleton – 100%
- Pelvis alone-95%
- Skull alone-90%
- Pelvis plus skull-98%
- Long bones alone-80%.

Age	Appearance of centre of ossification	Union of bone epiphyses
5 th year	Head of radius , trapezoid, scaphoid	Greater tubercle fuses with head of humerus
6 th year	Lower end of ulna, trapezium	Rami of pubis and ischium unite
6 th to 7 th year	Medial epicondyle of the humerus	
9 th year	Olecranon	
9 th to 11 th year	Trochlea of humerus	
10 th to 11 th year	Pisiform	
11 th year	Lateral epicondyle of humerus	
13 th year	Separate Centres In Triradiate cartilage of acetabulum	
12 th to 14 th year	Lesser trochanter of femur	
14 th year	Crest of ilium; head and tubercles of ribs	Medial epicondyle of humerus : lateral epicondyle ;patella complete
15 th year	Acromion	Coracoids with scapula;triradiate cartilage of acetabulum
16 th year	Ischialb tuberosity	Lower end of humerus ; olecranon to ulna;upper end of radius; metacarpals;proximal phalanges.
17 th to 18 th year		Head of femur;lesser and greater trochanter of femur acromion ; lower end of ulna
18 th 19 th year	Inner end of clavicle	Lower end of femur ; upper end of tibia and fibula; head of humerus ;lower end of radius
20th to 21 st year		Iliac crest ;inner end of clavicle ; ischial tuberosity, head of the ribs.

Traits diagnostic of sex from skeleton

Trait	Male	Female
1) General size	Larger, more massive.	Smaller, slender
2) Long bones	Ridges, despressions and processes more prominent bones of arms and legs are 8% longer.	Less prominent.
3) Shaft	Rougher.	Smoother, thinner with relatively wider medullary cavity.
4) Articular surfaces	Larger	Smaller
5) Metacarpal bones	Longer and broader	Shorter and narrower
6) Weight	4.5 kg	2.75 kg.

SKULL

Trait	Male	Female
1) General appearances	Larger, longer (dolichocrania)	Smaller, lighter, walls thinner; rounder (brachycrania), and smoother
2) Capacity	1500 to 1550 ml	1350 to 1400 ml
3) Architecture	Rugged; muscle ridges more marked, esp. in occipital and temporal areas	Smooth
4) Forehead	Steeper .(sloping), less rounded	Vertical, round, full, infantile.
5) Glabella	Rough and more prominent	Smooth, small or absent
6) Frontonasal junction	Distinct angulation	Smoothly curved
7) Orbits	Square set lower on the face, relatively smaller, rounded margins	Rounded, higher, relatively larger sharp margins
8) Supraorbital ridges	Prominent and rounded	Less prominent, sharper or absent
9) Check bones	Heavier, laterally arched	Lighter, more compressed
10) Zygomatic arch	More prominent	Less prominent
11) Nasal aperture	Higher and narrower margins sharp	Lower and broader
12) External auditory meatus	Bony ridges along the upper border is prominent	Often absent
13) Frontal eminences	Small	Large
14) Parietal eminences	Small	Large
15) Frontal sinuses	Much developed	Less developed
16) Occipital area	Muscle lines and protuberance prominent	Not prominent
17) Mastoid process	Wider, longer, round, blunt	Narrow, short, smooth, pointed
18) Base	Sites of muscular insertions more marked	Less marked
19) Digastrics groove	More deep	Less deep
20) Condylar facet	Long and slender	Short and broad
21) Occipital condyles	Large	Small
22) Palate	Larger, broader, tends more to U-shape	Smaller Tends more to parabola.
23) Foramina	Large	Smaller
24) Foramen magnum	Relatively large and long	Relatively small and round
25) Teeth	Larger	Smaller

MANDIBLE

1) General size	Larger and thicker	Smaller and thinner
2) Chin	Square (U-shaped)	Rounded
3) Body height	At symphysis greater .	At symphysis smaller
4) Ascending ramus	Greater breadth	Smaller beadth
5) Angle of body and ramus (Gonion)	Less obtuse (under 125); prominent , and everted	More obtuse; not prominent inverted
6) Condyles	Larger	Smaller
7) Mental tubercle	Large and prominent	Insignificant .

traits diagnostic of sex from skeleton

Trait	Male	Female
1) Bony framework	Massive , rougher, marked muscle sites . stands higher and more erect.	Less massive , slender , smoother
2) General	Deep funnel.	Flat bowl
3) Ilium	Less vertical ;curve of iliac crest reaches higher level and is more prominent	More vertical; distance between iliac crests is less ;iliac fossae shallow ; curves of crest well marked
4) Preauricular sulcus : (attachment of anterior sacroiliac ligament).	Not frequent , narrow, shallow	More frequent , broad and deep
5) Acetabulum	Large , 52 mm. in diameter : directed laterally : wider deeper	Small , 46 mm in diameter ;directed anterolaterally : narrower
6) Obturator foramen	Large , often oval with base upwards.	Small, triangular with apex forwards
7) Greater sciatic notch	Smaller, narrower , deeper	Larger, wider, shallower
8) Illeo – pectineal line :	Well marked and rough	Rounded and smooth
9) Ishnial tuberosity	Inverted	Everted ; more widely separated
10) Body of pubis	Narrow , triangular , thick	Broad, square pits on posterior surface if borne children
11) Ramus of pubis	It is like continuation of body of pubis	Has a constricted or narrowed appearance and is short and thick
12) Ischiopubic rami	More everted, thicker and rougher .	Less everted , thinner and smoother
13) Symphysis:	Higher, bigger and narrow in width margins of pubic arch everted.	Lower , wider and rounded . margins of pubic arch not everted ; distance between two pubic tubercles greater . the dorsal border is irregular and shows depressions or pits (scars of parturition).
14) Subpubic angle	V- shaped sharp angle 700 to 750	U – shaped , rounded broaded angle. 900 to 1000
15) Pelvic brim or inlet	Heart shaped	Circular or elliptical; more spacious diameters longer
16) Pelvic cavity	Conical and funnel – shapped	Broad and round

17) Pelvic outlet	Smaller	Larger
18) Sacroiliac articulation	Large, extends to 2 ½ to 3 vertebrae	Small, oblique, extends to 2 to 2 ½ vertebrae
19) Sacroiliac joint surface	Large and less sharply angulated	L-shaped and elevated anteriorly
20) Sacrum	Longer, narrower, with more evenly distributed curvature ; promontory well marked body of first sacral vertebra larger	Shorter, wider; upper half almost straight curve forward in lower half ; promontory less marked. Body of first sacral vertebra small
21) Coccyx	Less movable	More movable
22) Ishiopubic index pubic length in mm ------------------------ x 100 ischial length in mm	73 to 94	91 to 115
23) Sciatic notch index Width of sciatic notch ------------------------ x 100 Depth of sciatic notch	65+-8	54+-9
24) Pubic ramus ratio	1:1	2:1 or greater.
25) Sacral index breadth of base of sacrum ------------------------------ x100 Anterior length of sacrum	112	116

THORAX

1. General	Longer and narrower	Shorter and wider
2. Sternum	Body longer and more than twice the length of the manubrium (hyrtl's law);upper margin is in level with lower part of the body of second thoracic vertebra ; Breadth more .length more than 149 Mm (Ashley's rule)	Shorter and less than twice the length of the manubrium: upper margin in level with lower part of the body of third thoracic vertebra; breadth less. Length less than 149 mm. (Ashley's rule).
3. Sternal index Length of manubrium ------------------------------ x 100 Length of body	46.2	54.3
4. Ribs:	Thicker ; larger ; heavier ; lesser curvature and are less oblique.	Thinner; shorter ; greater curvature and more oblique.
5. Clavicle	Longer (151 to 153 cm) broader,heavier , less curved	Smaller , narrower (138cm) lighter , more

ESTIMATION OF AGE AS A WHOLE
- **FIRST FORTNIGHT** - Change in umbilical cord and skin
- **FIRST SIX MONTHS** - weight and height.
    - partial closure of anterior fontanelle.
    - fusion of the 2 halves of the mandible.
    - ossification centres in capitate – Appearance during 2nd month after Birth.

6 MONTH – 2 YEARS
- Eruption & calcification of "temporary "teeth.
- Certain ossification centre appear
- Certain ossification femur, tarsus carpus.

2-6 YEARS
- Ossification of tarsus & carpus.
- Appearance of centres in epiphyses of long bones.
- Number of carpal bones on X- ray is the Indication of approximate age (in years)

6 to 13 YEARS
- Eruption & calcification of "permanent" teeth.(very helpful)
- Alteration in already appeared centres.
- Additional centres appear.

13 to 16 YEARS
- Changes of puberty
- Ossification of bone - especially in elbow Joint region.

16 to 25 YEARS
- Union of epiphyses of most bones with the Shaft occurs.
- Union of epiphyses of clavicles, ends of ribs and iliac crest occurs.
- Incisors, tips of canines &cusps of premolar show slight to moderate wear between 20-30 years.
- Sternal rib shows a scalloped rim around a deepening V-shaped pit in both sexes in the early twenties.

25 to 35 YEARS
- Coronal sagittal & lambdoid sutures start to close.
- Changes in the symphysis pubis

35 - 50 YEARS
- Further progress in changes in symphysis pubis
- Between 30 to 40 years
    Tooth cusp wear:
    1.Moderate
    2.severe
- medullary cavity of humerus, may have increased upward upto the level of the lower end of the tuberosity
- Between 35 to 40 years , wrinkles appears in front of ears ,eyes , eyebrows.
- xiphoid process unites with sternum at about 40 years.

40 to 50 YEARS
- Between 35 to 40 years wrinkles
- in front of ears
- About eyes about eyebrows.

xiphoid process unites with sternum at about 40 years.
- Between 40 to 50 years – Vault sutures unites both Endocranially & ectocranially
- ortex of long bones becomes thinner & less dense.
- In the humerus medullary cavity may extent upward upto almost the surgical neck.
- Atrophic areas seen in scapula & iliac fossa becomes Moderate size
- Margins of bodies of lumbar vertebrae & inner borders of ischial tuberosities.

Lipping by 40 years.
↓
Well-marked by 45 years.
↓
More marked here & in joints of extremities later.

| END OF 5TH DECADE ||
MALE	FEMALE
Bony projection from superior and /or inferior rib margins-well marked.	Bone itself is thinner.
Pit deepens & widens	Relatively shallow pit

- Ossification begin
    1. Laryngeal cartilage
    2. costal cartilage
    3. Hyoid bone.
- Early changes in articular surfaces of many bones
    1. Lipping
    2. Reduction of joint space
    3. punched out areas of osteoporosis present (on the X-ray Examination).
- Skull bones: ivory like - Granular appearance & feel.

NOTE:
ARCUS SENILIS:

Due to degenerative changes.
↓
Gray opaque ring surround cornal margins
↓
But separated from margins by an area of clear cornea.

- In 50 years (or) later lipoid degeneration takes place and is followed by formation of Arcus senilis but not complete before 60 years.
- Called as Arcus juveniles when it occurs in young adults (<40 years) due to hyperlipidaemia

GREYING OF THE HAIR:
- Variable, not much valued.
- Greying of scalp hair occurs in 40 years
- 1st at the temples.
- later involves beard, chest hair & eyebrows .
- But pubic hair – Not becomes grey before 50-55 years.

50 to 60 YEARS:
- Slight thinning of external tables of vault
- Molar crowns of teeth -usually worn flat to a single.

AFTER 60 YEARS:
- Further sutural closure of skull occurs.
- Linea and tuberosities of muscle attachments shows small osteophytic 'spurs' or 'spikes' in 50's and 60's
- Joint changes becomes more extreme in character and marked osteoporosis seen.
- Fusion of joint between manubrium & body of the sternum and more visible calcification of laryngeal and costal cartilages seen.
- Pathological skeletal changes is considered as predominant feature.
- silvery white hair seen.
- Completely edentulous upper and lower jaws- Age of over 70 years

- Loss of collagenous stroma in old age and bone becomes lighter
- Stroma gets lost initially in outer corner zone around marrow cavity.
- Becomes fragile &brittle initially in ends of long bones adjacent to joints.
- Radiologically thinning of cortex:
- Progressive rarefaction of apex of Medullary cavity of humerus & femur and it is used in age determination
- Microradiographs of bone – useful (natural remodelling process correlates increasing age & loss of bone).

Indication of old age

Loss of elasticity of skin

wrinkling & discolouration of skin
1. Buttocks & abdomen
2. Atrophy of uterus & ovaries.
3. brown atrophy of heart
4. Atherosclerotic change in arteries.

Long continued fluoride ingestion causes mottling of teeth

Paraplegia:
Increase in density and weight of bones causes lipping of bones of vertebrae leads to increase in pressure on spinal cord.
- Age estimation -Uncertain after 25 years.
- Difficult to attain accuracy for even 5 years.

PROCEDURE FOR AGE DETERMINATION:

RADIOLOGY:
- 6-12 YEARS : Take X-ray of elbow joint and wrist joint
- 6 years: centers for lower end of ulna
- 6-9 years: Medical epicondyles of humeus .
- 9 years: Olecranon.
- 9-11 years: trochlea of humerus.
- 10th -11th years : pisiform.
- 11th year : lateral epicondyles of humerus
- 13 -16 years: X-rays of elbow joint and pelvis.
- 13th year: separate centres in triradiate cartilage of acetabulum
- 12-14 years: lesser trochanter of femur.
- 14th year: crest of ilium, fusion of medical epicondyle of humerus, lateral epicondyle with trochlea.
- 15th year: fusion of triradiate cartilage of acetabulum.
- 16th year: ischial tuberosity; fusion of lower end of the humerus, olecranon to ulna & upper end of radius.

Fusion of bones /joints in males:
- **16 years:** elbow joint
- **16-17 years:** ankle joint
- **17-18 years:** hip joint
- **18-19 years:** knee shoulder &wrist joints.
- **20-21 years:** fusion of the iliac crest ischial tuberosity & inner end of clavicle.

Fusion of bones /joints in females:1 year earlier than in males

```
                          Opinion about age
       ┌──────────────┬──────────┴──────────┬──────────────────┐
Physical findings  Dental findings  Physical examination  Multiple criteria of skeletal age
```

MEDICOLEGAL IMPORTANCE OF AGE:
1.CRIMINAL RESPONSIBILITY:
    a)Railway act :child (no age prescribed) may be held responsible for working train/ endangering safety of commuters of trains .
    b)SEC. 20, BNS: any act by child <5 years -not offence
    c)Sec.21, BNS: child 7-12 years – capable of committing an offence, if attained "sufficient maturity of understanding to judge nature & consequence of his conduct on that occasion. (maturity presumed unless proved otherwise by defence).
    d)<12 years child: can't give valid consent to suffer any harm from act done in good faith & for its benefits sec.83, I.P.C.
    e)SEC, 25, BNS:>18 years person can give valid consent to suffer any harm from unintended act / not known to cause death /grievous hurt.
    f)Persons with XXY chromosomal pattern is presented with aggressiveness and criminal nature.

2.RAPE: S.63, BNS - Age of Consent: 15 years is replaced by 18 years in BNS. Exception 2 of Section 63 states that "sexual intercourse or acts by a man with his wife, the wife not being under 18 years of age, is not rape".
3.KIDNAPPING :
    a)Sec.97, BNS:Offence to kidnap<10 years child with intention of dishonestly taking movable property
    b)Sec 137(1)b BNS:The IPC section is included as a clause in the BNS. Words "minor under the age of sixteen years of male or under eighteen years of age if a female" are replaced by "child" thus making it gender neutralc)Sec363,I.P.C:Offence to kidnap/make minor for begging.
    d)Sec87,BNS:Offence of kidnap, abduct or induce woman to compel her marriage.
    e)Sec96,BNS:Offence to procure <18 years child for prostitution
    f)Sec141, BNS:Offence to import into India from a foreign country a <21 years girl or Boy for illicit intercourse.
6.EMPLOYMENT :<14 years child not to be employed for any type of work
For person completing 15 years adolescent fitness certificate issued by certified surgeon tio allow him to work in factory.

7. ATTAINMENT OF MAJORITY:
Sec3, IND Majority Act,1875: A person completing 18 years is considered as major.
But if under guardianship of court of wards Or under a guardian appointed by the court majority will be attained on completing 21 years.

8. EVIDENCE :S.118, I.E.A:
All persons competent to testify unless they are prevented from understanding question put to them ,or from giving rational answers due to teenage years or extreme old age or disease of body /mind.

9. MARRIAGE CONTRACT :
<18 years female & <21 years male can't contract marriage
Child marriage restraint Act,1978:

10. INFANTICIDE: If infant proved under 7 months of intrauterine life charge of infanticide can't be supported.

10. CRIMINAL ABORTION:
Women passed child bearing age not charged for procuring criminal abortion

11. IDENTIFICATION:
In any chain of identity data approximate age is very important e.g. Few days old child – alleged to be a new born child.

12. IMPOTENCE &STERILITY : Boy before puberty is sterile not impotent .
women after menopause is sterile

AGE OF THE FOETUS:
- Developing ovum: 1st 7-10 days after conception (until implantation)
- Embryo: 1 week to end of 8th week
- Foetus: after end of 8th week.
- Infant: completely born.

Determining Gestational age:
- chorionic villi maturation
- foot length
- ossification centres.

END OF THE 1ST MONTH:
- 1cm length
- 2,5g weight
- Eyes -2 dark spots
- Mouth-cleft

END OF THE 2ND MONTH:
- 4cm length
- 10g weight
- Hands & feet -webbed
- Placenta- begins to form
- Anus -dark spot
- 1st ossification center in the clavicle(4-5 weeks)   Followed by maxilla (6 weeks)
- Ossification centres -in upper segment of sacrum &mandible.

END OF THE 3RD MONTH :
9cm length
30g weight
- Pupillary membrane -appears
- Eyes-closed
- Nails -appears
- Neck -formed

END OF THE 4TH MONTH:
- 16cm length
- 120g weight
- Sex-recognised
- Lanugo hair -seen on body
- Convolutions - Begins to develop in brains
- Meconium -found in duodenum.
- Between 2nd&3rd month and between 3rd& 4th month - NOT possible to draw hard and fast lines.

END OF THE 5TH MONTH:
- 25cm length
- 400g weight
- Nails -distinct and soft
- Light hair -appears on hand
- Skins -covered with vernix caseosa
- Meconium -at beginning of large intestine
- Ossification centres -middle segment of sacrum.

END OF THE 6TH MONTH:
- 30 cm length
- 700g weight
- Eyebrows eyelashes - appear
- Skin-red & wrinkled; subcutaneous fat begins to be deposited
- Vernix caseosa-present
- Meconium -in transverse colon
- Testes -close to kidneys.

END OF THE 7THMONTH: 35cm length
- Crown -rump length 23cm
- Foot length 8cm
- 900-1200g weight
- Nails thick
- Eyelids -open
- Pupillary membrane -disappear
- Skin-dusky red, thick fibrous
- Meconium -in entire large intestine
- Tests -at external inguinal ring
- Gall bladder -contains bile
- Caecum -in right iliac fossa
- Ossification centre -talus

END OF THE 8TH MONTH:
- 40cm length
- 1.5-2 kg weight
- Nails -reach finger tips
- Scalp hair -thicken ,1.5cm in length
- Skin - NOT wrinkled
- Left testis -in scrotum
- Placenta- 500g weight
- Ossification centre -lower segment of sacrum

END OT THE 9TH MONTH:
- 45cm length
- 2.2-3kg weight
- Scalp hair -dark &4cm long
- Meconium – at end of large intestine
- Scrotum - wrinkled; contains both testes
- Placenta -500g weight
- Ossification centre -lower end of female

END OF THE 10THMONTH :
- 48-52cm length
- 28-32cm crown-rump length
- 2.5-5 kg (avg-3.4kg) weight
- Male infant - 100g weight than female
- Head circumference -3.3 -38cm (Tape positioned at frontal and occipital prominence)
- 6fontanels -in neonatal skill Anterior fontanel (bregma)-at junction of sagittal & lambdoid Sutures &4x2.5cm
- Head of child - ¼ th of whole-body length
- Brains surfaces - convolution; grey matter begins to form
- Scalp hair -dark ,3.5 cm long
- Face -not wrinkled
- Lanugo -absent, except on shoulders
- Skin-pale; covered with vernix caseosa
- Nails -project beyond finger ends, but reach only toe tips
- Testis-in scrotum
- Labia majora – developed fully &covers the closed vulva & labia minora
- Rectum -dark brownish, green /black meconium present
- Umbilical cord -50-55cm long ,1 cm thick
- Limbs- firm, hard & rounded

OSSCIFICATION OF CENTRE:
1. **Sternum**- Placed flat on wooden board - cut along long axis in midline with cartilage knife.
2. **Lower end of femur & upper end of tibia:**

Leg flexed against the thigh

Transverse / vertical incision into knee joint

Patella-removed

Femur end pushed forward though wound

Several parallel cross-section made through epiphysis (from articular surface until largest part of ossification centre)

Centre -brownish -red nucleus surrounded by bluish -white cartilage

Further sections made through plain cartilage above it, until reaching the diaphyseal centre.

Centre -appears about 36th week

- 4-5mm diameter Of 37-38 weeks
- 6-8 mm diameter At full term

Upper end of tibia -similarly examined

80 % full term infants	other cases
Centre or upper end of tibia	centre appear after birth

3. BONES OF THE FOOT:

foot -grasped in the left hand behind heel, Toes pointing towards dissector
↓
Incision between interspace of 3rd & 4 toes with a long knife
↓
Backward through sole of foot & heel
↓
If centre in calcaneum & talus -not exposed
↓
Thin slices of cartilages of these bones cut until
↓
Present /absence shown.

RULES OF HASSE (1895):
- Rough method of foetal age calculation
- **Length of foetus (in cm):** Crown to heel
- During 1st month of pregnancy
- Square root of the length = approximate age of foetus in months
- e.g. 16cm foetus = 4 month

- **HAASES MODIFICATION OF MORISSON'S LAW:**
  During last 5-month - length in cm÷5
  e.g. 35cm foetus = 7 month
- **AFTER BIRTH:** the length of an infant = 50cm, 60cm at the end of 6 month
  END OF 1ST YEAR: 61cm length
  END OF 4THYEAR: 100cm length
  By 13 years 150cm length
- From 2- beginning adolescence -average growth of 5cm /year
- **BIRTH WEIGHT:** double by 4-5 months of age triples by about 1 year Quadruples at 24 months
- After 2-average weight gain until adolescence -2-3kg /annually
- **HEAD CIRCUMFERENCE:** increase by 12 cm in 1st year of life 90% of adult head size -by end of 2nd year
- **BRAIN:** at birth it is nearly in 80% of adult weight by 6 - 90%.
- In infants & children - height & weight - Compared with standard tables.

Stature

- Stature varies at different times of the day by one and half to two cum. It is less in the afternoon and evening due to reduced elasticity of the intervertebral discus and longitudinal vertebral muscles
- After the age of thirty, the natural processes of simile degeneration (A trophy and loss of elasticity of vertebral disks) cause gradual decrease in stature by about 0.6mm per year
- The Stature is greater by one to three cm on lying, the body lengthens after death by about two cm.
- Due to complete loss of muscle tone, relaxation of large joints and vertebral discs and loss of ten-sioning effect of per spinal muscles

Determination of stature from Disremembered body
1. The length from the tip of middle finger to the tip of opposite middle finger, when arms are fully extended, closely equals height.
2. Twice the length of one form with 30cm, added for two clavicles and four cm for the sternum, is equal to the height.
3. The height of forearm measured from tip of acromion process of tip of middle finger is equal to 5/19 of the stature
4. The length from the vertex to the symphysis pubis is roughly half of stature
5. After 14 years of age symphysis pubis lies about halfway of the body, before 14 years the trunk is longer than the lower limb.
6. The length from the sternal notch to symphysis pubis multiplied by 3.3 glosses the stature.

Anthropometry
1. Description data – colour of hair, eyes, complexion, steps of nose, ears, chin etc
2. Body orals – moles, scarps, tattoo marks
3. Body measurements
» Anteroposterior diameter of health
» Span of outstretched arms
» Left of length of left middle types

As a set means of identification, photographs are not always reliable, and they may be a source of error even when they are inspected by experts.

Dactylography (Dermatoglyphics)

Dermatoglyphics is the study of ridge pattern in the skin

Principle - Fingerprints are impressions of patterns formed by papillary or epidermal ridges of the fingertips.

Classification

1) Loops (60-70 percent)
- Radial
- Ulnar

2) Whorls (29-35 percent)
- Concentric
- Spiral
- Double spiral
- Almond shaped

3) Arches (6-7 percent)
- Plain
- Tented
- Exceptional

4) Composite (1-2 percent)
- Central pocket loops
- Lateral pocket loops
- Twinned loops
- Accidentals

Identification
- In practice 16-20 points of fine comparison are accepted as proof of identity.
- The patterns are not inherited and paternity cannot be proved through fingerprint patterns.
- The pattern is different even in identical twins
- The fingerprint system is the only guide to identify, which is unfailing in practice.

Poroscopy
- The ridges on fingers and halers are studded with microscopic pores, formed by mouths of duets of sub epidermal sweat glands.
- These pores are permanent and unchanged during life and vary in size, sharing with starting, stopping on occasion and branching at points.
- Position, extent and number, distribution and arrangement of the pores over a given length of ridge in each individual.
- The method of examining pores is called poroscopy and is useful when only fragments of finger prints are available in which there no specific pattern.

  Radiology - Study of friction ridges

  Edgeoscopy - Study of edges friction ridges (shows> characteristics)

  Quetlet's rule – Every mature- made objects present infinite variation in forms and no patterns are over alike.

Mode of production
- A constant stream of sweat covers the skin sweat contains 99% water (1% solids - sulphates, urea, fatty acid, lactic acid)
- Finger print may also contain oil exuded by sebaceous glades
- If finger applied to a smooth surface, a greasy impression of its pattern is made on it.

Techniques of fingerprinting
Hands are washed, cleared dried otherwise print will be blurred.

1. Plain print – applying ink to finger tips and placing the finger directly on paper

2. Rolled finger print – Rolling fingers on paper from outward to inward to obtain a impression of whole tip.

If rigor mortis is well developed, invasion into the palmer surface of fingers at the proximal interphalangeal joint will enable the fingers to be straightened, printing can be carried out.

Types
- Latent print (chance print) – invisible car Barely impression
- Visible print (patent print) - formed by fingers stained with blood car ink
- Plastic print – impression made on soap, mind, candles

Ridge impressions
- In manual lab our ears working with lime, sand and current the ridges on the bubbles get cur duly rubbed and become broken and indistinct
- Ridge impression get malformed if the quality of ink its poor, when the ink is too liquid and spreads into the depressions.

Development of latent print
- A latent print may be developed by dusting the area with coloured proverbs to provides

Contrast commonly used powder -
  1. Gray powder (chalk, measuring)
  2. White powder (lead carbonate or French stalk)
- Finger prints on paper, wood, fabrics are developed by treating then with 5% silver nitrate solution and fixing then with sodium thiosulphate.

Finger printers in decomposed bodies
- Histological sections up to a death of 0.6mm the surface of the skin give satisfactory finger prints
- In dead bodies, the palmer skin of the terminal palmate of each finger should be removed reportedly from both hands
- After labeling, placed in separate containers, containing 10% formalin and sent to fingerprint bureau.
- If fingers are shrivelled immerse it in 20% acetic acid for 24-48hrs (cause to swell to normal)
- If skin is dehydrated finger is soaked in 3% solution of potassium hydroxide in warm water until finger regain normal size
- Impressions may persist for years if undisturbed by learning.

Mutilation of finger prints
- Criminals sometimes attempt to mutilate the pattern by self-inflicted wounds or burns
- Applications of corrosives or erosion organist a hard surface, but they are not destroyed unless the true skin is completely destroyed
- Permanent impairment of the finger print pattern occurs in leprosy, electric injury and after exposure to radiation

COMPUTERISATION:
- Finger print reader (FINDER) can record each fingerprint data in half second.
- Printer up right fingers are recorded excluding little fingers.

MEDICOLEGAL IMPORTANCE:
- The recognition of impressions left at a scene of crime e.g. weapons, furniture, doors establish the identity of the criminal.
- The identification of suicides, deserters, persons suffering from loss of memory or those dead as unconscious after bring involved in accident.
- Identification in case of accident exchange of new born infants.
- Cheques, bank notes and other legal documents can bear a fingerprint.
- In criminals' impressions of all 10 fingers are taken, but for only civil purposes left thumb impression only is taken.

FOOTPRINTS (PODOGRAM)
- The skin patterns of toes and heels are as distinct and permanent as those of fingers.
- Footprints of newborn infants are used in some maternity hospitals to prevent exchange or substitution of infants.
- The first foot print of suspected persons is taken and compared with the original.
- Any peculiarities in the foot, such as a flat foot, supernumerary toes, scars or callosities are likely to be found in the footprint.
- A footprint produced by walking is usually larger than one produced by standing.
- Crime scene footprint are compared with the comparison prints made on similar surface by the suspect.
- Step length
    1. Adult woman 45-55cm
    2. Adult male 63-70cm

POTATO PRINTS:
- In the anterior part of the palate, the structural details like the rugae are individual specific permanent.
    a) Primary rugae (>5mm)
    b) Secondary rugae(3-5mm)
    c) Garmented rugae (2-3 mm) (Lyell)

LIP PRINTS (CHEILOSCOPY)
- The fissures and grooves on the lips are claimed to be characteristic of the individual.
- Lip prints are divided into six patterns (SUZUKI) which are specific to the in divided: vertical, branched, intersected, reticular pattern, etc.,24 characteristics.

EAR PRINTS:
- Ears have four basic shapes: oval round, rectangular and triangle. The shapes of ears tubes and the tips of ears of various types.
- Most of the ear prints are round are found on doors or windows. From the suspect three prints are taken
    1. Functional pressure
    2. Gentle pressure
    3. More pressure, on a glass pone
- If the tragus point, crus of the helix points and antitragus points fit, look at the lower and upper crura of the antihelix and the helix rim. If all details coincide the prints are from the same source.

NOSE PRINTS:
- The lines on the nose and the shape of the tip are helpful in identification. Chance impressions may be found over door wall etc.

RETINA SCAN IN IDENTIFICATION:
- Each person's retina has a unique pattern which is not changed from birth until death the pattern is different even is identical twins As such it appears to be the most precise and reliable biometric.
- A retinal scan is performed by casting an undetectable ray of low energy infrared light into a person's eye as he looks through the scanner's eyepiece focussing on a single point for a duration of 15 seconds, which outlines a circular path on the retina.
- Retinal blood vessels absurd light more readily than the surroundings tissue, but the amount of reflection fluctuates.
- The result of the scan is converted to computer code and stored in a doctor base.
- The retinal templates are one of the smallest of any biometric technologies.
- They are about 70 times more accurate than iris scans.
- Retinal patterns may be altered in cataracts, glaucoma, retinal degeneration and diabetes.

IRIS SCAN:
- The iris is a muscle within the eye that regulates the size of the pupil controlling the amount of light that enters the eye
- It is the coloured portion of the age
- Although the colouration and structure of iris are genetically linked, an individual's irises are unique and structurally district, purpose. The iris is locked using Landmark features.

SKULL PHOTO SUPERIMPOSITION
- It is a technique used to determine whether a skull is that of the patient /person in that photograph.
- A negative, with an view face photograph is appreciated
- The photograph is charged to standard size of a standard think in the photograph of the missing person
- If not, photograph is superposed by magnifying until interpapillary distances correspond
- The salient features of the face are traced dam from the photograph by a ground glass.
- The negatives of the photograph and the skull are superimposed by aligning characteristics points in the negative.

Points for comparison

1.The eyes,	2. Nasion,	3.Prosthion in central line,
4. Nasal space,	5.Lower border of nose,	6. Lower border upper jaw
7. Zygomas below eyes	8. Supraorbital ridge	9. Angle if jaw
10. External auditory meatus	11. Jaw	

- The two superimposable negatives are photograph on bromide paper. The outlines and landmarks should match if the face matches the skull
- A clear effect is brought by combining negative of skull and positive of portrait. This test is more of a negative value.

Video superimposition: Both the video of the skull and the portrait is superimposed with bunding and analysed for conformity. All the anatomical landmarks are compared.

Computer assisted superimposition: Both the skull and facial photograph are digitalise using a computer and compared by measurements by using dats measurements by mouse. Anterior teeth are mainly sun for positive comparisons.

Identification by Reconstruction of Facial features: A face is unconstructed by above skull features, but non-skull dependant parts the eyes, nose are not reconstructed. They are matched by verifying various varieties of stoical eyes, Cars and noses.

Computer pictures: several curves are generated by computers. Different features of face are generated, so that exact face is replicated.

Physiognomic Recoloration: 1. Sculptural to give 3-D burst 2. Artistic to give drawing in two views (facial and profile).

Normal and Abnormal bone comparisons:

When previous x-ray form is available, they can be compared with post mortem forms. It is useful in identification of adults.

1. The frontal shows are compared as no man's two sinuses are the same. They are individual specific
2. The Spain ait complex and mastoid area are also very useful criteria of individuality
3. The contours of the second rib are unique
4. Function of the ribs or vertebrae may be noted
5. Operative defects and cabovers in skull are very important

Skull suture pattern and vascular grooves:

- The sagittal and comodule sutures are especially complicated from one person to another
- The vascular grooves, such as those related to the middle meningeal verses, are more apt to be visible in x ray films than the suture lines.

SCARS

- A scar is a fibrous tissue covered by epithelium without hair follicles, sweat glands or pigment, produced from the healing of a wound.
- Injury to the dermis produces a scar, while superficial injuries involving only the epidermis does not produce a scar.
- Scars are permanent.

Examination:

- Good lighting is essential.
- The description should include:

• Number	• Site	• Size
• Shape	• Level it bears to the body surface	• Fixed of free Smooth or Irregular Surface
	• Colour	• Presence of absence of glistening
	• Tenderness	• Ends are Tapering or not

- Probable Direction of Original Wound
- The application of heat, filtered ultraviolet light or surface friction, makes faint scars readily visible.
- Old scars may become unrecognisable.
- Suspected scars in the dead body can be proved by microscopy, by a section stained to show the elastic tissue, which is absent in a scar.
- Elastic tissue is present in striae gravidarum.

Characters:

- Scars may indicate the type of injury which produced them.
1. Incised wounds produce linear scars. If healing is secondary, the scar is wider and thicker in the centre than in the periphery.
2. Scars from lacerated wounds, and from wounds which have suppurated are firmer, irregular, more prominent and adherent to the deeper. tissues.
3. Stab wound due to a knife-blade produces oval, elliptical, triangular or irregular scars (elevated - keloid formation).
4. A bullet wound causes a circular depressed scar.
5. Scars from scalds are spotted in appearance. tend to be continuous, often run downwards and show evidence of splashing about the main injury.
6. Scars clue to corrosive acids. burns or radiation, cause irregular scars, and keloid may develop in the scar tissue, especially in Negroes.
7. Vaccination scars are circular or oval, flat or slightly depressed.
8. Many skin diseases, smallpox. syphilis, etc., cause multiple scars on the skin.

Growth:

- Scars produced in childhood grow in size with the natural development of the individual, especially if situated on the chest or limbs.

Age of Scars:	
APPEARANCE	**TIME**
Reddish or bluish angry scar.	5 to 6 Days
Pale, soft, tender, sensitive.	14 days
White, glistening, Tenderness lost.	2 - 6 months
Tough.	6 months

Erasure:

The scar can be erased by excision and skin grafting, or suture of the edges of the excised area. This results in a scar which is less clearly seen.

Medicolegal Importance:

(1) They form important marks for identification of a person.
(2) The shape of the scar may indicate the nature of weapon or agent that caused the injury.
(3) The age of the scar is important in a criminal offence. If the age of a wound corresponds with the date of the attack it may have value as circumstantial evidence.
(4) Linea albicantes may indicate previous pregnancy.
(5) If a person is disfigured due to scars, it becomes a grievous hurt.
(6) Scar causing contracture at or around a joint restricting movement or functions of the joint becomes grievous hurt.
(7) The accused may attribute scars of wounds to disease or therapeutic procedures.
(8) Scar of various operative procedures also help in identification.
(9) To charge an enemy with assault, a person may claim that scars due to disease are those of wounds.

TATTOO MARKS

Mode of production:

- Tattoo marks are designs made in the skin by multiple small puncture wounds with needles or an electric vibrator dipped in colouring matter.
- The dyes commonly used are
  » Indian ink,
  » carbon (black),
  » cinnabar or vermilion (mercuric sulphide) red,
  » chromic acid(green),
  » indigo,
  » cobalt
  » Prussian blue (ferric ferrocyanide),
  » ultramarine (blue
- Most of the marks are found on the arms, forearms and chest, but may be present on any part of the body.

Natural disappearance:

- If the pigment has been deposited below the epidermis, it will very slowly become fainter and certain pigments, such as vermilion, and ultramarine may disappear after about ten years.
- If the dye is deposited into deeper layers of dermis, it will be removed by phagocytes.
- The rate of fading depends not only on the composition of the pigment, but also on the depth to which it penetrates the skin, and the site which is tattooed.
- Parts protected by clothing retain the design for longer period than the exposed parts of the body.
- Tattoos on the hands disappear early due to constant friction.
- A faded tattoo mark becomes visible by the use of ultraviolet lamp or rubbing the part and examining with a magnifying lens.
- Infrared photography makes old tattoos readily visible.
- The marks are recognised even in decomposed bodies when the epidermis is removed by wiping the area with a moist paper towel or a piece of cloth.

- Lymph nodes near a tattoo mark show a deposit of a pigment.
- The colour, design. size and situation of tattoo marks should be noted. Drawing or photography is more useful.

COMPLICATIONS:

- Septic inflammation,
- erysipelas,
- abscess,
- gangrene,
- syphilis,
- AIDS,
- leprosy
- tuberculosis

ERASURE

(1) SURGICAL METHODS:
(a) Complete excision and skin grafting,
(b) production of burn by means of red-hot iron,
(c) scarification,
(d) carbon dioxide snow.

(2) ELECTROLYSIS.

(3) CAUSTIC SUBSTANCES

remove pigment by producing inflammatory reaction and a superficial car, e.g., mixture of papain in glycerine, zinc chloride and tannic acid.

(4) LASER BEAM:

By exposure to laser beams, the particles of the dye get vaporised and expelled from the tissues in gaseous form.

(5) Confluent smallpox and sometimes chronic eczema in children can obliterate tattoo marks.

Medicolegal Importance:

(1) If there are a large number of tattoos, positive identification can be made by tattoos alone. Initials and dates, regimental or nautical details, identity numerals, one's own name, etc., provide more scientific basis for identification.
(2) Religion.
(3) God of worship.
(4) Indicate culture or life-style.
(5) The distribution of tattooing and the nature of designs and figures may indicate a particular country or region.
(6) The presence of indecent figures points to definite perversion in the individual.
(7) They reflect travel, history, war, occupation, sex interest, etc.
(8) Gang members may wear a tattoo of allegiance and symbolism to indicate status or other aspects relevant to their particular group.
(9) Illicit drug users may have tattoos that identify them as belonging to
a particular group or to obscure injection sites.
(10) Homosexuals may tattoo on the back of their hand between the base of their thumb and forefinger.

WOUNDS:

- Sometimes, the presence of wounds on the body may assist in connecting a suspected criminal to a given crime.
  e.g. a piece of skin adherent to a window glass may correspond with the wound on the thief, or rupture of fraenum of penis may be present in a person accused of rape.
- Dust, sand, etc., may be recovered from wounds and identified.

DISEASE:

- The finding of disease, e.g. gallstones, renal stones, calcified leiomyoma, silicosis, asbestosis and congenital anomalies like horseshoe kidney, are helpful.

The unidentified body should be checked for:
- amputations,
- body deformities,
- pacemakers,
- implanted heart valves,
- teeth, their fillings and restorations,
- degenerative changes,
- infection,
- enlarged joints of the fingers due to arthritis,
- immovable joints due to disease,
- bowed-legs and
- curvature of the spine.

X-rays will show the presence of:
- healed fractures,
- metal pins,
- plates, or
- screws used in treating fractures.

Commonly found missing organs at autopsy are
- tonsils,
- appendix,
- gallbladder,
- kidney,
- prostate,
- uterus and
- ovaries.
- Surgical scars may indicate hernia repair, circumcision or an operation upon the thyroid gland.

STAINS:

Stains found on body or clothing of the accused and the victim may be the same and may be derived from walls, doors, furniture, at the scene of crime.

OCCUPATION MARKS:

(1) RECENT AND TEMPORARY:
- Contact traces of some solid or liquid the person is working with may be found on the skin, beneath the nails, in the hair, ears or on clothing.
  They include:
- paint spots on painters,
- grease on engineers and mechanics,
- flour on bakers and millers,
- dyes on dye workers,
- saw dust on those engaged in timber cutting
- The microscopical examination of
- dust and debris on clothing,
- in the pockets and trouser turn ups,
- under the fingernails
- in the ear wax,

  is important in identification of unknown bodies.

(2) PERMANENT:
- Thickening of the palmar skin of fingers are seen on the right hands of butchers.
- Cuts, scars, callosities and hyperkeratosis of the hands indicate manual labourers.
- Tailors have marks of needle punctures on their left index finger.
- Coal miners have multiple 'blue scars' on the face and arms due to coal-dust contamination of small lacerations.
- Blacksmiths have scars on the back of the hand caused by burns from hot fragments.
- Opticians have small cuts on the tips of the index finger and thumb.
- Workers in chemicals and photography usually have discoloured, distorted fingernails.
- Carpenters have callosities on the thumb and index finger, on the palms, and one shoulder is usually higher than the other.
- Brick layers have a flattening of the thumb and index finger of the left hand due to constant picking up of bricks.
- The violinist has hardened tips on the fingers of the left hand.

COMPLEXION AND FEATURES:
- The complexion may be fair, wheat-coloured, dark, brown, pale-brown or pale-yellow.
- Details of the features regarding eyes, nose, ears, lips, chin, and teeth should be noted.
- The face may be oval, round, square or long.
- Eyes may be black, grey, blue or brown.
- Few persons can cleverly alter their features by changing the expression of their face.
- Expression is altered after death.

EYES:
MEDICOLEGAL IMPORTANCE:

(1) Identification:
(a) artificial eyes,
(b) absence of one or both eyes,
(c) shape,
(d) colour of iris,
(e) setting: deep set, bulging or prominent,
(f) squint,
(g) nystagmus,
(h) cataract
- The look of the person will show whether he is conscious, unconscious, frightened, confused

(2) ASPHYXIA:
(a) proptosis,
(b) congestion,
(c) petechial haemorrhages.

(3) INJURIES:
(a) Black eye (contusion of lids),
(b) in fracture of anterior cranial fossa involving orbits, there may be effusion of blood into the orbits, proptosis, limitation of movement of eyeball and subconjunctival haemorrhage,
(c) gouging of eyes,
(d) lacerated wounds,
(e) penetrating wounds,
(f) foreign bodies,
(g) chemical burns,
(h) ulceration and opacity of cornea,
(i) vitreous haemorrhages are likely to affect vision,
(j) rupture of choroid and retina,
(k) subluxation of lens and post-traumatic cataract.

(4) NATURAL DISEASE:
Blue sclerotics of osteogenesis imperfecta and odontogenesis imperfecta.

(5) ACUITY OF VISION:
for crimes committed during the night.

(6) WORKMEN'S COMPENSATION ACT.

HAIR

Trichology - study of hair

Hair growth rate – 0.4 mm/day

Purpose of examination of hair:
> To find out
> **1. Hair or some other fibre?**
> Hair = bulb /(root + shaft)

To pluck out a healthy growing hair from scalp
↓
Considerable force required
↓
If adult lifted (or) dragged by hair.
↓
Scalp may even be torn from the skull

Hair anatomy - 3 well defined layers

Cuticle	Cortex	Medulla
Outer layer	Middle layer	Inner layer
Consist thin, non – pigmented scales	Consist longitudinally arranged, elongated cells without nuclei	Composed of keratinised remains of cells

Fibres:

cotton fibres
- flattened & twisted tubes,
- consist long tubular cells, with thickened edges & blunt pointed ends

Linen fibres
- show cross lines (or) folds about which fibre is often swolle,
- narrow lumen

Jute fibres
- smooth without transverse lines.
- Cell cavity – not uniform
- Ends – blunt

Silk fibres
- long clear threads without any cells
- Smooth, finely striated

Wool fibres
- outer layer of flattened cells,
- overlapping margins
- interior – fibrous tissue, sometimes medulla

2. Human or animal:
> **Banding** - colour change along hair shaft
> **Medullary index of hair** – radio of diameter of medulla & diameter of whole hair shaft
> **Medullary index of hair** – Radio of diameter of medulla & diameter of whole hair shaft
> 1. < 0.3 in humans
> 2. > 0.5 in animals
> 3. varies in hair of different body parts
> 4. determines the part from which it is derived

3. From what part of the body derived?

Body part of the hair	Features of the hair
Hair from the head	Usually long, soft & taper gradually from the root to the tip
Beard & moustache hair	Usually thicker than the hair of any other part of the body
Hair of eyebrows, eyelashes & nostrils	Stiff, thick and taper to a point
Hair on the chest, axillae & pubic region	Short, stout & curly Hair from axillae & pubic region – split ends
Hair on other body parts	Fine, short & flexible. no pigment cells in the cortex

4. Sex:

sexing of human hair - difficult, except beard & moustache

Male hair – usually thicker, coarser & darker

Barr bodies in hair follicles of human head hair
- 29+-5 % in females
- 6+-2% in males

5. Age:

Determined sometimes from hair, only within wide limits as between that of an infant or an adult

Roots of hair
- **From children**: Dissolve rapidly in a solution of caustic potash
- **older people**: resist treatment

Age	Diameter
12 days	0.024 mm
6 months	0.036 mm
15 years	0.053 mm
Adults	0.07 mm

Body hair of human foetus & newborn child
1. fine
2. soft
3. non-pigmented (colourless)
4. non-medulated

Lanugo hair replaced by hair which is
1. coarser
2. pigmented
3. medullated
4. more complex scale

At puberty:
Growth of axillary and pubic hair is initially fine, soft and curly, later becomes coarse and pigmented.

In men:
loss of scalp hair starts from 3rd decade.

In women:
loss of axillary hair & facial hair at menopause

Grey hair
After 40 years

6. HAS THE HAIR BEEN ALTERED BY DYEING, BLEACHING OR DISEASE?
- **Bleached hair** - Brittle, dry and straw yellow
- **If coloured** - colour not uniform
- **roots** – different colour
- **hair** – rough, brittle & lustreless
- **scalp** – coloured
- **colour of head hair** - different from colour of hair of other body parts
- **length of extra follicular part of an uncoloured zone** - determine the time of colour last applied

Growth rate:

Scalp hair	Beard hair	Other hair
2-3 mm /weak – average is 2.5 mm	Slightly faster	Slightly slower

- Chemical examination of hair – identify the metal contained in the paint
- Dyed hair – characteristic fluorescence with UV light
- Undyed hair – much brighter than rest with polarised light microscope

7. IS THE HAIR IDENTICAL WITH VICTIM'S / SUSPECT'S HAIR?

By Careful Comparison
↓
HAIR OF PARTICULAR PERSON Debris, grease, etc -adherent to the hair
↓
very important Hair – usually mounted on a glass slide for examination in a comparison microscope
↓
embedded in wax / resin block & sliced finely (cross section preparation)
↓
cuticle scales impressions – on cellulose acetate
↓
microscopy – intimate structure of dyed hair
↓
Hazy, uniformity in general shade
↓
not seen in hair of natural colour
↓
Diet & drug intake and atmospheric conditions
↓
Traces of 18 elements deposited in hair in different proportion in different people
↓
Measured through neutron activation analysis
↓
Only 3 out of 1 lakh persons
↓
comparable amount of 9 major trace elements

8. DID IT FALL NATURALLY OR WAS IT FORCIBLY REMOVED:

Base examined to see if root present

Naturally fallen hair
Root – distorted & atrophied
Root sheath – absent

hair forcibly pulle out
hair bulb - larger, irregular
sheath – ruptured

9. WHAT IS THE CAUSE OF THE INJURY:
If hair not cut – pointed & non-modulated tip
But repeated tip injury – cuticle damaged – exposed & unprotected cortex splits & frays (refer fig 4-52)
Hair of axilla, pubis & frequently brushed hair – ragged ends
Blows with blunt objects – shaft crushed with flattening & splitting
Sharp weapon – clean uniform cut surface
Recently cut hair – sharply cut edge with projecting cuticle
End – square, smooth & later rounded but blunt   After 3 - 4 months: end – Elongated medulla – absent
Burns / firearm injury : -- singed hair – swollen, black, fragile turisted (or) curled, peculiar odour, carbon deposited, swollen tip

IDENTIFICATION:
- Distribution & concentration of trace elements along the shaft – varies with hair growth
- Hair - not a permanent record for identification
- Colour of hair – alter with disease

Lighter	Greenish	Blue	Bluish	Yellow
Patients with malnutrition, ulcerative colitis & kwashiorkor Normal colour on restored health	Copper smelters	Indigo workers and cobalt miners	Aniline workers	Picric acid poisoning

- Colour of hair alters sometimes after burial

BLOOD GROUPS:
- Modified absorption – elution technique (or) mixed agglutination technique (100 % accuracy)
- ABO groups determined in a single hair if hair bulb present, from any body part

MEDICOLEGAL IMPORTANCE:
1. Hair
    - Important in crime investigation
    - Identifiable on cloths, body and alleged weapon in crimes committed long before
    - Often only connection between weapon or even accused and victim of an assault

a) **Motor vehicles responsible for injuries**
     identified by hair on the vehicle

b) **Rape and sodomy**
     pubic hair of accused found on victim or vice versa

Bestiality
- animal hair on body/underclothing of accused
- His pubic hair found on genitals of animals

c) Stains on the hair
- indicate scene of crime
- Got from walls, doors, furniture, etc
- Indicate nature of the assault

Struggle
  Mud stains

sexual offences
  seminal stains

asphyxial deaths
  salivary stains

injury
  blood stains

2. Injuries to hair & hair bulb – identification of nature of weapon
3. Known peculiarity of the hair, dyeing, bleaching (or) artificial waving – hair useful in identification
4. Differentiating scales from burns

	Estimation of	Useful features
5	Age of a person	Growth of a hair on different body pats
6	Sex of a person	Distribution on body, texture & from barr bodies
7	Burns/close range firearm injury	Singeing & hair
8	Chronic heavy metal poisoning (e.g. Arsenic poisoning)	Poison detected in hair
9	Time of death	Length of hair on face

FORENSIC ODONTOLOGY

Science of dentistry to aid in administration of justice

- Analysis
- interpretation
- comparison of bite marks
- personal injuries
- malpractice

- Restorative work
- unusual features
- comparing antemortem with post-mortem X-rays

Comparison between records of missing persons & the findings in the body

DENTAL IDENTIFICATION

IDENTIFICATION OF AN INDIVIDUAL	
1. Number, spacing situation of the teeth.	a. Unerupted deciduous. b. Permanent teeth (surface &configuration) c. decayed teeth d. oversized/undersized teeth
2. Number & situation of absent teeth	
3. Extraction : evidence of old /recent healed / unhealed	
4. General condition of the teeth	a. Erosion b. Cleanliness c. Conservation, filling cavities d. Colour e. Periodontosis
5. Peculiarities of arrangement	a. Prominence b. growded/ectopic teeth c. Overlapping d. Deformities e. Rotation
6. Supernumerary teeth	
7. Denture	Full, partial, upper/lower, type, shape, restorative material
8. Recognisable width of the teeth	
9. Mesiodistal with of the teeth	Prognathism (prominence of lower jaw)
10. Old injury /disease	Recently dislodged, loosened, chipped/broken teeth
11. Special features, incisal edges, fractures, ridges, caries, etc	
12. Restoration & prosthesis	Surfaces, morphology, configuration material
13. Root canal therapy on X-ray examination	
14. Bone pattern on X-ray examination	
15. Oral pathology	Tori, gingival hyperplasia

MOST DENTIST'S BELIEF - NO 2 persons have identical identification
ADULT TEETH

160 surfaces

Dental treatment | bone pattern | bone pattern | tooth position

identification of persons

Most reliable identification

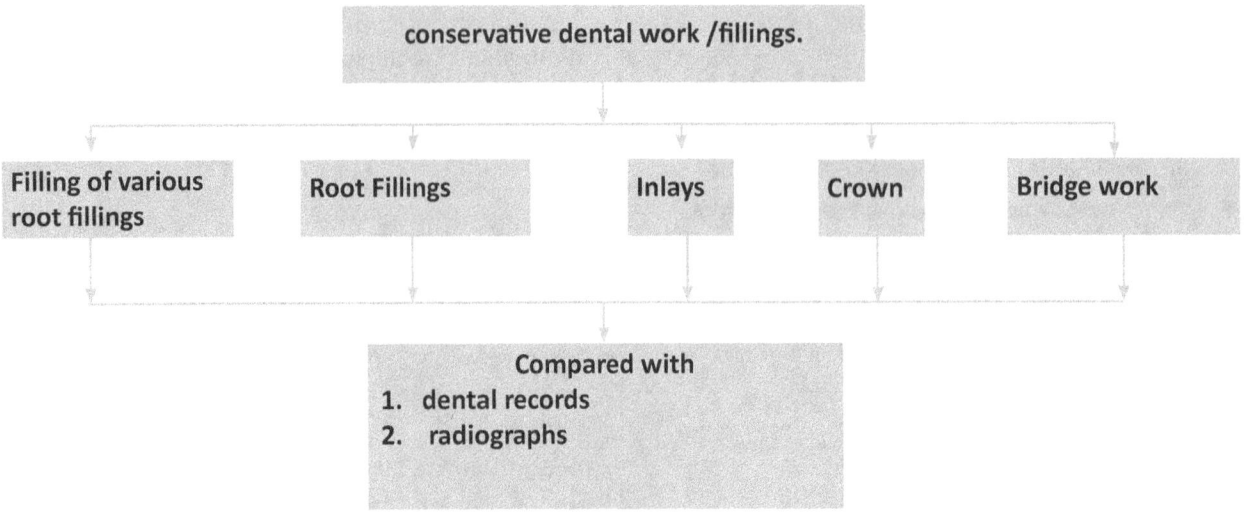

OVER BITE: protrusion of lower teeth beyond upper incisors

PINK TEETH:
- unknown cause (asphyxia /or poisoning as cause of pink teeth - disproved)
- Deposition of protoporphyrin near gum -line in a decomposed /skeletonised body

MOTTLED TEETH:
- state of regional chronic dental fluorosis.
- Opalescent pattern on enamel surface of permanent teeth during tooth calcification period

RADIOGRAPHY:
X-RAYS-antemortem vs postmortem comparison.
- Root shape
- pulp canal shape
- Shape of fillings
- Abnormalities & fractures
- Bone trapeculation
- Pattern & carries
- Tooth formation
- In mass disaster-list of possible persons involved
- More recent antemortem record -more reliable evidence
- If antemortem records -unavailable -dental information from relatives & friends.

MEDICOLEGAL IMPORTANCE:

1. Dental identification
1. most sophisticated in comparative identification.
2. except dactylography -if some features to compare some record of those features in a missing person.
3. Not much help in developing countries (dentists often don't keep records)
4. teeth jaws -usually protected from fire & mechanical trauma highly resistant to postmortem destruction &decomposition (refer table 4-12)
5. Established identification of single individual after accidental death /homicide & differential identification of large number of individuals after mass disasters, explosions, house fires, aircraft accidents, earthquakes, ship-wrecks.
6. made from intact, mutilated decomposed, skeletonised, burnt materials.
7. made by disease -caries, syphilis (Hutchinson's teeth)

2. Teeth - estimation of age of the individual.
3. Cells of pulp cavity - sex & blood group determined.
4. Loss of tooth due to assault - grievous hurt.
5. Dentures (partial/complete) - identification (especially if patient's name /code no, included).
6. Bite marks left in human tissues /food stuff- criminals
7. Poisons (arsenic, mercury)
8. Colour change - sulphuric acid/ nitric acid poisoning.
9. Yellowish- brown discolouration/mottling on enamels-fluorosis

ANTEMORTEM TOOTH LOSS/EXTRACTION:
- Bony -rim /alveolus-sharp & feathered.
- Blood clot within alveolar cavity & early organisation in 1-2 days.
- In a week-socket filled with organised clot.
    1. Replaced by fibrous tissue in 2 weeks.
    2. In 2-3 weeks -soft tissues healed socket partially filled with new bone.
- Reparative bone resorption of alveolar rim-smooth rounded rim of socket.
- In 6 months
- socket filled with new bone, but location of root outline -visible.
- In 1 year,
    1. whole socket is filled with a new bone.
    2. depression of bone outlet.
- If entire tooth -knocked out, irregular edges of remaining bone, splintering of buccal or lingual plates, areas of compressed bone or fracture of roots /crowns of adjacent teeth. Difficult to dislodge a healthy tooth without fracturing /loosening neighbouring.
- X-rays of jaw adjacent to dislodged teeth -Demonstration of these changes.

Advantages and disadvantages of comparisons of teeth and fingerprints

Trait	Teeth	Fingerprints
Burns	Fire resistant.	Destroyed by fire.
Putrefaction	No changes.	Subject to putrefaction.
Changes	Compatible inconsistencies	Unchanged.
Proof	No acknowledged criteria of proof.	Well established criteria.
Records	Useless without records.	Possible use of possessions

BITE MARKS:

Appearance: human bites
1. semi-circular /crescentic
2. caused by front teeth (incisors & canines).
3. gap at either side (separation of upper & lower jaws)
- Teeth - clear, separate marks /form continuous/intermittently broken line.
- Bite marks
    1. abrasions
    2. contusions
    3. lacerations
    4. combination of any 2/3.
- Forcible bite - 2 "Bows" with their concavities facing each other & gap at each end.
- Sucking action - reduce air pressure over centre & produce multiple petechial haemorrhages (rupture of capillaries & small venules in subcutaneous tissues)
- Forcible bite - petechiae
    1. confluent
    2. produce contusion
- Irregular /curved bitten area- only part of dental area comes in contact with tissues.
- Act of biting- twisted /distorted skin - distorted pattern

- Scraping of skin by upper incisors - parallel tracks - linear pattern of bite marks.
- Examination under UV light in a dark room
    1. More visible faint teeth marks.

SEXUAL BITES:
- Sucking - teeth as grip - central or peripheral suck mark - petechiae - reddening.
- In many such bites - teeth marks not seen.
- Love bites - breast, nipple, cheek, abdomen, arms, thigh, genitals.
- Sexual bites- breast, nipple
    1. tissue actually sucked into mouth before jaws close upon it .
    2. Affects shape of bites mark when skin released flattens out once more.
- Child abuse - bite marks - anywhere on the body.
- Self-inflicted bite marks - shoulders &arms.
- In living - these marks - 1-24 hours after infliction.
- Swabs of bite mark
1. taken immediately
2. swab moistened with sterile water used also used in taking.

RECORDING & REPRODUCING METHOD OF BITE MARKS:
1. Photography method
2. Casts
3. Digital imaging

1.Photographic method:
1. bite markfully photographed
2. scales -right angle in horizontal plane.
- Special mirrors
    1. inclusion of all teeth in upper &lower jaw in 1 photograph
    2. Photographs of teeth
    3. Matched with photographs /tracings of teeth (made from +casts of a bite impression, inking the cutting edges of front teeth)
    4. Transferred to transparent sheet
    5. Superimposed over photographs or (-) photograph of teeth superimposed over (+) photograph of bite.
    6. Exclusion -easier than positive matching.
    7. Human tissues &food stuffs - No exact reproduction of teeth biting character into them
    8. NOT always possible to relate teeth measurements to bitemarks with accuracy .

2.CASTS:
- Plastic substance (rubber /silicone) based medium containing catalytic hardener - laid over bite mark.
- Permanent (-) ve cast produced
- Plaster of Paris, modelling clay, plasticine, bees wax-also used
- Impressions of upper &lower teeth of suspect -taken.

3.Digital imaging of bite marks &rendering it as 3D data set.
  Image measured to high precision &accurately compared with measurements of case of dentition of suspect.
- Bite marks - useful in identification (teeth alignment peculiar to individuate)

MEDICOLEGAL IMPORTANCE:
  Bite marks -in materials left at place of crime., food stuff (cheese, bread, butter, sandwiches, fruit), or humans involved in assaults, when either victim or accused show the marks usually on hands, fingers, forearms, nose and ears)

CHARTING OF TEETH:
>150 different methods for Identification, numbering & charting of teeth.

CHARTING OF TEETH

Most widely used systems for permanent teeth.

- Universal system
- Palmer's notation
- Haderup system
- FDI 2 digit system
- Modified FDI system
- Diagramatic (or) anatomical chart

1. Universal teeth:
Plan advocated by the American & International society of forensic odontology
Teeth numbered
1. 1-16 from upper right - upper left
2. 17-32 from lower left - lower right.

	1	2	3	4	5	6	7	8	9	10	11	12	13	14	15	16	
Right																	left
	32	31	30	29	28	27	26	25	24	23	22	21	20	19	18	17	

2. Palmer's notation

	8	7	6	5	4	3	2	1	1	2	3	4	5	6	7	8	
Right																	left
	8	7	6	5	4	3	2	1	1	2	3	4	5	6	7	8	

3. Hader up system:
similar to palmer's notation system
(+) - upper teeth
(-) - lower teeth

4. FDI (federation dentaire international) 2-digit system:
- Slight resemblance to palmers' system (both utilises same numbers)
- But FDI system substitutes a number for quadrant side.

5. Modified FDI system

	1	2	
Right			left
	3	4	

6) Diagrammatic/ Anatomical chart:
1. In this each tooth
2. Pictorial symbol
3. Same number of teeth surfaces as those on same teeth in mouths
- Incisors and canines-4 surfaces; Premolars & molars- 5 surfaces (occlusal surface)
- Positions of crowns, caries, fillings, abnormalities, deciduous teeth
- Included in diagram

ANIMAL BITES:
- Rodents - Gnaw away tissue over fairly limited areas
- Shallow craters of borders of areas by nibbling
- Leave long grooves

1. DOG BITES
- Suddenly attacked dog bites- clear cut, narrow squarish arch anteriorly (animal bites to hold on attacked persons)
- Teeth impressions - Deep like stab wounds, small in area
- These animals - Long canines & 6 incisors

2. CAT BITES
- Small rounded arch with puncture marks by canines
- Scratch marks from claws

3. RAT BITES
- Very small & round
- Measuring intercanine distance - Differentiate between animal & human bites
- Distance between upper canines
    1. 25-40mm in adults
    2. <25mm in children

RACE
- Small nodules on lingual surface - of maxillary molars (Carbelli's cusps)
    1. most common in Caucasians.
    2. Rare in other racial groups
- Lateral incisors in upper jaw-Smaller than the central especially in females
- In Mongoloids
1. Shovel shaped upper incisors
2. Long & pointed canine roots
3. Frequent enamel pearls
4. Wide pulp cavity of molar (also deep)
5. Congenital lack of 3rd upper molar is most common (but can occur in any race)
    - In Negroids teeth - Large with more cusps in their molars 2 Lingual cusps on mandibular 1st premolars

SEX

MALE	FEMALE
Upper central & upper lateral incisors equal in size	The size varies
	Canines smaller more pointed comparatively; especially lower jaw
	Mandibular 1st molar has 4 cusps

- Y Chromosome - Isolated in tooth pulp cells up to 3-5 months post extraction / postmortem, Quinacrine staining useful.
- Teeth
    1. Markedly resistant to teeth
    2. Disintegrated & fractured if heated suddenly, severely
- Dead body - burnt - Oral cavity & teeth - Better chance of remaining intact
- Living persons - Lips - drawn back - Exposing the anterior teeth
- Temperature, intensity duration of fire Crowns of anterior teeth - Scorched, ashed (or) explode at gum line

OCCUPATION, HABITS & SOCIAL POSITION

Cobblers, Carpenters, Seamstresses, electricians, dress-makers
Holding of thread, nails, etc
Central notches in the incisal edge of front teeth
wide defects on front of the teeth
Defects on incisal edges

Pipe smokers & cigarette smokers
↓
use holders
↓
Visible loss of materials on the incisal edges of teeth mostly at angle of the mouth

- Heavy smokers - Deposition of black stain upon teeth
- Habitually bite various objects (or) hold them in their teeth- Loosening of certain teeth
- Workers exposed to corrosive acids - Labial enamel & later the exposed dentin are dissolved
- Excessive chewing of acid foods - Erosion of all surfaces of teeth
- Copper - Green
  Sliver - Black   -   Particularly at the neck of the teeth(or) at the marginal part of the gum

  Lead, Aniline & Bismuth - Bluish colour
- Social positions, country of origin - Ascertained from quality & type of restorations

CASE

1) Prinz (1915) - Reported the murder of a banker

- Cigar holder with a mouth piece of amber which had a tip worn down in a characteristic way-found near the body
- Lesion thought to be caused by teeth of owner of mouthpiece
- Judge saw this mouthpiece
- During trial when judge was questioning a witness
- ↓

He noticed a deformity in the teeth of that man
↓
Reminded him of the defect in cigar-holder
↓
Witness, a cousin of deceased his heir was shown how well the mouthpiece fitted the deformity in his own teeth
↓
Finally admitted to being a murderer

2) A train loaded with petrol & a passenger train

Ran into each other in Norway in 1944
↓
1st carriage of passenger train - Engulfed in burning petrol for 12 hours
↓
Only burnt remains of bodies left
↓
Teeth & dental restorations - Little affected in some cases

3) Ried (1884)-Reported the murder of a doctor & his mother
- Bodies found in kitchen
- Few dislocated teeth found - 2 didn't belong to murdered
- ↓
  Later proved to belong to murderer
  ↓
  (Lost during fight with his victims)

4) Paulik(1949)- Reported the murder of an old man by whose side was found an apple with characterstics bite mark
- Marks - 3 teeth close to each other
  1. 2 are broad
  2. 1- small, irregular (carious tooth)
- Bite - Didn't correspond to teeth of victim
- A prostitute was arrested & dental examination proved that bite marks produced by her teeth

5) Euler (1925) - Reported investigation of multiple murders in which a large number of extracted teeth were found
- An insane person - Collected only caries -free teeth from his victims
- Out of 351 teeth - Euler found 20 left lower canines
- He arrived at the number of 29 individuals - considering all the teeth in relation to the curves for caries development
- Later a note book was found - Containing the names &ages of all murdered. numbering from 1-31

CLOTHES AND ORNAMENTS
- Clothing -Indicate the social extent to a certain extent (from texture & value)
- Any variety of uniform   - very valuable for identification
- Clothing - Indicate occupation
- Examination of clothing & personal effects- Identification of victims in mass disasters - fire, explosions & aircraft crashes
- Detailed description to be given -size
  » colour
  » condition
  » type of each garment
  » Record of laundry marks
  » Name tags
  » Labels of tailors
- Photographs & examination for invisible laundry marks by UV light - useful
- keys
- letters
- bank books   - contained in clothing gives clue - Name and address of the individual
- visiting cards
- licenses
- Other documents

- watches   - These personal effects may be engraved with
- rings
                   Initials   Names   Dates
- keys

- Eyeglasses - also useful
- Belt buckle
- Bullet holes
- Tears   - On clothing gives the information regarding   - causes of death
                                                                                manner of death
- Cuts
- Type marks

- Design on ornaments- varies from region to region
- General cleanliness of person, state of the teeth, hand, & feet- idea of social status
- If shoes are worn
- Epidermis of soles of the feet
  1. Thin
  2. Smooth
  3. No fissures & cracks
- Criminal can interchange his identity with that of another person by clothing & personal effects

HANDWRITTING (CALLIGRAPHY)
- Characteristic of the individual, especially if written rapidly
- But may be disguised (or) forged
- Mental & nervous disease & Rheumatism -alter the character
- Evidence of handwriting experts
  1. not conclusive
  2. opinion evidence

SPEECH & VOICE:
- Certain peculiarities of speech
  » Stammering
  » Stuttering
  » Lisping
  » Nasal twang
- More evident when talking excitedly
- Nervous disease - Affect speech
- Recognise a person from voice - Risky
- Possible to alter his voice at will
- Tape recording - useful
- No 2 voices - Really alike
- **SPECTOGRAM**
  1. All the frequencies produced by utterance of a single syllable potted on time baseline
  2. Characteristic of speaker
  3. Trapping anonymous telephone callers

GAIT
- Any identification based on recollection of physical characteristics (lameness, particular body postures (or) movements) of person in question by friends & relatives - unreliable
- Gait - Altered by accident (or) design

TRICKS OF MANNER AND HABIT
- Frequently hereditary
- **e.g.:** left-handedness Jerky movements (of shoulders or face muscles)
- Individual characteristics

MEMORY & EDUCATION
- Sometimes useful
- Especially in cases of imposture

CHAPTER - 05
MEDICOLEGAL AUTOPSY

into:
- Autopsy which is also called necropsy, means postmortem.
- In each and every case the autopsy must be complete, all the body cavities should be opened and every organ must be examined.
- This is because the evidence that is contributing to the cause of death may be found in more than one organ.
- A complete autopsy is necessary to prove the truth of the evidence of eyewitnesses.

PARTIAL AUTOPSY:
- Partial autopsy has no place in forensic pathologic practice.
- It is worser than no autopsy at all and it leads to miscarriage of justice.

ROLE OF DOCTORS:
- Autopsy should be performed only by the doctors and not left to a mortuary attendant.
- The doctor should remove the organ himself.
- The attendants should prepare the body & help the doctor where required such as sawing the skill cap etc.,

Types:

The approach of forensic pathologist to the investigation of death is different from that of the hospital pathologist.

The types of autopsy

1. Pathological autopsy.
The hospital pathologist has easy access to relevant information about the history, physical condition and course of the disease leading to death.

2. Medicolegal autopsy.
In this case, the clinical history is absent, sketchy, doubtful or misleading and in some cases identity may not be known.

3. Psychological autopsy :
- It is a form of counseling for relatives of the deceased who die of suicide.
- Especially, when there is a history of suicides among their family members.

4. Verbal autopsy :
Done in infant deaths for data on infant mortality.

Main aim of Pathological autopsy:
1. To find morphologic changes(extent of a known disease)
2. Explaining signs or symptoms of the disease
3. Explaining effectiveness of treatment

Advantages of Pathological autopsy:
- It helps to determine the cause of death, the extent of natural disease or the combination of comorbidities(more than a disease that occurs at a time)that leads to death
- It detects the previously unrecognised disease and helps the family to know of inheritable conditions present in the the deceased.
- It offen relies on histologic assessment and it is academically oriented.

Medicolegal autopsy

Role of pathologist in Medicolegal autopsy:
- To determine the time of death, age of injuries, cause, manner and mechanism of death.
- If there are any inconsistencies between the apparent death scene and his actual findings, he has to visit scene of crime.
- Carry out careful external examination including clothing, pattern of injuries and their relationship to the object or weapon causing them and collect trace evidences.
- it has evidentiary and confirmatory value for public interest.

Object:
To find out,
1. The cause of death, whether natural or unnatural. This is done by detecting, describing and recording any external or internal injuries, abnormalities and diseases.
2. How injury occurred.
3. Manner of death, whether accidental, suicidal or homicidal.
4. Time since death.
5. To establish identity when not know.
6. Collect physical evidence in order to identify the object causing death and to identify the criminal.
7. To retain relevant organs and tissues as evidence.
8. Innewborn infants to determine the question of livebirth &visibility.
9. To find factual & objective information for police and court.

Importance of autopsy:
If it is not done then the exact cause of death, the presence and extent of disease or injury the capacitation produced by them and whether there was any pain or suffering becomes only speculation.

Rules for medicolegal autopsy:
1. The body should be labelled as soon as it arrives in the mortuary.
2. The autopsy should be conducted in a mortuary and never in a private room.
- However, it may be necessary to do an autopsy at the site, when the body is an advanced state of decomposition (by microbes).so, the transportation becomes difficult and materials of evidential value may be lost in transport.
- It is also done when immediate examination of body is essential due to any special reason.
3. It should be conducted only when there is an official order authorizing the autopsy, from the police or magistrate.
4. It should be performed s soon as possible after receiving official order without delay.
5. The medical officer should read the injure report carefully and find out the apparent cause of death.
6. He should obtain all the available details of the case from the case sheet, accident register etc....,
7. By doing this, attention may be the significant points while doing the post-mortem examination and to carry out appropriate investigation ex: toxicology, microbiology.
8. Lack of such information may result in loss of vital evidences.

Role of case sheet:
I. It helps to know the, nature of wound if stitched or if the patient survives for few days.
II. If surgical incision passes through an injury during operation.
III. Therapeutic wounds e.g.: surgical stab wounds of chest or abdomen for insertion of drainage tubes,
IV. tracheostomy, venesection etc..,. and operative procedures.
V. A drainage tube may be introduced through stab to chest or abdomen.
VI. Injuries that occurred while correcting the physiological disorders of person(resuscitation injury) like artificial respiration ,cardiac massage etc..,.
VII. In gunshot wounds to know the wound of entrance and exit, if there was surgical intervention
VIII. Not to mistake collection of blood in chest and abdominal cavities due to operation.
IX. Areas of tenderness for the detection of an injury in which skin is not damaged(confusion)
X. If after head injury, the patient is maintained on respiration, lung shows areas of collapse, haemorrhages and hyaline membrane.
XI. To detect the fracture in which the bones are broken on one side only & not all way through bone (green stick) and the fractures which are too small that they are not detected by x-ray (fissured fracture).
XII. To detect the cause of death ex: diabetes, asthma, epilepsy, uraemia, etc..,.
XIII. The actual poison consumed or to suspect a particular poison from the signs and symptoms observed during life

9)
•The examination should be conducted in daylight as far as possible, because colour change as jaundice, change in bruises (discoloration due to Breakage of Blood vessels under skin), change in postmortern staining etc.. that Cannot be detected by artificial light.
•If the body is received late evening done preliminary examination is done to note the external appearances, the Body temperature, extent of postmortem lividity and rigor mortis etc.
•The actual postmortem may be conducted on the next day as early as possible.
•There is no law, which prevents autopsy. Being conducted during night
10) The Body must be identified by the police constable who accompanies it and relatives of the deceased. The name of those who identified the body must be recorded.
•In unidentified bodies, the marks of identification, photographs, fingerprints should be taken.
(11) No unauthorized person can perform autopsy. The investigating police officer may be present
(12) If the doctor does not find injuries recorded in the injure report, he should state that such injuries are not present, or are misinterpretation or PM changes and not injuries.
•Difference in injuries in wound certificate and autopsy report benefits accused (as to weapon used, injuries& time of injuries).
13) As the autopsy is conducted, details of examination should be noted literally by an assistant or voice activated tape recorder made of all important injuries.
14) Nothing should Be should be erased. And all alterations should be initiated in the report
15) Even if the body is decomposed, autopsy should be performed as certain important lesions may still be found.
16) Both positive, negative findings should be recorded & the body should be handed over to the police constable after completion of autopsy
17) PM report should not be issued to the party.

Autopsy room:
- It should be properly ventilated, illuminated and cleaned with plenty of running water daily.
- Disinfection must be done with weekly fumigation, Phenol, savlon or glutaraldehyde of can be used for disinfection.
- During autopsy care must be taken to prevent unnecessary soiling of floor, walls& instruments and splashing of body fluids &water.
- All instruments must be washed with disinfectant after use.
- Biomedical & other materials must be disinfected & disposed according to biomedical waste management rules, 2016 universal court precautions should be followed.
- Staff must be immunized for tetanus ,hepatitis B

Autopsy room photography:
Objects:
1. To provide a visual record for the pathologist to refer to at a later time
2. To allow other professionals to review the pathological findings and to formulate their own opinions.
3. To show to the judge in trial, and for teaching purpose.

Procedure:
1. Photographs should be taken from above and at right angles to the body to avoid perspective distortion
2. All the objects, such as scalpels & scissors should be excluded.
3. The case number should be placed in a corner or along one edge of the photograph
4. A pointer ex: a narrow triangle of thin cardboard, may be used if a lesion is not readily visible.
5. In violent death, front & back views of the uncleaned body with clothes & also after the removal of clothes should be taken.
6. Then the body should be washed and in the naked body, a distant shot to indicate the location of injuries & close-up shot major wounds should be taken by placing a scale to show the dimensions.
7. In an unknown body photograph of the face should be taken.
8. Victim's hands should be photograph to demonstrate electrical burns , defence arts etc..,.
9. Ligatures negatively charged polysaccharide compounds & bindings should be photographed before removal.
10. The photograph shot should be vertical in lesion
11. Isolated organs should be cleaned with a sponge & placed on a green cloth and photographed.

The autopsy protocol:
A protocol is a signed document containing a written record which serves as a proof of something.

Autopsy protocol is used in two basic forms:
1. Narrative (in story form)
2. Numerical (by the numbers)

The advantages of numerical protocol are:
1. It provides a guide for an orderly description of all autopsy findings and tends to prevent the omissions of minor details.
2. It is objective & impersonal

Autopsy report:
It consists of:
1. The preamble:
This should mention,
- The authority ordering the examination
- Time of arrival of the body at the mortuary
- Date & place of examination
- Name , age & sex of the deceased
- The means by which the body is identified

2. **The body of the report:**
   It should contain,
   - Complete description of external & internal examination of the body.
   - Natural, direction, situation and dimension of the wounds.
   - Numbers assigned for all the wounds & diagrams of them.
   - All the negative and positive findings.
3. **Conclusion:**
   - The cause of death must be given, based on the postmortem findings.
   - Clear language and quality of being short is of high value.
   - It should be detailed, comprehensive, honest, objective and scientific.
   - It should have signature and qualifications of the doctor.

   A properly performed autopsy furnishes objective facts which can disprove the weight and worth of misleading statements.

   According to the special condition of the case eg: instab wounds of the chest or abdomen, the usual incision may have to alteaed to avoid such wounds

   Photographs can be used to demonstrate & correlate external injuries & internal injuries

Internal examination:
   This is started from the cavity chiefly affected.

Noted:
   In a case of suspected cranial injury, the skull should not be opened until the blood has been drained out of opening the heart.

Opening of body cavities:
1) **Abdomen:**
Procedure:
   - The pathologist should stand on the right side of the body, if he is right handed and on one side of autopsy table an instrument trolley with instruments is kept.
   - The recti muscles of the abdomen are divided about 5 cm above symphysis.
   - A small cut is made in the fascia big enough to admit the left index and middle fingers, palmar surfaces up The fingers are separated in a V. (to protect the underlying structures) and a sharp-bladed knife is inserted between them
   - The peritoneum is cut up to the xiphoid.
   - The thickness of the fat in the abdominal wall is noted.

Note:
   - In factly people, a few transverse incisions can be made on the inner side of the abdominal wall to divide muscle, and fat, which allows lateral faps to gape widely, to have a full view of the abdomen.
   - The condition of the abdominal cavity and organs is observed before. anything is disturbed or altered.

Note:
   - If blood, pus or any other fluid is present, its quantity is measured & perforations are also noted.
   - If this precaution is not taken, there will be a doubt, as to whether any blood or damage to organs found at a later stage is a result of the opening of the body, or whether it was already present to the examiner.

Things to be noted:
   - Amount of fat in the mesentery and omentum.
   - Abnormalities and position of abdominal organs, adhesions, old operations, pathological processes, injuries and height of diaphragm in relation to the ribs.
   - Adhesions, congestion, inflammation or exudation in peritoneum is noted.
   - The course, direction and depth of injuries and enumerable structure involved by the injury is described.

- Identify and label any foreign object, bullets, fragments of knives. Etc….. and specify its relation to a given injury.
- Photograph injuries to document their location and a scale is included to show their size.
- Photographs can be used to demonstrate & correlate external injuries & internal injuries.

2) Neck:

- A block 12 to 20 cm high, is placed under the shoulders. The head is allowed to fall back and thus the neck is extended.
- The skin is held with a toothed forceps and with a sharp, long-handle scalpel, the dissection is carried out immediately deep to the skin through the platysma.
- The subcutaneous dissection should be carried up to the lower border of the lower jaw, well laterally on the side of the neck & clavicle. The deep cervical muscles & the submandibular gland.
- The sternomastoid muscle is freed from its clavicular and sternal attachments, separate from its underlying fascia and reflected on each side.
- The omohyoid, sternothyroid & thyrohyoid muscles are exposed, they are inspected & reflected on each side
- Thyroid gland and the carotid sheaths are freed by blunt dissection from their investing connective tissues.
- The larynx, trachea, pharynx & esophagus mobilized and pulled away from the prevertebral tissue by blunt dissection.

3. Mouth:

Procedure:

- The mouth is opened, and the tip of the tongue is pushed upwards and backwards with forceps.
- The knife is inserted under the chin through the floor of the mouth.
- Cut along the sides of the mandible to the angle of mandible.
- This causes the division of the neck muscles attached to the lower jaw.
- At the angles of the mandible, turn the blade inward to avoid cutting the carotid artery.
- The tongue is pushed down under the mandibular arch with the index and middle fingers.
- The soft palate is then cut to include the uvula and tonsils with tongue and neck organs to be removed.
- The knife is carried backwards and laterally on the both sides of the midline to divide the posterior pharyngeal wall.
- The middle finger of the left hand is passed into the larynx and with a scalpel.
- The pharyngeal tissues are dissected from behind forwards and laterally and the pharynx is pulled down to the upper part of the neck.
- The dissection is then carried distally through the prevertebral muscles on the anterior surface of the cervical vertebrae.
- As a result, the whole of the neck structures are free to the level of suprasternal notch.
- The great vessels including the carotid should be divided in the neck.

4. Pneumothorax:

- Cases of pneumothorax are demonstrated before the chest wall is opened by various methods.

Methods to demonstrate various cases of pneumothorax.

- The pocket is dissected on the affected side between the chest wall and the skin and is filled with water.
- The wall is punctured with the knife under the water.
- The scalpel should be twisted a few times to make sure that the wound is open.
- If air is present, it will bubble out of the opening through the water.
- A wide-bore needle [16-gauge] attached to a 50ml syringe without the plunger is introduced into subcutaneous tissue, over an intercostal space and then the syringe is filled with water.
- The needle is pushed to enter the pleural cavity.

- If air is present, it will bubble out.
- One of the intercostal muscles is carefully removed until the underlying parietal pleura is seen.
- If there is no pneumothorax, the visceral pleura of the lung will be seen immediately below the parietal pleura.
- If there is a pneumothorax, visceral pleura will not be seen.

5. chest:
- The edge of the knife is kept directed inwards towards the ribs, carried back to the mid axillary line, down to the costal margin and up on the clavicles and the chest muscles are dissected away.
- The ribs, sternum and spine should be examined for fractures, and the chest is opened by cutting the costal cartilage with a cartilage knife.
- Begin at the upper border of the second cartilage, keeping very close to the costochondral junctions.
- The knife should be inclined about 30° to the vertical.
- In old persons where the rib cartilages are calcified, a pair of rib shears or hand saw are used.
- Then, the sternoclavicular joint is disarticulated on each side by holding the knife vertically and inserting the point into the semicircular joint.
- The position of this joint can be made out by moving the shoulder tip with the left hand which causes the joint capsule to move.
- To divide the joint capsule, the knife is put in vertically and turned in a circular manner.
- The diaphragm is divided as its attachment to the lower ribs and sternum up to the spine.
- Before the complete removal of the sternum the pleural cavity should be examined, to prevent leakage of blood from subclavian and jugular veins into the pleural cavity before inspection.
- Do not pull the sternum and ribs to avoid negative pressure resulting in aspiration of air into the vessels.

Before removal of the thoracic organs, insitu inspection should include:
1. Observation of the lumen of the main pulmonary vessels.
2. observation of the right atrium and ventricle for air embolism.
3. The state of distension or collapse of the lungs.
4. pleural cavities for the presence of fluid, blood or pus and pleural adhesions.
5. pericardium for cardiac tamponade.
6. collection of the blood sample from the heart for toxicological examination.

Pericarditis:
- The pericardial sac normally contains 20 to 50 ml of straw coloured fluid and the pericardium is smooth and glistening.

Causes in pericarditis :
- While spots (milk spots) on the surface of the heart indicate healed pericarditis.
- In acute pericarditis, the sac contains large collections of serous or purulent fluid and fibrin deposits (bread and butter pericardium).
- Hemorrhagic fluid in the sac is seen in malignancy & rarely in tuberculosis, uremia, bleeding disease and secondary to myocardial infarction.

6) Air embolism:
- If air embolism is suspected, the head should be opened first and the surface vessels of the brain examined for gas bubbles.
- It must be prominent and definite .but not segmental break up of the blood in the vessels with collapsed segments between.
- Care should be taken to avoid pulling the sternum and ribs to avoid creating negative pressure in the tissue which may result in aspiration of air into vessels.

It can be demonstrated by:
- Before handling the thoracic organs, the pericardium is opened, the heart is lifted upwards and the apex is cut with a knife.
- The left ventricles are filled with frothy blood, if air is present in sufficient quantity to cause death.

- If the right ventricles contain air, the heart will float in water.
- Another method of demonstrating air embolism is by cutting the pericardium anteriorly and grasping the edges with hemostat on each side.
- The pericardial sac is filled with water and the right heart is punctured with a scalpel & twisted a few times.
- Bubbles of the air will escape if air is present.
- A wide – bore needle attached to a 50ml syringe filled with water is inserted into the right ventricle.
- If air is present, it will bubble out through the water.
- Air in inferior vena care can be demonstrated by puncturing it under water and looking for escape of bubbles of gas.
- Chest x-ray
- Pyrogallol test
- 4ml of 20% freshly prepared pyrogallol solution is collected into two 10 ml syringes.
- To the first syringe four drops of 0.5M sodium hydroxide solution is added.
- Gas is aspirated from the right side of the heart, the needle is removed and replaced with a stopper, and the syringe shaken.
- If air (oxygen) is present, the mixture turns brown. In the second syringe some air is introduced and the test repeated as a control.
- The solution should turn brown. This test helps to differentiate gas present in the heart from gas formed due to decomposition.

Fat embolism :
- If fat embolism is suspected, the pulmonary artery should be dissected under water & the escape of fat droplets noted.

Method of removal of organs:
1. Virchow's technique
2. Rokitansky's technique
3. Lettulle's technique
4. Ghon's technique

TECHNIQUES	APPROACH	IMPORTANT POINTS
Virchow	Individual organs are removed one by one.	Cranial cavity is exposed first, followed by thoracic, cervical abdominal organs. Spinal cord is removed from the back. In this the anatomico-pathologic relations are not preserved.
Rokitansky's	It involves in situ dissection in part, combined with en block removal.	It is preferred choice in patient with highly transmissible disease like HIV, hepatitis B
Lettulle's	Cervical, thoracic, abdominal & pelvic organs are removed en masse & dissected as organ blocks.	It has the advantages of leaving all attachments intact.
Ghon's	Cervical, thoracic, abdominal, organs and urogenital system are removed as a organ block neural system is removed as another block	

Removal of small & large intestine:
- The greater omentum lying across the small intestine is pushed upwards across the liver
- The upper part of the small intestine is grasped in the left hand, and followed upwards until it disappears retroperitoneally to become the duodenum.
- The mesentery is penetrated with the point of the knife at the duodenojejunal flexure.and two pieces of string are passed through the hole.
- They are then brought upwards, tied separately and tightly around the gut & it is divided between these two ligatures.
- The coils of the intestine are pulled forward by the left hand and the mesentery is cut close to the mesenteric border of the gut until the ileocaecal valve is reached.
- The caecum is mobilized and the ascending colon pulled forwards and medically by the left hand, and its attachments, with the posterior abdominal wall, are cut with the knife up to the hepatic flexure.
- The omentum is pulled down and the transverse mesocolon is cut through with a knife, until the splenic flexure is reached, then the descending colon is freed in a similar manner until the sigmoid colon is free.
- The upper part of the rectum is mobilised and cut through between two ligatures below the brim of the pelvis.
- The entire small & large intestine are removed.

Removal of thoracic organs:
- The axillary bundles which lie behind the clavicles and the first rib are cut, by passing the knife upwards on each side from the thoracic cavity into the neck.
- If there is any pleural adhesions between the lungs and the chest wall,it should be cleared of by fingers or knife.
- Slip the fingers of both hands between the lateral portion of the lung and the inner side of the chest wall.
- The left hand works up to apex, the right down to the base and they meet at hilum, after cutting the structures on the front of the spinal column to the level of diaphragm.
- The neck structures are grasped enmasse in the left hand and pulled downwards.
- After this, the thoracic organs are put back in the thorax.
- The stomach and spleen are pulled medially by the left hand and the diaphragm is removed by cutting through its attachment to the ribs on both sides.
- The thoracic organs are pulled down gently along the surface on the neck structure & the cruciate ligament which attaches the diaphragm to the spine is cut.

Removal of abdominal organs:
- The spleen and the tail of the pancreas are held in the left hand and dissection is carried behind them to the midline.
- The diaphragmatic surface of the spleen is held in the palm.
- The vessels at the hilum are cut after they have been inspected.
- The liver is pulled medially and the knife is passed behind it to free it from attachments.
- The peritoneum and fat are cut just outside the lateral border of the kidney,which is then grasped in the left hand and mobilised by dissection behind it to the midline,freeing it from the anterior surface of the iliopsoas muscle.
- The ureter is identified and freed all the way down to its entry to the bladder.
- Both kidneys are then taken in the left hand,and the knife is carried down midline behind the aorta to the pelvis.
- The knife is passed around the side wall of the pelvis,dividing the lateral attachment of the bladders, each side of the pelvis being dissected downwards to the midline.
- The anterior surface of the bladder is freed with the finger from the public bone.
- The femoral vessels are cut at the level of the brim of the pelvis.
- The contents are pulled upwards and the urethra & vagina divided as low as possible.

Removal of organs in dorsal cavity [cranial and spinal cavities:
- The atlanto-occipital joint should be examined by moving the head on the spine to note any fracture -dislocation and the cervical spine is examined for fracture.
- The so-called "undertaker's fracture" is caused due to the head falling backward forcibly after death which tears open one of the intervertebral discs usually around c-6 & c-7 due to which subluxation of the lower cervical spine occurs.
- The thoracic and lumbar spine should be examined by pushing a hand under the body to raise up the spine forward, which will show any abnormal movement to the site of fracture.
- The cervical spine can be tested by manual manipulation.
- To detect the fracture of the sacroiliac joints or of the pelvic bones the pelvic bones, the pelvis should be squeezed from sides to side by pressure on each iliac crest.

Examination of organs:
- The enmasse chest and abdominal organs are kept on a wooden board with posterior surface upward and the tongue facing the operator.

Description of an organ:
- A description of the organ system should be limited to a clear, concise, objective description of shape,colour,and consistency and the presence or absence of any lesions other than those systematically described under trauma.
- The microscopic description may be limited to the positive finding.
- The pathologists should indicate those tissues he had examined and the number of sections he has taken in any tissue.

CRITERIA	THINGS TO BE NOTED
1) Size	Measure by tape In liver, blunting of the inferior border points to enlargement and sharpness to atropy. A usually tense capsule is in favour of enlargement,and loose capsule with lames. A straight course of superficial vessels as on heart shows increased size, while undue tortuosity means decrease.
2) Shape	Note whether there is any departure from normal.
3) Surface	Most organs have a delicate smooth glistening transparent capsule of serosa. Look for any thickening,roughening,dullness or opacity.
4)Cohesion	**Definition:** It is the strength within the tissue that holds it together. It is judged by the resistance of the cut surface to tearing pressure or pulling. **Things to be noted:** An organ with reduced cohesion is triable,while when it is increased ,the tissue seems to be tough or leathery. If a small toothed forceps bites info a testis it should pull away threads composed of tubules if it is normal.
5)Consistency	The softness or firmness as measured by pressure of the fingers.
6)Cuf surface	A) Colour: every organ is basically some shade of grey,but this is altered by the red contributed by blood supply. Other colour can be added by i) Jaundice or fatty infiltration (yellow) ii) Lipofuscin or hemosiderin (brown) iii) Malarial pigment (grey brown) iv) Anaemia (pallor) v) Congestion (blue tinge) B) Structure : This is a factor of the particular organ eg : cortex,medulla in the kidneys .In disease these may become indistinct or greatly exaggerated.

ORAL CAVITY:
- Examination of organs should be done systematically from above downward so that nothing is missed.
- It is examined for any disease or injuries, especially bite marks which are usually seen along sides,and less commonly at the trip.
- A small haemorrhage is seen under instant mucosa in bite marks.
- Serial incisions should be made through the tongue for the presence of bruises.

Examination of pharynx ,Epiglottis and glottis :
It should be examined, especially a foreign object and the condition of the tonsils is noted.

Neck structure:

Structure	Examination
1) Oesophagus upto cardiac portion	A large blunt pointed scissors is used to cut open the oesophagus from the posterior surface upto the posterior surface upto the cardiac end of the stomach. The lower end shows postmortem lesion, due to the regurgitation of gastric juice through the relaxed cardiac sphincter. Things to be noted: It is should be noted for the presence of any capsule,tablets ,powders etc.,
2) Varices	Special precautions should be taken in this case. If the esophagus is cut at the lower end,blood will drain from varices ,which would then collapse and may be missed. When death occurs from rupture of esophageal varices the break should be demonstrated.
3) Larynx,trachea,bronchi	Location: It lies opposite third to sixth cervical vertebra in the adult mole & litile higher in the adult female and children Laryngeal prominence is 2 to 5 cm below the hyoid bone when the chin is held up. Examination: It is examined by cutting them open from the posterior surface & the presence of blood, mucus,foreign bodies, vomitted matter, tumour, inflammation, mucopus etc., in them should be noted.
4)Thyroid	It is removed and examined .sections are made in both lateral lobes along their longest diameter.
5)Parathyroid	It is also examined.
6)Carotid artery	It is examined for the presence of thrombosis particularly at the bifurcation near the skill. The hyoid bone thyroid & cricoid cartilage is examined for any fracture or contusions.

- If rigor is present, to remove mandible, autopsy incision is extended into a neck 'y' and the skin of the lower part of the face is dissected.
- The masseter and temporalis muscles are divided above their insertion into the mandible, to allow the jaw to become mobile.
- The maxilla, palate and inferior part of facial skeleton is removed by sawing horizontally across the maxilla at the level of lower margin of nasal aperture taking care to saw above tooth roots.

Lungs:
1) Procedure for dissection:
Place the lungs with anterior surfaces uppermost and open the pulmonary artery and continue into the lungs tissue.

Disease to be noted: thrombi, emboli, antheroderosis

Important point:
Trace the course of pulmonary veins into the lungs looking for evidence of thrombus
- An antemortem embolism may sometimes be coiled and when straightened out resembles a cast of the vessels from which the thrombus originated usually in the leg.
- Those may be side branches but it does not fit the vessel in the lung.'
- Massive pulmonary emboli completely blocks either the main trunk of the pulmonary artery or impart in one of the major pulmonary vessels.

2) Procedure for dissection :
To separate the lungs the long bladed knife is placed blunt edge upward under the hilum of each lung and turned around so that the sharp is upward.
- Then with a short sawing motion ,the hilum is completely cut through.
- The lung is held on the upper surfaces by the left hand (or by an interposed sponge) and the organs cut across from apex to base with a large brain knife held parallel to the board.
- This produces an anteroposterior slice.

Things to be examined :
- Consolidation ,edema,emphysema, atelectasis,congestion,tardieu spots emboli,tumour etc.,
- The smaller bronchi are examined for mucosal thickening ,infection,blockage.
- The smaller pulmonary arteries are examined for thrombosis or embolism.

Important points:
For fixation of lungs a cannula is held or tied into the bronchus and 10% formal-saline is held one meter above the lungs ,the lungs is then put in formalin solution.

AORTA :
The scissors is passed into the iliac vessels and the whole length of the aorta is cut on its posterior surfaces around the arch ,up to the aortic valve.

Things to be noted :
Chronic aortitis with plaque formation which obstructs the mouths of coronary arteries.

HEART

External examination - look for:
- » adhesions
- » pericarditis
- » discolouration of infarct
- » aneurysms

- Pulmonary arteries palpated for presence of thrombus or emboli before they are unit
- If thrombus felt – right ventricle &pulmonary trunk opened insitu& the size & extend of thrombus noted
- Size varies from clot to massive coiled thick structures

In pulmonary trunk
- large ones saddle shaped
- Bifurcating into pulmonary arteries
- Pink coloured
- Firmly adherent to vessel wall

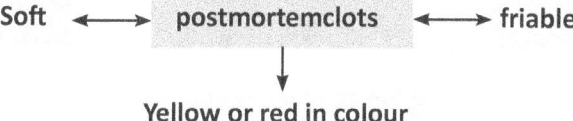

Examination for thrombi & emboli :-
- superior& inferior venacava
- pericardium

Study of isolated heart

Opened in direction of inflow – outflow method

Right atrium cut between opening of superior & interior venacava

Auricular appendage is opened (100 k for any thrombi)

Opening of right ventricle along lateral margin by cutting through tricuspid orifice
1. lateral margin towards dissector
2. Atrium towards him

- Circumference of intact value of heart measured by graduated cones at various
- To check pulmonary value competency in shouldn't be stretched or collapsed - so held it in the palm
- The competence of tricuspid& mitral value can't be satisfactorily tested postmortem
- Enterome is introduced into right ventricle close to the apex & the conus & pulmonary valve cut about 10mm right & parallel to interventricular septum

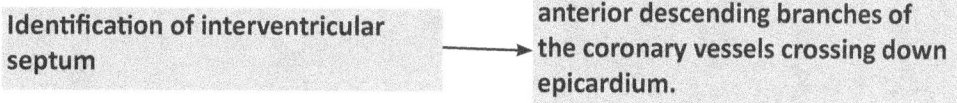

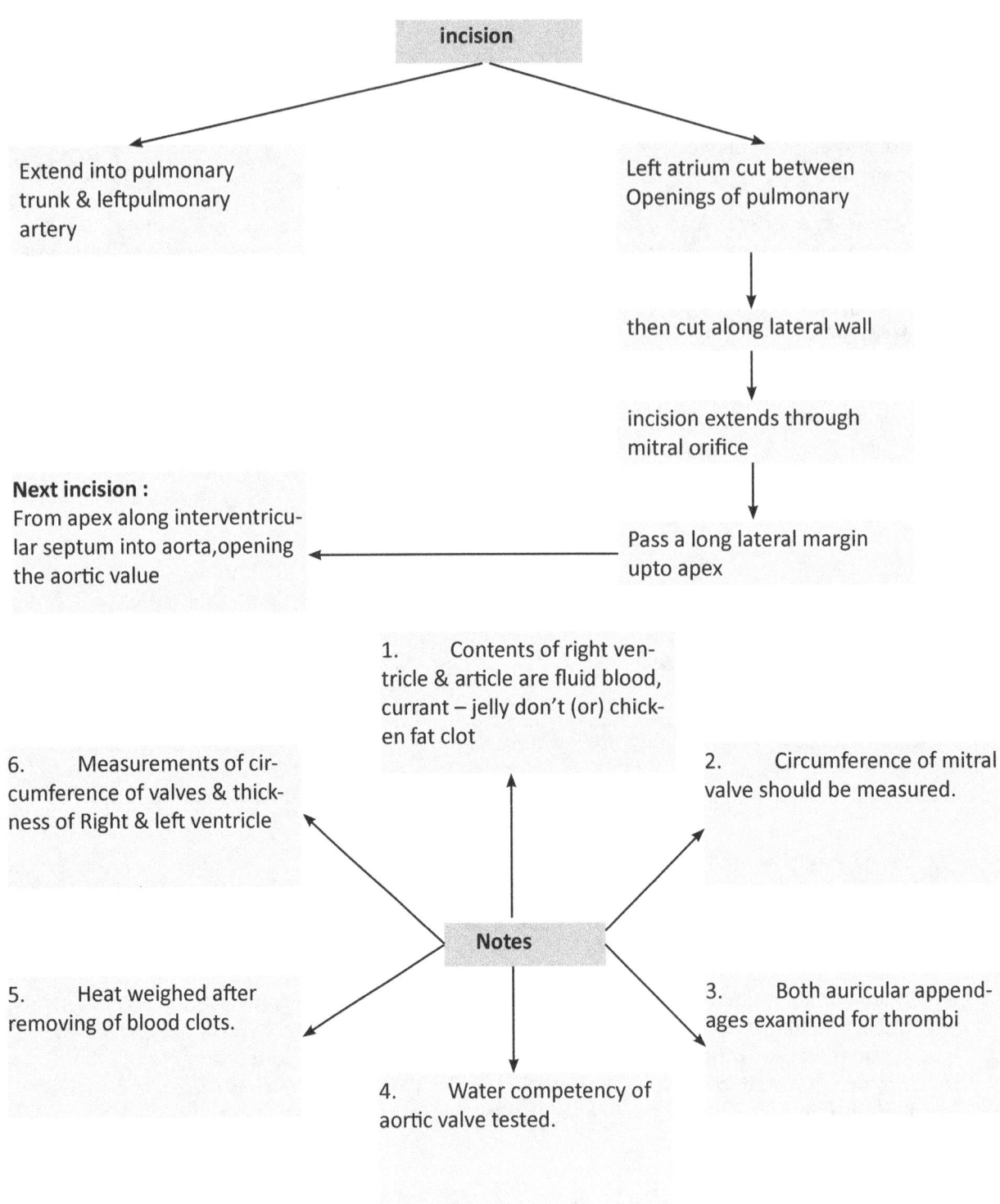

- Flabby heart – death due do ventricular fibrillation

Coronary arteries:
- Their anatomy varies considerably
- Examined before opening the heart by serial cross sections along the entire course of major vessels 2-3 mm by scalpel.
- It demonstrates narrowing (percentage stenosis) of the vessel, and any antemortem throumbus in its lumen, without danger of dislodging it
- Coronaries shouldn't be opened by scissors as they have rushing & cutting action & may be the thrombus pushed along with the point of the scissors.

Arteries	cutting
Anterior descending branch of left coronary artery	cut along the front of septum
Circumflex branch	opposite side of mitral valve
Right coronary artery	near pulmonary valve above tricuspid valve

- Look for any acute coronary lesions
- Eg. plaque rupture, plaque hemorrhage thrombus.

Calcified coronary vessels :
Can't be cut with scalpel. it should be stripped off the heart & decalcified for at least, 24 hours before cutting

SUBENDOCARDIAL HEMORRHAGES:
Site : left ventricle, upper part of the left side of the interventricular septum opposing papillary muscles & adjacent columnae carnae
Shape : flame shaped confluent, one continuous sheet rather than patches it bleeding severe -> raise the endocardium into a flat blister

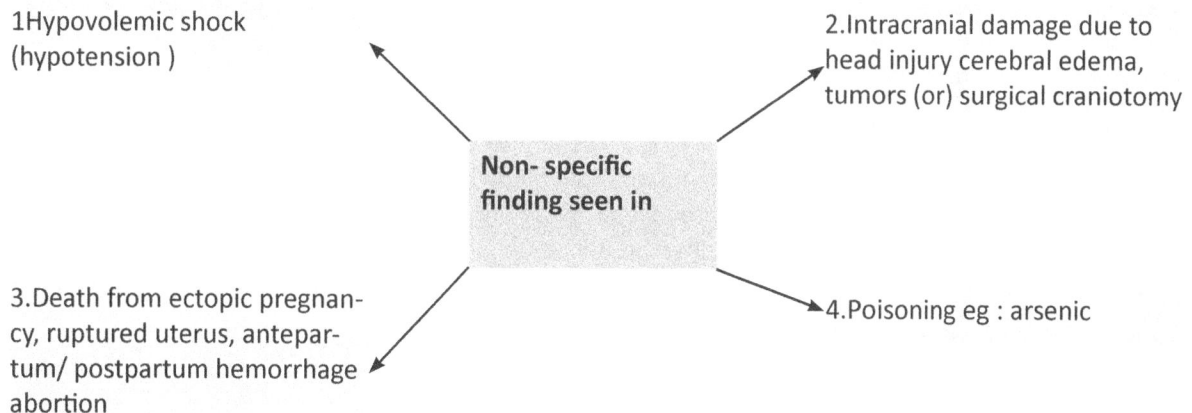

Antemortom blood clots thrombi :-
-Dark red firm but friable, dry, pale granular, adherent to vessel wall of section showsalternate layers of platelets of fibrin (coralline platelet thrombus).
Dark line – red cells & a network of fine white lines of fibrin
Older thrombi – grayish red & vary from place to place
-In sliced lung, emboli slightly project above

Postmortem thrombus :-
-Dark red glistening, soft, jelly – like & very friable

Antemortem thrombi	Postmortem thrombi
Dark, red, firm	Dark red, glistening
But friable, dry, place granular	Very friable, soft, jelly like
Adherent to vessel wall 7 knows alternate layer & platelet & fibrins	Pulled out of the vessel forms case of the branches
Sliced lung – emboli slightly project above	Sliced lung – clot doesn't pour out of cut small vessels

AGONAL THROMBI:
　Case : person dying of slow circulatory failure
　Thrombus nature : firm, stringy, rough
　Colour of thrombus : pale yellow
　Site : cavities on rigth side of heart
　Beginning of thrombus formation : a trial appendage, in the apex of ventricle / angle a tricuspid valve
　Extend of thrombus: right article & ventricle & spread into pulmonary artery & branch like a tree – like cast.

Postmortem clots

1. Red currant jelly :-
- Nature - soft, lumpy, slippery moist
- Colour – dark, red
- Blood clots rapidly

2. Chicken fat :
- Nature : fibrin clot may be soft (or) jelly like fibrin – elastic
- Colour : pale 1 bright yellow layer of serum
- RBC sediment before coagulation

What is cardiac polyps?
Postmortem clots :
- Moist, smoothy, shiny, rubbery, homogenous loosely (or) not attached to underlying wall
- No fine white lines of fibrin (striae of zahn)

Postmortem fluidity of blood :
- Shortly after death – blood usually fluid
- Autopsy done few hours after death – blood partly clotted & partly fluid
- Healthy person dies suddenly – uncoagulable fluid blood in limb vessels
- Death due to asphyxia – fluid & incoagulable (due to fibrinolysins)
- Death due to infections & cachexia, slow natural death – abundant clots seen death

Fluidity of blood :-

　Agonal period ⟶ vasoactive materials ⟶ release of plasminogen activation

　　　Release of fibrinolysins from vascular endothelium ⟵ fibrinolysin activation

　Excessive acidosis ⟶ degeneration & neurosis of cell membrane ⟶ permeability of cell

　　　Activation of fibrinolysis ⟵ leakage of plasminogen activator

- Certain condition, fibrinolysin so active & destroy fibrin rapidly

Unclotted blood :
- Sudden death – clots greatly reduced

Fluid blood
- septicemia
- co poisoning
- asphyxia
- amniotic fluid embolism (hypofibibrinogenaemia)
- retained abortion
- puerperal sepsis
- large dose of anticoagulant

Condition of blood at autopsy depends upon :
- Concentration of fibrinolysin
- Rate of intravascular coagulation

Fluid (blood	Thrombi
Activate fibrinolysin	Less active fibrinolysin
Rate of coagulation is slow	Rate of coagulation is rapid

Abdomen:
Keep the organs on the board with the liver away from the operator & the anterior surface upwards.

Stomach:
- After applying double ligatures at each end stomach is removed & placed in clean dish
- Open from cardiac to pyloric end along greater curvature

Examine:
- Size of pyloric ring with a finger
- The contents for nature of food present stage of digestion ,smell ,colour , character & also presence of foreign or suspicious matter
- The mucous membrane for presence of congestion ,haemorrhage ,ulceration or other abdominal conditions.

Stomach contents:
- 1.Regurgitation of bile from duodenum- gastric contents are yellow or yellow –green
- 2.Paralytic ileus- foul smelling,copious thick fluid ,dirty green ,brown or black
- 3.Gastrocolicfistula- faecal material may found
- 4.Massive haemorrhage- large soft clots,take the form of a cast of gastric outline

Intestine:

Examine small & large intestine are:
- Serosa
- Diameter of various portions
- Colour
- Consistency of wall
- Adhesions
- Hernia
- Other abnormalities

- Superior mesentery vessels examined for any disease ,thrombi or emboli
- Inferior mesenteric vessels are examined
- Transverse colon& pelvic mesocolon are separated from mesentery open small intestine along- line of mesenteric attachment
- Large intestine along – anterior taenia
- Large intestine along – anterior taenia
- They are examined for congestion,inflammation ,erosion ,ulcers ,perforation
- Also examine the contents

Liver:
Note for:
- » Weight
- » Size
- » Colour
- » Consistency
- » Presence of any pathologic process
- » Injury
- » Cut into 2cm thick slices

CUT SECTION	
Chronic venous congestion	granular (nutmeg) appearance
Fatty liver	greasy
Biliary cirrhosis	granular & olive green
Pyogenic abscesses	multiple
Amoebic abscesses	single ,large confined to right lobe
Portal cirrhosis	studded with nodules(1 to 3mm)
Post hepatic cirrhosis	varying size nodules 4-10mm

- Ampulla of vater is identified by opening the anterior wall of second part of duodenum
- Squeeze the gall bladder gently & note if bile enters duodenum
- Look for tumors calculi & structures in common bile duct
- Note the condition & nature of lymph nodes in neighbourhood

Spleen:
- Removed by cutting through pedicel
- Note:
- » Size
- » Weight
- » Consistency
- » Condition of capsule
- » Rupture
- » Injury or disease
- » Character of parenchyma
- » Follicles & septa

PULP NATURE	
Congestive splenomegaly	very soft & scraped ear
Portal hypertension	firm & enlarged
Malaria,kalaazar,portal vein thrombosis leukaemia,reticulosis,schistosomiasis	enlarged

Pancreas:
- They are sliced by right angles to log axis to get best exposure of ductal system
- Probe the duct before cutting
- Acute haemorrhagic pancreatitis- areas of fact necrosis seen as small round,opaque area around pancreas & mesentry

Kidney:
Abdominal aorta is opened along its anterior midline

Examine:	for:
Renal artery ostia	thrombi, emboli or atherosclerosis
Renal veins	thrombus
Pelvis	calculi and inflammation

- Note size & weight of kidney
- Strip the capsule with toothed forceps
- Chronic nephritis, hypertensive nephrosclerosis, pyelonephritis- capsule strip with difficulty
- The kidney is holded in left hand b/w thumb & finger the ureter passing between ring & middle finger
- The kidney is sectioned longitudinally to spirt in half & open the pelvis

Adrenals:
- Identified by their relationship to the upper pole of each kidney
- The periadrenal fat is gripped with forceps & cut & adrenal removed
- Gently cut the gland with scalped without applying under pressure
- Haemorrhage seen in meningococcal septicemia, bleeding disease hypertension, birth trauma, pregnancy etc

Bladder:
Examine:
- » The condition of wall
- » Amount & character of urine
- Open from fundus
- Auto cystitis – mucosa is red, swollen & covered with fibrin & pus
- Chronic cystitis – mucosa is covered with much mucus & pus & may show ulcerations

Prostate:
Examine :
> Any enlargement or malignancy

prostatitis	Carcinoma
Organ is firm	Hard & granular

Testes:
> Incise inguinal canal from peritoneal aspects
> ↓
> Pull out the loop of vas with finger
> ↓
> Free the vas into inguinal ring
> ↓
> Push the testis up out of the scrotum & pull vas with Left hand

- Testis comes out without any difficulty or damage
- Testis &v epididymis cut longitudinally

Note for:
- Presence of clotted blood is scrotum & around testis
- Seminal tubules can be lifted like thin long filaments by toothless pointed forces

Acute orchitis & epididymitis	Chronic orchitis
• Organ is swollen & firm • Show small abscess	• Organ is firm, nodular & reduced in size

Female genitalia:
- Tubed, ovaries & uterus are freed & removed
- Expose the cervix by cutting the anterior vaginal wall
- Examine the fornices
- Uterus opened
    - » From: external os
    - » To : the fundus
- For exposing the endometrium, 2 short incisions are made in the fundus from main longitudinal incision towards earn cornu
- Ovaries – seitioned longitudinally
- Tube- cut across at intervals
- If uterus contain fortus, age should be determined

HEAD:
Head is fixed by a head rest & shoulder is placed above the wooden block.

1. Scalp incision :
    Type : coronal incision
    Starting : mastoid process just behind one ear
    Ending : over the vertex to the back of the opposite ear (intermastoidal incision)

Reflection of scalp :
    Forward - Superciliary ridges
    Backward - occipital protuberance
- Any bruising of deeper tissues of the scalp or bone injury should be noted.

2. Removal of skull cap :
- Temporal & masseter muscles - out on either side
- Slightly v-shaped direction (sawline)
- Saw line go through cline extending horizontally on both sides, from centre of fore head to the base of mastoid process
- Avoid sawing through the meanings & brain
- Avoid using chisel & hammer to loosen the skull completely
- Skull structures elicited by tapping of skull gives **"cracked pot"**
- Gently removed skull cap b inserting & twisting thechisel through cut at various places

3. Examination of skull cap :
Meninges :-
- Examined for congestion disease, etc
- In old persons, they are write & thickened with little calcified patches (arachnoid granulations)
  - Extradural of subdural hemorrhage measured & also of intracranial tension
  - Describe variation in thickness of the material is semi – liquid & not easily collected
  - Superior longitudinal sinus is examined for antemortem thrombus
  - Antemortem thrombus lead to back pressure in the bridging veins crossing the subdural space & cause subdural hemorrhage
  - The duramater is removed & the surface of brain is examined

Dissection of head in infants:
ROKITANSKY'S method is the autopsy technique for infants

> Put incision on anterior fontanelle at its posterior margin (5mm)
>
> The knife point is pushed parallel to the inner aspect of parallel bone (1-2mm)
>
> Between dura & leptomeninges)
>
> The incisions is extended to lateral angle (opposite side & both anterior margins cut similarly)
>
> One blade of scissors passed under original
>
> Parietal bone cut longitudinally about 5 mm (parallel to sagittal upto lambdoid & suture) other side also cut similarly
>
> Reflect the flaps , the vertex of brain & terminations of pial veins into superior longitudinal sinus (look for any hemorrhage)

- Haematoma – foundbetween falx & medial aspect of hemispheres (or) between 2 dural layers of falx
- Superior longitudional sinus – examine for thrombi tentorium – examine for tears & for haematoma
- The dural sinuses are opened & the dura is detained from the base & sides of skull by forceps, or held the part of dura with towel & is pulled

Removal of brain :
- Cut dura along the line of cleavage of skull & fold it back to midline
- Free flax cerebri from cribriform plate & pull dura& flax back ward
- Insert four fingers of left hand between frontal lobes & skull & drawing frontal lobes backwards & cut the vasculonervous structure
- Cut cervical cord &cervical nerves & cerebral arteries by passing knife into occipital foramen
- Grasp cerebellum with right hand & brain is removed from vault
- Child's brain attains mature size & weight at about 6 years of age

Examine :
- Surface & base – hemorrhage injury , disease
- Circle of willis – arteriosclerosis, minute aneurysms , etc
- Ruptured berry aneurysm, easily dissected under flow of running water by blunt dissection from the greater intercerebral vessels origin
- **Berry aneurysm site :** junction of posterior cerebral arteries , the posterior communicating vessel middle cerebral artery & the anterior communicating artery.

Note :
- cerebral infarction due to increased intracranial pressure thrombus or atheroma cause obstruction to venous outflow
 Hemorrhagic infarction - pinkish purple discolouration of cortex with stippled hemorrhages.

Fixation of brain :
- For complete examination of brain it is fixed in 10 % formalin for one week.
- In foetuses & infants acetic acid may be added to formalin which makes tissue firmer
- The weight of the brain is increased by about 8% due to fixation in formalin.

Dissection of brain :
- Place it in normal anatomical position

1.Single incision pass through corpus callosum midbrain pons, medulla
↓
2.Incision on midline , pass through septum lucidum cavity & expose its internal surface
↓
3.It pass through 3rd ventricle aqueduct of sulvius & 4 th ventricle
↓
Lateral ventricles opened by - dissection of anterior posterior & inferior horns
• Ependymal lining is examined
4.Turn cerebellum & cut through vermis to expose the 4th ventricle
↓
5.Expose dentate nucleus , cut obliquely
6.Stem is sectioned transversely at few mm interval, to demonstrate hemorrhages
↓
7.Cerebral hemispheres serial sections made in coronal plane at 1 cm interval other method : horizontal cut through cerebrum at level of tips of the frontal 100e & temporal to occipital lobes
↓
8.Inspect choroid plexus , thalamus caudate nucleus , locate interventricular foramen , fornices & corpus callosum bent backwards
↓
9.3rd ventricle exposed pass probe through aqeuduct of sylvius
↓
10.Expose 4th ventricle by cutting along vermis that lead to exposure of basal ganglia & lateral ventricles

Injury to brain successive sections parallel to the wounded surfaces should be made till the whole depth of lesion seen.
- The dura is stripped from the base of skull (forceps used) to look for basal fractures
- Washable: Sub dural hemorrhage
- Non washable: sub arachnoid hemorrhage
- For personal identification & determination of type of violence , electric drill & copper wire used for replacement & fixation of bone fragments .

Cerebral oedema:
- Flattening of cerebral convolutions obliteration of sulci, glistening white matter
- Herniation of inner portion of temporal poles through tentorial hiatus, & portions of cerebellar lobe & cerebellar tonsils through foramen magnum (coning)
- Coning – discoloured (or) necrotic cerebellar tonsils
- Increased bulk of hemisphere cause tentorial herniation
- Severe injury white matters shows pools or lakes of pale staining fluid

Middle ear examination :
Done by chiselling out the wedge shaped portion of petrous temporal bone
Mastoid : nipping away the bone with bone forceps
Orbits: remove the orbital plates : open the sphenoid and frontal sinuses by chisel
Remove the pituitary & also look for any abuses or septic condition in the jaws & teeth.

Vertebral column:

Pants	Examined for
Atlanto – occipital joint	Fracture dislocation
Anterior surface of spinal ligaments	Hemorrhage
Cervical spine	Examine it
Thoracic & lumbar spine	Show movement at site of fracture
Pelvis (mobility it present)	Fracture of sacro – iliac joints or pelvic bones
Thorax	Recent or old fractures of ribs

Removal of spinal cord:
- Not routinely examined, unless theme is indication of disease or injury
  Beginning : midline extending from occipital protuberance
  Ending : lower end of sacrum

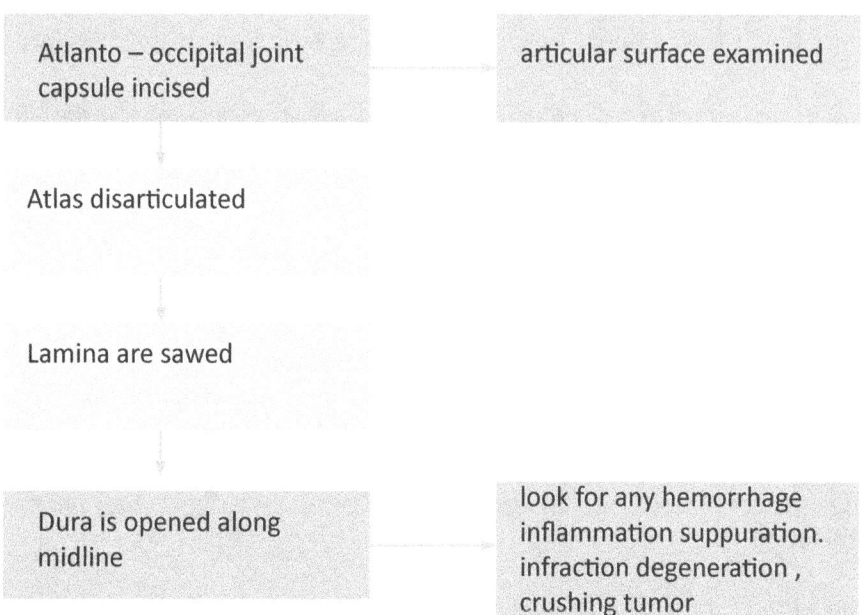

- Vertebral column – examined for fractures or dislocations
- Empty spinal cord – look for any disc protrusion tumors fractures dislocations & vertebral collapse

Extremities:
    1. Femoral vessels – longitudinal incision below inguinal ligament
    2. Popliteal & calf veins – vertical midline incision
    3. Achilles tendon – divided
    4. Calf muscles – separated from the bones transverse sections about 2 cm apart are then made in the calf muscles.

- If thrombi present – they protrude as firm, solid, tube like masses
- All the organs & parts removed from the body should be returned to the dead body for the purpose of burial

ENDOSCOPIC TECHNIQUE OF POSTMORTEM DIAGNOSIS:
- It requires use of rigid Hopkins – endoscope of 4mm & 8 mm diameter with 00,900, & 1300,, light source from fiberglass cable
- Sinuses, fundus, external auditory meatus, larynx, etc
- Hepatic, splenic & diaphragmatic injuries & intraperitoneal & thoracic hemorrhage can be visualized
- Natural orifices dearly examined

VIRTUAL AUTOPSY (VIRTOPSY):
- Non – invasive technique of examining dead bodies to find out the cause of death
- A combination of CT & MR imaging
- CT – information about morbid anatomical findings
- MR – soft tissue injury, organ trauma, state of blood vessels, tissue & bones.
- Emphysema, air embolism, pneumothorax, hyberbaric trauma & decompression effects can be better appreciated
- **CT scanning :** track of projectile inside the brain& other internal organs with hemorrhage & damage to tissue can be viewed.

Psychological autopsy :
- It is a set of postmortem investigation procedures that help ascertain & evaluate the role that physical & psychological factors play in the death of a victim suicide
- Description of scene of death, position of body evidence at the scene such as weapons, poison & notes etc
- It involves systemic collection of psychological data through interviews of the deceased's family members friends coworkers, employers & fellow students who had dealt with deceased
- Most commonly introduced in those involving custodial (are taking police custody & prisons) & those of contested life insurance claims.

Function :
1. Determination of mode of death
2. To determine the state of mind at the time of death
3. To gain information that will be helpfuk in treating future patients
4. To retrieve the most honest information possible in a way that will be healing for survivors
- Psychological autopsy have also been introduced in criminal cases (suicide or homicide) worker compensation (unsafe job conditions), product manufactures depressents & professional negligence proximate cause of suicide, the gathered may be biased, but it significantly improves manner of death determination

Collection of blood :
- After death most of the concentration variation of a substance is caused by uneven distribution by enzymatic & microbiological activity & by diffusion from sites of higher concentration
- Before autopsy 10 to 20 ml of blood can be drawn from the femoral vein in the groin by a syringe.

Blood can be collected from :
- Femoral vein
- Jugular (or) subclavian vein
- Subclavian vein
- Iliac veins

Note :
- *Blood should never be collected from the pleural or the abdominal cavities it can be contaminated with gastric or intestinal contents , lymph , mucus, urine , pus (or) serous fluid*
- *Alcohol & barbiturates they diffuse passively into organs leading to erroneous results*

C.S.F:
- Collected from lumbar puncture or from the cisterna magna by inserting a needle between atlas & the occipital bone
- Direct aspiration from lateral ventricles (or) third ventricle can be done

VITREOUS HUMOUR:
- fine hypodermic needle is inserted through outer canthus into the posterior chamber of the eye
- 1 to 2 ml of fluid aspirated from each eye
- To restore the tension , water can be re – introduced

Lungs :
- Solvent abuse & death from gaseous or volatile substances , lung mobilized & the main bronchus tied off tightly with a ligature
- After dividing the hilum , immediately the lung is put in to a nylon bag, which is sealed
- Polythene bags (plastic) are not suitable as they are permeable to volatile substances
- After completing the autopsy , the body cavities should be cleaned of blood , fluid,,etc
- The organs are replaced in the body , dissected flaps brought close together & well sutured , scalp is pulled back over the calvarium &it is stitched with strong twine
- Any excess space is packed with cotton cloth etc the skull should be filled with cotton or other absorbent material
- Body should be washed , dried & covered with clothes & handed over to the police constable

Indian penal code:
S.297,IPC tells that whoever offers any indignity to any human corps shall be punished (or) imprisonment for one year

Autopsy of a case of aids & infection:
Infectious diseases transmitted by direct contact contact with infected materials:
- Cholera
- Rabies
- Tetanus
- Poliomyelitis
  1.Patent with persenile dementia may have creutzfeldt – Jakob disease (CJD) caused by virus ,highest concentration in nervous & lymphoid tissues.
  2.Hepatitis B & C concentrated in hepatic tissue & present in blood stream

HIV:
- High concentration remain viable for 3 weeks from liquid blood after 2 months
- Not association with air borne
- Present mostly in lymphoid tissue & brain and also in colon & lungs
- High risk of transmission through needle prick injury while collecting the blood sample

Prosector's wart:
- Inoculation tuberculosis of skin seen in person engaged in post-mortem examinations
- It is better to leave some organs insitu in cadaver rather than eviscerating en masse

Universal work precautions:

1. Tag of biologically hazardous:
All infected bodies should be tied & wrapped in double layer tough plastic bag, label them with red color tag as biologically hazardous it also should mention name, age, sex, registration number etc

2. Persons prohibited to handle AIDS victims:
Workers having exudative lesions or weeping dermatitts or external injury

3. Protection:
- Proper protective clothing, double gloves (heavy autopsy gloves over surgical gloves), waterproof of rubber gumboots upto knee length with shoe covers
- Plastic visor for eyes & mucosal surface (splash injury)
- High efficiency particulate air – filled respirator or powered air- purifying respirator should worn

4. Handling sharp instruments:
- Avoid accidental pricks & cuts from needles scalpels etc..
- Hands & other skin surface should be washed immediately & thoroughly of contaminated with blood or other body fluids
- Infection of AIDS can be acquired by transdermal involution through cuts & needle punctures
- Transmission rate 10 to 30 times higher for serum hepatitis than for AIDS
- 0.3 – 0.5 % of individuals will become seropositive

5. specimens for laboratory examination:
- Mucocutaneous Handling contact with the body fluid& aerosol inhalation should be avoided
- They should be sealed & filled with 10% formalin solution & handled with gloved hands

6. Disposal of used instruments:
Dipped in 20% of glutaraldehyde (cidox) for ½ an hour washed with soap or detergent & water dried & then rinsed in methylated spirit & air dried

7. Incineration:
All solid gauze & cotton etc collected in double plastic bag for incineration

8. Laundary material:
Aprons towels etc.. soaked in 1% bleach for ½ an hour wash with detergent and autoclaved

9. Clean up procedure:
- Wear disposal gloves
- Small spatters & spills of blood & other body parts (fluid) wiped with disposable towels & discorded in proper biohazard bags
- Autopsy table cleaned with 1% bleach solution followed by washing with soap & water

10. Disinfectants:
- 1:10 dilution of common household bleach or freshly prepared sodium hypochlorite
- Liquid chemical germicides areeffective against HIV

11. Sudden cut injury:
Instruments contaminated with blood or body fluid was working on body wound should be washed thoroughly under running water bleeding encouraged & disinfected

12. to minimize aerosol splatter, skull opened with electrical oscillating saw attained to vacuum dust exhaust & filter / band saw under transparent anti- slash cover
Tag attached body covered with double layer heavy plastic sheet bag to prevent leakage
13. After autopsy completed, face & hands washed with soap & water and rinsed in70% methylated spirit
14. The body should be burnt or incinerated

Universal precautions

Applicable	Not applicable
Blood	Feces
Semen	Nasal secretions
Vaginal secretions	Sputum
CSF	Sweat
Synovial fluid	Tears
Pleural fluid	Urine
Pericardial fluid	Vomitus
Amniotic fluid	Can less contain visible blood

The autopsy and disposal of radioactive corpse:
- No extra precaution necessary- if amount of radioactivity <5 millicuries
- Between 5 to 30 millicuries- doctors must wear heavy rubber gloves ,plastic aprons ,plastic shoe covers & spectacles
- Organs & fluid – more radioactive should removed first & placed in covered glass jars ,labelled & examined for radioactivity from time to time
- Contaminated wearing dress should be thoroughly cleaned with soap & water & stored for suitable decay of radioactive material
- Instruments are soaked in water & soap or detergent ,spilled fluid cleaned with dry disposable water
- If the radiation level is high a team is required special organs may be removed first,detailed dissection done
- If more than 300 millicuries of activity after autopsy ,it should be embalmed in hospital morgue
- Cardiac pacemaker is recorded if it is one which might contain mercury was radioactive substance
- As explosions incrematoria from the heating of mercury batteries have proved hazardous

National human rights commission's recommendations on autopsy:
The doctors who have access to the scone of death should:

    1.Photography the body
    2.Record body position
    3.Determine time of death
    4.Protect desceased's hand with paper bags
    5.Examine the scene for blood
    6.Obtain information from scene witness ,friends , relatives
    7.Place the body in body pouch
    8.Become familiar with types of torture or violence

Autopsy:

    1.Record names of all person present during autopsy
    2.Throne should ne principal prosector
    3.Photography – full frontal &right & left profiles of face
    4.Colour photographs should be comphrehensive
    5.Radiography the body
    6.Obtain dental x ray.
    7.Photograph 100% of body area
    8.Examine clothing & photography
    9.Determine the time of death
    10.Photography all injuries

11. Photograph scars, keloides, moles etc
12. Identify & label recovered foreign objects
13. Look for deep injuries in the length of back, buttocks extremities, wrist & ankle
14. Conduct through complete autopsy
15. Take colour photographs of all injuries found during internal examination
16. Record the specimens which have been saved
17. Send viscera for chemical examination
18. Preserve all foreign objects .eg: nail scarping, public hair(sexual assault)
19. The autopsy report should be a summary of the findings & the cause of death

Laboratory procedures:

1. Histopathology:
- Various internal organs are examined
- Affected area removed along with a portion of normal borderline
  ↓
  It should be cut into pieces 1cm in thickness for preservation
  ↓
  Specimens fixed in 10% neutral

Formalin or 95% alcohol
- Amount of preservation 6-10 times the volume of tissue to be fixed

Negri bodies:
- Intracytoplasmic deeply eosinophilic inclusion found in pyramidal cells of hippo campus & uncus & purkinje cells of cerebellum
- 1 to 2cm preserved in 50% glycerol saline

2. Bacteriological examination:
Blood for culture should be collected before organs are distributed

Blood:
The anterior surface of right ventricle is seared with heated knife and 10ml of blood aspirated using sterile needle & syringe

CSF:
- The subarachnoid space is opened & the specimen is taken by sterile swabs
- The samples should be stored in sterile stoopered containers

Death due to septicemia:
- Spleen is the best organ for culture
- The surface of organ (2*2 cm) is seared with not spatula & the area is punctured with sterile instrument & pulp is scraped

3. Smears of brain cortex, spleen & liver:
- They are stained for material parasites
- Bone marrow from ribs & sternum is stained for blood dyscrasias
- Smears from chancers & mucous patched are examined fresh by dark field or stained

4. Virological examination:
- Tissue is collected & the sample is freezed or preserved in 80% glycerol in buffered saline
- Kept in sterile container & sealed tightly

5. Blood, urine vitreous and C.S.F:
They are collected for biochemical examination

Blood:
- Femoral vessels > subclavian vessels > root of aorta > pulmonary artery > superior venacava > heart
- Blood collected for volatile substance, glass bottles with aluminium foil lined should be used stored at 4c
- Valued if collected within 4 to 6 hrs after death but not later than 12 hrs

6. Enzymes:
Collected (tissue) in thermos flask containing liquid nitrogen

7. Faeces:
- Examined for protozoa & helminths
- 5 to 10gm without any preservative sent for bacteriologic examinations

8. Urine:
- Can be obtained by catheter or suprapubic puncture before autopsy
- It can also be collected by making an incision on the anterior surface of the bladder during autopsy

9. Cyst fluid:
Examined for Ecchinococcus hooklets

10. Bite marks:
Saw the bite site with saline – moistened cotton swab, dry & place in a test tube & plug with cotton

11. Vaginal & anal swabs:

12. Urethral discharge:

13. Rectal swabs:
Swab from rectal mucosa are suitable for bacteriological examination

Preservation of viscera in cases of suspected poisoning:
1. If the death is suspected to be due to poisoning
2. Deceased was intoxicated or used to drugs
3. Cause of death of death not found after autopsy
4. An unusual smell, color or an unidentifiable material is detected in stomach contents
5. Anaphylactic deaths
6. Death due to burns
7. Advanced decomposition
8. Accidental death involving driver of a vehicle or machine operator

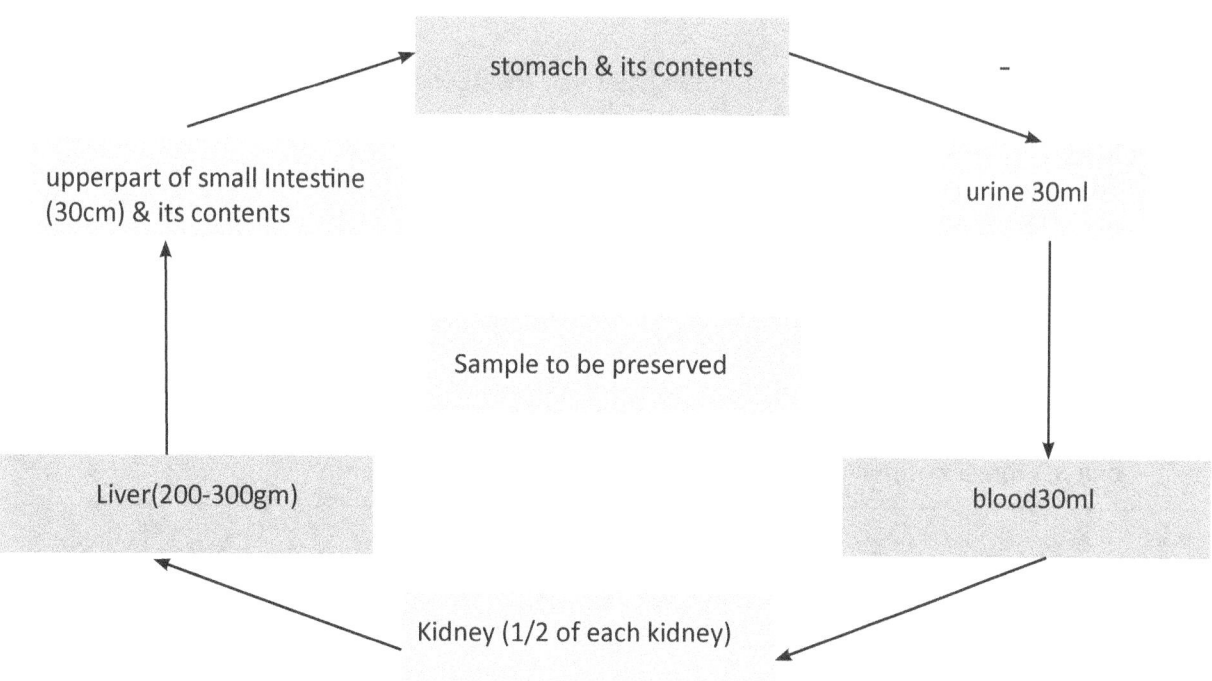

- Most of the poisons are taken orally so they most likely to present in the stomach liver majorly & has the power of concentrating them &making them identifiable
- Kidney being the organ of excretion contains large amount of poison

---

Note:
- *Levels of drug in the muscle best reflects the blood level than the liver r kidney*
- *It is essential to prevent contamination of the solid viscera with the contents of GIT*
- *It is important to keep the contents of the alimentary canal in separate bottles*
- *Poison found in urine unless added with evil intention is a proof of absorption & excretion*
- *The stomach contents are of primary value for estimating the quantity ingested in acute overdoses &qualitatively in identifying substances which have been recently ingested*

Containers:
- 1l capacity glass bottle should be used it should be clean ,wide mouthed white & fitted with glass stoppers
- Chloroform & phenols get extracted into rubber inserts ,so they shouldn't be used under caps
- Clean glass containers with H_2SO_4 chromate solution rinsed with distilled water & dried
- Volatile substance difference through plastic ,instead of plastic nylon bags should be used
- Blood collected in screw –capped bottle (30ml)

Preservatives:

1. Saturated NaCl solution:

They used except in poisoning from corrosive acids ,alkalis,corrosive sublimate and aconite

2. Rectified spirit:

Except in cases of suspected poisoning by (a) alcohol,kerosene(b) chloroform ,ether (c) chloral hydrate (d) formic acid €formaldehyde acetic acid(f) phenol (g) phosphorous & (h) paraldehyde

3. 10mg 1ml of sodium or potassium fluoride:
- Prevent glycolysis,inhibit enolase & also bacterial growth
- Blood- potassium oxalate
  Urine ,CSF, - fluoride added
  Vitreous humour
  For analysis for cocaine ,cyanide&co
- Oxalic acid ethyleneglycol ,fluoride and co poisoning 30mg sodium citrate should be added for 10ml
- 1ml of conc .HCL or 100mg of thymol or 100mg of sodium fluoride can be used for 10ml urine as a preservative toluene is better

Preservative not necessary if:
- Viscera can be analysed within 24hrs
- Sample can be kept in refrigerator or ice box
- Bone ,hair ,nails
- lung for detecting inhaled poisons

Note:

The viscera shouldn't be preserved in formaldehyde because extraction of poison ,especially non-volatile organic compounds becomes difficult

---

Instructions for preservation and despatch of viscera:

1. Stomach, small intestine & its contents - one bottle
   Liver kidney - another bottle
   Blood & urine - separately
2. Stomach & intestines - opened before they are preserved
   Liver & kidney - they cut into small piece of 0.5 to 1cm
3. Quantity of preservation = viscera in bulk
4. 2/3 rd of bottle filled with viscera & preservative to avoid bursting (gases formed)
5. The stoppers of bottles well – fitted covered with a piece of sealed
6. Labelling the bottle:

- Name of the victim, age, sex, autopsy number, police station, crime number the organ it contains the date & place of autopsy preservative used & signature
- Warning should be put on label

7. A sample of preservative used i.e 25ml of rectified spirit or 25gm of Nacl is separately kept in bottle
8. The sealed containers is locked & lock is sealed using personal or departmental seal
9. A copy of inquest report, post-mortem report & the authorisation from the magistrate sent to the forensic science laboratory along with viscera

- Viscera are not analysed unless there is an authorisation letter from the magistrate or a police officer not below the rank of deputy superintendent

10. The key of the box & a sample seal or a piece of paper, corresponding to the seal used on bottles lock kept in envelope, sealed & sent with viscera box
11. Viscera box is handed over to the police constable after taking receipt who delivers it personally in the office of the ESL after obtaining a receipt for the same.

viscera	Case of poisoning
Heart	Strychnine, digitalis, yellow oleander
Brain	Alkaloids; organophosphorous opiates co cyanide, barbiturates, strychnine volatie organics
Spinal cord	Strychnine, gelsemium
C.S.F	Alcohol
Bile	Narcotic drug cocaine, metaodone glutathione, barbiturates, tranquilisers
Vitreous humour	Alcohol chloroform, cocaine morphine, tricylic anti-depressants
lung	gaseous poisons, hydrocyanic acid alcohol, chloroform etc
trachea	Collect bronchial air & heat sealed
viscera	Case of poisoning
skin	Insulin, morphine, heroin, cocaine & illicit -drugs
Bone	Subalute or chronic poisoning by arsenic, antimony, thallium or radium
Hair	Head hair removed with a tweezer to remove the roots tied in locks
Nails	All nails removed by spencer – wells forceps under nail plate, grasping & twisting
Uterus	Criminal abortion
muscle	Embalmed body –skeletal muscle from the buttock (best spelimen)
fat	Pesticides & insecticides

Cause of death:

The doctor must consider:
- History
- Description of fatal environment
- Circumstanced (provided by primary source)
- Treatment leading upto death
- Manipulation of body after death which cause injuries ,before arriving an autopsy interpretation
- Clinical records must check if he victim admitted in the hospital
- After the completion of post-mortem a complete but concise report written in duplicate using carbon papers
- 1st copy to – investigating officer
- Another way- for future reference
- Autopsy report should contain list of specimens & samples retained for further examination
- If lab tests have to be carried out,an interium report should be written after obtaining reports supplementary report is written
- The autopsy reveals the disease & lesions that the person lived with and not necessary those which killed him
- If the cause of death cannot be found viscera should be preserved & histological & bacteriological examinations carried out
- In poisoning case ,opinion should be kept reversed until chemical examiner's report received
- If the cause of death not found in autopsy the opinion should be given as " undermined or unascertained " the manner of death is unknown
- Opinions are based on the facts & findings as they are known at the time the opinion is given
- If the facts which forms the basis for the opinion change ,the opinion can & often will change

Autopsy of decomposed bodies:
- All human remains should be examined even when they arent' likely to provide information
- In case of advanced decomposition also through examination shows gross traumatic or pathological lesion
  1. Antemortem injury – localised of redness
  2. Incision into discoloured area- dark red ecchymoses in subcutaneous fat & muscle
  3. Bullet wound lacerated wound or incised wound- discoloured skin
- Fractured easily detected
- Antemortem thrombi may persist

Effacement or obliteration of identity

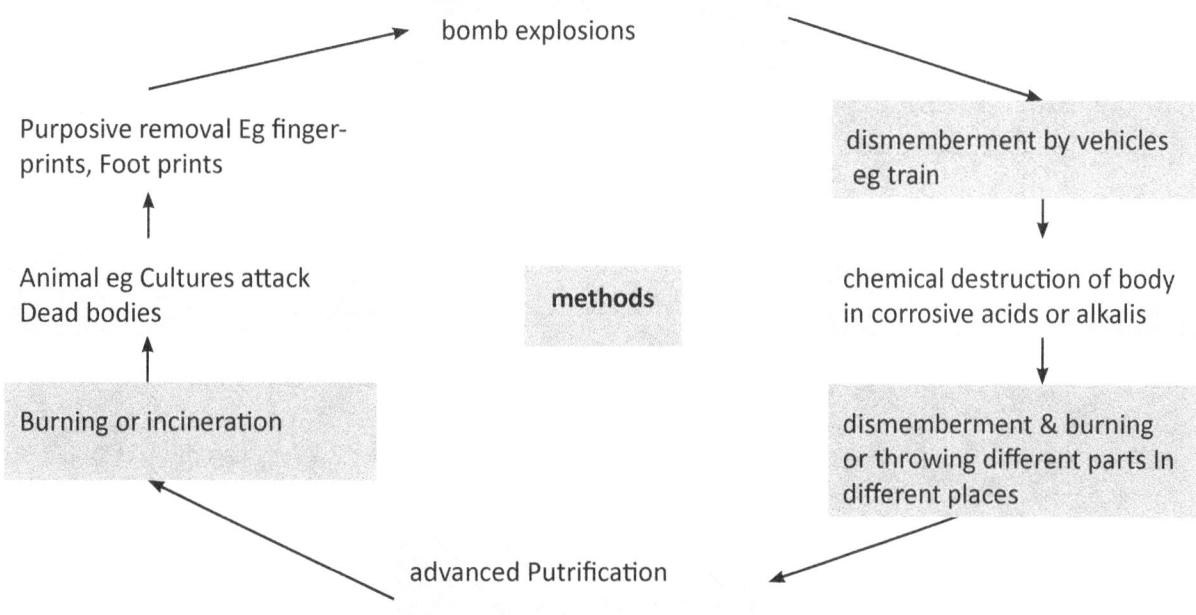

5. alkaline hydrolysis use lye 150 c heat & 60 pounds of pressure a square inch to destroy bodied in big stainless steel cylinders

Examination of multilated bodies or fragments:
- multilated bodies are extensively disfigured, or in which a limb or a part is lost but the soft tissues muscles and skin are attached to the bones
- sometimes only a part of body may be found eg: trunk head
- scene should be photographed first

Human or animal	If only muscle piece available without attached skin or viscera, it is difficult Test: Precipitin test or antiglobuin inhabitation test using blood
One or more bodies	Determined by fitting all separated parts color of skin in all parts
Sex	- Distribution or absence of hair, pelvis, skull etc -Recognition of prostatic or uterine tissue
Age	Skull, teeth, bone ossification
stature	Measurement of long bones
Identity	Fingerprints tattoo, scars, moles, hair, teeth deformities etc.. articles of clothing and superimposition technique
Manner of separation of parts	Examine the margins of the parts whether they had been cleanly cut swan, hacked lacerated disarticulated at the joints or gnawed through by animals
Time since death	Condition of parts they determined
Cause of death	Made out if there is evidence of fatal injury to vital organ, blood vessels deep cut marks of burning bone fracture – skull cervical vertebrate hyoid bone or ribs
Antemortem or postmortem	Examine the margins of parts for evidence of vital reaction decomposing bodies haemorrhage along with wound talk on dissection indicates antemortem nature

Examination of bones

Forensic anthropology – branch of physical anthropology, deals with the identification & analysis of skeletonised remains known to be or suspected of being human

- Sand dust or earth present on bones removed with brushed & wooden picks & scrape
- Light applications of acetone help to remove tight dirt
- Note for ant putrefaction of soft tissues attached to bone
- Examine the skeletal muscle,& note whether the bones are moist & humid or dry & their smell
- If soft tissues are attached, boil the bones in water or immersed un dilute aqeous solution of trisodium phosphate & household detergent (sodium hypochlorite 5 to 6 %)
- Disarticulation is usually done by filling the cranial cavity with a substance that swells when moistened & forces the bone apart through expansion
- The specific gravity of a bone, which forms the densest part in the human body is two

1. Are the remains actually bones?	Sometimes stone or even pieces of wood mistaken by the public for bones
2. Human or animal	Find out whether particular bones are human or not - Precipitin test useful when bone is fairly fresh, some of the blood constituents are still present. - Fresh bone- DNA analysis useful. - Serological tests are not useful not having extractable plasma proteins. - Non human bones contain sheets of plexiform structures in cross section. - Human & animal bones can also be distinguished by chemical analysis of bone -ash
3. One or more individuals	- Determined by reconstructing the skeleton - No disproportion in size of various bones, reduplication articulation is correct, if the age sex & race of all boned they belong to one individual - When the surface of bones are exposed to uv radiation, they reflect variety of colours - Radiated colour is derived from fluorescence of organic elements in bones, inorganic substances in the surface ones and to a lesser extend reflected light
Sex	- Recognisable sex difference aren't present before puberty. - Examination of pelvis skull, manubrium –gladiolus ratio, diameter of head of femur & numerus & measurements of femur, tibia, humerus & radius. - Parous women, public symphysis become irregular & have scars of parturition.
Age at death	- Examination of teeth ossific centres, amount of wear and tear in teeth, length of long bones, epiphyseal union public symphysis, closure of skull structures cortical resorption bony lipping, osteoporosis calcification osteoarthritic changes. - Foetal age can be determined by measuring the length of the ossified portion of long bones. - Broken bones, measurement of external diameter of the long bones at midshaft

- Most resorptive activity is found in the medullary third of the cortex
- The general age can also be estimated by the resorption patterns in the cortex of the long bones
- Kerley has described for the quantifying

Cortical elements for estimating age:
    1. Osteons
    2. Osteon fragments
    3. Lamellar bone
    4. Non- haversian canals
- Advancing age, gradual fatty replacement of red bone marrow
- Loss of cancellous tissue, proximal end of medullary cavity of human assumes a cone shape

5. Race:
    Racial differences in the skeleton skull, face measurements teeth, lower extremities

6. Stature:
- Stature is calculated by applying mathematical formulae to the length of the long bones
- Long bones must be measured by means of osteometric board
- "pearson's formulae" – used for number if years(1899)
- " trotter &gleser formulae" more satisfactory(1958)
- "Harrison &dupertuid&Hadder" but not accurate for Indians
- The formulae are different for dry bones & wet bones for white persons & negroes & for males& females
- A single formula can't suit all parts of india due to different morphological features & racial chatators

Osteometric board:
- A rectangular base with a sector fixed along one of its long sides
- An upright is fixed at one end of the board ,a second one slides along the board
- The bone is placed with one of its ends against the fixed upright & the movable upright is brought up to the other end of the bone
- Hepburn osteometric board modified by trevor is commonly used
- Osteometric board is not available ,measured on a flat bench with maximum lengths taken between two vertical parallel boards placed in contact with bone ends
- Bones covered with articular cartilage,substract for radius &humerus 3mm tibia 5mm & femur 7mm before applying the formulae
- Right side bones are normally measured in the dry state without cartilages
The results obtained are not quite accurate & the error may be up to 2.5 cm

Bone length:
Femur: head to medical condyle
Tibia: lateral condyle to tip of medical malleolus
Fibula: tip of head totip of lateral malleolus
Radius : medial margin of head to tip of styloid process
Humerus: trochlea to head

Rule of thumb:
Humerus – 20%
Tibia-22%
Femur-27%
Spine-35%
- Absence of long bones – articular length of the 5 metacarpals

7. Identification:
Identity established from teeth ,disease& deformities of bone ,old healed or healing fractures ,ortnopedic surgical procedures ,regional atrophy,spinal deformities ,flat feet ,supernumery ribs Congenital defects etc..
Skull = 1-2% reduced by drying

Dimensions
Vertebral column = 2.7% reduced
- Useful identification stuff are previous x ray dental charts ,dental radio graphs
- Certain disease & developemental problems can lead to asymmetry of skeleton such as polio ,paget's disease neurofibromatosis
- It is possible to identify ABO group of skeletal material

8. Nature of injury:
- Examine the long bones for act by sharp cutting instruments or hacked or swan or gnawed by animals

Animal bites:
1. Rodents- chisel marks
2. Dog,fox,wolf- heavy damage
3. Carnivore- puncture ,pits or indentation
4. Canids- spiral fracture
5. Deer & sheep-forks shaped or double pronged
6. Crabs ,fish,turtle- shallow marks

- Post-mortem conditions may cause fractures & fragmentation due to continued & repeated freezing & thawing& from pressure of shifting soil weight

Burnt bones:
- Heat makes bone brittle ,so breakage occur during collection
- Burnt skull ,cracking has circular pattern with sharp edges which looks like cuts
- Unprotected bone when burnt undergoes charring ,cracking ,splintering & may be reduced to ashes
- Bone embedded in thick soft tissue shows melted guttered condition (fusion by heat)
- Bone burnt in open – white
- Burnt in closed – black or ash grey fire

9.Time since death:
- Determination of the time of death by the appearances of the skeletal remains such ad presence or absence of ligaments cartilages etc
- The answer depends upon the circumstances under which the bones have found
- Eg: burial & cold weather will diminish decomposition

Plastic deformation:
- When force is applied on living or recently dead bone particularly those of skull ,bending twisting & distortion are possible
- Force applied to dry dehydrated ,brittle bone it will fracture &fragment
- A fairly recent bone is slightly greasy to the touch & is heavy bone due to persistent collagen & normal apatite matrix
- Odour is a goof indication of relatively recent death
- After lost the covering tissue odour of decomposition lost bone appear fresh
- Repeated freezing thawing of the bones when buried superficially ,cause bone to expand & crack within few years
- Older burials ,cancellous bone at the metaphyses &epiphyses eroded by weathering
- Ground water seepage learn the calcium phosphate or may deposit excess calcium carbonate
- Mineral –rich areas leached areas are found in some parts of the skeleton & heavily mineralised bone
- They can be detected by examining histological ground section of lung bones or microradiographs of un decalcified ground section of those bones
- After many years ,they are dark in colour & weight more than the original dry bone because attend to absorb iron salts ,pigments & tine sand from percolouration of water

Dating of bones:
1.Recent bone: nitrogen content
4 to 5g% of nitrogen between 50 to 100 years nitrogen content more than 3.5g% if it is more than 2.5g% age will be loss than 350 years

2.Fresh bone: amino acids
- Fresh bone- 15 aminoacids (mostly collagen) (glycine &alanine are predominant)
- More than 100 years – contain 7 aminoacids
- Proline&hydroryproline tend to disappear after 50 yrs

3. Fluorescence:
   Less than 100 years old –fluoresces in uv light over most of its cut surface, progressive loss & absent in 500-800 years

4. Blood pigments:
   They persist upto 100 years in temparate zones

5. Precipitin test:
   They are negative after 10 years

6. Carbon dating
- No significant fall in the c14 content during 1st century
- After prolonged burial, over 50 years, histological examination show globular pockets of resorption
- Ancient bones tend to ne dry brittle chalky & marrow cavity is dry, free of fat & contains particle of earth or sand

Diagenesis:
- Minerals in the bone may be replaced chemically by minerals in the sediments while maintaining the original shape of the bones
- This occurs over long time periods & leads to fossilisation

EX HUMATION:
- it is the legal digging out of an already buried body egally from the grave..
- No Time limit for exhumation in India.

Autopsies performed:

1) CRIMINAL CASES
   Homicides, suspected Homicides, disguised as suicide, suspicious poisoning, Criminal abortion & criminal negligence.

2) CIVIL CASES
   Accidental death claim, insurance, workmen's compensation claim, liability for professional negligence, survivorship & inheritance claims or disputed identity

AUTHORISATION:-
   Exhumed only when, there is a written order from the Executive Magistrate. The body can be exhumed by any government doctor.

PROCEDURE
- Detailed information about the 'alleged deceased & the clothes worn at the time of burial is necessary before, starting exhumation.
- The body is exhumed under, supervision of Medical officer & Magistrate in presence of police officer
- The grave should be blocked from the public visibility...
- The Magistrate, should inform, the relatives of the deceased & allow them to remain present at the injury [176 (4) Cr.pc].
- The distance of grave from some of in permanent objects Like trees, road un fence should be noted
- It should be conducted in natural light
- The burial should be uncovered 10-15cm" notes should be made about the....... condition of soil, water & vegetable growth.
- Measure the depth of grave of rom skull surface & from the surface of the feet
- Open the burial pit, upto 30cm. on all. sides of body.
- Use soft brush or which to expose the body
- Photograph the body the position in which it was found.

Note the details

E.g
- Draw the grave's body or skeleton & mark
- if face is up, or to right
- arm extended
- lower limbs fixed like that.

- If decomposition. is not advanced, gently shift the body on to planks or shoot & then removed from the grave.
- if skeletonisation advanced, dig down beside &then beneath the body insert, a hardboard gradually inserted under the body, lifted & transported.
- After removing remains, shift the soil in a finely-moshed screen to; relover small objects .eg., teeth, epiphyses, bullets, etc.
- Note the condition of the burial clothes & surface of the body.
- In case of suspected mineral poisoning, samples of the earth (1/2kg) in actual contact with the body & also from above, below & from each side should be collected
- Collect any fluids or debris in coffin
- Remove a portion of coffin & burial clothes before contamination from external source
- The body should be identified by dose friends of relatives
- All personal effects, clothing, hair, nails ere should be picked up for examination

AUTOPSY:
- Don't sprinkle disinfectants on body.
- Recently buried body, Postmortem conducted in usual manner
- Made an attempt to establish Identity in much putrified body
- Preserve all viceras for chemical. analysis
- Examine the bone if skeleton only present

SECOND AUTOPSY:
- Obtain all the available documents relating to the case in 1st autopsy report before starting
- Eg:- Hospital reports, photographs of of death SLOND..
- If possible call the get1st autopsy pathologist to correlate the findings..
- It is difficult to the intrepret the finding in2nd and autopsy due to progressive decomposition changes,& serious alterations resulting from 1st autopsy.
- The findings should be documented. In great details, whether the findings arecorifirmatory or contradictory from the result of 2nd autopsy
- Even if no new information is obtained from the second autopsy, it will help in putting an end, to rumors or suspicions.

Fig(5.1) Removal of scalp

Courtesy: Professor, Dr. Chandrasekar, MMC, Madurai.
Associate professor, Dr.Sadhasivam, MMC, Madurai.

CHAPTER - 06
DEATH AND ITS CAUSES

Definition
   No legal definition of death

Thanatology:
   Deals with death in all its aspects including changes that occur with and after death

Moment of death
   Death is not an event, it is a process.
   There is a progression from clinical death to brain death, then biological death and finally cellular death.
   Clinical death – lack of oxygen

Brain death
   1st – cerebral cortex dies
   2nd – cerebellum dies
   3rd – lower brain centers die
   4th – brain stem and vital centers die

After this, cellular death begins.

Types
   1. Somatic, systemic or clinical
   2. Molecular or cellular

   Death denotes death of a human being unless the section 2(6), BNS contrary appears from the contact

Registration of Births and Deaths Act. Sec -2b
   Defines death as the permanent disappearance of all evidence of life at any time after live-birth has taken place.

Somatic death:
   It is the complete and irreversible stoppage of the circulation, respiration and brain functions, but there is no legal definition of death.

> **Bishop's tripod of life**
> Circulation
> Respiration
> Brain functions

- The question of death is important in resuscitation and organ transplant.
- As long as the circulation of oxygenated blood to vital organs persists, life exists.
- Whether a person is alive or dead can only be tested by the withdrawal of artificial maintenance.
- The person who cannot survive upon withdrawal of artificial maintenance, is dead.

Note :

Historically, the concept of death was that of 'heart and respiration death', but by the invent of heart-lung bypass machine, mechanical respiration and other devices, the concept has changed medically in favour of a new concept 'brain death' that is the irreversible loss of cerebral functions.

Brain death

Types: permanent cessation of functions of cerebrum, cerebellum and brain stem

Cortical or cerebral death:

- Brain stem is intact.
- causes vegetative state in which respiration continues but there is total loss of power of preparation by the senses
- This condition produced by
1. Cerebral hypoxia
2. Toxic conditions
3. Widespread brain injury

Brain stem death:
- Cerebrum is intact, though cut off functionally by stem lesion
- Loss of vital centers that control respiration and the ascending reticular activating system (ARAS) causes the victim to be irreversibly comatose and incapable of spontaneous breathing.
- This condition is caused by
1. Raised intracranial pressure
2. Cerebral oedema
3. Intracranial hemorrhage

Functions of brain stem:
1. A functioning paramedian tegmental area of the brainstem is a precondition for full consciousness which enables the cerebral hemispheres to work in an integrated way.
2. Respiratory drive
3. Maintenance of blood pressure
4. All motor output from the brain travels through the brain stem.
5. Apart from vision & smell, all sensory traffic coming in to the brain arrives through the brain stem.
6. Brain stem also mediates cranial nerve reflexes.

VARIOUS CRITERIA FOR DETERMINING BRAIN DEATH:

Harvard criteria for determining brainstem death
1. Unreceptiveness & Unresponsiveness
    - Total awareness to externally applied stimuli and inner need
    - There is complete unresponsiveness even to the most intense and painful stimuli.
2. No movements
    - No spontaneous muscular movements in response to stimuli such as pain, touch sound or light for a period of at least one hour
3. Apnoea
    - Absence of spontaneous breathing for at least one hour
4. Absence of elicitable reflexes
5. Irreversible coma with abolition of activity of the central nervous system
    - It is the past history in which there is absence of elicitable reflexes.
    - The pupils are fixed and dilated and do not respond to a direct source of bright light.
6. Isoelectric ECG
    - It has confirmatory value.

Note:

All these tests should be repeated after 24 hours with no change.
Further, it is stressed that the patient be declared dead before any effort is made to take the ventilator off him if he is already on ventilator.

Diagnosis of brainstem death:
There are two distinct schools of diagnosing death:
1. French and English schools that are similar to Harvard
2. Austro – German school that includes Harvard - criteria and bilateral serial angiography of internal carotid and vertebral artery criteria - a negative angiogram for more than 15 minutes proves death.

Precondition for diagnosis:
- Patient must be deeply comatose.
- Patient must be maintained on a ventilator.
- Cause of the coma must be known.

Personnel who should perform the tests:
- Brainstem death tests must be performed by two medical practitioners.
- Doctors involved should be experts in this field. Under no circumstances should these tests be performed by a transplant surgeon.
- At least one of the doctors should be of consultant status, junior doctors are not permitted to perform these tests.
- Each doctor should perform the tests twice.

Tests to be performed:
- Before the tests are performed, the core temperature of the body is taken to ensure that it is above 35^0C.
- The diagnosis of brainstem death is established by testing the function of the cranial nerves which pass through the brainstem.
- If there is no response to these tests, the brainstem is considered to be irreversibly dead.

Exclusions:
- When the patient may be under the effect of drugs e.g. therapeutic drugs or overdose
- When the core temperature of the body is below 35^0C.
- When the patient is suffering from severe metabolic or endocrine disturbances which may lead to severe but reversible coma
  E.g. Diabetes

Certification:
When the doctors have performed these tests twice with negative results, the patient is pronounced dead and a death certificate can be issued.

Vegetative state:
1. Whole or part of the brain can be irreversibly damaged due to hypoxia, cardiac arrest, intracranial hemorrhage, poisoning and trauma to the brain.
2. When cortex alone is damaged, patient goes into deep coma but brainstem will function and maintain spontaneous respiration.
3. This is called 'persistent vegetative state'
4. Death may occur months or years later due to extension of cerebral damage of from intercurrent infection.
5. They are not in need of life sustaining treatment but require nutrition and hydration.
6. In this, the patient breathes spontaneously, has a stable circulation and shows cycles of eye opening and closing.
7. This may simulate sleep and waking, but he is unaware of the self-environment.

Causes:
1. Diffuse axonal injury
2. Diffuse ischaemic brain damage
3. Underspread bilateral damage to the neocortex.
4. Diffuse damage to white matter
5. Bilateral damage to the thalami

Tissue and organ transplant:
The success of the homograft mainly depends upon the type of tissue involved and the rapidity of its removal after circulation has stopped in the donor.

THE DURATION FOR EACH ORGAN TO BE COLLECTED:

Cornea	-	within 6 hour from dead body
Skin	-	within 24 hours from dead body
Bone	-	within 48 hours from dead body
Blood vessels	-	within 72 hours from dead body
Kidney, hearts, lungs, pancreas, intestines, liver	-	obtained as soon as circulation has stopped as they deteriorate rapidly

1. The body does not reject the transplanted cornea
2. Most bone transplants last the life of the individual

Types of grafting/donation:

Homologous donation

Homologous donation means grafting of the tissue from one part of the body to another in the same patient.

E.g. skin (or) bone

Live donation:

1. Live donation includes blood and bone marrow transfusion.
2. Live organ donation includes kidney and parts of the liver.

Cadaveric donation:

Most organs must be obtained while the donor's heart is still beating to improve chances of success.

Xenograft

Xenograft is the grafting of animal tissues into humans, which has limited success.

THE BEATING HEART DONOR:

After brainstem death has been established, the retention of the patient on the ventilator facilities a fully oxygenated cadaver transplant the so called **'beating-heart donor'**

1. The result of the transplant is much desirable.
2. This has no legal sanction.

Some important terms:

1. **Supravital period or intermediary life:**

    it is the period of survival of some tissues after irreversible circulatory arrest.

2. **The latency period:**
    - It is an undisturbed period characterized by continuing aerobic energy production which is limited by the oxygen reserve.

3. **The resuscitation period:**
    - it is the duration of complete ischemia after which the ability to recover expires.
    - During this period, there is a breakdown of ATP below 60% of normal value and a steep increase of lactic acid.
    - The resuscitation period of heart is 3-4 minutes.

4. **Molecular death:**
    - It means death of the cells and tissues individually, which takes place usually one to two hours after the stoppage of the vital functions
    - Molecular death occurs piece meal.

Mechanical excitability of skeletal muscles:

Tendon reaction or zasko's phenomenon:

Procedure:

Take a reflex hammer.

Strike the lower 3rd of quadriceps femoris muscle, about 10 cm above the patella.

An upward movement of patella results because of the contraction of whole muscle.
- This can be seen upto 1-2 hours after death.
- It seems to be a propagated excitation of muscle fibres.

Idiomuscular contraction or bulge:

Procedure:

With the back of a knife, strike at the biceps brachii muscle.

It produces a muscular bulge at the point of contact due to local contraction of muscle.
- In the second phase, which lasts for 4-5 hours a strong and typically irreversible idiomuscular pad develops.
- In the last phase which lasts between 8-12 hours, a weak idiomuscular pad develops and it can persist upto 24 hours.

Note:

Electrical excitability of skeletal muscles of the face may be observed for few hours after death.

ANOXIA:

Anoxia means lack of oxygen.

Anemic anoxia:

Here oxygen carrying capacity of blood gets low.

E.g. acute massive hemorrhage poisoning by
- carbon monoxide,
- chloride,
- nitrates &
- coal tar derivative.

Stagnant anoxia

In this type, impaired circulation results in reduction of oxygen delivery to the tissues.

E.g.
- heart failure,
- Embolism &
- shock

ANOXIA

Anoxic anoxia:

Here, oxygen cannot reach the blood because of lack of oxygen in the lungs.

This occurs when breathing in a contaminated environment.
- **E.g.** from explosive to the fumes in wells & tanks,
- from exposure to sewer gas
- From mechanical interference with the passage of air into or down the respiratory tract

E.g. in smothering ,Choing, Hanging ,Strangulation, Drowning ,Traumatic asphyxia Acute poisoning

Histotoxic anoxia

Here the enzymatic processes through which tissues use the oxygen in blood are blocked.

E.g. acute cyanide poisoning

Note:
- *Normal level of oxygen in arterial blood (po2) is 90 to 100 mmHg at 30 years and 65 to 80 mmHg at 60 years*
- *Reduction to 60 mmHg results in hypoxia*
- *At 40 mmHg, there is severe hypoxia and death may occur at 20 mmHg.*

Modes of death:

According to Bichat, there are three modes of death, depending on whether death begins in one or other of the three systems, irrespective of whatever the remote cause of death may be.
These modes are

1. Asphyxia
2. Coma
3. Syncope

Asphyxia

Asphyxia is the condition caused by interference with respiration or due to lack of oxygen in the air respired, due to which the organs and tissues are oxygen (O2) deprived, causing unconsciousness or death.

- The term asphyxia indicates a mode of dying rather than a cause of death.

Age	Oxygen saturation
Young & middle age	90-100 mmHg
Above 60 years	60-85 mmHg
Sever fatal hypoxia	20-40 mmHg

- The brain weight is about 1.4% of body weight, but it uses 20% of total available oxygen.
- Therefore, nerve tissues are 1st affected by deficiency of oxygen and their functions are disturbed even by mild lack of oxygen.
- In total ischaemia of the brain, cessation of nerve cell function in the cerebral cortex starts after 8-15 seconds and in the brainstem ganglia after 25-30 seconds.
- Irreversible damage of cells occur.
  - In cortex, about 3 minutes
  - In basal ganglia, after 6-7 minutes
  - in vagal centers, after 9-10 minutes
- Subnormal oxygen in the blood supply to the brain causes rapid unconsciousness.
- In all forms of asphyxia, heart may continue to beat for several minutes after stoppage of respiration.

The rule of thumb is:

- Breathing stops within twenty seconds of cardiac failure, and Heart stops within 20 minutes of stopping of breathing.
- If the heart function for several minutes after stoppage of breathing, the weight of the lungs may increase to 450 to 500 g.

Types and causes:

1. Mechanical:

In this, the air passages are blocked mechanically.

a. Closing of external respiratory orifices by closing the nose and mouth with hand or a cloth (or) by filling these openings with mud or other substances
b. Closure of air passage by external pressure on the neck as in hanging strangulation, throttling etc.
c. Closure of the air-passage by the impaction of foreign bodies in the larynx or pharynx
d. Prevention of entry of air due to the air-passage being filled with fluid, as in drowning
e. External compression of the chest and abdominal wall interfering with respiratory movements as in traumatic asphyxia

2) Pathological:

In this, the entry of oxygen to the lungs is prevented by disease of upper respiratory tract or the lungs.

E.g.
- Bronchitis
- Acute edema of glottis,
- Laryngeal spasm,
- Tumors &
- Abscess

- Paralysis of respiratory muscles may result from acute poliomyelitis.

3) Toxic substance:

Poisonous substance prevents the use of oxygen.
a. Poisoning by CO - the capacity of hemoglobin to bind oxygen is reduced
b. Poisoning by cyanides - enzymatic processes that utilize oxygen in blood are blocked
c. Poisoning by opium barbiturates strychnine - respiratory center may be paralyzed
d. Poisoning by gelsemium - muscles of respiration may be paralyzed

4) Environmental:
a. insufficiency of oxygen in the inspired air
   E.g. enclosed spaces, Trapping in disused refrigerator or trunk
b. Exposure to irrespirable gases in the atmosphere
   E.g. sewer gas, CO, CO2
c. Cxposure to high altitude

5) Traumatic:
a. pulmonary thrombo-embolism from femoral vein thrombosis due to an injury to the lower limb
b. pulmonary fat embolism from fracture of long bones
c. pulmonary air embolism from an incised around of internal jugular vein
d. bilateral pneumothorax from injuries to the chest wall or lungs

6) Postural asphyxia:

This is seen where an unconscious (or) stuporous person either from alcohol, drugs or disease, lies with the upper half of the body lower than the remainder.

7) Iatrogenic:

It is mainly associated with anesthesia.

Pathology:

Compression of neck:

There are two types of consent

| Jugular veins get occluded Prevents venous drainage from the head, but arterial supply continues through the carotid and vertebral artery. | Air passage are occluded Impair oxygenation to lungs Decrease in oxygen content of arteria blood. Reduction in oxygen tension causes capillary dilation Stasis of blood in dilated capillaries and venules Capillo-venous engorgement |

- This blood stasis causes congestion of organs and venous return to the heart is diminished leading to anoxia, which causes capillary dilation and the vicious cycle goes on.

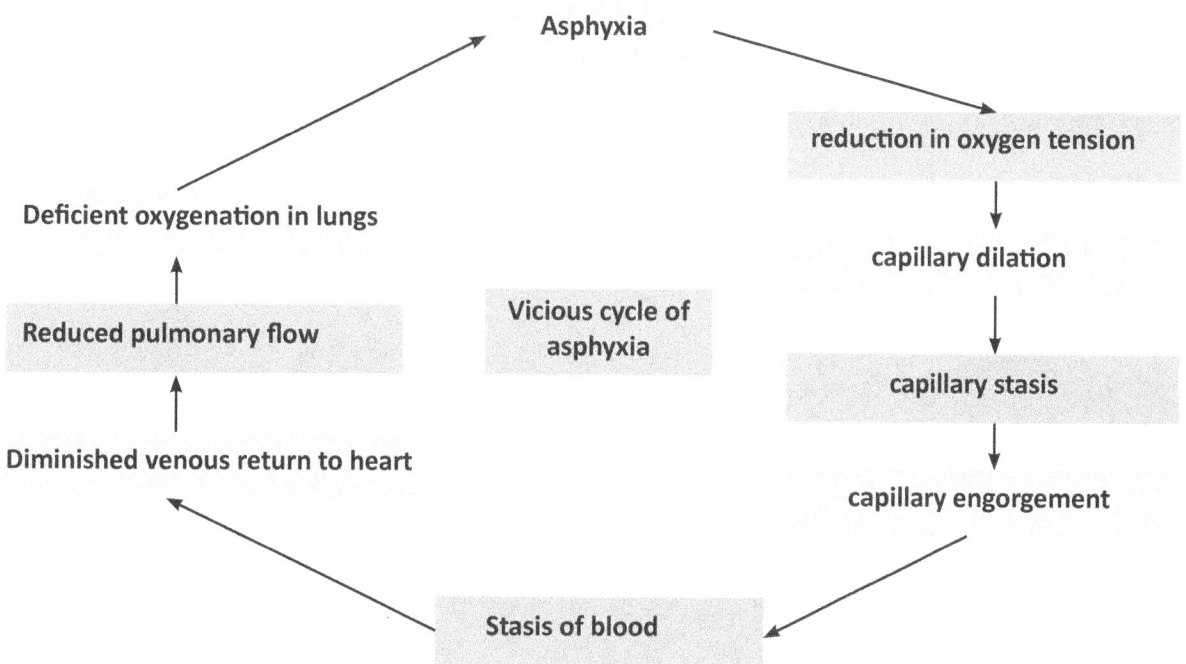

Vicious cycle of asphyxia

1. **Petechial hemorrhage:**
   It is caused due to increased venous pressure from impaired venous returned resulting in overdistension and rupture of venules especially in lax tissues and not to hypoxia of the vessel wall.

Time required:
   A minimum of 15-30 seconds is required to produce congestion and petechiae.

Size of petechiae
   - Petechiae vary in size from 0.1 to 2.2 mm
   - If larger than this, they are called ecchymoses areas where petechial are seen:
   - Skin, sclera, conjunctiva, outer and inner surface of the eyelids and on the mucosal surface in mouth
   - Petechial hemorrhages may be found in the substance of viscera but readily seen in serous membranes particularly in visceral pleura in the interlobar fissure and around the hilum and pericardium
   - In infants & children, thymus may show numerous petechiae.
   - In brain, they are seen in white matter.
   - When carotid arteries are obstructed, intensity of cerebral, facial and orbital petechiae are much less prominent than that seen in venous obstruction.

Points to know:
   In sudden complete carotid obstruction, facial pallor can be striking.

Areas where petechiae rarely seen:
   In parietal pleura and peritoneum petechial hemorrhages are rarely seen, except in hemorrhagic diathesis.

Interpretation of petechial hemorrhage
- Numerous petechiae may be produced as a common autopsy artefact during reflection of scalp flaps in all types of death and are of no significance.
- They are often present in normal post-mortem hypostasis, especially where the mode of death was congestive as in heart disease.
- Petechiae can develop after death in dependent areas of the body

2. **congestion:**
   - Congestion occurs due to obstructed venous return and capillo-venous distention.
   - When the neck is compressed, face, lips and tongue become swollen and reddened.
   - The colour change of congestion is usually darkened by the onset of cyanosis.

   If neck gets compressed the following conditions may occurs:
   i. Stasis of blood in head and hypoxia
   ii. Increased CO_2 tension in blood
   iii. Capillary dilatation and loss of tonicity of vascular walls
   iv. Increased capillary and venous permeability
   v. Transudation of fluid into tissues

In early stages, transudation is followed by increased lymphatic drainage and oedema does not develop.
If the hypoxia continues oedema of the tissues develop
- Oedema of the lungs is common and is usually caused due to combination of hypoxia and raised pulmonary vessel pressure.
- Oedema of the brain occurs due to back pressure and hypoxia.
- Generalized edema is not prominent.
- Congestion and oedema are non-specific and result due to obstructed venous return.

3. **cyanosis:**
   - Cyanosis means bluish discolouration of skin, mucous membrane and internal organs due to increased concentration of reduced hemoglobin more than 5g/100ml of hemoglobin.
   - The essential cause of cyanosis is diminished oxygen tension in the blood with a rise in proportion of the reduced hemoglobin.
   - Oxygenated blood is brightly red, it becomes purplish-blue when oxygen is given up.
   - In constriction of neck, cyanosis follows congestion of the face.
   - Cyanosis produced during life may be partly or wholly overshadowed by hypostasis which may be a deep-purple or blue and may be mistaken for true cyanosis.
   - If the airway is blocked, the impaired oxygenation in the lungs causes decrease in the oxygen content of the arterial blood, which causes darkening of all organs and tissues and will increase the cyanosis of the face.
   - cyanosis is marked in skin where hypostatic livid stains develop and lips, ears, tip of nose, fingernails, cheeks and internally the lungs, liver, spleen, kidney and meninges are cyanosed.

Note:
Methemoglobin and sulfhemoglobin also cause cyanosis.

Transudation of fluid into tissues

In early stages, transudation is followed by increased lymphatic drainage and oedema does not develop.

If the hypoxia continues oedema of the tissues develop
- Oedema of the lungs is common and is usually caused due to combination of hypoxia and raised pulmonary vessel pressure.
- Oedema of the brain occurs due to back pressure and hypoxia.
- Generalized edema is not prominent.
- Congestion and oedema are non-specific and result due to obstructed venous return.

3. cyanosis:
- Cyanosis means bluish discolouration of skin, mucous membrane and internal organs due to increased concentration of reduced hemoglobin more than 5g/100ml of hemoglobin.
- The essential cause of cyanosis is diminished oxygen tension in the blood with a rise in proportion of the reduced hemoglobin.
- Oxygenated blood is brightly red, it becomes purplish-blue when oxygen is given up.
- In constriction of neck, cyanosis follows congestion of the face.
- Cyanosis produced during life may be partly or wholly overshadowed by hypostasis which may be a deep-purple or blue and may be mistaken for true cyanosis.
- If the airway is blocked, the impaired oxygenation in the lungs causes decrease in the oxygen content of the arterial blood, which causes darkening of all organs and tissues and will increase the cyanosis of the face.
- cyanosis is marked in skin where hypostatic livid stains develop and lips, ears, tip of nose, fingernails, cheeks and internally the lungs, liver, spleen, kidney and meninges are cyanosed.
- When the deceased is found with the head lower than the body, marked congestion, cyanosis and petechial hemorrhages are common.

Heart:

Dilatation of the heart chambers on the right side and fluidity of the blood in deaths due to asphyxia are obsolete and should be disregarded.

This is seen in any type of congestive death including primary heart failure from many diseases.
-Generalized rise in venous and intracardiac pressure
- Distension of the atria and ventricles is a common postmortem finding and may result from secondary muscular flaccidity.

Lungs:

-The light lungs (about 300 gm) are more compatible with sudden rhythm disturbance and cessation of the action of the heart.
-Heavier lungs (450 to 500 gm or more) indicate cessation of respiration with continuance of the heart beat for several minutes.

Histology:
1. Partial disruption of alveolar septa with distinctive hemorrhage within the alveoli and in the intra alveolar oedema fluid
2. Brick red discolouration of nerve cells in cerebral cortex seen in stained neurological sections
3. Pallor and vaccuolar degenuation of purkinje cells in the cerebellum
4. Vacuolar degeneration of liver cells in prolonged suffocation.

Asphyxial stigmata

Asphyxia is not a pathological entity, and cannot be clearly recognised from morbid anatomical findings alone.

The triad of
(1) cyanosis,
(2) facial, palpebral, bulbar,
subpleural and subepicardial petechiae,
(3) visceral congestion,
are all due to raised venous pressure.

- They are merely consistent with but not diagnostic of asphyxia from anoxic anoxia.
- Reliable indications of fatal obstructing trauma must be demonstrated to establish that death occurred from mechanical asphyxia.
- Parenchymatous degenerative changes develop in rapid hypoxic and rapid anoxic deaths, but they are non-specific.

SYMPTOMS:

(1) STAGE OF DYSPNOEA:

The excess of carbon dioxide in the blood stimulates the respiratory center.
- The respiratory movements become increased in rate and amplitude,
- blood pressure is increased,
- pulse rate increases and
- there is slight cyanosis.

(2) STAGE OF CONVULSIONS:
- The effort to breathe is mostly expiratory,
- The face is deeply congested,
- Blood pressure is increased,
- Pulse is fast,
- Veins in the neck become swollen.

There are frequently convulsions
which cease as the victim becomes insensible and the reflexes are abolished.

(3) STAGE OF EXHAUSTION:
- The respiratory center is paralyzed,
- the muscles become flaccid.
- There is complete insensibility,
- reflexes are lost and the pupils are widely dilated.
- The breathing is gasping, mostly inspiratory with long intervals between the gasps.
- The blood pressure falls, muscles relax, respiration ceases, and death takes place.
- The pulse is imperceptible, but the heart may continue to beat for some minutes after respirations have ceased.

The three stages last for 3 to5 minutes before death takes place.

Postmortem Appearances:

External:
- Postmortem hypostasis is well developed.
- The face is either pale in slow asphyxia, or distorted, congested, often cyanosed and purple, and sometimes swollen and oedematous.
- Ears and fingernails are bluish.
- The eyes are prominent; the conjunctivae are congested and the pupils are dilated.

- The tongue is protruded in most cases, and frothy and bloody mucus escapes from the mouth and nostrils.
- Petechial hemorrhages, known as Tardieu spots (when seen externally) are most marked where for mechanical reasons, capillary congestion is most prominent.
- They are produced by simple mechanical obstruction to the venous return of blood from the parts, resulting in acute rise in venous pressure and overdistension and rupture of thin walled peripheral venules, especially in lax, unsupported tissues, such as forehead, skin behind the ears, eyelids, circumoral skin, conjunctivae and sclerae, neck, buccal mucosa, epiglottis, visceral pleura, pericardium, Thymus and Rarely in the serosa of the bowel
- Their distribution lies above the level of obstruction.
- They appear commonly in the scalp, eyelids and face in hanging and strangulation and in the zone above the level of compression in traumatic asphyxia.
- A hand lens is useful to identify petechial hemorrhages
- In many cases unconsciousness can occur in several seconds.

Internal

- The blood is fluid and dark because of the increased amount of CO_2.
- The large veins are full of blood.
- Vessels may burst in the eardrum and in the nose causing bleeding.
- The larynx and trachea are usually congested, and contain a varying amount of slightly frothy mucus.
- The lungs are dark and purple.
- If the backpressure persists, there is exudation of serous or serosanguineous fluid in the alveoli, producing oedema.
- The amount of pulmonary oedema does not indicate the time interval between injury and death.
- Accumulation of fluid in the posterior and dependent parts of the lungs after death, should not be mistaken for pulmonary oedema.
- Some of the marginal portions of the lungs may show emphysematous changes.
- The abdominal viscera show marked venous congestion.
- The brain is often congested.
- The cranial sinuses are usually filled with dark blood.
- Tardieu spots (when seen internally) are numerous where the capillaries are least firmly supported, as in subconjunctival tissues and under the pleural and pericardial membranes, but they can appear almost anywhere if the degree of congestion and cyanosis is sufficient.

- Tardieu spots are usually round, dark and well-defined, varying in size from a pin's head to two mm.
- They may occur as isolated minute hemorrhages or present in large numbers, and at times fuse to form patches of red colour, especially at the back of the heart.
- They are numerous in the region of auriculoventricular junction of heart and the lower lobes and the interlobar fissure of the lungs and thymus.
- In the brain, petechiae occur in the white matter, and there may be larger patches of bleeding in the subarachnoid space, because of acute venous engorgement.
- Often profuse petechiae and ecchymoses are seen under the scalp due to the same mechanism.
- The time taken for these various signs to occur depends on the circumstances, from a few seconds to several minutes.
- Petechiae and ecchymoses are common non-specific autopsy findings and may be seen in many non-asphyxial deaths beneath the pericardium, pleura, interlobar fissures and around the hilum.
- Petechiae are likely to occur in association with cyanotic congestion and may not be visible until the area is drained of blood during autopsy.
- Sometimes, it is difficult to distinguish petechiae from the cut ends of congested vessels, especially in the brain.
- Microscopic examination will confirm the nature of hemorrhage.
- Cutaneous and visceral petechiae, especially the latter can appear and enlarge as a postmortem phenomenon.
- They are seen on the front or back of corpses who have died from causes other than mechanical asphyxia.
- They are often seen in normal postmortem hypostasis, especially where the mode of death was congestive as in many types of natural heart disease.
- As such petechiae are highly unreliable indicators of an asphyxial process.

Natural diseases:
- The natural disease which produce hemorrhages in the skin include:
  » bacterial endocarditis
  » meningococcal septicaemia and
  » blood dyscrasias, especially purpura and hemophilia
  » in deaths from coronary thrombosis, acute heart failure, secondary shock, and rapid anoxia.
- Petechiae can be seen following any severe increase in intrathoracic pressure including
  » asthmatic attack,
  » heart failure,
  » respiratory failure,
  » straining at stool, and
  » soon after delivery.
- These conditions produce relatively large hemorrhages which tend to combine.
- Their distribution is general, whereas Tardieu spots are present above the level of obstruction.
- Asphyxia causes vomiting due to medullary suboxia, due to which the air-passages may be filled at the end of asphyxial event by the inhaled vomit.
- This finding especially in infants, should not be assumed to be the cause of asphyxia as it is more likely the result of asphyxia.
- About 20 to 25% of all individuals aspirate food agonally whatever may be the cause of death.

Variations:
- There are variations in the intensity of asphyxial signs.
- When the asphyxial process is
  » slight and prolonged, –the congestive element will be diminished;
  » when intense and short– lividity and congestion are marked.
- During the process of asphyxia, if heart failure occurs before respiratory failure, the asphyxial signs may be less marked.
- Sometimes, the finding are not sufficient to use an accurate term and the cause of death has to be given within a broad framework such as "consistent with asphyxia".
- In the presence of putrefaction. mechanical asphyxia is indicated by presence of petechial hemorrhages under the eyelids, conjunctivae, sclerae and facial skin.

DELAYED DEATHS:
- In asphyxia the higher cortical centers suffer first from hypoxic injury, followed by basal ganglia and ultimately the vegetative centers, which explain delayed deaths.

Order of damage
1st - cortical centers
2 nd- basal ganglia
3rd- vegetative centers

- Such delayed deaths usually follow periods of unconsciousness, resulting from anoxic cerebral damage and subsequent hypostatic pneumonia.
- Other lethal sequelae include, massive subcutaneous and mediastinal emphysema from tracheal and laryngeal lacerations or occlusion of airway due to oedematous or haemorrhagic swelling of pharyngeal tissues or the aryepiglottic folds.
- When death occurs hours, days or weeks after the asphyxial episode, the proximate cause of death is the traumatic incident.

COMA:
- It is a state of unarousable unconsciousness determined by the absence of any psychologically understandable response to external stimuli or inner need.
- It involves the central portion of the brain stem.
- Coma is a clinical symptom and not a cause of death.

CAUSES:
(1) Compression of the brain,
e.g., effusion of blood on or in the brain,
inflammation, abscess or neoplasm of the brain.
(2) Drugs;
opium,hypnotics, cocaine, alcohol, anesthetics, cyanide, atropine, phenol, oxalic acid, CO, etc.
(3) Metabolic disorders and infections:
uraemia,cholaemia,eclampsia,diabetes,pneumonia,infectious fevers,heat stroke, etc.
(4) Other causes:
embolism and thrombosis in the cerebral vessels, epilepsy, hysteria, etc.

AUTOPSY:
- Injuries or disease of the brain may be present as noted in the causes of coma.
- The lungs, brain and the meninges are congested.
- Splanchnic pooling of blood occurs.

SYNCOPE:
- Syncope is a sudden stoppage of action of the heart, which may prove fatal.
- This term is also not used as a cause of death.
- Syncope or fainting is due to vasovagal attacks resulting from reflex parasympathetic stimulation.
- Syncope is caused by

reflex bradycardia or asystole, or by reflex splanchnic vasodilation.
- Due to the acute reflex circulatory changes, blood pressure falls suddenly causing cerebral anemia and rapid unconsciousness.
- Recovery is common.

CAUSES:
Put as mind map
(1) Anaemia due to sudden and excessive hemorrhage.
(2) Aesthenia from deficient power of heart muscle as in

fatty degeneration of the heart, myocardial infarction and certain poisons.
(3) Vagal inhibition.
(4) Exhausting diseases.

AUTOPSY:
- The heart is contracted and the chambers are empty when death has occurred from anemia, but chambers contain blood when death occurs due to asthenia.
- The lungs, brain and abdominal organs are usually pale.
- Splanchnic pooling of blood occurs.

Chamber empty - death (anemia)
Chamber with blood - death (aesthenia)

CAUSE OF DEATH:
- The cause of death is the disease or injury responsible for starting the sequence of events, which are brief or prolonged and which produce death.

It may be divided into:

(1) IMMEDIATE CAUSE,
the injury or disease present at the time of terminal event,
e.g., bronchopneumonia, peritonitis, trauma, etc.

(2) BASIC CAUSE,
pathological processes responsible for the death at the time of the terminal event or prior to or leading to the event,
e.g., gunshot wound of abdomen complicated by generalized peritonitis.

(3) CONTRIBUTORY CAUSE
the pathological process involved in or complicating, but not causing the terminal event.
- In some cases, the basic and the immediate cause may be identical.

The MANNER OF DEATH:
- It indicates the circumstances under which the person died.
- It is established from the

personal and family history, circumstantial information from the scene of death, witnesses of the event, information from family members and others, and by the autopsy findings.
- If death occurs exclusively from disease, the manner of death is natural.
- If death occurs exclusively by injury or is hastened due to injury in a person suffering

from natural disease, the manner of death is unnatural or violent.
- Violence may be suicidal, homicidal, accidental or of undetermined or unexplained origin.

MECHANISM OF DEATH:
- It is the physiological or biochemical disturbance, produced by the cause of death which is incompatible with life,

e.g., shock, sepsis, toxemia, severe metabolic acidosis and alkalosis, ventricular fibrillation, respiratory paralysis, etc.

AGONAL PERIOD
- It is the time between a lethal occurrence and death.
- Determination of the cause of death following autopsy is an interpretive and intelligent procedure and depends upon

sound evaluation of all data, circumstances surrounding the death, morphological evidence of disease and injury and additional laboratory investigations.
- In fact, the more a forensic pathologist knows about the total investigation, the more he can contribute from his autopsy.
- The effectiveness of the doctor would be greatly diminished,
1. if he had to work alone
2. receives bodies for autopsy without clothing
3. receives bodies for autopsy without the knowledge of the circumstances surrounding death.
- The recognition of the structural organic changes or chemical abnormalities, which cause stoppage of the vital functions is the first step.
- Understanding the mechanism by which the anatomical and chemical deviations that have caused death, i.e. how they produced or initiated the sequence of functional disturbance which were sufficient to cause respiratory or cardiac arrest, which are the two ultimate lethal processes, is the second step.

CLASSIFICATION OF THE CAUSE OF DEATH:
According to the autopsy findings, the cause of death may be grouped as follows.

(I) NATURAL CAUSES:
(a) Where a lesion is found at autopsy which is incompatible with life.
(b) Where a lesion is found at autopsy which is known to cause death.

(II) UNNATURAL CAUSES:
(a) Where a lesion is found at autopsy which is incompatible with life.
(b) Where a lesion is found which may have caused death or which may have precipitated death, but which is also known to be compatible with continued life.

(III) OBSCURE CAUSES:
Where no lesion is found at autopsy, or if a lesion is found it is of a minimal or indefinite nature.

\# receives bodies for autopsy without clothing,

\# receives bodies for autopsy without the knowledge of the circumstances surrounding death.

- The recognition of the structural organic changes or chemical abnormalities, which cause stoppage of the vital functions is the first step.
- Understanding the mechanism by which the anatomical and chemical deviations that have caused death, i.e. how they produced or initiated the sequence of functional disturbance which were sufficient to cause respiratory or cardiac arrest, which are the two ultimate lethal processes, is the second step.

CLASSIFICATION OF THE CAUSE OF DEATH:

According to the autopsy findings, the cause of death may be grouped as follows.

(I) NATURAL CAUSES:

(a) Where a lesion is found at autopsy which is incompatible with life.

(b) Where a lesion is found at autopsy which is known to cause death.

(II) UNNATURAL CAUSES:

(a) Where a lesion is found at autopsy which is incompatible with life.

(b) Where a lesion is found which may have caused death or which may have precipitated death, but which is also known to be compatible with continued life.

(III) OBSCURE CAUSES:

Where no lesion is found at autopsy, or if a lesion is found it is of a minimal or indefinite nature.

NATURAL CAUSES:

(A) WHERE A LESION IS FOUND AT AUTOPSY WHICH IS NOT COMPATIBLE WITH LIFE:

- In this category, the structural abnormalities establish beyond any doubt the identity of the disease which caused death.
- It is apparent that the lesions observed are incompatible with life because of its nature, site or extent, and they are antemortem in origin.
- The examples are:

massive pulmonary, thromboembolism, spontaneous intracerebral hemorrhage, ruptured myocardial infarct, rupture of an aortic aneurysm.

(B) WHERE A LESION IS FOUND AT AUTOPSY WHICH IS KNOWN TO CAUSE DEATH:

- This category includes deaths in which some lesion is found at autopsy which may have caused death, but which is also compatible with continued life,

e.g.,
- » arteriosclerosis of the coronary arteries,
- » advanced chronic heart diseases,
- » lobar pneumonia, etc.

- The autopsy does not reveal any other reasonable explanation for death, and the location, nature, severity and extent of the anatomical changes are sufficient to cause death, but it is not a conclusive proof.
- In such cases, the clinical history is important.
- In the case of coronary arteriosclerosis, if the deceased had several attacks of angina pectoris before his death, it can be reasonably assumed to be the cause of death.
- If the clinical history is unusual, the possibilities suggested by the history should be excluded before the death is attributed to the lesion.
- Stenosing coronary atherosclerosis can cause sudden death, in which the autopsy may reveal a few scattered foci or only a single site of significant luminal narrowing, and there may be no recent vascular occlusive lesion.

- In most cases of sudden coronary death, a fresh thrombus or a recent myocardial infarct is not found at autopsy.
- In these cases, correlation of the morbid anatomy with the suddenness of death must be based on hypotheses.
- Emotional stress, e.g., anger, fear, joy, apprehension, etc., can precipitate acute failure in persons with organic heart disease, especially of the coronary atherosclerotic type.
- Emotional excitement significantly increases the workload of the heart which can overtax the limits of tolerance of damaged, labouring heart.
- In a normal person sudden release of adrenaline due to extreme terror can initiate ventricular fibrillation and death.
- Sudden deaths following assaults or even threats may occur due to existing heart disease.
- Such events may be encountered in criminal charges arising out of collapse during fights, in minor assaults upon old persons, in litigation related to death from work stress, etc.
- Sufferers from asthma and epilepsy can die suddenly and unexpectedly for no obvious reasons.

UNNATURAL CAUSES:
(A) WHERE A LESION IS FOUND AT AUTOPSY WHICH IS NOT COMPATIBLE WITH LIFE:

In some deaths, injuries may be found at autopsy which are incompatible with life in any person,

e.g., decapitation, crushing of the head, avulsion of the heart from the large blood vessels.
- If they are antemortem, they are the definite cause of death.

(B) A LESION IS FOUND AT AUTOPSY WHICH MAY HAVE CAUSED OR PRECIPITATED DEATH, BUT IS COMPATIBLE WITH LIFE:

- At autopsy certain injuries may be found which from their nature, site or extent may not appear to be sufficient to cause death in a healthy person.
- But such injury may be the cause of death due to some complication resulting directly from the injury, but which is not demonstrable at autopsy.
- The degree of shock or the extent of hemorrhage following an injury cannot be assessed at autopsy.
- In such cases, the absence of any other adequate cause of death, and a consideration of the circumstances of the injury and of the symptoms found, may enable the doctor to attribute death to the injury with reasonable certainty.
- In some cases, an injury may not appear to be sufficient to cause death, but some natural disease may be present which is known to cause death,

e.g., coronary arteriosclerosis.
- In such cases, the circumstances of death and the symptoms found at the time of collapse may suggest that the death was precipitated by the injury.

NEGATIVE AUTOPSY:
- When gross and microscopic examination, toxicological analyses and laboratory investigations fail to reveal a cause of death; the autopsy is considered to be negative.
- 2 to 5% of all autopsies are negative.
- In teenagers and young adults up to the age of about 35 year, there is a higher proportion of negative autopsies than in older group.
- A negative autopsy may be due to:

(1) Inadequate history:

Deaths from vagal inhibition, status epilepticus, hypersensitivity reaction, laryngeal spasm in drowning, etc.

These conditions may not show any anatomical findings.

(2) Inadequate external examination
- The presence of fresh and old needle marks may be missed on cursory examination in a drug addict.

- Death from snake bites and insect bites cannot be explained unless the bite marks are identified.
- The burn may be missed in electrocution.

(3) Inadequate or improper internal examination:
- Air embolism and pneumothorax are often missed.

(4) Insufficient laboratory examinations.

(5) Lack of toxicological analysis.

(6) Lack of training of the doctor.

OBSCURE AUTOPSIES

- Obscure autopsies are those which do not show a definite cause for death, in which there are minimal, indefinite or obscure findings, or even no positive findings at all.
- They are a source of confusion to any pathologist.
- Frequently, these deaths are due to obscure natural causes, but they may be due to certain types of injury or complications of injury, or to poisoning.

The obscure causes are:

(1) Natural diseases:
   (a) With obscure or some microscopic findings.
   (b) Death precipitated by emotion, work-stress, and
   (c) Functional failure, such as epilepsy, paroxysmal fibrillation.

(2) Biochemical disturbances:
   (a) Uraemia, diabetes, potassium deficiency.
   (b) Respiratory pigment disorders, such as anemic anoxia, porphyria.

(3) Endocrine dysfunction:
   (a) Adrenal insufficiency.
   (b) Thyrotoxicosis or myxoedema.

(4) Concealed trauma:
   (a) Cerebral concussion.
   (b) Self-reduced neck injury.
   (c) Blunt injury to the heart.
   (d) Reflex vagal inhibition.

(5) Poisoning:

Without macroscopic change:
   (a) Delayed subtoxic or narcotic poisoning.
   (b) Anesthetic overdose or maladministration.
   (c) Neurotoxic or cytotoxic poisons.
   (d) Plant poisoning.

(6) Miscellaneous:
   (a) Allergy,
   (b) drug idiosyncrasy.

- Obscure autopsies are usually seen in a younger, healthy person who dies suddenly and unexpectedly.
- Non-medical persons believe that the cause of death can always be determined by autopsy.
- The police may press the doctor for giving a positive statement with regard to the cause of death.
- In such cases, the doctor should admit his inability to give a positive opinion.
- Such obscure cases require clinical and laboratory investigations and interview with persons who had observed the deceased before he died, to know the signs and symptoms shown by the deceased before his death.
- Laboratory investigations may be bacteriological, virological, histological, biochemical and toxicological.
- In these cases, re-examine the body and look for tongue bite, foreign body in respiratory tract, fat or air embolism, sepsis, cardiac hypertrophy, coronary ostia patency, atherosclerosis, severe narrowing of coronary arteries, pancytopenia or leukemia, sickle cell thrombi in the brain, heart, etc. drug reaction, small electrical burns, needle marks, etc.
- Review, available history and obtain more if possible.
- In cases where general senile atrophy of most organs is present without any other positive finding and the history is not helpful for a specific cause of death and natural causes are excluded, cause of death can be certified as "myocardial degeneration due to senility".
- When circumstances are unequivocally those of a natural death, the cause of death can be given as "undetermined natural circumstances".
- When circumstances are equivocal, the cause and manner of death should be given as "undetermined".
- In the absence of positive findings from these sources, a careful assessment of possible functional causes of death must be made, before any cause of death is given as undetermined.
- The presence of infectious, malignant, occupational and other diseases are also excluded.
- Though the pathologist cannot establish the cause of death, he can exclude many conditions which have been incorrectly attributed to have caused death.

(1) NATURAL CAUSES:
CARDIAC LESIONS:
- Acute rheumatic carditis may cause sudden death in a young adult.
- In some such cases, naked-eye changes may be absent, but typical Aschoff bodies of rheumatic fever are found in the myocardium on microscopic examination.
- Acute toxic myocarditis of diphtheria may cause sudden death, in which the primary lesion in the nose or throat may be overlooked.
- Idiopathic myocarditis may cause sudden death.
- Brown atrophy of the heart and senile heart may prematurely fail suddenly.
- Myocarditis, fibrosis, and necrosis of conducting tissue may escape detection.
- Small coronary thrombosis and easily dislodged emboli may be overlooked.
- Acute occlusion of the coronary artery may result from thrombosis or hemorrhage within the wall of the artery.
- Zones of occlusion are usually less than 5 mm. in length, and most of the occlusions occur within 3 cm. of the orifices of the vessels.
  » First part of the anterior descending branch of left coronary artery within 2 cm. of its origin is commonly affected, followed by
  » the proximal part of the right coronary artery,
  » first part of the circumflex branch of left coronary artery, and
  » the short main trunk of the left coronary artery.
- Fresh thrombi are dark-brown, and attached to the vessel walls.
- Old thrombi appear as homogeneous yellowish or grey, firm plugs blocking the vessels.
- Most infarcts occur in the left ventricle in the anterior wall.
- Posterior infarcts may be due to blockage of either the right vessel or the circumflex branch of the left artery.
- Infarction usually occurs when the lumen is reduced to 20% or less.
- Right ventricle is involved in less than 10% cases.
- Coronary insufficiency from narrowing of the lumen of major vessels may lead to chronic ischaemia and hypoxia of the muscle distal to the stenosis.
- Hypoxic myocardium is electrically unstable and liable to arrhythmias and ventricular fibrillation, especially at moments of sudden stress, such as exercise or an adrenaline response, such as anger or emotion.

MYOCARDIAL INFARCTION:
(1) A laminar infarct in which the subendocardial region of much or even all of the left ventricle is involved, sometimes extending through half or more of the thickness of the wall.
- It produces minimal gross changes than the transmural infarct.
- It occurs due to generalized stenosis in the major branches of coronary vessels.

(2) A regional or focal infarct is more commonly caused by localized occlusion or severe stenosis in a coronary artery.
- A well demarcated zone of necrosis is seen here.
- There is usually a thin rim of preserved subendocardial myocardium which is directly perfused by the blood in the ventricular chamber.
- Right ventricle and atria are involved in less than 10% of cases.
- The papillary muscles are usually involved.
- There is no need for the ischaemia to be severe enough to produce a myocardial infarct. At autopsy,
- no naked eye changes are seen for the first 12 to 18 hours.
- After this period, there is oedema and pallor of the affected area which is the first sign, and the cut surface looks granular and dull.

- After 24 hours to 3rd day, the area becomes better demarcated, and turns yellow and is surrounded by an area of hyperaemia.
- By the end of 1st week, the entire infarct is bright yellow or yellow-green, soft and has a thin hyperaemic border.
- By 10 days, the periphery of the infarct appears reddish-purple due to growth of granulation tissue.
- In one to three days there is a progressive softening and thinning of the infarcted area, which is maximum about the 10th day, and rupture may occur during this period.
- With breakdown of myocytes, red streaks appear due to dilated vascular channels and area of inter-fibre hemorrhage, giving rise to "tigroid" appearance, though sometimes the yellow element is virtually uniform or red streaks may fade after a few days.
- There may be a red zone in the less damaged muscle around the periphery.
- From the 3rd week and later, the center of the infarct becomes gelatinous and the colour become grey.
- Later, the necrotic muscle is resorbed and the infarct shrinks and becomes pale grey.
- During the next month or two, fibrosis replaces the dead muscle to form a scar.
- By the end of 6 weeks, the infarcted area is replaced by a thin grey-white, hard, shrunken fibrous scar which is well developed in about three months.

Histology:
- No changes are seen in the first 6 hours.
- After 6 hours, some oedema fluid appears between the myocardial fibers.
- The muscle fibers at the margin of infarct show vascular degeneration called myocytolysis.
- By 12 hours, coagulative necrosis of myocardial fibers sets in and neutrophils begin to appear at the margin of the infarct.
- There is loss of striations and intense eosinophilic hyaline appearance and may show karyolysis, pyknosis and karyorrhexis.
- Hemorrhages and oedema are present in the interstitium.
- During the first 24 hours, shrunken eosinophilic cytoplasm and pyknosis of the nuclei occurs.
- Slight neutrophilic infiltration is seen at the margins of infarct.
- During 48 to 72 hours, coagulative necrosis is complete with loss of nuclei.
- The neutrophilic infiltrate is well developed and extends centrally into the interstitium, which is more marked by 4th day and some of them undergo degenerative changes.
- Resorption of necrosed muscle fibers by macrophages begins at the end of the 1st week.
- Proliferation of capillaries and fibroblasts begins from the margins of infarct, and most neutrophils are necrosed and gradually disappear.
- By 10th day, most of the necrosed muscle at the periphery of infarct is removed.
- The fibrovascular reaction at the margin of infarct is more prominent.
- Many pigmented macrophages containing yellow-brown lipofuscin and golden-brown hemosiderin are seen.
- Eosinophils, lymphocytes and plasma cells are seen.
- By the end of 2nd week, most of the necrosed muscle in small infarcts is removed, neutrophils disappear and newly laid collagen fibers replace the periphery of the infarct.
- During the 3rd week, necrosed muscle fibers from larger infarcts continue to be removed and replaced by ingrowth of newly formed collagen fibers.
- Pigmented macrophages, lymphocytes and plasma cells are prominent, while eosinophils disappear gradually.
- During 4 to 6 weeks

- » further removal of necrotic tissue occurs
- » there is increase in collagenous connective tissue,
- » decreased vascularity and
- » fewer pigmented macrophages, lymphocytes and plasma cells.

- At the end of 6 weeks a contracted fibrocollagenic scar with diminished vascularity is formed.
- Firm fibrosis occurs in about 3 months.
- Pigmented macrophages may persist for a long time in the scar, sometimes for years.

Enzyme Histochemistry:

- Immersion of tissue slices in a solution of triphenyl tetrazolium chloride (TTC) gives brick-red colour to intact area (where dehydrogenase enzymes are preserved) and the infarcted area appears pale.

TTC–intact area (brick red)

–infarct area(pale)

- This is seen in about 4 hours, but the results are variable.

Cardiomyopathies account for the 2nd largest number of sudden deaths after coronary artery disease.

Histochemical methods:

In H&E staining, increased cytoplasmic eosinophilia is seen in 8 to 12 hours after infarction.

Fluorescent Method:

- Acridine orange stained cryosections of intact myocardium show golden-brown fluorescence which turns into greenish fluorescence with increasing ischaemic time.
- Eosin fluorescence of normal myocardium in paraffin embedded samples show olive green fluorescence which turns into yellow in injured tissue.
- High percentage or wrong positives are seen.
- The rule of thumb is, that the more sensitive methods are used, the greater the probability that agonal period and autolytic changes may be difficult to differentiate from intravital changes.
- Severe narrowing of coronary arteries (at least 75%) without thrombosis or myocardial infarction is the common cause of sudden death.
- A physical or emotional stimulus may demand sudden increase in cardiac effort, and if the circulation of the deceased is unable to satisfy the immediate need for increased oxygen, death may result (acute coronary insufficiency).
- Any person with a heart in excess of 420 gm. is at risk of sudden death, even though the coronary arteries are normal.

ADDITIONAL POINTS:

- Fresh thrombotic lesions are seen in less than 25% of the cases.
- Transitory coronary artery spasm can cause death in persons suffering from angina without narrowing of the coronary arteries and without significant atherosclerosis or congenital anomalies.
- Spasm of the coronaries may lead to cardiac arrhythmia and death.
- A thrombus or an occlusive lesion in the terminal part of the artery may be overlooked.
- The ostia of the coronary arteries may be occluded by atherosclerosis of the aorta.
- A ventricle which is overworked and under-nourished may suddenly go into ventricular fibrillation or asystole.
- This can occur even if the arteries are not completely blocked and is often precipitated by a sudden demand for an increased cardiac output.
- The lesions of the conducting system of the heart may sometimes cause arrhythmias and death.
- In these cases a state of electrical instability occurs from chronic hypoxia, so that sudden

stresses, such as exercise or emotion can suddenly cause the arrhythmias.
- Sympathetico-adrenal stimulation causes increased myocardial irritability resulting in ventricular extrasystoles and ventricular fibrillation and death occurs after several minutes.
- At autopsy, coronary artery sclerosis, fatty heart, chronic valvular disease, etc. may be seen.
- Lungs are congested and oedematous with pleural petechial hemorrhages.

Concealed Trauma:

(a) Cerebral Concussion:
- This may cause death without any external or internal marks of injury.

(b) Neck Injury:
- Cervical spinal fracture-dislocation may occur in diving, fall on head, impact downstair with a wall-facing, from oblique impact or by fall of some object on the head, in such a way as to cause the dislocation especially with the head thrown back.
- The dislocation may be associated with tears of the ligaments and with the displacement of the skull from the spine.
- Sudden movements of the head over the spine with displacement may cause contusion and laceration of the spinal cord and rapid death.
- If death is delayed, there may be oedema, softening and necrosis of the cord.
- Injury to the spinal cord causes spinal concussion and may cause death.
- Unconsciousness is not seen in all persons, but all get up with residual tingling, numbness, weakness of arms or legs and gait defects.
- Routine autopsy and X-ray may not show any abnormality.
- The dislocation of the cervical segments is often self-reducing, and externally there may not be any injury, or there may be abrasions on the brow or chin.
- Complete dissection of the spine is essential.
- The spinal cord, cut longitudinally, may show internal bruising.
- Death may be instantaneous.

(c) Blunt Injury to the Heart:
- Contusion of the chest as in steering-wheel impacts, head-on collisions, from blast or heavy punching, may temporarily or permanently derange the heart without much evidence of trauma.
- Contusion of the heart may cause death.
- Trauma may cause arterial spasm and it is likely that a functional inhibition or coronary spasm may cause sudden death that sometimes follow upon blows to the chest.

(D) INHIBITION OF THE HEART:
1. Vagal Inhibition;
2. vaso-vagal shock;
3. reflex cardiac arrest;
4. nervous apoplexy or Instantaneous physiological death

- Instantaneous physiological death means death of a person with no abnormality sufficient to be presumed to have caused death and where death occurs within a few seconds.
- Sudden death occurring within seconds or a minute or two due to minor trauma or relatively simple and harmless peripheral stimulation are caused by vagal inhibition.
- Pressure on the baroreceptors situated in the carotid sinuses, carotid sheaths, and the carotid body causes an increase in blood pressure in these sinuses with resultant slowing of the heart rate, dilatation of blood vessels and a fall in blood pressure.
- Carotid sinus is intimately connected with the control of blood pressure and heart rate.
- In normal person pressure on the carotid sinus causes minimal effect with a decrease in heart rate of less than six beats per minute, and only a slight reduction (less than 10 mm. Hg) in blood pressure.

- Some individuals show marked hypersensitivity to stimulation of the carotid sinuses, characterized by bradycardia and cardiac arrhythmias ranging from ventricular arrhythmias to cardiac arrest.
- Stimulation of the carotid sinus baroreceptors causes impulses to pass via Hering's nerve to the afferent fibers of the glossopharyngeal nerve (9th cranial nerve) ; these in turn link in the brainstem to the nucleus of the vagus nerve (10th cranial nerve).
- Parasympathetic efferent impulses then pass to the heart via the cardiac branches of the vagus nerve.
- Stimulation of these fibers causes profound bradycardia.
- This reflex arc is independent of the main motor and sensory nerve pathways
- Parasympathetic stimulation of the heart can be initiated by
  » high neck compression,
  » pressure on carotid sinus or
  » by direct pressure over the trunk of the vagus nerve.

Causes:

(I) The commonest cause of such inhibition is pressure on the neck particularly on the carotid sinuses as in hanging or strangulation.

(2) Unexpected blows to the larynx, chest, abdomen, or genital organs.

(3) Extensive injuries to the spine or other parts of the body.

(4) Impaction of food in larynx or unexpected inhalation of fluid into the upper respiratory tract.

(5) Sudden immersion of body in cold water.

(6) The insertion of an instrument into the bronchus, uterus, bladder or rectum.

(7) Puncture of a pleural cavity usually for producing a pneumothorax.

(8) Sudden evacuation of pathological fluids,

e.g., ascitic or pleural fluids.

(9) Sudden distension of hollow muscular organs,

e.g., # during attempts at criminal abortion,

when instruments are passed through the cervix or fluids are injected into the uterus.

(10) In degenerative diseases of the heart,

e.g. # sinus bradycardia and

partial or complete A-V block;

–parasympathetic stimulation further depress the heart rate and may induce a Stokes-Adams attack which may be fatal.

- –There is great variation in individual susceptibility.
- Death from inhibition is accidental and caused by microtrauma.
- The stimulus should be sudden and abnormal for the reflex to occur.
- The reflex is exaggerated by fear, apprehension, struggling, a high state of emotional tension, any condition which lowers voluntary cerebral control of reflex responses, such as a
  » mild alcoholic intoxication,
  » a degree of hypoxia or
  » partial narcosis due to incomplete anesthesia.
- The release of catecholamines during such adrenal responses may well sensitise the myocardium to such neurogenic stimulation.
- The victims are usually young adolescents of nervous temperament.

Autopsy:
- When death results from inhibition, there are no characteristic postmortem appearances.
- The cause of death can be inferred only by exclusion of other pathological conditions, and from the accurate observations by reliable witnesses, concerning the circumstance of death.

CASE:
A soldier was dancing with his girlfriend in the presence of many others in a hall. While dancing, he playfully "tweaked" (pinched) her neck. She dropped down dead on the spot.
- There were no injuries or signs of asphyxia.
- Death was as a result of vagal inhibition.

ANAPHYLACTIC DEATHS:
- Anaphylaxis is an acute immunologic reaction characterized by cutaneous gastrointestinal, respiratory and cardiovascular signs and symptoms that can rapidly progress to shock and death.
- Deaths due to allergic reactions are rare.
- Most deaths occur within 1 to 2 hours and are preceded by signs and symptoms suggesting hyperacute bronchial asthma.
- Sometimes, deaths are delayed for several hours with nervous symptoms, such as coma or with symptoms of circulatory failure resembling traumatic shock.

AETIOLOGY:
Allergic reactions may occur due to:
(1) Drugs: penicillin, aspirin, horse-serum products, iodine-containing agents.
(2) Insect bites.
(3) Foods: fish, shell-fish, eggs, nuts, fruits.
(4) Hormones: insulin, ACTH.
(5) Enzymes; trypsin.

- When an allergen is injected into the body, the antibodies formed by plasma cells combine with their antigens to form antigen-antibody complexes (allergens), which stimulate mast cells to release histamine and similar substances.
- About 75% of patients dying of penicillin anaphylaxis do not have allergic reactions during earlier course of penicillin therapy.
- Patients should be observed for 30 minutes after receiving the injection of antibiotics.
- The anaphylactic syndrome is caused by local and systemic release of endogenous active substances.
- These include leukotrienes, C, D, E histamine, eosinophilic chemotactic factor and other vasoactive substances, such as bradykinin and kallikrein.

- Anaphylactic shock is due to bronchospasm with contraction of the smooth muscle of the lungs, vasodilation, and increased capillary permeability.
- Death occurs due to laryngeal oedema, bronchospasm and vasodilation.
- Serum tryptase levels are an indicator of mast cell activation and if elevated suggest, an allergic mediator release, particularly in anaphylaxis.
- Peak levels of tryptase occur 1 to 2 hours after anaphylaxis and then decline with half life of about 2 hours.

SIGNS AND SYMPTOMS:
- The onset of symptoms is within 15 to 20 min.

General:
1. malaise,
2. weakness,
3. sense of illness,
4. oedema of face.

Mucosal:
1. periorbital oedema,
2. nasal congestion,
3. angio-oedema,
4. cyanosis.

Respiratory system:
1. sneezing,
2. rhinorrhoea,
3. dyspnoea.

Lower airway:
1. dyspnoea,
2. acute emphysema,
3. asthma,
4. bronchospasm.

Upper airway:
1. laryngeal oedema,
2. hoarseness,
3. stridor,
4. oedema of tongue and pharynx.

- Gastrointestinal System:
  » nausea,
  » vomiting,
  » dysphagia,
  » abdominal cramps,
  » diarrhoea

- Cardiovascular System:
  » tachycardia,
  » palpitation,
  » shock.
- Central Nervous System:
  » anxiety,
  » convulsions.

AUTOPSY:
- Search for injection sites or sting marks.
- The sting area should be excised and frozen at -70°C and submitted for antigen-antibody reactions.
- Findings are non-specific.
- There is usually
  » oedema of the larynx (recedes soon after death),
  » oedema of epiglottis, trachea and bronchi,
  » emphysema, cyanosis, petechial hemorrhages, congestion and oedema of the lungs,
  » focal pulmonary distension alternating with collapse and bronchiolar constriction,

froth in the mouth and nostrils, visceral congestion, and infiltration of bronchial walls with eosinophils.
- History is very important.
- In cases of insect bites, Ig E antibodies are found in the serum.
- Ig E binds to the mast cells and basophils.
- Then the cells interact with specific antigens, they release a number of potent compounds, including histamines and an eosinophilic chemotactic factor, which causes an immediate hypersensitivity reaction.

DIAGNOSIS:
- To establish diagnosis of death from allergic shock, the following should be established:
(1) The injected material must be non-toxic to normal persons.
(2) Characteristic allergic symptoms should be present before death.
(3) Autopsy should not reveal the presence of any other lesion capable of causing death.
(4) By the passive transfer technique, a specific sensitizing substance corresponding to the allergen must be demonstrated.

DRUG IDIOSYNCRASY:
- The administration of drugs in amounts which are known to be harmless to normal person may cause death due to drug idiosyncrasy,

e.g., many persons are hypersensitive to cocaine.
- The diagnosis is based mainly on clinical history.

DIABETES:
- Glucose levels above 200 mg% are diagnostic of diabetes mellitus even if i.v., glucose infusions were administered.
- An elevated vitreous glucose level is an accurate reflection of an elevated antemortem blood glucose level.
- Glucose level in vitreous falls gradually as the time after death increases.

ASTHMA:
- Asthma can cause sudden death without being in status asthmaticus or even an acute attack.
- If airflow obstruction is not relieved, there will be steady progression to elevated CO_2, metabolic acidosis, exhaustion and death.
- The mechanism is obscure.
- At autopsy, the lungs appear over expanded, and completely occupy the chest cavity.
- A sticky tenacious white mucus deposit fills the bronchi.
- Microscopically, chronic inflammatory infiltrate with numerous eosinophils are seen around the bronchi.
- The basement membrane of the bronchi is thickened and has a wavy appearance.
- In chronic cases, there is protrusion of bronchi above the cut surfaces of the lungs.

EPILEPSY:
- Very few persons die in status epilepticus.
- Bite marks in the tongue are seen in about 25% of cases.
- Death is caused due to postictal respiratory failure.
- Sudden death due to epileptic seizures is most likely due to a lethal cardiac arrhythmia induced or propagated by the disorganized neural discharges of seizure.
- Sudden death can occur without being in a status epilepticus or even without a typical fit.
- In such cases the mechanism is obscure.
- Repetitive seizures can cause bilateral hippocampal sclerosis.

AIDS/HIV
- HIV attaches itself to the T-receptor molecule on T-helper lymphocytes in order to infect them.
- T-helper lymphocytes are found in most body fluids, such as semen, saliva, tears and breast milk.
- After infection with HIV, blood becomes positive after 2 to 18 months.
- AIDS is usually communicated by sexual intercourse or from blood transfusion.
- HIV causes profound depression of cell-mediated immunity.
- This suppression exposes patients to a variety of opportunistic infections and malignant conditions.
- Mandatory testing, i.e. without consent of the person is done for screening donors for blood, semen, organs or tissues.
- According to guidelines laid by the Government of India, the status of HIV should not be disclosed to blood donor.
- The intention is to spare him of the agony of knowing the helplessness of his situation.
- If the blood drawn is positive, it should be discarded.
- Once blood sample is drawn, the register of patient identities should be kept quite separate and sample identified only with a code number.
- If the donor wants to know the result of HIV test, he should be referred to an accessible HIV testing center where supplemental tests with counseling will be offered to him.
- HIV testing requires both pre-test and post-test counseling.
- Patient bas to be informed face to face about the test result and not over the telephone or by a third party.

- HIV positivity should not be revealed to unauthorized persons.
- The Centre for Disease Control (CDC). estimates that 5.5% of all HIV positive persons are employed in the health care field.
- According to the guidelines issued by CDC, with the exception of health care workers and personal service workers who use instruments that pierce the skin, no testing or restriction is indicated for workers known to be infected with HIV, but otherwise able to do their jobs.

- Doctors in government service are obliged to treat AIDS cases.
- The treating doctor has the duty to inform the paramedical staff involved in the treatment of such patients, the mortuary staff, pathologist and the staff of the crematorium so that due precautions can be taken by these people, who are likely to come in direct contact with the infected biological material.
- WHO guidelines state that there is no public health rationale to justify isolation, quarantine on discrimination based on a person's HIV status.
- A person testing positive for HIV cannot be removed from service, if he is physically fit to discharge his duties.
- If pregnant, they should be allowed to decide whether to continue or terminate the pregnancy.
- HIV positive women should be advised to avoid pregnancy as there is one in three chance of having an infected child.
- Breast feeding may result in transmission of HIV from mother to child.
- Recently, Supreme Court of India has ruled that the sexual partner of an AIDS/HIV positive patient to be informed of the fact.

SUDDEN DEATH
- Death is said to be sudden or unexpected when a person not known to have been suffering from any dangerous disease, injury or poisoning is found dead or dies within 24 hours after the onset of terminal illness (WHO).
- Some authors limit sudden deaths as
  » those occurring instantaneously
  » within one hour of onset of symptoms.
- Emphasis is placed more on the unexpected character, rather than suddenness of death.
- The incidence is approximately 10 percent of all deaths.
- No period in life is exempt.
- Natural death means that the death was caused entirely by the disease, and the trauma or poison did not play any part in bringing it about.

Causes:

(I) Diseases of the Cardiovascular System (45 to 50%):
(1) Coronary atherosclerosis with coronary thrombosis.
(2) Coronary atherosclerosis with hemorrhage in the wall causing occlusion of the lumen.
(3) Coronary artery disease (narrowing and obliteration of the lumen by atherosclerosis).
(4) Coronary artery embolism.
(5) Occlusion of the ostium of the coronary artery associated with atherosclerosis or syphilitic aortitis.
(6) Arterial hypertension with atherosclerosis.
(7) Rupture of the fresh myocardial infarct.
(8) Spontaneous rupture of aorta.
(9) Angina pectoris.
(10) Pulmonary embolism.
(11) Systemic embolism occurring in bacterial endocarditis.
(12) Rupture of aortic or other aneurysm.
(13) Cardio-myopathies, alcoholic myopathy, asymmetrical hypertrophy of the heart.
(14) Lesions of the conducting system: fibrosis, necrosis.

(15) Valvular lesions: aortic stenosis, aortic regurgitation, mitral stenosis, rupture of the chordae, ball-valve thrombus.
(16) Fatty degeneration of the heart.
(17) Acute endocarditis.
(18) Acute myocarditis.
(19) Acute pericarditis.
(20) Congenital heart disease in the newborn.
(21) Senile myocardium.

(II) Respiratory System (15 to 23%):
(1) Lobar pneumonia.
(2) Bronchitis and bronchopneumonia.
(3) Rupture of blood vessel in pulmonary tuberculosis with cavitation.
(4) Pulmonary embolism and infarction.
(5) Air embolism.
(6) Influenza.
(7) Diphtheria.
(8) Acute oedema of the glottis.
(9) Acute oedema of the lungs.
(1 0) Lung abscess.
(11) Massive collapse of the lung.
(12) Pleural effusion
(13) Pneumothorax Caused by rupture of emphysematous bleb.
(14) Neoplasm of the bronchus.
(15) Bronchial asthma.
(16) Impaction of foreign body in the larynx and regurgitation of stomach contents into air-passages and bronchioles.

(III) Central Nervous System (10 to 18%):
(1) Cerebral hemorrhage.
(2) Cerebellar Haemorrhage.
(3) Pontine hemorrhage.
(4) Subarachnoid hemorrhage.
(5) Cerebral thrombosis and embolism.
(6) Carotid artery thrombosis.
(7) Brain abscess.
(8) Brain tumour.
(9) Meningitis.
(10) Acute polioencephalitis.
(11) Cysts of third or fourth ventricle.
(12) Epilepsy.

(IV) Alimentary System (6 to 8%):
(1) Hemorrhage into the gastrointestinal tract from peptic ulcer, esophageal varices, cancer esophagus, etc.
(2) Perforation of ulcers, e.g., peptic, typhoid, amoebic or malignant.
(3) Acute hemorrhagic pancreatitis.
(4) Strangulated hernia.
(5) Twisting and intussusception of the bowel.
(6) Paralytic ileus.
(7) Appendicitis.
(8) Bursting of the liver abscess.
(9) Rupture of enlarged spleen.
(10) Intestinal obstruction.

(11) Obstructive cholecystitis.

Genitourinary System(3-5%)

(1) Chronic nephritis.
(2) Nephrolithiasis.
(3) Obstructive hydronephrosis and pyonephrosis.
(4) Tuberculosis of the kidney.
(5) Tumours of the kidney or bladder.
(6) Rupture of ectopic pregnancy.
(7) Toxaemia of pregnancy.
(8) Uterine hemorrhage due to fibroids.
(9) Cancer vulva eroding femoral vessels.
(10) Twisting of ovary, ovarian cyst or fibroid tumour.

(VI) Miscellaneous (5 to 10%):

(1) Addison's disease.
(2) Diabetes mellitus.
(3) Haemochromatosis.
(4) Hyperthyroidism.
(5) Blood dyscrasias.
(6) Cerebral malaria.
(7) Shock due to emotional excitement.
(8) Reflex vagal inhibition.
(9) Anaphylaxis due to drugs.
(10) Mismatched blood transfusion.

- The majority of sudden deaths caused by atherosclerotic coronary artery disease are not associated with a coronary thrombus or an acute myocardial infarct.
- Coronary artery spasm can occur in persons with normal coronary arteries.
- Myocardial infarction and rare cases of sudden death do occur.
- Hypertension is the most common cause of concentric left ventricular hypertrophy which can cause sudden death even in the absence of significant atherosclerotic coronary artery disease.

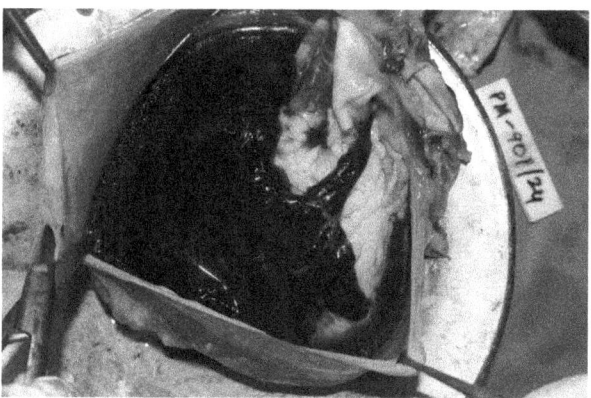

Fig(6.1) Cardiac tamponade

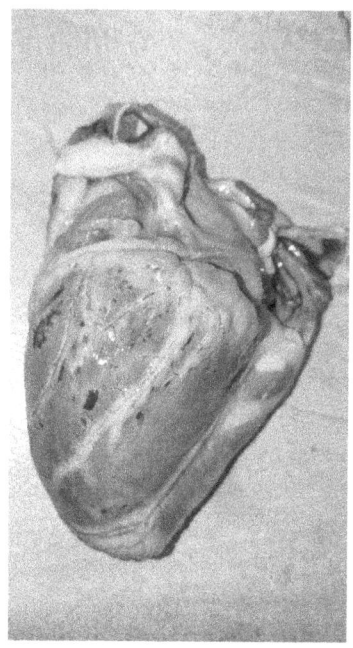

Fig(6.2) Petechial Hemorrhage

Courtesy: Professor, Dr. Chandrasekar, MMC, Madurai.
Associate professor, Dr.Sadhasivam, MMC, Madurai.

CHAPTER - 07
POST-MORTEM CHANGES

Forensic Taphonomy:
Forensic taphonomy is defined as the history of changes of a body after death.
- It is used to differentiate the signs of death from the suspended animation.
- The changes that take place are helpful for determining the time of death.

Post-mortem changes

Immediate changes (somatic death)	Early changes (Cellular death)	Late changes (Decomposition and decay)
Insensibility & loss of power	Pallor and loss of elasticity of skin	Putrefaction
Cessation of respiration	Changes in eye	Adipocere formation
Cessation of circulation	Primary flaccidity of muscle	Mummification
	Cooling of body	
	Postmortem lividity	
	Rigor mortis	

Immediate changes:

1. **Insensibility and loss of movement:**
    » It is the earliest sign of death.
    » There is loss of reflex, no response and loss of tone in muscle.
       E.g. prolonged fainting attack
   - Vagal inhibitory phenomenon
   - Epilepsy
   - Electrocution

2. **Cessation of respiration:**
   Complete stoppage of respiration for more than five minutes usually causes death.
   It can be observed by using stethoscope placed over the upper portion of lungs and larynx
   Even respiration can stop without death.
   E.g. voluntary breath holding
   - Cheyne – stokes breathing
   - Newborn
   - Drowning

3. **Cessation of circulation:**
   - Stoppage of heartbeat for more than five minutes is irrecoverable, which results in death.
   - It can be observed by playing a stethoscope on the pericardial area of the heart.

Test for respiration:
- It has a historical importance but it is not utilized now.
- **Feather test:** No movement is observed if a feather is placed at the nose of a dead person.
- **Winslow test:** No movement of chest is observed when reflection of light shone on the mirror.
- **Mirror test:** No vapour is seen on the reflecting surface of mirror when it is held in front of the nose & nostrils.

Test for circulation:
- **Magnus test :** Finger fails to show bluish dis-colouration when pressure is applied on the base.
- **Diaphanous test :** Finger web space doesn't show redness when we transilluminate from behind.

I card's test:

Fluorescein dye injected on the given site of dead body fails to produce yellowish green discolouration, but it is usually seen in a living person.

Pressure test- Fingernails appear pale and fail to show reddish colour on removal of firm pressure over it.

Suspended animation:
- Suspended animation or apparent death
- Suspended animation is the condition where signs of life are not found and the vital signs like heartbeat & respiration are interrupted for some time or reduced.

Mechanism:

The metabolic rate is reduced greatly so that requirement of oxygen to cell is satisfied by the presence of dissolved oxygen in the body fluid.

Types
1. **Voluntary:** Seen in the practitioner of yoga in a trace
2. **Involuntary:** It lasts for about a few seconds to half an hour.

Condition for involuntary suspended animation:
- Anesthesia
- Poisoning
- Electrocution
- Vagal inhibition'
- Severe syncopal attack
- shock
- New born infants
- Sunstroke

The patient can be resuscitated by cardiac massage.

Mediolegal importance:

Doctor may wrongly determine the person to have died.

Early changes:

All post-mortem changes depend on temperature: high temperature accelerates the changes.

Changes in skin:
- Skin becomes pale and white ash colour due to cessation of circulation.
- Skin loses its elasticity.
- Lips appear dark red to black & dry

Changes in eyes:

Loss of corneal reflex:

It may be seen in cases of deep insensibility and it is not a reliable sign.

E.g. Epilepsy, Narcotic poisoning, general anesthesia

Opacity of cornea:
- There is opacity of cornea due to drying & deposition of debris.
- This may be delayed if the lids are closed after death, and cornea remains clear for about 2 hours.
- (Tachy noire - the formation of yellow triangle if the eyelid remains open for about 3-4 hours after death)
- Yellow Triangle formed
- Base at the limbus
- Apex at medial & lateral canthus
- Sides are formed by margins of upper and lower lids.
- Tachy noire formed because of cell debris and mucus upon which dust settles and the surface become wrinkled.

Flaccidity of eyeball:
- Due to reduction of intraocular pressure in the eye, the eye ball is shrunken.
- Intraocular pressure at death becomes zero at the end two hours.
  In living person – Intraocular pressure ranges between 14 to 25 gm

Pupils:

The pupils are dilated after death due to relaxation of iris muscle. Later due to onset of rigor mortis, the iris becomes constricted and evaporation of fluid starts.
- Such a case is not an indication of death in the antemortem appearance.
- Occasionally rigor mortis affects ciliary muscle, so size of pupil is larger than that of the other eye.
- Pupil reacts with atropine & serine for first 30 minutes after death, after that pupil doesn't react to strong light.
  During life, pupil shape cannot be shaped.
  After death if we give pressure on two or more sides of the eyeball, pupil shape changes to oval, triangular or polygonal.

Retinal vessels:
- The blood column of retinal vessels is fragmented or segmented ,trunkling or shunting within seconds to minutes after death and if it persists for about an hour - it is called Kevorkian sign - occurs due to loss of blood pressure.
- It is observed in ophthalmoscope.
  Retina is pale for initial two hours around optic disk, it is yellowish and becomes blurred in 7-10 hours.
  Chemical changes - steady rise in potassium &hypoxanthine in vitreous after death.
  Cooling of the body (algor mortis)
- The cooling of body is a complex process which doesn't occurs at the same rate throughout the body after death.
- After death, the temperature of the body falls and after some hours it tends to be equal to the immediate surrounding's temperature.

Mechanism:
- The fall of temperature of body due to cessation of energy and inactivity of heat regulation centre in the brain.
- Loss of the body heat occurs by conduction, radiation and evaporation.
  Features of curve
- It is a sigmoid, biexponential or inverted S shape
- Initial phase – No loss of heat or fall of temperature of the rectal temperature for the 1-2 hours this due to thickness of skin & the subcutaneous tissue which is a good insulator of heart. It is also called as Isothermic phase.

- Some hours after death, the fall of temperature at the inner core of body achieves a regular, linear andconstant phase (intermediate).
- Fall in temperature gradually becomes slow as the temperature of the environment is reached, the last part of the curve (Terminal) is slightly above the base line.

Methods for measurements of core temperature:
- Laboratory thermometer ranges from 0-50°C
- Site for recording the temperature is rectum except in case of sodomy.

Procedure:
A thermometer should be inserted 8 to 10 cm into rectum and left there for two minutes.

Temperature can also be recorded by making small opening into the peritoneal cavity and inserting the thermometer in contact with inferior surface of the liver.

External auditory meatus or the nasal passages also can be used.

Reading should made at the interval of 1 to 2 hour in order to obtain fall in number.

Note:

The temperature of this reading and the temperature of the environment should be recorded at the same time.

The formula for obtaining the rough idea of time in hours:

$$\frac{\text{Normal body temperature} - \text{rectal temperature}}{\text{Rate of temperature fall per hour}}$$

Variation in temperature:
- Rectal temperature after death ranges between 36.5° C to 37.5° C.
- Difference of rectal and oral temperature in about 0.5° C to 1° C higher than the oral temperature.
- Daily variation of this temperature is upto 1^0C to 1.5^0C
1. It is lowest in early morning
2. It is highest in late evening

Some of the conditions there were sharp rise in rectal temperature
1. Air embolism
2. Infection
3. Heat stroke
4. Neuroleptic medication
5. Co poisoning

Note :
- *Rectal temperature higher upto 1.5 to 2° C in case of struggle or exercise prior of death*
- *Lower rectal temperature is seen in congestive heart failure, collapse ,hypothermia, hypothyroidism.*

Factors affecting rate of cooling:
1. **Difference in temperature of body & medium**
2. Rate of temperature fall is directly proportional to the temperature of body & medium
3. In tropical climates the heat loss is roughly 0.4 °C to 0.6°C in temperature countries 1°C per hour
4. Built of cadaver and physique of cadaver
5. Obese people cool slowly, lean people cool rapidly so the rate of heat loss is directly proportional to weight and the body surface
6. Children and old person cool rapidly
7. Environment of the body:
8. Air movement of the body tend to cool the body very rapidly due to evaporation
9. A body is kept at well ventilated room will cool rapidly than one in closed room
10. Cooling is rapidly in a humid rather than the dry environment
11. Cooling is earlier in water and late in buried body

The rate of fall of temperature in different media
   Cooling twice faster as in air then it is about three times faster
1. Covering on (or) surface of body
2. Rate of cooling is slow in well clothed than naked or thinly clothed body

---

Note:
- *If the body is exposed to heat shortly after death, the temperature will rise.*
- *When a body is in zero temperature, it undergoes freezing, becomes stony hard and formation of ice in cavities and blood vessels occurs.*

Mediolegal importance:
- It helps in the estimation of time of death which is not reliable.
- Determination of temperature of body is important only in cold and temperature climates.
  Post-mortem caloricity
  In this condition, instead of cooling the temperature will rise for the first two hours.
  This occurs due to
  * excessive bacterial activity in case of septicemia
- great increase in heat production in muscles due to convulsion, strychnine poisoning
- regulation of heat production is severely distributed as in sunstroke

Post-mortem hypostasis:
- Post-mortem hypostasis is defined as bluish purple or purplish red discoloration, which appears under the skin in the most superficial part of the dermis due to gravitational setting of toneless capillary and venules in the dependent part.
- It is also called post-mortem staining, livor mortis, subcutaneous hypostasis.

Mechanism
- After the stoppage of circulation, there is a stagnation of blood in the vessels and it tends to sink by force of gravity.
- Blood tends to accumulate in the toneless capillaries & venules in the dependent part of body.
  It causes bluish purple discoloration by filling the vessels.
- The upper portions of body drained of blood are pale.
- The intensity of reduced hemoglobin in blood is upon the intensity of the colour.
  [In recently dead person or died tissues, oxygen dissociation takes place until the equilibrium takes place between tension of the
  oxygen in the capillaries and the surrounding tissues.]
- It is not possible to distinguish PM staining from cyanosis seen in the living.

Development:
- It develops shortly after death but it may not be visible for 30 minutes -1 hour after normal death and for anemic person it is about 1 to 4 hours.
- It consists of dull patches of length 1 to 2 cm in diameter that appear in 20 to 30 minutes.
- The small patches increase in size and merge with each other, increase in intensity and it is well-developed within 1-4 hours.
- The areas then enlarge and combine to produce extensive?
  [In some bodies, isolated patches of staining remain separate from large area of staining.]
- Frost – Erythema, Hypothermia induces purple spots on the prominent part of shoulders and knee joint. It usually mistaken as hypostatic patches.
- Circulatory stasis in aged resembles as effect of violence
- When staining develops by applying the thumb pressure against the skin and held for a few seconds, the staining at the part will disappear it will be pale or white when the pressure is released staining appears

- Plasma tends to cause edema of the dependent parts contribute cutaneous blisters of early putrefaction
- In early states – patches of hypostasis may be seen on the upper surfaces of body
- It is usually well developed within four hours completed 6 to 12 hours (primary lividity)
- But lividity (staining) to be lighter degree remains in the original area due to staining of the tissue hemolysis (complete staining)
- If the body in moved within few hours after death, patches of staining disappears and the new ones will form on the dependent parts of the body

Intensity:
- In intense asphyxia where blood neither may not coagulate in sudden death within short period and a great circulating blood volume.
- It is less marked in death from hemorrhage, anemia and wasting disease due to reduced hemoglobin.
- It is less marked in lobar pneumonia.
- Sometimes bluish staining becomes pink along the upper margin and dark in lower part.

Extent of PM staining
- Depends upon
- Volume of blood at circulation at the time of death
- Length of time that the blood remains

Note – PM hypostatic may been seen in the case at few hours before death.(ie) person dying a slowly with circulatory failure (ie: Cholera, Typhus, Tuberculosis, uremia, morphine / barbiturate poisoning).

Petechial hemorrhages
- Numerous fine petechial hemorrhages on the dependent part of hypostatic area
- Common in Narcotic poisoning and acute cardiac arrest
- Petechial hemorrhages may in staining area in 18 to 24 hours due to rupture of small vessel

Distribution of PM staining
- It depends on the position of the body
- In a body lying supine – it appears in the neck and then spreads entire back with exception of the areas directly pressed on the ground (or) the bed (i.e. occipital area, shoulder, buttocks, posterior aspect of thigh, calves and heels) which don't show staining is known as contact pallor /contact blanching.
- The vessels in this area are pressurized and the blood is compressed similarly any pressure that prevents the capillary filling (i.e.collar, waist) remain free from colour this phenomenon is called bands or stripes, it mistaken as beating or strangulation on neck.
- In a body in lying position as in drunken person intense staining seen in front
- Eyes may suffuse and numerous conjunctional hemorrhages.
- If a body lying on the side, blood will settle on the side.
- If the body suspended vertically as in hanging, PM staining will be mostly in legs and gentalia, lower part of for arms, hands and upper margin of the ligature mark on the neck.
- When the body remains submerged in water as drowning, the staining is usually found in face, upper part of chest, feet and the calves.

Note: Vibices,Tiny spots, sometimes merge round to oval bluish due to rupture of subcutaneous capillaries.

Fixation of PM Staining:
   If the body is undistributed, the PM standing gets fixed in 6 to 12 hours after the complete formation of PM staining,
- Alteration in the position of the body doesn't change the position of staining and remain as such though the colour usually fades away.
- It occurs earlier in summer, delayed in asphyxia death and intracranial lesion.

Calorimetric:
- It is used to find out time since death.
- Increasing in pallor of staining occurs during the first 24 hours.
- Rate of colour changes decreases as PM interval increases.
- It is the analysis to determine the relationship between PM interval and colour of skin.

Hemorrhages:
- It is also called death spots / postmortem ecchymoses.
- Commonly seen in back of the shoulders, neck and sometimes in front of back even when the body is lying on its back.

Absences of hypostasis:
- Blood loss of at least 65% of circulating blood volume in adults and 45% in infants
- Occurs before death due to trauma

Internal hypostasis:

Cause	Colour change
Asphyxia	Deep bluish or purple
Hypothermic, Drowning, Refrigerated bodies	Bright pink
Infection with intravascular coagulation	Blothy purplish, red and pink
Poisoning	
Carbon monoxide	Cheery red
Nitrates, potassium, chlorates etc	Chocolate or brownish red
Phosphorous	Dark brown or yellow
Hydrogen sulphide	Bluish green
Carbon dioxide	Deep blue

Mediolegal importance
- It is a sign of death
- Estimating of time of death which unreliable due to difference in appearances
- It may indicate the moving of body to another position after death
- Colour change may indicate the causes of death
- Distribution of staining may indicate manner of death

Various types of colour change
- Ante mortem origin – Trauma – Bruises, asphyxia Asphyxia - Cyanosis. Inflammation- congestion
- Postmortem origin – hypostatis, putrefaction, poisoning
- Artificial – paint, mud, grease,etc

Difference between Congestion and PM staining

Feature	Congestion	PM staining
Situation	Uniform all over the body	Irregular and in dependent part
Mucous membrane	Normal	Dull
Exudate	May be seen	Inflammatory exudates
Hollow viscus	Uniform	Stomach and intestine when stretched show alternate area of discolouration

Muscular changes
Three phases of muscular changes
1. Primary flaccidity
- During this stage death is somatic
- It lasts for about one to two hours are begin to relax soon after death
- All the muscles begin to relax soon after death
- The Lower jaws falls ,Eyelids loose tension and joints are flexible
- Body flattens over area which are contact with surface and rests is called Contact flattening
- Muscle may respond to mechanical, chemical and electrical stimuli
- Peristalsis may occur in the intestine with ciliary movement of intestinal cells.
- After death ATP presents, muscles are relaxed
- ATP is produced by anaerobic glycolysis
- Pupils react to atropine or physostigmine but not Light.

2. Rigor mortis /Death stiffening /Cadaveric rigidity

Rigor mortis is a state of stiffening of muscles with small degree of shortening

Mechanism:

Muscle fibres contains bundles of myofibrils which consists of two types of protein filaments
- » Actin
- » Myosin
- At rest actin filaments interdigitate myosin filaments only to a small extent .muscle fibers also soft
- Maintenance of this condition of muscles is due to the presence of ATP (Adenosine triphosphate) above certain level.
- on nervous stimulation hydrolysis of ATP to ADP (Adenosine diphosphate) and phosphate with liberation of energy which causes contraction of the muscle fibres and extension of actin filaments more inside the myosin filaments

After death.
- There is continuous hydrolysis of ATP and as long glycogen available in muscle,there is resynthesis of ATP
- Once ATP is exhausted , there No futher synthesis ATP so the muscle losses softness,elasticity and extensibility due to actomyosin complex gives rights to rigor mortis
- After the PH of the muscle becomes 5.5 of the automatic enzymes stored in Lysosomes
- The enzymes are cathepins and calpins
- The enzymes act as myofibrillar proteins and hydrolyze them ,As a result actomyosin complex broken down and muscle becomes soft again this is called as resolution of rigor mortis

---

Note:
- *When ATP is redued to a critical level (85% of the normal) and the formation of rigid acto-myosin comple cause loss of extensibility,hardness and rigid*
- *The rigidity is maximum when ATP level is reduced to 15% and lactic acid level is 0.3%.*

Order of rigor mortis:

Both of voluntary & involuntary muscles are affected but all muscles don't affected simultaneously
- order of Rigor mortis follows **NYSTEN'S RULE**

Rigor mortis first appears.in heart muscles. (Myocardium) within a hour of death in involuntary muscles

Among involuntary muscles;
1. First it appears at eyelid muscle
2. Face ,Jaw and Muscles in neck then passes downwards
3. Muscles of chest, upper limbs and abdomen and lower limbs.
4. lastly fingers & toes

Note:
- *In individual limb it Progresses above downwards and it is not constant or regular*
- *It disappears in same order in which it has appears*

Shaipro Suggest;

Rigor mortis is a physiochemical Process it more likely develop in smaller muscle than the larger muscle
- the proximo distal progess - rigor mortis usually devlops sequentially and follows descending pattern called Nysten's Rule

Development of rigor mortis:
- Development of rigor mortis is concerned within muscles only
- Rigor mortis develop slowly in paralyzed muscle.Before rigor mortis we can move the body to any posture so that after rigor mortis body can fix at the posture
- After fixing the new position fixing of the extremities when the rigor mortis is developing,the rigidity is less likely in other Symmetrical group
- skeletal muscles contain two muscle fibre.

Type 1 (Red) - Rich in Mitochondria, dominant in oxidative metabolism

Type 2 (White) -Poor in Mitochondria , dominant in glycolytic metabolism
- Rigor mortis can occur in different times in different fibres
- Some fiber which are still slack and some other are not fully contracted and retain the capacity of binding of actin and myosin filaments and re-establishment of rigor mortis occur due to contraction of muscles fibre
- If force is applied to fully development of rigor mortis in the body, stiffness is permanantly broken down causes. Postmortem ruptures ,frequently breaking of rigor mortis causes pathy distribution

Features
- Fully development of rigor mortis in the body
- Entire body is stiff
- Muscle shortened, hard & Opaque
- Knees,Hips and shoulders are slightly flexed
- Fingers & toes are flexed

1) Goose skin appearance with elevation of cutaneous hair known as cutis anserina or goose skin
2) Rigor mortis of dartos muscle may cause post mortem ejaculation of Semen
3) Pupils are partially get Contracted
4) Rarely Rigor mortis of uterine muscles is in labour at the time of death cause uterus to contract and expell the fetus.

Testing of rigor mortis
- It is testing by lifting the eyelids, Depressing the jaw and gently bending of the neck and various joints
- **Heart** - Ventricles get Contracted which may be mistaken as ventricular hypertrophy it may be excluded by measuring the relative size of left side and ventricular thickness
- Face may the appearance of grimacing
- secondary muscle flaccity may result in dilation of Atria & Ventricles which may be mistaken as antemortem dilation of Chamber due to myocardial degeneration
- Soppage of Systolic and Diasystolic blood pressure it is not possible to determine in autopsy
- Muscle relaxation immediately after death with opening of eyes and mouth and later it got fixed

Onset & duration
- In tropical country like India it commences in one to two hours after death and get well established in the entire body in six hours in summer
- In Temperate countries it commences in three to six hours and further it takes two to three hours to develop
- This is called rule of 12 (Rigor of March)
- In Northern India the duration of rigor mortis is 18 to 36 hours in summer and 24-38hours in winter
- Which rigor mortis set early it passes off quickly and vice versa

Condition altering Rigor Mortis
1. **Age:** Commonly found at still born infants at full term and it is develops very slowly and well marked
* It is rapid at old age
2. Nature of death
3. Wasting disease like tuberculosis, Cancer, Typhoid and cholera
4. Violent deaths, cut throat injury and firearms
5. Strychnine, HCN poisoning
6. Asphyxia due to CO poisoning, hanging
7. Hemmorrhages
8. Paralyzed muscles
9. Cold, Refrigerated Muscle

Muscular State
- Violent or vigorous exercise prior to death may slows down the onset
- Onset is slow, duration is long- Muscle are healthy, rest before death
- onset is rapid, duration is short -Fatigue, vigorous exercise
- Rigor is rapid in legs compared to other parts
- Rigor may be delayed in weak person

Atmospheric condition
- Onset is slow, duration is long in cold weather
- Rigor persits longer in fresh dry air and prolonged in dry air (Cold)
- onset is rapid is hot air
- If body in an extreme hot environment, decomposition begins and rigor mortis disappears after 12 hours of death
- If refrigerated bodies - rigor mortis persits for 3 - 4days.

Medico legal importance
- Sign of death
- Help in estimation of time of death
- It indicates the position of the body at the time of death

Trait	Rigor mortis	Cadaveric spasm
Production	Freezing and exposure to temperature 75C	cannot produced by any method after death
Mechanism	Break down of ATP	Not exactly known
Predisposing factor	Nil	Sudden death, excitement, fear, fatigue
Muscles	All muscles in the body	Restricted to selected group of voluntary muscles
Muscle stiffening	Not marked	Marked
Molecular death	Occurs	Not occurs
Body heat	Cold	Warm
Muscle reaction	acidic	alkaline
Medicolegal importance	Time of death	Mode of death

For example

If the body lying on its back with it lower limb is raised in air, it indicates that the body reached full rigidity.

Condition stimulating rigor mortis
- Heat stiffening.
- It is seen in deaths from burning, high voltage electric shock and falling from hot liquid
- Heat causes stiffening of the muscle, because the tissue proteins are denatured and coagulated in cooking
- Muscles are contracted or even carbonised on the surface
- the body assumes an attitude commonly called as pugilistic attitude (Boxer attitude) with lower limbs and arms are flexed and hands are like claw
- The heat stiffening cannot be broken down by extending the limbs as in rigor mortis
- Stiffening remains until the muscles and ligaments get soften due to decomposition
- In such state rigor mortis don't occur
- cold stiffening
- When body is exposed to freezing temperature the tissues become frozen and Stiff
- Freezing of body fluids and solid formation of the subcutaneous tissue fat stimulating rigor
- when joints are forcibly flexed, the ice breaks in the synovial fluid with a sudden sharp sound
- If the body is placed in warm atmosphere the stiffness disappear and after a time the normall rigor mortis occurs rapidly and passes quickly.
- Hardening of subtaneous of fat particularly in infants may render the skin rigid and may be mistaken as ligature mark

Cadaveric spasm / Instantaneous rigor:
- Cadaveric spasm is a well recognized but quite rare phienenomenon
- Primary flaccidity doesn't occur in case of Cadaveric spasm and the muscle undergo stiffening at the moment of death.
- This is usually limited to a group of voluntary muscles
- Adrenocortical exhaustion which interfers with the resynthesis of ATP may be the possible cause of cadaveric spam
- It is associated with the violent deaths occuring under the circumstances of intense emotions
- No other condition stimulates cadaveric spasm and it cannot be produced by any method after death
- It passes without interruption of rigor mortis
- Circumstances of cadaveric spasm,
- Cases of drowning
- Death from violent disturbance of nervous stimulation
- Strychnine and cyanide poscaving
- Case of accidents such as mountain fatalities

Medicolegal importance of cadaveric spam
- Presence of indicates cadaveric spas indicates Person was alive at time of Cadaveric spam
- It indicates the antemortem nature of drowning
- Succidal - when the some weapon are clenched tightly in the hands of died person which gives the clue of succidal evidence
- If the deceased dies due to assault some part of clothing of this person who attacks
- It helps in indicating the mode of death whether it is succidal/ homicidal/ accidental

Gas stiffening
- The stiffening occurs in dead bodies shows signs of decomposition
- Gases evolving during Putrefaction also stiffen the body to due of accumulation of gases in the tissues
- Usually this process has no problem in distinguishing true rigor

Secondary relaxation (or) flaccidity
- Rigor mortis disappears and the muscle becomes soft and flaccid
- Muscle don't respond to mechanical or electrical stimuli
- This is due to myosin being dissolved by the excessive production of acid during the stage of rigor mortis
- It is caused due to action of the alkaline liquid produced by putrefacation
- Enzymes are developed in dead muscle which dissolves myosin by a process of autodigestion
- The sign of decomposition start appearing on the body
- The body become totally relaxed and flaccid and can be put in any position

DECOMPOSITION
- Two processes of decomposition
  » Autolysis
  » Putrefaction

Autolysis
Autolysis defined as self digestion of tissue
- Soon after death the cell membrare are permeable and breakdown with the release of cytoplasm containing enzymes and lysozymes and the enzyme (Hydrolyases) released from the cell
- The proteolytic, glycolytic & lipolytic action ferments causes autodigestion and disintegration of organs and occurs without bacterial influence
- The earliest autolytic changes occur in parenchymatous, glandular tissues and in the brain
- Chemical processes are increased by heating and it is stopped by freezing.

- In fetus, In dead born maceration - an aspetic dead fetus autolysis in utero is seen . Maceration occur when the dead child surrounded by liquor with exclusion of air
- The macerated fetus is usually in Brownish pink in colour
- In adults such digestion occur before start of death in cases of intracranial lesion and terminal pyrexias

» Autodigestion in gastric mucosa causes perforation of stomach
» Earliest external sign is a whitish, cloudy appearence in cornea

Putrefaction
- It is the final stage of death.
- It is a process in which destruction of soft tissues in the body occurs
- Putrefaction usually follows the disappearance of rigor mortis
- During hot season it may commences before rigor mortis has completely dissappeared from the lower extremity

Mechanism
- Proteolytic , Glycolytic and Lipolytic enzymes from the cell act on the body tissues
- Their softening and liquefaction (auto digestion of organ)
- Aerobic & Anaerobic organisms present in the intestinal tract invade the mucous membrane after death and spread all over are after the body
- They produce enzymes that breakdown body tissues with gas evolution

Features
Changes in the colour
- The first external sign of Putrefaction is usually a greenish discolouration of the skin over the region of ceacum which lies superficially and the content of the bowel are more fluid.
- After Death the bacteria can invade directly from the bowel into the abdominal wall , hemoglobin diffuses stains the surrounding tissue as reddish brown

Mechanism -
- Microorganism invade through the intestinal wall and reach the blood vessels releases hydrogen sulfide gas and the gas combines with hemoglobin and forms the sulfhaemoglobin which causes discolouration
- The change in colour appears by about 12-18 hours and one to two days in winter
- The discolouration spreads all over the Abdomen , External genitalia and on the patches appears on chest, Neck ,Face,Arms and Legs
- The Patches become dark green but latter purple and dark blue. The patches scattered and join together and the whole skin become discoloured
- Putrefactive bacteria tend to colonize in venous blood
- Wrinkling fingertips occur early but latter become leathery and the nails become prominent
- Internal seen in undersurface of liver ,anterior peritoneal surface of liver ,adipose tissue around bladder

Marbling of Skin
- Area seen in Superficial vein especially over the roots of limbs ,thighs, sides of abdomen, chest and the neck
- It depends on the total amount the amount of sulphaemoglobin formation in affected vessels due to hemolysis of red cells
- It is a marbled appearance (Red then greenish pattern resembling the branches of tree)
- Starts in 24 hours and prominent in 36 to 48 hours
- The clotted blood becomes fluid as such postmortem staining altered and the fluid collects in serous cavity.
- Putrefactive effusion of foul smelling fluid (blood) starts which the skin becomes macerated in Pleural cavity
- The reedish green colour of the shin may become dark green or black in 3-4 days

Internal

1) Discolouration
- Reddish brown colour in inner surface of vessels especially in aorta
- Decomposition proceeds slowly in the surface
- The same colour change seen in viscera but the colour varies from dark red to black rather than green
- Visera become softer,greasy to touch , finally they breakdown into soft disintegrating mass

2) Development of foul smelling gases
- Reduction of complicated proteins and carbohydrate. being split into simpler compound
- Simpler compound formation of amino acids, ammonia, carbon monoxide,carbon dioxide,H2S, phosphorated hydrogen ,methane & mercaptans.
- the gases are inflammable in early but later it will burn
- Gases collected in intestine 12-18 hours in summer, 1 to 2 days in winter
- Abdomen become tense & distended
- Eyeballs become soft
- Cornea become white, flattened
- Compressed later it become collapsed
- The gas formation in the blood vessels may force blood stained fluid ,air and fat between epidermis and dermis leads to formation of blisters in 18-24 hours
- Blisters form at the lower surfaces of trunk earlier leads to edema
- Gases collect in the tissues , cavities,hollow viscera causes bloation and distoration

Pressure effects
- Due to presence of gas in the abdomen, the diaphram forced upwards compressing the lungs and heart and blood stained frothy exudes from the mouth is called as postmortem purge which is mistaken as artemortem bleeding
- Swelling in the face ,genitalia and the abdomen,Limbs are free from the putrefactive changes and well marked in face and trunk and it was mistaken as sign of strangulation
- In 24 to 48 hours, the subcutaneous tissue become emphysematous.
- In males the gas causes scrotal swelling.
- The breast and Penis are distended
- Eyes are buldged
- Tongue are swollen
- Discoloured lips

Maggots
- Maggots are produced in one to two days which have proteolytic enzymes that dissolve the tissues
- As they eat they may create holes that resembles as gunshot wounds
- Large acumulation of maggots in one area may indicate pre existing antemortem wound
- Activities of maggot may raise the temperature.
- The junction of epidermis and dermis are weakened. Which causes epidermal layer to slip produces large, fragile sac or pink red and join together and it rupture
- The exposed subdermal tissues a yellow parchment appeerences
- The sphincter relax , Urine and feces may escape ,wounds caused before or after death due to bleed to pressure effects of gases in the heart and blood vessels
- The anus & uterus prolapse after 2 to 3 days
- Blood stained fliud may leak from the mouth,nostrils,rectum and vagina
- In 3 to 5 days the suture of skull separated and the liquid from the brain comes
- Teeth become loose and fall off
- postmortem luminescence due to contamination of bacteria
- when the nutritive substances are used the gas production stops and swelling subsides

Distribution
It follows the order
Abdomen, chest, neck, face, shoulders and arms
- The distribution of Putrefactive changes may be influenced by the position of the died person after death

For example
- Person dies with his head as dependent position, Putrefaction is fast in head and neck
- Rigidity due to inflation of the tissues with gases
- In this condition the changes well marked in 2 to 3 days
- Position -The lower limbs are flexed, abducted and rigid The arms are abducted and flexed
- False rigidity is produced due to acumulation of gases in the tissues because rapid decomposition
- Seen in bodies recovered from water

Liquefaction of tissue
- Colliquative Putrefaction beings from 5 to 10 days after death
- The abdomen will burst, stomach, & intestine will protrude and In children throax will burst
- The tissues becomes soft, loose, converted into semifluid mass
- The tissues will be separated from bone.
- The cartilage ligaments softened and the bones are destroyed
- Decomposition may differ from body to body, from environment to environment and one part to another part is called as differential decomposition
  i.e. some parts are mummified and the rest may show liquefying phenomenon

Internal phenomenon
- Decomposition is slowly at surface
- As the blood decomposed it's transudes into the tissue show change in colour of yellowish, greenish blue, greenish black
- Viscera becomes greasy and softened
- The organ composed of muscular tissues and those containing large amount of fibrous tissue resists the Putrefaction longer than the parenchymatous organ with exception of soft tissue and intestine

various organ putrefaction
- Depending on the vascularity, structure access of air and bacteria in the following order
- Larynx and trachea: Early the mucous membrane becomes brownish red, later greenish and soft in 12 to 24 hours in summer and 2 to 3 days in winter
- stomach & intestine: Occurs in 24 to 36 hours in summer and 3 to 5 days in winter
- Deep red iregular patches in the whole thickness of wall
- Gas blebs are formed in sub mucous layer
- Small multilocular cyst in lumen
- The become softned dark brown and change into dark soft, pulpy mass
- The muosa eaaily peeled off
- Intestine there much of blood and bile pigment
- Spleen -Soft, pulpy liquefes in 2 days
- omentum and mesentry it putrefy early
- they become greyish green and dry in 1 to 3 day in summer
- Liver - Soft & flabby in 12 to 24 hours in Summer
- Multiple blisters appear in 24 to 36 hours
- The lesion appear first as yellowish, Opaque, Yellowish, dendritic fingers in the parenchyma
- When the bubble develop organ has a honeycombed, Vesicular or foamy apperance gives a greenish colour
- In advanced putrefaction it gives green or black in colour

Gall bladder
>It resists the putrefaction for long time but the bile pigment diffuses to adjacent tissues

Pancreas
>Softened and hemmorrhagic

Heart
>Soft, flabby cavity appears dilated. Rarely white granules seen is endocardial surfaces below the capsules of Liver and kidney. The nodules is called as millary plaques
>This consist of caluim and soapy material

Lungs
>Gaseous bullae formed under pleura which are pale red , scattered later the lungs become soft collapsed reduced to small black mass

Brain
>The leptomeninges appear red, Liquefy brain may be grey green

kidney
>The renal tissue becomes flabby and the surface are dull. The cortex darkens and become green

Adrenals
- The cortex softens, soft medulla.
- Later medulla liquefies and the interior of gland appears like a narrow slit

Bladder
- It resists puutrefaction for long time if it is empty and Contracted bladder
- Uine show albumin due to transduction of serum protein from the blood within 48 hour of death

Prostate
>It resists putrefaction for long time

Uterus
- It is a last organ to putrefy in virgin
- In gravid uterus it occurs soon after delivery

Body farm
- It is a the rearearch facility for the estimation of time of death
- The body are exposed to different condition that ways to decompose
- In all stages animal activity ,smell ,body temperature and weather condition is recorded for gaining the knowledge about decomposition
- The facility exist in USA but not relevant to India

Conditition affecting the putrefaction

External factor
>**Environment:** The temperature for decomposition is 21 -38°C, increase range of temperature ,decomposition occurs at slow rate [delayed when the temperature is less than 10°C & 38°C]
- Decomposition stops less than 0°C and greater than 48°C
- The rate of decomposition in doubles as rapid in summer as in winter
Optimum temperature helps in
- chemical breakdown of tissues
- promoting growth of microorganisam

Moisture
- Presence of moisture promotes decomposition by promoting the growth of microorganisms
- If the body dries is quickly. Putrefaction stops and mummification occurs
- Body the is taken from air body and it left in air the body decompose readily

Air
- Free access of air hastens putrefaction because air conveys organisms. into the body
- Stagnant air promotes decomposition whereas movement of air retards the decomposition

Clothing
- Cothing reduce the rate of decompostion by preventing entry of the body by air borne organism
- In winter, clothing hastens putrefaction by maintaining body temperature for a longer period

Clothing
- Cothing reduce the rate of decompostion by preventing entry of the body by air borne organism
- In winter, clothing hastens putrefaction by maintaining body temperature for a longer period

Manner of burial
- If the body is burried soon after death Putrefaction is less
- In the surface burial the rate of decompostion is more than the deep burial because of more bacteria in surface
- Putrefaction is delayed if body is buried in dry sand soil or the body in a coffin because of exclusion from water,air and the action of insects and animals

Age
- In still born fetus or infants who are unfed or not breathed ,the process of decomposition is slow
- Bodies of of children putrefy rapidly and old people slowly

Sex

Doesn't have much influence but in female sex the process of decomposition occur faster because of large amount of subcutaneous fat,moisture content and heat for longer period

condition of the body

Emaciated body decomposes later than the well nourished bulky fatty body

Cause of death
- when the death is due to infection or septicemia decomposition in rapid
- putrefaction is delayed in wasting disease, anemia,poisoning of carbolic acid ,Zinc, Chloride, Strychnine or heavy metal

External injury of body

Dead body having external injuries will decompose earlier because injured area will allow the entry of microorganisms easily

Odour mortis

About 50 volatile compounds were identified as being associated with human remains which are unique for decomposition of human remains

Field portable instruments can as used to locate the human remains in burial

Putrefaction in water.
- Casper's dictum is related to Putrefaction
- Body decomposes in air twice as rapidly in water
- It is real but no practical value
- Purtrefaction is rapid in warm,fresh water than in cold salt water
- It is more rapid in stagnant water than water
- Putrefaction is delayed in deep burial and clothing
- As the submerged dead bodies decomposition starts early in the head and face because being heavy they assume the lowest level in the water and blood content is maximum
- As the submerged dead bodies floats with the head lower than the trunk gaseous distention and postmortem discolouration is seen on the face,neck ,upper extremity,chest, abdomen and the lower extremity

Adipocere (saponification)
- It is a modification of decomposition
- It is formation of soft ,whitish,crumbly,waxy ,greasy material occuring in the fatty tissues of dead bodies
- Commonly seen in body immersed in water and in warm temperature

Mechanium:
- Adipocere consists of fatty acids due to hydrolysis and hydrogenation of of pre-existing fat
- Water is essential for the bacterial and enzymatic process invblued in adipoure formation
- The chemical reaction essential involves in conversion of fatty acid to higher fatty acids which combines with calcium and ammonium ion to form insoluble soap which is acidic inhibit putrefactive bacteria
- Whole of fat like palmitic acid ,oleic, stearic and hydroxystearic acid with glycerol and the mixture of substances forms a adipocere.

Factor influencing adipocere formation
- Heat accelarates and cold retards the adipocere formation
- Warm and Moisture is essential for the reactions to occur ,it occur rapidly in body immersed in water than the soil
- In Obese people and mature newborn, the adipocere formation occur rapidly
- Early activity of of bateria like Clostridium perfringens less this bacteria produce lecithinase enzyme which facilitates adipocere formation
- In buried body ,The body is enclosed in water tight coffin for many years may be converted into adipocere even in absence of water
- Running water retards the formation of adipocere

Note: water is essential for adipocere formation

Properties
- Adipocere has a offensive smell during early stages.
- The smell remains in the clothing of handling such bodies
- Fresh adipocere is soft, moist and translucent but old samples are dry,hard, crackled yellowish and brittle
- It shows fragments of fibrous tissue and muscles in fracture
- It is inflammable but it burns with faint yellow flame
- It floats in water and dissolves in ether and alcohol

Distribution
- It forms in any site where the fatty tissues are present
- It forms first in subcutaneous tissues, usual sites are face buttocks , abdomen and breast
- Sometimes limbs and chest wall may be affected
- The epidermis disappears as adipocere forms
- Internally small muscle are dehydrated and become thin and have a uniform grayish colour
- The depth of large muscle have a pink or red colour with complete conversion of fat into adipocere
- The intestine and lung are usually parchment like consistency and thickness
- The liver is prominent and retains its shape
- Even adipocere persits for a decades

Time required for formation
- It depends upon temperature and humidity
- In Temperate countries the formation is about 3 weeks
- Over a period of time stiffening, hardening of fat occurs
- Complete conversion in adult limb occurs about 3 to 6month
- In India it has been observed to begin in 4 to 5 days

Medicolegal importance
- When the process involves the face this features are preserved. which helps for identification
- The cause of death is determined since the injuries can be recognized
- It gives the estimation of time since death

Mummification
- It is the modification of decomposition
- Dehydration or drying and shrivelling of the dead body occurs from the evaporation of water but the natural appearences and the facial features. are preserved

Features
- It begins in the exposed part of body like face, hands, feet and extends to entire body including the internal organ
- The skin may be translucent due to absorption of liquefied subcutaneous fat. It is usually Shurken and contracted, dry, brittle, leathery, rusty brown in colour
- The skin is stretched in the bony prominences such as such bones of cheeks,chin, coastal margins and hips ,adheres closely to the bones and often covered by fungal growth
- Internal organ become shurken, hard, dark brown and black and become single mass
- Collagen, elastic tissues, cardiac muscle ,skeletal muscle ,bones and cartilages has as demonstrable histologically features in Mummified bodies
- Sometimes body shows evidence of mummification in a certain parts and adipocere changes in others
- Thus there may be adipocere in cheeks , Abdomen,legs and Mummification of arms and legs

Time required for mummification
3 months to years and it was influenced by size of body, atmospheric condition and the place of disposal

Factors necessary for mummification
- Absence of moisture in air
- Continuous action dry or warm air
- Marked dehydration before death.
- Bodies burried in shallow graves in dry sandy sail in deserts
- chronic Arsenic or antimony poisoning favours mummification

Medicolegal importance
same as adipocere formation

Note:
- *When the body is removed from the water the rate is rapid and the temperature is required for the growth of microorganisms*
- *The epidermis of the hand and feet become swollen,bleached ,wrinkled after immersion*
- *Fish ,crustacea,water rats in water may destroy the body*
- *Moulds located anywhere in the body but generally in exposed area*
- *Fungus grows with vary in colour from white and yellow to green and black*

Skeletonisation
- Skeletonisation of dead bodies takes place in varying time depending on several factors
- In buried bodies total skeletonisation takes place in one year
- When disposed off carefully on land or water , skeletonisation occur within few days to few months
- Destruction of bones ordinarly takes several years.

Note: Decompostion changes is divided into five stages

1. Fresh
Starts as early 24 hours and as late as 7 days after death in cold winter

2. Early
Begins with onset of skin slippage and hair loss, maggots infestations, Marbling, purging and offensive odour

3. Advanced
Appearance of loose, sagging skin and the collapse of abdominal cavity, extensive maggots, loss of organ, adipocere formation

4. Skeletonisation
Exposure of more than half of skeletal structure with soft tissue attachment

5. Extreme
Seen only in remains that have exposed to the environment leads to erosion of skeleton

Preservation of dead bodies

1. Embalming:
It is the art and science of Preservation of dead body with antiseptics and preservatives to delay the putrefaction

Goals of embalming
- sanitation
- Presentation
- Preservation

This treatment results in coagulation of protein fixation of tissues, bleaching and hardening of organ and that leads to conversion of blood into brownish mass and it produces a Chemical stiffening similar to rigor mortis & normal rigor doesn't develop

Reason for embalming
- Required for public display at funeral, religious reasons for using as anatomical specimens and legal requirements
- Anatomical embalming is performed into a closed circulatory system. The fluid is injected with a machine into a artery at high pressure
- Then it is allowed to swell and saturate the tisues. This cadaver have a typical uniform grey discolouration due to high formaldehyde mixed with the blood

Procedure:
- The content of the intestine is syringed or taken out by suction
- Then six part injection is made through illiac or femoral arteries, Subclavian or Axillary vessels and common carotid with the viscera treated separately with cavity fluid
- the evacuation of the intestine clears out the prevailing microorganism and fomalin fixes the tissues protein and renders it unsuitable for bacterial invasión
- Autolysis is also prevented due to chemical fixation of tissues.

Typical embalming fluid.

Formalin (preservative)-1.5L
Methanol (preservative)-500ml
Phenol (Germicide)-500ml
Thymol (Fungicide)-5gm
Sodium borate (Buffer)-600gm
sodium citrate (Anticoagulant) -900gm
Glycerin(Wetting agent)-600mL
Sodium chloride (controls PH)-800gm
Eosin1% (Cosmetic)-30ml
Soluble wintergreen (Perfume)-90ml
water (vehicle)-upto 10 ml

Note:
Sodium borate & sodium citrate should be dissolved in a hot water and allowed to cool. Add rest of the component and dilute to make up 10L and allow to stand for few hours and filtre
Autopsy cases embalming differs from Standard embalming since postmortem disrupts the circulatory system due to removal of organ and viscera

---

Disadvantages of embalming
- Difficult to interpret any injury or disease
- Determination of cyanide, alcohol, organic poisoning and drugs become difficult
- Blood grouping may not be possible.
- Thrombi and emboli are dislocated

Other methods
1. use of of dry ice is common traditional technique . for Preservation at home.
2. Dry ice is applied in different part of body and the ice should be changed every 24 hours
3. Freezing of body below 0°C and at -20°C in refrigeration equipment The body is treated with chemical agents like lead, arsenic and potassium carbonate which prevent bacterial action and autolysis

Time since death/Estimation of Postmortem interval
- The time interval between time of death and the time of conducting autopsy is called the time since death (TSD).
- The exact time of death cannot be fixed in any case, but a range of time between which death was presumed to have taken place, can be estimated. It is more of a scientific guess, rather than a precise opinion.
- The longer the postmortem interval, less accurate is the estimated time since death.
- Determination of TSD is an indispensable component of Corpus Delicti.

Objectives:
- To know when the crime has been committed.
- A starting point for the Police in the investigation of the crime.
- Exclude some subjects and to search for the likely culprit.
- To check on a subject's statement.
- To give opinion on time of death
- Go through all the available history.
- Local physical and environmental factors at the scene of crime (e.g. fire, open windows, environmental temperature, etc.)

External examination
The body is throughly examined for
(i) Algor mortis (cooling of the body)
(ii) Livor mortis (postmortem staining)
(iii) Rigor mortis (cadaveric rigidity)
(iv) Decomposition and/or its modifications
(v) Entomology of cadaver (maggots).

Entomology of cadaver
- Flies lay eggs on the fresh corpse, in the moist areas of the body, e.g. eyelids, nostrils, angle of mouth, etc, soon after death.
- Once skin decomposition begins, eggs are laid down anywhere on the body.
- Larvae and maggots are produced from the eggs in 8 to 12 hours.
- These maggots crawl into the interior of the body and produce powerful proteolytic enzymes and destroy the soft tissues.
- Maggots become pupae in 4 to 5 days. They become adult flies in another 3 to 5 days.

Medico legal importance
- To estimate the time since death based on the stage of development of the insect.
- To identify the cause of death, in certain poisoning cases.
- To corroborate the scene of crime, by identifying the species of the insect.

Internal examination.

I)Stomach emptying time
- Stomach starts emptying by within 10 minutes.
- Bulk of the food is emptied in 2 hours.
- Light meal in 2 hours,Medium meal in 3 to 4 hours and heavy meal in 5 to 6. hours
- Digestion is delayed in sleep and suspended in Coma
- Emotional disturbances Causes hypermotility and can result in rapid emptying
- Diet rich in Carbohydrate empties faster than protein, which is faster than fat
- Head of the meal reaches hepatic flexure in 6 hours and splenic flexure in 9 to 12 hours and pelvic colon in 12 to 18 hours
- If stomach is full and containsundigested food, the time since death would be approximately 2 to 4 hours

II)Urinary bladder

Bladder emptying time
- Average urine volume of healthy adults is 1.5litres / day half of which occurs at night
- Depending upon the volume of urine in the bladder a rough estimation of time of death can be made out the rate of formation of urine in adult is 1ml/minute ,the amount of urine present in the bladder will indicate the approximate time of death.If the previous bladder emptying time is known.
- If the bladder is full it can be said that the individual has lived for a reasonable period of time after going to bed. (Since its customary with most people to evacuate the bladder before going to bed).

Other useful indicators which can be assessed only by laboratory techniques are:

1.Cerebrospinal fluid:
- Lactic acid concentration raises from 15 mg% to 200 mg% in 15 hours
- Non-protein nitrogen shows steady raise 15 mg% to 40 mg% in 15 hours
- Amino acid evenly raises from 1 mg% to 12 mg% in 15 hours.
- Depending upon the rate of increase the approximate time of death can be assessed.

2.Blood
- Potassium, phosphorus, magnesium increase after death.
- Sodium and chloride-decrease after death
- Other compounds the concentration of which increase after death are: Non-protein nitrogen, amino acid nitrogen, lactic acid and bilirubin
- Certain enzymes like acid phosphatase, alkaline phosphatase, amylase, lactic dehydrogenase also increase after death.

3.Bone marrow
- During life up to 40% of cells are neutrophils
- After death, nuclei begin to swell within 1 hour; becomes round in 4 hours; formation of vacuoles in the cytoplasm, cell outline becomes obscure in about 10 hours.

4.Vitreous humor
- Gradual increase in potassium and reduction in sodium occurs for the first 85 hours (3 to 4 days) after death.
- The level of glucose and pyruvic acid decreases and lactic acid increases after death.

5.Hair Growth

During life, hair grow at the rate of 0.4 mm/ day. After death hair and nails stop growing. If the time of last shave is known, then an approximate interval of the time of survival can be made out.

6. Non-Scientific data:

Examination of scene of crime for time since death: Certain scene markers like newspapers, dates on a postal mail, the degree of coagulation of milk, state of food on a table will indicate the approximate time since death.

If the body lies on growing grass, underlying grass and vegetations soon dries and turns yellow or brown. This will indicate how long the body was lying at the scene.

7) Carbon dating: (Radioactive Carbon)

- C14 content of the bone is steadily maintained during life
- After death radioactivity of C15 gradually weakens with the half of life being 5600 years
- Radioactive carbon is useful only for cases which data back to several centuries it is not useful for the bones which are less than a century old
- Postmortem changes with approximate time since death
- Postmortem changes. Time in hour
- Body warm, transparent cornea-within 1hour
- Postmortem lividity in patches-2 to 3 hour
- Body cold, uniform postmortem staining,
- fixed rigor mortis in upper part of body-6 to 8 hours.
- Rigor mortis all over body-Around 12 hours
- Body cold and stiff ,eggs and flies
- Greenish discolouration in right illiac fossa-12 to 24 hours
- Rigor mortis passing off and
- abdominal distension-24 to 36 hours
- Greenish discolouration on abdomen and
- chest ,marbling, distention
- postmortem blisters and maggots-36 to 48 hours
- whole body bloated, face unrecognizable,
- Nails and hair easily pulled off,
- grown maggots/pupae all over body-3 to 5 days
- Putrefaction, internal organ reduced to black -2 weeks
- Skeleton exposed-1 to 3 months

Presumption of death

- Arises in connection with civil cases
- A person is presumed to be alive, if there is nothing to to suggest death the probability of his death within 30years, But if proof is produced that the same person is not been heard for 7 years by his relatives and friends and the death is presumed

Presumption of survivorship

- Arises in connection with inheritance of Property
- when two or more person die in a common disaster for example earthquake, plane crash .
- The question of who survived longer may arise ,The case is decided on the fact and evidence available
- In the absence of such evidence age,sex,built, nature, severity of injuries and mode of death are taken into consideration in deciding the survivorship.

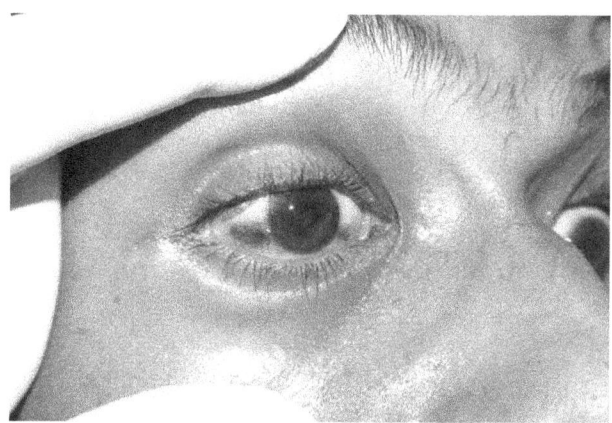
Fig(7.1) Tache noire

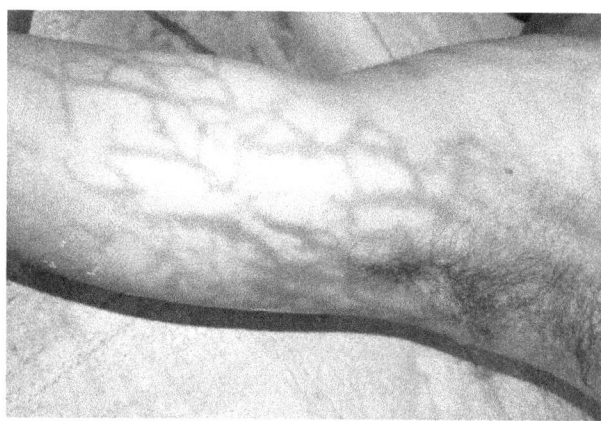
Fig(7.2) Marbling (putrefactive network)

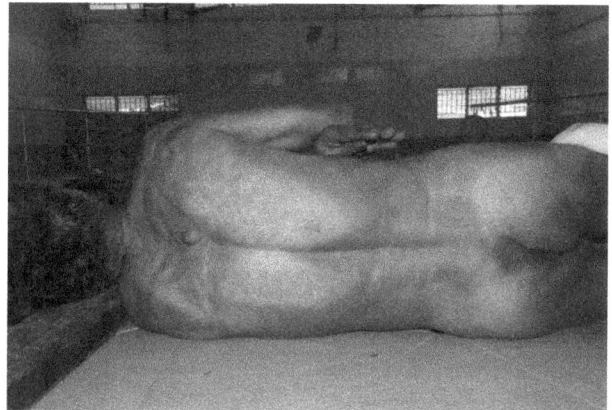
Fig(7.3) Postmortem hypostasis

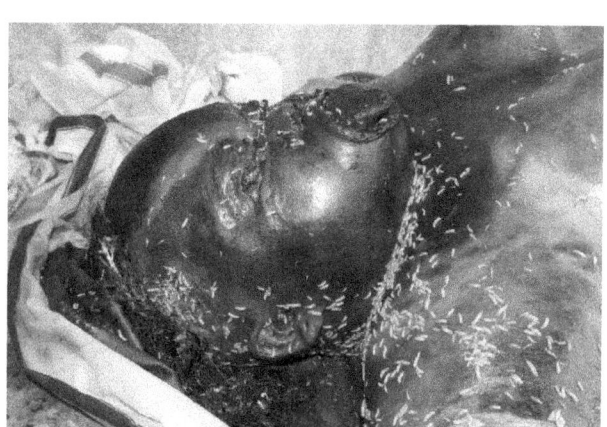
Fig(7.4) Maggots infestation

Courtesy: Professor, Dr. Chandrasekar, MMC, Madurai.
Associate professor, Dr.Sadhasivam, MMC, Madurai.

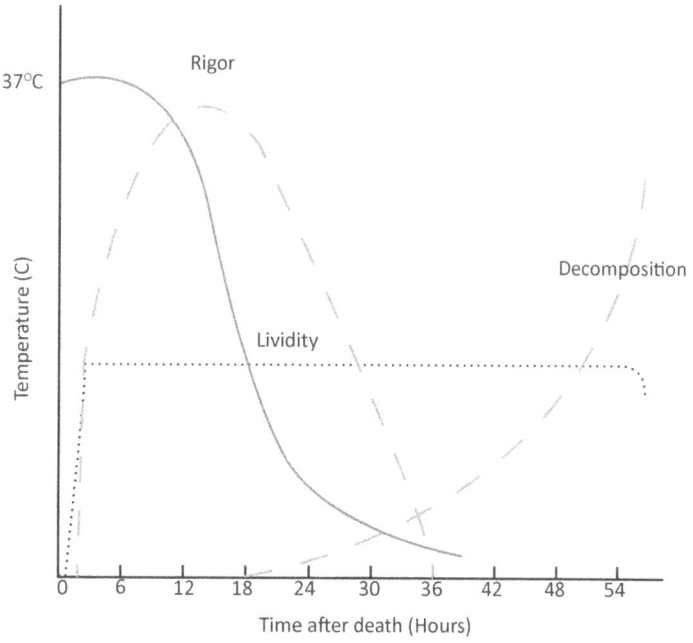

Fig. (7.5). Chart showing the major changes to estimate time since death.

CHAPTER - 08
MECHANICAL INJURIES

Injury:
- An injury means any harm, whatever illegally caused to any person in body, mind, reputation or property (Sec. 2(14), BNS).
- Medically a wound or injury is a break of the natural continuity of any of the tissues of the living body.
- **Mechanical injuries** (wounds) are injuries produced by physical violence.

Classification of injuries :

Medical :

I. Mechanical or physical Injuries:
   A. Due to blunt force:
      1. Abrasions.
      2. Contusions.
      3. Lacerations.
      4. Fractures and dislocations.
   B. Due to sharp force:
      1. Incised wounds.
      2. Chop wounds.
      3. Stab wounds.
   C. Firearms:
      1. Firearm wounds.
      2. Blast injuries.

II. Thermal Injuries:
   A. Due to cold:
      1. Frostbite.
      2. Trench foot.
      3. Immersion foot.
   B. Due to heat:
      1. Burns.
      2. Scalds.

III. Chemical Injuries:
   1. Corrosive acids.
   2. Corrosive alkalis.

IV. Explosions

V. Miscellaneous:
   Electricity, lightning, X-rays, radioactive substances, etc.

Legal:
1. Simple.
2. Grievous.
3. Dangerous.

Medicolegal :
1. Suicide.
2. Homicide.
3. Accident.
4. Fabricated.
5. Self-inflicted.
6. Defence.
7. Ante mortem or post mortem.

GENERAL PRINCIPLES:

A wound is caused by mechanical forces.

Mechanical forces

Moving weapon object & (give force) Reasting body. (give conunter force)

Stationary weapon object & (give conunter force) moving body (give fouce)

Due to the impact

Energy has been transferred to tissues of body

Change in state of rest or motion

The human body contains many complex tissues and this forceful impact does not affect the tissues uniformly.

Affected tissues subjected to compression or Traction strains or Both

- All the body tissues are resistant to compression, except those which contain gas,, i.e., they resist force tending to reduce their volumes.
- Mechanical force does not cause compression of the tissue but causes their displacement and deformation, and traction strains are produced in the affected tissues.
- A shear strain is a strain which is produced in a body by the forceful alteration of its shape but not its volume.
- The rigid tissues like bones resist deformation, but if the limits of their elasticity is exceeded fracture occurs.
- The soft tissues are plastic, and as such, mechanical force alters their shape, which is limited by
  » the cohesion between the tissue cells,
  » connective and vascular tissue frameworks and
  » capsules of organs.
- Soft tissues rupture when they are stretched beyond the limits of their tensile strength.

FACTORS GOVERNING THE NATURE AND EXTENT OF WOUNDS:

1. **THE NATURE OF THE OBJECT OR INSTRUMENT CAUSING THE WOUND:**
   - In a blow from a sharp-edged object, the force is concentrated to a very limited area or a point or a line deep penetrated or clear separation of the tissues.

1. The hardness of the tissues will resist the passage of the object.
- In a blow from a blunt instrument having a flat surface,
  2. Force is concentrated in large area of body,
  3. dissipation of the energy in the adjacent tissues
  4. damage caused to a unit mass of the tissue within that area is less than that due to a narrow object.
- Irregularities in the shape of the instrument, or curvature of the part of the body struck such as at the top of head, may limit the area of the actual impact to a small size and damage will be more.
- A fall against a projection may produce more serious injury than a similar fall against a flat surface.
- If a blow is struck with a plastic instrument, some energy will be spent in deforming or breaking the instrument, increases the size of the area of impact and increases the period over which the energy is discharged, Less damage

2. AMOUNT OF ENERGY DISCHARGED DURING IMPACT:
- Kinetic energy is measured in a moving object by:
- $KE = 1/2\ mv^2$, where m = mass and v = velocity.
- When the mass doubles, kinetic energy is also doubled.
- However, when velocity is doubled kinetic energy increases four times.
- A light bullet has a relatively great destructive power because of its high velocity.

3. THE CONDITION UNDER WHICH THE ENERGY IS DISCHARGED:
- In an impact, most of the energy may be spent in moving the body and the person may be knocked down, but local injury may be minimal.
- If the body or the part of the body struck is immobilised, therefore the greater part of the force is spent in causing localised tissue damage.

Example :
- If the head is free to move, a blow may cause little damage, but a similar blow to a head resting on the ground may cause marked injury to the skull.
- Any factor which increases the period of time over which the energy is discharged will also decrease the destructive effect of a blow,

e.g. a punch with a fist if withdrawn quickly will produce more damage than one where the fist stays in place.

4. THE NATURE OF THE AFFECTED TISSUES:

A. THE SKIN:
- The skin readily changes shape when it is struck, as it bends easily and is elastic.
- It is also resistant to traction forces.
- Because of these factors, when it is struck by a blunt object it won't damage, but the underlying structure may be severely damaged.
- The skin may easily split when crushed against rigid bone.

B. THE SUBCUTANEOUS TISSUES:
Elasticity and plasticity:
- The subcutaneous tissues are very plastic due to their fat content and connective tissues are more pliable, these provide a cushioning effect and protect the body
- when the body gets a blow the incompressible fat of the subcutaneous tissues may be crushed and undisplaced between the skin and underlying structures producing bruises due to severe blows from blunt instruments (Hooke's law of elasticity).

C. THE MUSCLES:
- The muscles are usually not damaged due to blows, because of their great plasticity and elasticity and their strong encapsulating sheaths.
- They may be crushed against bone or deeply cut by fragments of displaced and broken bone.
- The muscles may rupture, if they are unduly stretched.

D. THE BONES:
When a force is applied to a bone it may bend without breaking, but when it is bent beyond the limits of its elasticity it fractures.

E. BODY FLUIDS:
- Fluid is incompressible, but is readily displaced.
A blow over a hollow organ which contains fluid.

powerful hydrostatic forces developed in that fluid.

Force is transmitted equally and uniformly in all directions.

rupture of anatomically distant and mechanically weak tissues
e.g. a sudden compression of the chest may rupture distal venules and capillaries, as seen in traumatic asphyxia.
- The violent displacement of fluid in the gastrointestinal or urinary tract may cause distant ruptures of portions of these tracts.

F. GASES:
- Gases are readily compressible
- lungs may be extensively compressed without any structural damage
- But when compressed suddenly and violently, sufficiently powerful pneumostatic forces may develop and cause damage to tissues.

APPLICATION:
- Different wounds may be caused from equal forces when applied to the same region of the body in different circumstances.
- Sometimes, minor forces may produce severe wounds, and relatively severe forces may cause minor wounds.
- Because of these, often on scientific grounds it is not possible to give an opinion as to the amount of force which must have been used to cause a particular wound.
- It is also not possible to predict the amount of damage which could be caused by the application of a certain force.
- The doctor should give his opinion in broad qualified terms.

ABRASION
- An abrasion (gravel rash) is a destruction of the skin, which usually involves the superficial layers of the epidermis only.
- Thickness of the skin is 1.6 mm.

Mechanism :
- They are caused by friction against a rough surface or by compression
- For abrasions to occur some pressure and movement by agents on the surface of the skin is essential.
- If sufficient friction is applied, partial or complete removal of the epithelium may occur and the superficial layer of Dermis is damaged.
- The rougher the surface, and the more rapid the movement of the skin over it, the deeper the injury is.
- Sometimes, full thickness of the skin may be damaged in places, but usually in an interrupted, irregular manner, and intact epidermis remains within the area of the abrasion.
- The exposed raw surface is covered by exudation of lymph and blood which produces a protective covering known as a scab or crust.

Features:
- Abrasions vary in size, depending on the abrading force and the body surface exposed.
- They are simple injuries, bleed slightly, heal rapidly and scar is not formed, Large abrasions can cause severe pain and bleeding.
- The size, situation, pattern and number of abrasions should be noted.

Types :
Point scratch
1. Scratches. Fingernail scratch
2. Grazes. Brush burn or gravel rash
   Abrasions are of Friction burn
   Four types.
3. Pressure abrasion
   Patterned abrasion
4. Impact abrasion.

1. Scratches :
- A scratch (linear abrasion) is a very superficial incision with significant length but no significant width.
- They are caused by a sharp or pointed object, not sharp enough to incise, but pointed enough to make a hole or scratch,
  i.e. remove a portion of the skin's surface, while passing across the skin,
  for example : fingernails, pin, thorn.
- A scratch produced from the tip of the knife or razor can be called a point scratch.

Fingernail abrasions:
They may be parallel linear scratches if the fingers are dragged down the skin.
- When the skin is gripped in a static fashion, fingernail abrasions may be
  » straight or curved
  » 1 to 2 mm breadth,
  » about 0.5 to 1 cm. long,
  » wide at the start,
  » narrow at the end.
- When skin is indented by nails, lateral tension develops in it and it may distort the skin and when the tension is released, the elasticity of the skin makes it return to its original position with the nail mark in the skin.
- The curve may then reverse to form either a straight line or a convexity, but this is always not true.
- Pointed nails are more likely than those with straight edges to give these paradoxical results.

2. Grazes
- Also called sliding, scraping or grinding abrasion
- They are the most common type.
  They occur when there is movement between the skin and some rough surface in contact with it.
- Usually, the skin is uniformly striped off at the start or may be serrated.

- The furrow may be broad at one end, and narrow in the opposite direction
- This is seen in road accident, glancing kick with a boot.
- Many abrasions extend into the dermis, because of the corrugations of the dermal papillae, and bleeding occurs.
- Deep abrasions have a typical punctate or spotty appearance.
- Brush burn or gravel rash -An abrasion caused by violent lateral (tangential) rubbing against a surface.

  e.g. in dragging over the ground .
- It is a scraping injury over a large area.
- "Friction burn" (scuff or brush abrasion) -
  » an extensive, superficial, reddened excoriated area without serous ooze or bleeding and
  » With little or no linear mark.
- It may occur due to tangential contact with a smooth surface or when the skin is covered by clothing.
- Brush burns and friction burns are seen in motor cyclists, persons ejected from vehicles, pedestrians, cyclists thrown forward after the primary impact from a motor vehicle.

3. **Pressure Abrasions**
   - Also known as crushing or friction abrasions
   - They are caused by crushing of the superficial layers of the epidermis and are associated with a bruise of the surrounding area.
   - If the movement of the instrument is around 90° to the skin, a pressure type of abrasion occurs.
   - In this type, the movement is slight and largely directed inwards.
   - **Example**:
     » ligature mark in cases of hanging and strangulation
     » teeth bite

4. **Impact Abrasions**
   - Also known as contact or imprint abrasions
   - They are caused by impact with a rough object, when the force is applied at or near a right angle to the skin surface.
   - If the impact is forcible, the dermis is damaged with an underlying bruise
   - The abrasion is slightly depressed below the surface, unless there is bulging due to underlying contusion or local oedema.
   - If a person strikes a flat and relatively smooth surface, an abrasion can be produced which shows little or no linear markings, as in traffic accidents
   - Example :
     When a person is knocked down by a motor car, the pattern of the radiator grille, a headlamp rim or the tread of the tyre may be seen on the skin, which may contain road dirt, paint flakes, grease, etc

Patterned abrasions:
- Patterned injury is any injury that suggests an inflicting instrument or unique means of its causation.
- Patterned abrasions are produced when the force is applied at right angle to the surface of skin.
- Impact abrasions and pressure abrasions reproduce the pattern of the object causing it and are called patterned abrasions.
- The skin may be compressed into the cavities of the pattern with capillary damage leading to an intradermal bruise,
- The epidermis is scraped away, destroyed or detached.
- They show uneven, longitudinal parallel lines (grooves or furrows) with the epithelium heaped up at the ends of these lines, which indicate the direction in which the force was applied.

- Examples of patterned abrasion are :
  » Skin struck with a weapon having a patterned surface
  » Body falls against a patterned surface
  » When a motor tyre passes over the skin
  » Imprint of bicycle chain,
  » Weave of coarse fabrics,
  » The spiral of electric wires, ropes,
  » Serrated knife,
  » Multi-thonged whip, such as a cat-o-nine-tails, leaves a series of linear abrasions or superficial tears.
- Usually, the pattern and shape are non-specific.
- If there are multiple minor abrasions on a particular area, they can be described together as present over an area of (giving dimensions) on the particular anatomic region.

Age of the Abrasions :
Abrasions heal from the periphery by new growth of epithelial cells.
- The exact age cannot be determined.

Fresh :
- Bright red.

12 to 24 hours:
  » Lymph and blood dries up leaving a bright red scab.

2 to 3 days
  Reddish-brown scab.

4 to 7 days
  Dark brown to browinsh-black scab.
  » Epithelium grows and covers defects under the scab.

After 7 days :
  » Scab dries,
  » shrinks and falls off,
  » leaving a depigmented area underneath, which gets gradually pigmented.

Antemortem and Postmortem Abrasions:
- Postmortem abrasions may be produced after death when a body is dragged away from the scene of crime.
- The distribution of such abrasion depends upon the position of the body while it is being dragged.
- Postmortem abrasions are typically found
  » over the forehead,
  » the prominent points of the face,
  » anterior trunk,
  » backs of hands and
  » the fronts of the lower legs.
- Facial injuries ooze blood, mimicking ante-mortem wounds.
- After death, the abraded epidermis becomes stiff, leathery and parchment-like, brown, more prominent and may be mistaken for burns.
- This is classically seen in ligature mark of hanging and strangulation. Condition where identification is difficult:
- Abrasions produced slightly before or after death cannot be differentiated even by microscopic examination.
- In superficial lesions or when decomposition is advanced, differentiation is difficult.
- On drying, abrasions become dark-brown or even black.
- In a body recovered from water, abrasions may not be seen on first inspection, but they are easily seen after the skin dries.

Difference between antemortem and postmortem abrasions:
  Trait. Antemortem changes. Postmortem changes
  Site: Anywhere on the body. Usually over bony prominence.
  Colour: Bright-reddish brown. Yellowish, translucent, and parchment like.
  Exudation: More; scab slightly raised. Less; scab often lies slightly below the level of skin.
  Microscopic: Intravital reaction and No Intravital reaction and Congestion seen. No congestion.

CIRCUMSTANCES OF INJURIES :
- Abrasions are usually seen in accidents and assaults.
- Suicidal abrasions are rare.
- Sometimes, hysterical women produce abrasions over accessible areas like the front of forearms or over the face to fabricate a false charge of assault.
- Abrasions on the face or body of the assailant indicate a struggle.
- Persons collapsing due to heart attack tend to fall forward and receive abrasions to the eyebrow, nose and cheek, but there will be no injuries on the upper limbs.
- A conscious person when falling puts out his hands to save himself, and abrasions may be produced on the palmar surfaces of the hands.
- The alcoholic tends to fall backwards and strikes his occiput on the ground.

Medicolegal Importance:
1. They give an idea about the site of impact and direction of the force.
2. They may be the only external signs of a serious internal injury.
3. Patterned abrasions are helpful in connecting the wound with the object which produced them.
4. The age of the injury can be determined, which helps to corroborate with the alleged time of assault.
5. In open wounds, dirt, dust, grease or sand are usually present, which may connect the injuries to the scene of crime.
6. Character and manner of injury may be known from its distribution.
a. In throttling, crescentic abrasions due to fingernails are found on the neck.
b. In smothering, abrasions may be seen around the mouth and nose.
c. In sexual assaults, abrasions may be found on the breasts, genitals, inner side of the thighs and around the anus.
d. Abrasions on the face of the assailant indicate a struggle.
e. Abrasions on the victim may show whether the fingernails of the assailant were long, irregular or even broken.

Differential Diagnosis:
1. **Erosions of the Skin Produced by Ants :**
   - Ants produce brown erosions with minute irregular margins of the superficial layers of the skin.
   - They are most commonly found at mucocutaneous junctions, about the eyelids, nostrils, mouth, ears, knuckles, axillae, groin, genitalia and the moist folds of the skin.
   - Examination by hand lens shows multiple crescent-shaped, sand-like bite marks.
   - Each one is separated by normal skin.
   - Vital reaction is not seen.
2. **Excoriations of the Skin by Excreta:**
   - In infants, slight inflammation with excoriation may be seen in the napkin area at the time of the death.
   - After death, these areas become dry, depressed and parchment-like and the colour varies from pale-yellow to deep-copper.

3. Pressure sores.
4. Drying of the skin of the scrotum produces hardened, reddish-brown colouration resembling abrasion.

CONTUSIONS (BRUISES)

Mechanism:
- A contusion is an effusion of blood into the tissues, due to the rupture of blood vessels (veins, venules and arterioles),
- caused by blunt trauma, such as fist, stone, stick, bar, whip, hammer, axe, wooden handle, poker, shod foot,. boot, etc.

Types:
1. Intradermal.
2. Subcutaneous.
3. Deep.

Situation:
- Contusions may be present in all tissues ,but commonly seen in skin , lungs, heart, brain , and muscles.
- The bruise is usually situated in the dermis and subcutaneous tissues, above the deep fascia, often in the fat layer.

Features:

In contusion,
- » there is a painful swelling, and
- » crushing or tearing of the subcutaneous tissues usually without destruction of the skin.
- The extravasated blood is diffusely distributed through the tissue spaces, and the margins are blurred.
- Bruises may be seen in association with abrasions (abraded-contusion) or lacerations.
- When a large blood vessel is injured, a tumour-like mass called haematoma is formed.
- Petechial bruises are finely mottled or stippled.
- If the petechiae become larger and more confident, they are called ecchymoses.
- A fresh bruise is usually tender and slightly raised above the surface of the skin, and even a deep-seated bruise shows some swelling when compared with the opposite limb or part of the body.
- A bruise has lighter colour in the centre because extravasated blood is pushed outward by the impact.

Mongolian spot
- It is a hyperpigmented skin in the lumbosacral region
- It should not be confused with contusion.

Size :
- Bruises vary in size from pinhead to large collections of blood in the tissues.
- The size of a bruise is slightly larger than the surface of the agent which caused it, as blood continues to escape into the area.
- Development of marked tissue swelling in the vicinity of a bruise usually results in loss of its original shape.
- As a general rule, the greater the force of violence used, the more extensive the bruise will be.

Factors modifying size and shape:

1. Condition and Type of Tissue :
- If the part is vascular and loose, a slight degree of violence may cause a large bruise, as there is sufficient space for blood to accumulate.
  Example : in face ,vulva, scrotum.

- If the tissues are strongly supported, and contain firm fibrous tissues and covered by thick dermis, a blow of moderate violence may produce a comparatively small bruise.
  Example : abdomen, back, scalp, palm and soles.
- In boxers and athletes, bruising is much less because of good muscle tone.
- Bruising is relatively more marked on tissues overlying bone, which acts as anvil, with the skin between the bone and the inflicting force.
- Chronic alcoholics bruise easily.
- Bruising of the scalp is better felt than seen.
- Bruising of the scalp with fluctuant centres can simulate depressed fracture.
- Even a severe injury may produce little haemorrhage, if it was preceded by an injury which produced deep shock.
- Resilient areas, such as the abdominal wall and buttock bruise less.
  Condition where bruising is not seen:
- Bruising is not seen if the injured part is thickly covered, or if the weapon used is a yielding one, such as a sand bag.
- Bruising may be absent if the pressure is continued until death occurs.

2. **Age:**
   - Children and old persons bruise easily
   - Softer tissues and loss of subcutaneous tissues
   - Loose delicate skin and flesh
   - cardiovascular changes

3. **Sex :**
   - Women bruise more easily than men, because the tissues are more delicate and subcutaneous fat is more.
   - Fat people bruise easily, because of greater volume of subcutaneous tissue.

4. **Colour of Skin :**

   Fair skinned persons. Dark skinned person
   Clearly seen. Better felt than seen
   - The areas of extravasated blood appear darker even on heavily pigmented negroid skin.
   - If the body is embalmed, skin bruises become more prominent probably
   » by forcing of additional blood into the damaged area,
   » increased transparency of overlying skin, and
   » formation of a dark pigment complex.
   - Contusions appear much more clear in black and white photographs than by direct observation.
   - Colour photographs more truly reproduce contusions

5. **Natural Disease :**
   - When the vessels are diseased as in arteriosclerosis, bruising occurs very easily and may even result from coughing or slight exertion.
   - In children, small bruises may be caused by the violent coughing as in whooping cough.
   » purpura haemorrhagica,
   » leukaemia,
   » haemophilia, in these conditions prominent
   » scurvy, bruising is seen even after a
   » vitamin K deficiency minor trauma
   » prothrombin deficiency
   » phosphorus poisoning.
   - Many old persons, especially those on systemic steroids develop senile ecchymoses all over their bodies, especially on extremities.

6. **Gravity Shifting of the Blood :**
   - Bruises do not always appear at the site of impact.
   - If a deep bruise develops due to crushing of soft tissues against the bone take long time to become visible

   If appear/visible so
   » It may not appear below the actual point of impact
   » It may not appear below the actual point of impact
   » Blood will track along the facial planes
   » Appears where the tissues layers become superficial
   » Ectopic bruising (or) percolated (or) migratory contusion

Black eye (pectacle hematoma)
   - Haemorrhages in the soft tissues around the eyes and in the eyelids may be caused by
   1. direct trauma, such as a punch in the eye,
   2. blunt impact to the forehead, the blood gravitating downwards over the supraorbital bridge,
   3. fracture of the floor of the anterior fossa of the skull.

Battle's sign
   - A bruise behind the ear may indicate a basal fracture, rather than a direct blow behind the ear.

Other examples:
   - In fracture of the jaw, a bruise may appear in the neck.
   - In fracture of the pelvis, a bruise may appear in the thigh.
   - In fracture of the femur, a bruise may appear on the outer side of the lower part of the thigh.
   - A blow to the upper thigh may appear as a bruise above the knee.
   - A kick on the calf of the leg may appear as a bruise around the ankle.

Note:

The site of bruising does not always indicate the site of the violence.

Patterned Bruising :

A patterned contusion is one in which the size and shape of the contusion resembles the mirror image of a portion of the object which caused it.

1. A bruise is usually round, and indicates the nature of the weapon especially when death occurs soon after infliction of injury.
   If the person is living, this pattern may become obscure as the area of bruising tends to extend and merge with adjacent structures.
2. Solid body -round bruise eg: hammer, closed fist
3. Thick stick
   - End-round bruise
   - Length- elongated and irregular bruise
4. Rod

- Stick Two parallel linear haemorrhages
- Whip (railway lines or tram lines)
- The intervening skin appears unchanged, because the rod forcibly dents the tissues inwards and momentarily stretches each side of the dent .
- At line of bruising base of dent compressed tissue
- Vessels gets ruptured vessels not injured
- Blood gets displaced to the sides due to pressure effect

- When the rod is removed and the skin comes back to its normal position, the two sides of the depression remain as contused lines.
- In a bruise produced by a long rigid weapon, e.g., stick, the edges of the bruise may be irregular and the width may be greater due to infiltration of blood in the surrounding tissues along the edges of the bruise.
- A blow with a rigid weapon like a stick on a curved surface of the body, in a region where the soft tissues are particularly pliable, e.g., the buttocks, the contusion is not limited to the maximum convexity of the affected part, but it may extend over the whole of the curved surface.

5. When the body is struck by a broad flat weapon, such as a plank, the edges of the plank may cause parallel bruises in the skin, separated by apparently normal tissue.
6. Bruises caused by blows from whips are elongated, curve over prominences, and may partially encircle a limb or the body. They are seen as two parallel lines, the distance between which is roughly equal to the diameter of the whip.
7. Bruises made by pliable canes are similar to those due to whip, but never encircle a limb or curve round the sides of the body.
8. Bruises from straps, belts or chains, leave a definite imprint.
9. A woven, spiral or plaited ligature may sometimes produce a patterned bruise.
10. Contact injuries from firearms may produce abrasion with bruising indicating the outline of the muzzle of the weapon.
11. Patterned bruising is also seen in motor car accidents.
12. Suction or biting on sides of the neck or the breasts, during erotic love-making or sexual intercourse produces elliptical patterned bruises.
13. In a bruise caused by impact with a patterned object, the haemorrhage which is relatively small, may be sharply defined if it lies in the immediate subepidermal layer, and the pattern is distinct due to translucency because of the thin layer that overlies it.
    - Such contusions are commonly seen when the impacting object has alternating ridges and grooves (such as the tread of a motor tyre in a traffic accident, kick with ribbed, rubber soles of shoes, impact from whips), as the skin will be forced into the grooves and distorted.
    - Intradermal bleeding will occur and the red lines may be produced not by the ridges which are pale as the pressure forces the blood from the small vessels, but by the grooves, by a squeezing or bursting effect on the cutaneous capillaries.
14. Forceful compression with the sole or the heel may imprint an intradermal bruise of the pattern of the sole or heel of the shoe. Kicking and jumping on a person combined is known as **'stomping'**.
15. If a violent blow is struck on a clothed area of the body, or if the clothing is grabbed and twisted over the skin, petechial haemorrhages occur within the skin reproducing the texture of clothing

Delayed Bruising :
- A superficial bruise appears immediately as a dark-red swelling.
- A deep bruise may take several hours, or one or two days to appear and deeper extravasation of blood may never appear.
- Therefore, one more examination should be carried out 48 hours after the first examination, to note bruises of slower development.
- Occasionally, when an injury is produced before death, the bruise may appear some time after death, due to further escape of blood from the ruptured vessels due to gravitation, mainly due to percolation, and rapid haemolysis of stagnant blood, the pigment diffusing locally and producing a stain on the surface (come-out bruise).
- This may explain the difference of opinion between two observers, who have examined the person or the body at different times.

- The pressure of the gases of putrefaction may cause the extravasated blood to extend along the tissue spaces and give rise to a false impression of the extent of antemortem bruising.
- Haemolysis of extravasated red cells and diffusion of pigment into the surrounding tissues may also cause postmortem extension of bruise.
- Therefore, in assessing the extent of bruising, the postmortem interval should be considered.
- The examination of whole body by ultraviolet light will sometimes clearly show otherwise undetectable areas of bruising.
- At autopsy, when the superficial tissues are drained of blood, contusions may become more prominent and extensive than before.
- Surgical removal of the corneas for transplant purposes can cause haemorrhage in the eyelids simulating antemortem trauma.
- Removal of the vitreous soon after death can also cause scleral haemorrhage

Deep Tissue and Organ Contusions:
- All organs can be contused.
- Deep contusions are clearly seen during autopsy, as the blood is drained from blood vessels and also due to postmortem autolytic changes.
    1. A contusion of the brain
    2. initiate enough swelling with gradual accumulation of acid by-products of metabolism,
    3. further swelling and impairment of function,
    4. confusion, coma and death.
- Contusions in vital centres, can be fatal ,even when very small
  e.g Centers which control respiration and blood pressure
  Contusion
  Small contusion of heart Large Contusion
  Serious disturbance of normal.
  Rhythm or stoppage of Inadequate cardiac emptying
  Cardiac action
  Death. Heart Failure
  Of other organs
  Ruptured of that organ
  Slow or rapid bleeding into body cavity
  Death

Additional points
- Sometimes, haemorrhages are seen in areas of lividity on the arms or shoulders of fat persons without evidence of trauma on other parts of the body.
- These haemorrhages are produced by tearing of small veins in the skin when the body is lifted from the scene of death.
- At autopsy blood drains from blood vessels so that the deep bruises may show up against the white areas as the blood in the contusions will not drain

The Age of Bruise:
- A bruise heals by destruction and removal of the extravasated blood.
- The more vascular the area, the smaller the contusion, and the healthier the individual, the more rapid will be the healing.
  Red cells
  Hemolysis
  Haemoglobin
  Hemosiderin. Haematoidin. Bilirubin

Factors affecting colour of contusion include:
1. depth of bleeding,
2. amount of bleeding,
3. environmental lighting, and
4. overlying skin colour.
- The colour change starts at the periphery and extends inwards to the centre.
- At first: Red.
- Few hours to 3 days : Blue.
- 4th day : Bluish-black to brown(hemosiderin).
- 5 to 6 days : Greenish (haematoidin).
- 7 to 12 days : Yellow (bilirubin).
- 2 weeks: Normal.
- The rate of colour change is quite variable, not only between persons, but in the same person and from bruise to bruise
- Bruises in children change colour rapidly and may be completely absorbed in a few days.
- In old people, the healing of bruises is very slow.

IMPORTANT NOTE
- In interpreting the age of a bruise by colour changes, one should be very cautious.
- Subconjunctival ecchymosis does not undergo usual colour changes due to diffusion of atmospheric oxygen through the conjunctival tissue.
- They are at first bright red, then yellow before disappearing.
  A bruise sustained at the time of carbon monoxide poisoning is likely to have a bright-red colour.
- It is difficult to estimate the exact age of bruise with any degree of certainty even by microscopic examination.

Antemortem and postmortem bruising
- Appreciable bruising does not occur after death due to arrest of circulation, but by using great violence, small bruises can be produced up to 2 to 3 hours after death, in areas where the tissues can be forcibly compressed against bone and also in hypostatic area,
  e.g., the back of the scalp, if the body is dropped by on the ground, or on trolleys or postmortem tables.
  Decomposed bodies:
  If a body lies on its back
  If any contusion is present in if blood accumulates in
  the scalp. posterior or dependent half
  of scalp due to gravity
  (hypostasis)
  Leakage of red cells into Blood vessels break down
  Soft tissues with leakage of red cells
  into soft tissues

Erythrocytes in soft tissues are Erythrocytes are hemolyzed
hemolyzed. due to decomposition
Produce a diffuse discoloration of the soft tissues
Becomes impossible to differentiate between
Antemortem contusion and postmortem hypostasis
Table (8-2)difference between hypostasis and bruise

Demonstration of Bruising :
- At autopsy, bruises may not be readily detected or they may be obscured by patches of postmortem lividity, or by the dark colour of the skin.

Medicolegal Importance :
1. Patterned bruises may connect the victim and the object or weapon, e.g., whip, chain, cane, ligature, vehicle, etc.
2. The age of the injury can be determined by colour changes.
3. The degree of violence may be determined from their size.
4. Character and manner of injury may be known from its distribution.
    a. When the arms are grasped, there may be 3 or 4 bruises on one side and one larger bruise on the opposite side, from the fingers and thumb respectively, indicating the position of the assailant in front of, or behind the victim.
    b. Bruising of the arm may be a sign of restraining a person.
    c. Bruising of the shoulder blades indicates firm pressure on the body against the ground or other resisting surface.
    d. In manual strangulation, the position and number of bruises and nail marks may give an indication of the method of attack or the position of the assailant.
    e. Bruising of thigh especially inner aspect, and of genitalia indicates rape.
5. In open wounds, dirt, dust, grease or particles of stone or sand are usually present, which may connect the injuries to the scene of crime

Bruises are of less value than abrasions because:
- Their size may not correspond to the size of the weapon.
- They may become visible several hours or even one to two days after the injury.
- They may appear away from the actual site of injury.
- They do not indicate the direction in which the force was applied.

Complications:
- A contusion may contain 20 to 30 ml. of blood or even more.
- Multiple contusions can cause death from shock and internal haemorrhage.
- Gangrene and death of tissue can result.
- The pooled blood can serve as a good site for bacterial growth, especially by clostridial group.
- Rarely, in severe sudden compression of the subcutaneous tissue, pulmonary fat embolism may occur.

Artificial Bruises :
- Some irritant substances, when applied to skin produce injuries, which simulate bruises.
- They are produced to make a false charge of assault.
  Table (8-3) difference between true bruise and artificial bruise

LACERATIONS
- Lacerations are tears or splits of
  - skin,
  - mucous membrane
  - muscle or internal organs

  produced by application of blunt force to a broad area of the body, which crushed or stretched tissues beyond the limits of their elasticity.
- They are also called tears or ruptures.
  Mechanism:
  impact of the blunt force,
  Sets up traction forces
  Localised portions of tissue are displaced
  tearing of the tissues.
- Unless great force is used, most lacerations require a firm base to act as an anvil for the skin and underlying tissues to be pinned against.
- In lacerations of soft areas, such as the buttock, thigh, calf, abdomen, upper arm, etc., the lacerating agent is either a projecting point or edge, or a completely blunt object is pulled obliquely against the tension of the skin until it tears.
- The object causing a lacerated wound crushes and stretches a broad area of skin, which then splits in the centre.
- The edges are irregular and rough, because of the crushing and tearing nature of the blunt trauma.
- Frequently, the skin, at the margins is abraded due to the flatter portion of the striking object rubbing against the skin as it is indented by the forceful blow.
- A single blow with a blunt weapon may produce more than one lacerated wound, e.g., a single blow over the side of the head may produce lacerated wounds over the parietal prominence, ear and the lower jaw.
- Some lacerations are caused by jagged projections ripping into the skin in the same manner as a blunt knife or axe.

Causes:
They are caused by
- blows from blunt objects,
- by falls on hard surfaces,
- by machinery,
- traffic accidents, etc.

Contused-laceration or bruised-tear.
- In an injury if the force produces bleeding into adjacent tissues, it is called contused-laceration or bruised-tear.

Abraded laceration or scraped tear.
- If the margins are abraded it is called abraded laceration or scraped tear.
- If the blunt force produces extensive bruising and laceration of deeper tissues, it is called "crushing" injury

Types :
Split Lacerations :
- Splitting occurs by crushing of the skin between two hard objects.
- Scalp lacerations occur due to the tissues being crushed between the skull and some hard object, such as the ground or a blunt instrument.

Splits are not undermined, but show tissue bridges.

Incised-like or Incised-looking Wounds :
- Lacerations produced without excessive skin crushing may have relatively sharp margins.
- Blunt force on areas where the
- skin is close to bone, and
- the subcutaneous tissues are scanty,
may produce a wound which by linear splitting of the tissues, may look like an incised wound.
- The sites are the scalp, eyebrows, cheek bones, lower jaw, iliac crest, perineum, and shin
A wound produced by a fall on the knee or elbow with the limb flexed, and by a broken glass or sharp stone also simulates an incised wound.

Stretch Lacerations :
- Overstretching of the skin, if it is fixed, will cause laceration.
- There is localised pressure with pull which increases until tearing occurs and produces a flap of skin, which is peeled off the underlying bone or deep fascia.
- This is seen in the running over by a motor vehicle, and the flap may indicate the direction of the vehicle.
- They can occur from kicking, and also when sudden deformity of a bone occurs after fracture, making it compound.

3. **Avulsion (shearing laceration) :**
   - An avulsion is a laceration produced by sufficient force (shearing force) delivered at an acute angle to detach (tear off) a portion of a traumatised surface or viscus from its attachments.
   - The shearing and grinding force by a weight, such as lorry wheel passing over a limb may produce separation of the skin from the underlying tissues (avulsion) over a relatively large area. This is called "flaying".
   - The underlying muscles are crushed, and the bones may be fractured.
   - The separated skin may show extensive abrasions from the rotating frictional effect of the tyre, but one portion is still in continuity with adjacent skin.
   - Internally, organs can be avulsed or torn off in part or completely from their attachments.
   - Avulsion of scalp is also caused by traction from hair being trapped in machinery.
   - In lacerations produced by shearing forces, the skin may not show signs of injury, but the underlying soft tissue is avulsed from the underlying fascia or connective tissue, producing a pocket which may be filled with blood.
   Example:This is seen usually on the back of the thighs of pedestrians struck by motor vehicles.
   - In a case of extreme avulsion, an extremity or even the head can be torn off the body.

4. **Tears:**
   - Tearing of the skin and tissues can occur from impact by or against irregular or semi-sharp objects, such as
   » door handle of a car.
   » blows bybroken glass,
   » fall over a rough projected object.
   - A tear is deeper at the starting point than at the termination.
   - This is another form of overstretching.

5. **Cut Lacerations :**
   - Cut lacerations may be produced by a heavy relatively sharp-edged instrument such as
   » axe,
   » hatchet,
   » chopper. etc.

The margins are usually abraded with bruising.
- In an impact over the scalp, external laceration may not occur due to the hair, but inner layers of scalp may be lacerated.
- If the instrument is padded or has a broad striking surface, severe fractures of the skull may occur without external laceration.

   Lacerations of the internal organs may be caused by :
- direct injury of the viscera by fragments of fractured bone,
- development of traction shears or strain shears in the viscera,
- stretching of the visceral attachments, and
- hydrostatic forces

   The margins are usually abraded with bruising.
- In an impact over the scalp, external laceration may not occur due to the hair, but inner layers of scalp may be lacerated.
- If the instrument is padded or has a broad striking surface, severe fractures of the skull may occur without external laceration.

   Lacerations of the internal organs may be caused by :
- direct injury of the viscera by fragments of fractured bone,
- development of traction shears or strain shears in the viscera,
- stretching of the visceral attachments, and
- hydrostatic forces

   At point of impact. Other edges
   sharp and turned inwards. Everted , exposing
   hair follicles in the depth.
- Tearing at the ends of lacerations, at angles diverging from the main laceration itself, so-called swallowtails, are frequently noted.

2. Bruising is seen either in the skin or the subcutaneous tissues around the wound.
- If the force is exerted by an object with a downward course, the lower margin of the wound is likely to be bruised more and undermined than the upper.
- Equal undermining of all sides indicates a perpendicular impact.

3. Deeper tissues are unevenly divided with tags of tissues at the bottom of the wound bridging across the margin because different components of soft tissue have different strengths .
- Tissue bridges (bridging fibres) consist of nerves, blood vessels and elastic and connective tissue fibres.

4. Hair bulbs are crushed.
5. Hair and epidermal tags may be driven deeply into the wound.
6. Haemorrhage is less , except in wounds of the scalp, where the temporal arteries bleed freely as they are firmly bound and unable to contract.
7. Foreign matter may be found in the wound.
8. Depth varies according to the thickness of the soft parts at the site of the injury and degree of force applied.
9. The shape and size may not correspond with the weapon or object which produced it.
- A laceration is usually curved; the convexity of the curve points towards the direction of application of force.

a. A blunt round end may cause stellate laceration.
b. A blunt object with an edge, such as a hammer head, may cause crescentic laceration (patterned laceration).
c. Long, thin objects, such as pipes, tend to produce linear lacerations, while objects with flat surfaces produce irregular, ragged, or Y -shaped lacerations

10. If the impact is from an angle, the skin on the side of the wound opposite to the direction of motion is usually torn free or underlined for a variable distance.
- The other side, i.e. the side from which the blow was delivered, will be abraded and bevelled.

- Gaping is seen due to the pull of elastic and muscular tissues.

Age:

Age determination of laceration is difficult unless there are clear signs of healing, such as
- granulation tissue,
- fibroblast ingrowth,
- organising infiltrate.

Medicolegal Importance :
1. The type of laceration may indicate the cause of the injury and the shape of the blunt weapon.
2. Foreign bodies found in the wound may indicate the circumstances in which the crime has been committed.
3. The age of the injury can be determined.

Combinations of Abrasions, Contusions and Lacerations :
- Abrasions, contusions and lacerations are frequently seen together or as integral parts of one another.
- The same object may cause
  » a contusion with one blow,
  » a laceration with second, and
  » an abrasion with a third.
- Sometimes, all three types of injury may result from a single blow.
- Sometimes, an imprint may result from an object, and it may be difficult to determine whether the imprint is primarily an abrasion or a contusion.

Punching:
- Punching, i.e. blows with the clenched fist will produce abrasions and contusions; laceration may occur over bony prominences
  Punches on the face may split the lips, fracture the teeth, nose, jaw or maxilla and produce black eyes.
  Kicking:
- Kicking and stamping injuries are caused by a foot which is either swung or moved downwards (compression) with some force.
- They will produce abrasions, contusions and sometimes lacerations, which are more severe than punching.
- The feet may be used to stamp down on the recumbent body, causing deep injuries to abdominal organs and fractures of ribs and sternum.
- The pattern of the footwear may be imprinted on to the skin

INCISED WOUNDS
- An incised wound (cut, slice) is a clean cut through the tissues, usually the skin and subcutaneous tissues, including blood vessels and caused by sharp- edged instrument.
- The wound is longer than it is deep.

Mechanism:
- It is produced by the pressure and friction against the tissue, by an object having a sharp cutting edge,
  such as knife, razor, scalpel, scissors, sickle, cleaver, sword, etc.
- In this, the force is delivered over a very narrow area, corresponding with the cutting edge of the blade.

Causes:
1. Striking the body with the edge of sharp-cutting weapon,
2. by drawing the weapon, against the body surface, and
3. by using the weapon like a saw in which case there may be more than one cut in the skin at the beginning of the wound which merge into one at the end.

Characters :

1. **Margins :**
   - The edges are
     » cleancut,
     » well-defined and
     » usually everted.
   - The edges may be inverted, if a thin layer of muscle fibres is adherent to the skin as in the scrotum.
   - The edges are free from contusions and abrasions.
   - A dull irregular-edged or nicked cutting edge may produce a wound with irregular, contused, and/or abraded margins, as the wound is caused more by the pressure applied by the weapon than by the cutting edge.
   - A serrated knife may produce a saw-toothed cut on the body, if the blade passes obliquely or at a shallow angle
     The depth of the wound will not show any bridging tissue.

2. **Width :**
   - The width of the wound is greater than the thickness of the edge of the weapon causing it, due to retraction of the divided tissues.

3. **Length :**
   - The length is greater than its width and depth, and has no relation to the cutting edge of the weapon.[L > W,D]
   - A curved weapon like a sickle, produces a stab from the pointed end, and an incised wound from the blade, sometimes with an intervening intact skin.
   - Rarely, there may be a superficial tail (a shallow scratch) at the termination known as tailing of wound which indicates direction.

4. **Shape:**
   - It is usually spindle-shaped due to greater retraction of the edges in the centre.
   - Gaping is
     » greater if the underlying muscle fibres have been cut transversely or obliquely, and
     » less when cut longitudinally.
   - Incised wounds crossing irregular surfaces may be irregular in depth, but will be linear.
   - The wound may take zig-zag course if the skin is loosely attached as in axillary fold,
   - If the blade is curved, the edges will be crescentic.
   - If the surface is convex, the straight-bladed weapon may also produce a crescentic wound.
     Example in occipital region , buttocks.

5. **Haemorrhage:**
   - As the vessels are cut cleanly, the haemorrhage is more.
   - If the artery is completely cut, the bleeding will be more due to its inability to contract or retract.

6. **Direction**
   Incised wounds are deeper at the beginning, because more pressure is exerted on the knife at this point.
   - This is known as the head of the wound.
   - Towards the end of the cut the wound becomes increasingly shallow.
   - This is known as the tailing of the wound, and indicates the direction in which the cut was made.

7. **Bevelling cut**
   If the weapons blade enters obliquely, the wound will have a bevelled margin on one side with undermining (undercut) on the other side so that subcutaneous tissue is visible, indicating the direction from which the blade entered

Beveling can be produced by sharp weapons only.
- If the blade is nearly horizontal, a flap wound is caused.
- It is usually homicidal and may indicate the relative position of the assailant and the victim.

Age of Incised Wound :
In an uncomplicated wound, healing occurs as follows:
- Fresh: Haematoma formation.
- 12 hours: The edges are red, swollen and adherent with blood and lymph; leukocyte infiltration.
- 24 hours : A continuous layer of endothelial cells covers the surface; overlying this a crust or scab of dried clot is seen.

WOUNDS BY GLASS :
- Wounds produced by glass are lacerated, but can resemble incised and stab wounds.
- If a sharp-pointed piece of glass enters by its point, the wound has a stab-like appearance.
- Margins of the wound will almost always show tiny side cuts due to irregularities of the glass.
- Particles of glass may be found in the wound
  Assault with broken glasses or bottles show multiple irregular incised-type wounds of variable depth and severity.
  Medicolegal Importance:
1. They indicate the nature of the weapon (sharp-edged).
2. The age of the injury can be determined.
3. They give an idea about the direction of the force.
4. Position and character of wounds may indicate mode of production, i.e., suicide, accident, homicide.

Features of self-inflicted wounds:
1. They are multiple and parallel or nearly so, in any one area.
2. They are uniform in depth and direction.
3. They are relatively minor.
4. The fatal wounds are present on several limited accessible areas of the body,
5. such as the front of the neck, wrists, groin, and occasionally on the back of legs or on chest.
6. They avoid vital and sensitive areas like eyes, lips, nose, and ears.
7. Hesitation marks or tentative cuts or trial wounds:
- They are cuts which are multiple, small and superficial often involving only the skin and are seen at the beginning of the incised wound .

Additional important points:
- The sites of election of suicidal incised wounds are:
  » throat,
  » wrist and
  » front of chest.
- The fatal incisions are usually made with great violence, and the large gaping wound produced by suicide should not be mistaken for homicidal wounds.
- When a safety razor blade is used, unintentional cuts are found on the fingers, where the blade has been gripped
  In a decomposed body, it is difficult to differentiate a laceration from an incised wound.
- When a body with incised wounds, stab wounds, or lacerations is immersed in water soon after infliction of injuries, the blood in the wounds is lysed by water and passes into the water, and whether the injuries are antemortem or postmortem cannot be made out.Table(8-4) Difference between suicidal and homicidal cut throat wounds

CHOP WOUNDS (Slash wounds):
- They are deep gaping wounds caused by a blow with the sharp-cutting edge of a fairly heavy weapon, like a hatchet, an axe, sword, broad heavy knife, chopper, sabre, or meat cleaver.
- The dimensions of the wound correspond to the cross section of the penetrating portion of the blade.
- Undermining occurs in the direction towards which the chop is made
- Usually the lower end (heel) of the axe strikes the surface first, which produces a deeper wound than the upper (toe) end.
- The deeper end indicates the position of the assailant.
- The margins are sharp and may show slight abrasion and bruising with marked destruction of underlying organs.
- If the edge is blunt, the margins are ragged and bruised.
- In the skull, the undermined edge of the fracture defect is the direction in which the force is exerted, and the slanted edge is the side from which the force was directed.
- In case of long bones, the bone fragments get loosened on the opposite side of the force.
  With axe and heavy cutting weapons,
  the initial impact slices cleanly through the bone on one edge.
  The rebound removal of the weapon is at a slightly different angle,
  either from deliberate intention or from relative movements between bone and blade.
  This cracks off an irregular fragment of bone of the opposite side
  the defect has one smooth and one rough edge particularly near the ends of the chop wound.
- If the extremities are attacked, there may be complete or incomplete amputation of the fingers or other bones, and the joints may be separated or disarticulated.
- If the chopping blow is tangential, a disk-shaped portion of bone or skin or soft tissue may be cut away
  The neck may be almost completely separated.
- Most of these injuries are homicidal and usually inflicted on the exposed parts of the body like the head, face, neck, shoulders and extremities.
- Accidental injuries are caused by
  » power fans,
  » band saws or ship
  » aeroplane propellers, which may lacerate the soft tissues extensively or amputate parts of the body.
- Suicidal chop injuries are very rare

STAB OR PUNCTURED WOUNDS

- A stab wound is produced when force is delivered along the long axis of a narrow or pointed object, such as
  » knife, dagger, sword, chisel, scissors, nail, needle, spear, at Tow, screw driver, etc. into the depths of the body.
- The wound is deeper than its length and width on the surface of skin.
- The most common stabbing instruments are
  » kitchen knives,
  » sheath knives
  » pen-knives.

Types :

They are called
1. Puncture wounds
- When soft tissues are involved.
2. Penetrating wounds,
- when they enter a cavity of the body or a viscus.
- When the weapon enters the body on one side and comes out from the other side,
3. Perforating wounds or through-and-through puncture wounds .
- The wound of entry is larger with inverted edges, and the wound of exit is smaller with everted edges, due to tapering of blade.
- The victim of a fatal penetrating injury may not show signs and symptoms of injury until many hours have passed.

Characters :

1. Margins:
- The edges of the wound are clean-cut and inverted.
- The margins can be everted when the wound is situated over the fatty area, such as protuberant abdomen or gluteal region.
- There is usually no abrasion or bruising of the margins, but in full penetration of the blade, abrasion and bruising(hilt mark) may be produced by the hilt-guard (metal piece between the blade and handle) striking the skin
- The margins may be abraded and ragged if the cutting edge is blunt.
- The mark will be
  » symmetrical. - if the knife strikes the skin at the right angle.
  » Prominent above the stab wound- if the knife strikes in a downward
  » angle.
  » Below the stab wound - if the knife strikes in an upward angle.
- In oblique stab wounds, a knife striking from the right will have an abrasion on the right side and vice versa.
  In such cases, the suspected knife should be examined to determine the compatibility of the shape of the abrasion around the stab wound, with the handle of the knife in question.

2. Length :
- The length of the wound is slightly less than the width of the weapon up to which it has been driven in, because of stretching of the skin.
  [Length of wound<width of weapon]
- For measuring the length of the stab wound, the edges of the wound should be brought together.
- Deliberate lateral, forward, or backward movement of the weapon during its withdrawal from the body tends to widen the wound, and the length will be more than the maximum width of the blade.
- If the instrument is thrust in, and is then completely withdrawn with the cutting edge dragging against one end, the wound would be extended superficially, producing a tail.

3. Width:
    - The maximum possible width of the knife blade can be approximately determined if the edges of a gaping wound are brought together
    - Elasticity or laxness of the skin can change the width by one to two millimetres
    - Shape is most commonly elliptical
    - A stab wound inflicted when the skin is stretched will be long and thin, which becomes shorter and broader when the skin is relaxed.
4. Depth
    - The depth (length of track) is greater than the width and length of the external injury.
    - The depth of a stab wound is usually equal to, or less than the length of the blade that was used in producing it,
    but on yielding surfaces like the anterior abdominal wall, the depth of the wound may be greater, because the force of the thrust may press the tissues underneath
    - The breast, buttocks and thigh are indented by a full thrust, and the depth of wound may exceed the length of the weapon.
    - It is not safe to find out the depth of a stab wound by introducing a probe, because it may disturb a loose clot and may lead to fatal haemorrhage, or cause serious damage and may produce multiple false wound tracks.
    Important note:
    - Many of the internal organs are not fixed but have a variable degree of mobility.
    - This should be taken into account when estimating the depth of the wounds.
    - After the withdrawal of the weapon, the wound tends to close by expansion of the tissues along the track.
    - The depth should be determined in the operation theatre when the wound is repaired.
    Variations in position of viscera:
    - The viscera of a dead body on the autopsy table are not in the same positions, as when the same person was alive and in standing position, or was bent over in a state of emotional tension, at the time of an assault.
    - Example:
    » When tense, the abdomen is usually contracted, and the distance between the abdominal wall and the spine is reduced.
    » When the same body is on the autopsy table, the abdominal wall is relaxed and this distance increases.
    » Similarly, the anatomical relationship between the lungs, liver and other viscera is not the same as when the person is bent at the hips and when lying flat.
    - stab wound on
    anterior wall of the chest.   back of the chest,
    the postmortem depth is greater   the depth of the
    than it was during life.   wound is less
    Due to lung collapse.   . As the lung collapse
                                         posteriorly
    The force required to inflict stab wound:
    - It is subjective, and can only be stated in comparative terms, such as
    - slight force,
    - moderate force,
    - considerable force, and
    - extreme force.

The depth of stab depends on:
1. Condition of the knife:
   - The sharpness of the extreme tip of the knife is the most important factor in skin penetration.
   - A thin, slender, double-edged knife will penetrate more deeply than an equally sharp, wide, single-edged blade inserted with the same force.
   - A blunt-pointed instrument requires considerable force to puncture the skin and penetrate the soft tissues.
2. The resistance offered by the tissues or organs:
   - Most resistance to knife penetration is given by
     » Bone
     » Calcified cartilage
     » Skin followed by muscles
   - Uncalcified cartilage is easily penetrated by a sharp knife, though more force is required.
   - A Forceful stab from a strong, sharp knife can penetrate the rib, sternum or skull.
3. Clothing:
   - The amount of clothing and its composition,
     e.g. multiple layers of tough cloth,
     leather belts,
     thick leather jackets,
     coats, etc
     Require greater forces.
4. The speed of thrust of the knife.
5. Stretched skin
   - It is easier to penetrate than lax skin, e.g. chest wall.
6. When the knife strikes the skin at right angle,
   - it usually penetrates more deeply than when it strikes from some acute angle.

7. When the knife penetrates the skin rapidly,
     e.g. if the body falls or runs on to the blade,
     The momentum of the forward moving body is sufficient to cause fatal injury.
   - However, the knife must be sharp-pointed and held firmly so as to penetrate easily, as a blunt knife held loosely will be turned aside by the approaching body.
     Track of stab wound:
   - A piece of pliable tube
     introduced gently into the stab wound
     if it goes in easily
     reveal the true track.
   - Later, the tubing can be made more rigid and straight by inserting a probe into it.
   - Dissection in the tissues parallel to, but away from the wound, will reveal the track.
   - Radio-opaque material or dyes can be injected into stab wounds to demonstrate the wound track by X-rays.
   - Rarely, a single stab may produce multiple skin wounds:
     Example:
     » A tangential stab of the arm, which passes through superficial tissues and then re-enters the chest wall,
     » A knife passing through the edge of a sagging female breast re-entering thorax.

5. Shape:
    - The size and shape of a stab wound in the skin is dependent on
        » the type of implement,
        » cutting surface,
        » sharpness,
        » width and shape of the weapon,
        » body region stabbed,
        » the depth of insertion,
        » the angle of withdrawal,
        » the direction of thrust,
        » the movement of the blade in the wound,
        » cleavage direction,
        » the movement of the person stabbed, and
        » the condition of tension or relaxation of the skin .

Cleavage lines of Langer:
- Stab wounds and incised wounds are slit-shaped with two acute angles, or gape open depending on their location and their orientation, with regard to the so-called cleavage lines of Langer.
- The pattern of fibre arrangement of the intermingled dermal collagen and elastic fibres is called the cleavage direction or lines of cleavage of the skin, and their linear representation on the skin are called Langer's lines, which is almost the same in all persons.
- In the dermal layer of skin ,
    » Cleavage lines are mostly in parallel rows
    » In extremities they run longitudinally
    » In the neck and trunk circumferentially
- A stab wound
    » which runs parallel to the cleavage lines will remain slit-shaped and narrow and the dimensions of the blade will be represented with considerable accuracy.
    » which cuts through the cleavage lines transversely will gape.
    » If the knife is inserted in an oblique plane, the skin defect is wider and the wound may gape asymmetrically and assume a semicircular or crescentic shape.
- To ascertain the shape of the instrument, the edges of a wound may be manually approximated with slight twisting or they may be held together with a transparent adhesive tape.
- The resulting slit is considerably longer than the original oval-shaped wound
- This will counter the claim of the defence that the suggested knife could not have produced a stab wound of the type as seen before reconstruction.
- The dimensions of the gaping wound are not useful to assess the shape of the blade. Weapons causing stab wounds:
- The shape of the wound usually corresponds to the weapon used, but the shape of the wounds made by the same weapon may differ on different parts of the body.

1. single-edged weapon:
   - If it is used,
     » the surface wound will be triangular or wedge-shaped, and
     » one angle of the wound will be sharp,
     » another angle rounded, blunt or squared off.
   - Blunt end of the wound may have small splits in the skin at each end of the corner, so-called "fishtailing", if the back edge of the blade is stout.
   Some stab wounds caused by single-edged weapons have bilateral pointed ends like those due to double-edged weapons.

This is due to:
   a. The initial penetration by the knife point to a depth of about one cm., first produces a dermal defect with sharp angles at each end.
      As the knife penetrates more deeply,
      the end in contact with the end in contact with
      cutting edge of the blade noncutting surface of
      . Knife
      continues to be sharply   Also sharply angulated
      angulated.
      Because dull surface does not
      Imprint it's shape to the skin defect
      further separation of the skin which
      continues to be torn along the course of its original direction.
   b. he knife penetrates the skin at an oblique angle.
   c. Many single-edged knives have a cutting edge on both sides at the tip.
   - In some single-edged knives, both ends are blunt.
   - This is caused if the knife penetrates to full length up to the guard, because of ricasso (short, unsharpened section of blade between the cutting edge and guard).
   - By examination of a single wound, it is not possible to say whether it was caused by a single-edged or double-edged weapon.
   - If multiple stabs are produced by a single-edged weapon, examination of all the stab wounds will reveal the single-edged nature of the weapon.
2. double-edged weapon
   - If a double-edged weapon is used, the wound will be elliptical or slit-like and both angles will be sharp or pointed.
   - If the knife penetrates to full length up to the guard, one or both edges may be blunt because of ricasso.
3. A round object like the spear may produce a circular wound.
4. A round blunt-pointed object, such as a pointed stick, or metal rod may produce a circular surface wound with inverted ragged and bruised edges.
5. A pointed square weapon may produce a cross-shaped injury, each of the 4 edges tearing its way through the tissues.
6. A fall on a pointed article, e.g., pieces of broken glass, will produce a wound with irregular and bruised margins, and fragments of glass may be found embedded in the soft tissues.
7. Stab wounds inflicted with a broken bottle, appear as clusters of wounds of different sizes, shapes, and depth, with irregular margins, and varying depth.
8. Stabbing with a fork produces clusters of 2 or 3 wounds depending upon the number of prongs on the fork.
9. A screwdriver will produce a slit-like tab wound with squared ends (rectangular) and abraded margins.

10. A stab wound through a crease or fold in the skin, such as through a sagging abdomen or female breast, crease of the armpit or groin near the scrotum are likely to result in an atypical injury.
11. Thick relatively blunt-edged blades, e.g., bayonets, may produce cross-shaped stab wounds,
12. Ice-picks or similar instruments produce stab wounds, resembling small calibre bullet wounds.
13. Irregularly-shaped stab wounds such as L or V -shaped may be mistaken to be produced by two distinct stabbings in the same location.
14. If the scissors is closed, the tip of the scissors splits rather than cuts the skin, producing a linear stab wound with abraded margins.
- Deep penetration will produce 'Z'-shaped wounds.
- If the screw holding the two blades is projecting, there are small lateral splits in the wound centre.
- If the two blades of the scissors are separated, each thrust will produce two triangular stab wounds.
15. A knife with a serrated back edge will produce a stab wound, the back edge of which may be torn or ragged.

6. **Direction :**

   When the knife penetrates at an angle, the wound will have a bevelled margin on one side unde mining (undercut) on the other so that subcutaneous tissue is visible, indicating the direction from which the knife entered.
   - In solid organs like the liver, the track made by the weapon is better seen.
   - The principal direction should be noted first and other next, e.g., backwards and to the right.

   - If the weapon is partially withdrawn and thrust again in a new direction, two or more punctures are seen in the soft parts with only one external wound.
   - If the wound is perforating, it should be described in sequential order:
     » the wound of the entrance,
     » the path of the wound track, and
     » the wound of exit.
   - If the wound is penetrating it s described as,
     » the wound of entrance,
     » the depth
     » direction of wound track, and
     » specific termination.

Complications :
1. External haemorrhage is slight but there may be marked internal haemorrhage or injuries to internal organs.
2. The wound may get infected due to the foreign material carried into the wound.
3. Air embolism may occur in a stab wound on the neck which penetrates jugular veins.
- Air is sucked into the vessels due to the negative pressure.
4. Pneumothorax.
5. Asphyxia due to inhalation of blood.

Concealed Puncture Wounds :
- These are puncture wounds caused on concealed(hidden) parts of the body, such as nostrils, fontanella, fornix of the upper eyelids, axilla, vagina, rectum, and nape of the neck.
- Fatal penetrating injuries can be caused without leaving any readily visible external marks,
  e.g .. thrusting a needle or pin into the brain
- through the fontanelles,
- through the inner canthus of the eye, or
- into the medulla through the nape of the neck.
- These injuries may not be detected unless searched carefully.

Examination :
The following points should be noted :
1. Identification and labelling of cuts and damage to clothing.
2. Distribution of blood stains.
3. Removal of clothing, layer by layer.
4. Identification and labelling of wounds.
5. Wounds:
a. Position (height from heels),
b. location (measurements from fixed anatomical landmarks),
c. description including margins, size, shape, ends, extension,
d. direction,
e. depth,
f. trauma to viscera,
g. estimation of force required,
h. foreign bodies.
- To indicate the general character of the instrument which inflicted the stab wound, the term "incised' or 'lacerated' should be included in the description of the stab wound, e.g., 'incised-stab wound', 'lacerated-stab wound', etc.
- Probes should not be thrust into deeper tissues before examination of thoracic and abdominal organs in situ.
- Organs should not be removed until they are examined in situ for injuries associated with the wound track.
- The relationship between the wound and weapon can be established by the shape,width,length, and presence of blood on the weapon.
- When a victim is stabbed multiple times and bleeds heavily, the last stab wound inflicted may appear bloodless. This causes difficulty in deciding whether this wound was inflicted before. during, or soon after death.
- If the knife is found embedded in the body, the thumb and index finger should grasp the sides of the handle immediately adjacent to the skin to remove it, to preserve fingerprints of the assailant on the handle of the weapon.
- When multiple stab wounds are present, they should be numbered and photographed.
- A sketch or a printed body diagram should be used.
  Incised-stab wound:
- Incised-stab wound is a wound, which
  » starts as an incised wound and
  » ends as a stab wound by the sudden thrust of the blade into the body, (or)starts as a stab wound and

- » becomes an incised wound as the knife is pulled out of the body at a shallow angle to the skin surface producing an incised wound .
- If a nick or a pork-shaped cut is present at the end of the stab wound opposite to the incised portion, then the wound has started as an incised wound and ended as a stab wound.
- If the fork is at the end of the stab wound where the incised wound arises, then the wound has started as a stab wound .
- The external and internal appearances of a stab wound help to give an opinion upon:
- » dimensions of the weapon,
- » the type of weapon,
- » the taper of the blade,
- » movement of the knife in the wound,
- » the depth of the wound,
- » the direction of the stab, and
- » the amount of force used.
  An example of description of stab wound:
- Stab wound, wedge-shaped on the right upper chest, placed obliquely, with the inner end lower than the upper outer end.
- Length was 4 cm.
- The maximum width at the centre was 5 mm.
- The centre of the wound was just below the line joining the nipples, being 5 cm. from the midline, 6 cm. from the right nipple, and 18 cm. below the right collar bone.
- The inner end was sharp and the outer blunt.
- The lower margin was undermined.
- A track is established on the right anterior thoracic wall, passes through the fifth interspace, through the upper lobe of the right lung to a depth of 7 cm.
- A right haemothorax of 400 ml of fluid and clotted blood is present

Examination of the Weapon:

The doctor should note :
- the length, width and thickness of the blade,
- whether single-edged or double-edged,
- the degree of taper from hilt to tip,
- the nature of the back edge in a single"edged weapon, e.g. squared-off. serrated, etc.,
- the face of the hilt guard adjacent to the blade,
- any grooving, serration or forking of the blade, and
- sharpness of the extreme tip of the blade and the cutting edge.

Absence of blood stains on knife:
- In some cases of stabbing, the blade of the knife may not be bloodstained.
  Example:
- In solid organs, bleeding occurs only after the knife is withdrawn, because bleeding is prevented by the pressure of the knife.
- In such cases, analysis of wiping of the blade might still yield sufficient tissue to perform at least limited DNA analysis and typing.
- If clothing is present, it may also wipe off the blood.
- An injury may cause deep shock and severe circulatory collapse.
- Subsequently, even if a deeply penetrating wound is produced, there may be little bleeding.
- When a victim is stabbed multiple times and bleeds heavily, the last stab wound inflicted may appear bloodless
- Some injuries cannot be divided clearly into stab or incised wounds, but may exhibit features of both.

Medicolegal Importance :
1. The shape of the wound may indicate the class and type of the weapon which may have caused the injury.
2. The depth of the wound will indicate the force of penetration.
3. Direction and dimensions of the wound indicate the relative positions of the assailant and the victim.
4. The age of the injury can be determined.
5. Position, number and direction of wounds may indicate manner of production, i.e., suicide, accident, or homicide.
6. If a broken fragment of weapon is found. it will identify the weapon or will connect an accused person with the crime.

Autopsy:

Clothes:
- Examine Clothes while still on the body and its relation to injuries on the body.
- Sketches / photographs should be taken
- Cuts in clothes should be measured and described.
- Describe blood stains on clothes site , shape ,direction,margins,etc.of injuries should be described.
- Length of the injury should be measured with and without edge opposition.
- Distance of injuries from heel level should be measured.
- Hair and blood samples should be retained.

Internal:
- Dissection of tissues layer by layer parallel to, but away from the wound will reveal the track .
- Measure blood in the cavities.

CIRCUMSTANCES OF INJURIES:

SUICIDE :
- Suicidal stab wounds are found over accessible areas of the body.
- The common site is the chest over the heart region.
- The depth is variable, some are superficial and others enter the pericardium or heart.
- The suicide may not withdraw the point of the weapon from the skin, and stab himself repeatedly in different directions through the same skin wound.
- Rarely one stroke is fatal, and the knife may be found sticking in the wound.
- In many cases, even multiple stabs do not cause death and the person may resort to other methods which present a puzzling picture.
- Stab wounds of the head are rare.
- Suicidal stab wounds of the spine, abdomen, neck and extremities are rare.
- In suicide, there are no corresponding cuts or rents on clothings on part of the body which is normally covered by clothes, as a person who commits suicide exposes his body by opening his clothes and then inflicts wounds.
- In some suicides, the victim may be able to conceal the weapon.
- Common methods of suicide are:
- poisoning,
- hanging, burning,

- » drowning,
- » jumping from a height,
- » stabbing and cutting and
- » railway injuries.

HARA-KIRI:
- It is an unusual type of suicide.
- Here the victim inflicts a single large wound on the abdomen with a short sword while in a sitting position (or) falls forward upon a ceremonial sword and pulls out intestines.
- To produce impalement on a knife, there should be enough momentum by the victim moving toward the knife and it would need to be fixed firmly in some way.
- The sudden evisceration of the internal organs causes a sudden decrease of intra-abdominal pressure and cardiac return, producing sudden cardiac collapse.

HOMICIDE:
- Most deaths from stab wounds are homicidal, especially if found in an inaccessible area.
- The wounds are multiple, widely scattered and deeply penetrating, involving the chest and abdomen.
- In case of a sudden surprise attack, a single wound is found at a vital spot.
- If there is a struggle, there may be a number of wounds, sometimes associated with defence cuts on the hands.
- These wounds are usually seen on the face or neck, and may be far away from the fatal injury.
- Homicidal stab wounds of the chest may have any direction, but the common direction is at an angle from left to right and from above downwards.
- Fatal stab wounds of the right chest usually injure the right ventricle, aorta or right atrium.
- Stab wounds of the left chest usually involve the right ventricle when parasternal, and left ventricle as the stab wounds become more lateral and inferior.
- Severing of the left anterior descending coronary artery is rapidly fatal.
- Most stab wounds of the heart and lungs occur over the front of the chest, rarely the sides, and least on the back.
- Stab wounds of the lower chest can injure the heart and lungs and also abdominal viscera.

OVERKILL HOMICIDE
- In overkill homicide, the assailant continues stabbing beyond the victim's death .
- When a knife is thrown at a person, the skin resistance will cause significant loss of its kinetic energy and the stab may not be deep because of further resistance of the internal tissues.
- Post Mortem stab wounds do not show bruising and are often yellow, or tan, due to absence of tissue perfusion, parchmented and sharply defined.

ACCIDENT:
- Accidental wounds are rare.
- They are caused by falling against projecting sharp objects like glass, nails, etc., or a person may be gored by the horns of a bull, buffalo, etc.
- When the knife penetrates the skin rapidly, eg. if the body falls or runs on to the blade, the knife does not need to be held rigidly in order to prevent it being pushed backwards.
- Its inertia, if the tip is sharp, is quite sufficient to hold it in place.
- A moving sharp object striking the person may produce a stab wound.
- In accidental stabbing, the weapon should be anchored or held firmly.
- The following factors are helpful to determine whether the wounds are suicidal, accidental or homicidal.
1. The nature, direction, extent and situation of the wounds.
2. The presence of foreign matter in the wound or adherent to the margins.
3. The nature of the suspected weapon or instrument.
4. Scene of the crime.

Table (8-7) Difference between suicidal, homicidal and accidental wounds:

DEFENCE WOUNDS :
- Defence wounds result due to the immediate and instinctive reaction of the victim to save himself.

They are classified into two types:
1. Active defence wounds are caused when the victim tries to grasp the weapon.
2. Passive defence wounds are caused when the victim raises the hands, arms or legs.

Active defence wounds:
- If the weapon is sharp, the injuries will depend upon the type of attack, whether stabbing or cutting.
- In stabbing with a single-edged weapon, if the weapon is grasped, a single cut is produced on the palm of the hand or on the bends of the fingers or thumb.
- If the weapon is double-edged, cuts are produced both on the palm and fingers.
- The cuts are usually irregular and ragged, because the skin tension is loosened by gripping of the knife.
- A typical knife defence wound may be seen in the web between the base of the thumb and index finger, when the blade is grasped.

Passive defence wounds:
- When attacked with a blunt object, most persons will attempt to protect their eyes, head and neck by raising their arms, flexing their elbows and covering the head and neck, or try to grasp the weapon.
- As a result bruises and abrasions are produced on the extensor or ulnar surfaces of the forearms, wrists, backs of the hands, knuckles and lateral/posterior aspects of the upper arms.
- Fractures of the carpal bones, metacarpals and digits may occur.
- Defence wounds may be found rarely on the shins and feet if the victim was lying on the ground usually face up, as he kicks at the assailant.
- The arms and posterior aspects of lower limbs and back may be injured as the victim curls into a ball with flexion of spine, knees and hips to protect the anterior part of the body and genitals.

Important points :
- Defence wounds indicate homicide.
- In the female, they suggest sexual assault.
- Defence wounds are absent if the victim is unconscious, or is taken by surprise, or attacked from the back, or under the influence of alcohol or drugs.

Offensive Manual Injuries:
- Abrasions and contusions over the knuckles can be sustained due to offensive efforts by the victim, or by his defensive efforts.
- Ragged knuckle lacerations on the victim indicate that his fist struck the assailant's anterior teeth when he struck a blow on the latter's open mouth.
- Fractures of the fourth and fifth metacarpals (knuckle fractures) may occur when the assailant is punched on his head or chin.
- In manual assault, the hands of the suspected assailant may show injuries indicative of or compatible with his involvement in assault.

SELF-INFLICTED AND FABRICATED WOUNDS:
- Self-inflicted wounds are those inflicted by a person on his own body.
- Fabricated wounds (fictitious, forged or invented wounds) are those which may be produced by a person on his own body (self-inflicted), or by another with his consent.

Motive :

They may be produced for the following reasons.
1. To charge an enemy with assault or attempted murder.
2. To make a simple injury appear serious.
3. By the assailant to pretend self-defence or to change the appearance of wounds, which might connect him with the crime.
4. By policemen and watchmen acting in collusion with robbers to show that they were defending the property.
5. In thefts by servants or messengers for the above reason.
6. By prisoners, to bring a charge of beating against officers.
7. By recruits to escape military service.
8. By women to bring a charge of rape against an enemy.

Types of wounds :
- Fabricated wounds are mostly incised wounds, and sometimes contusions, stab wounds and burns.
- Lacerated wounds are rarely fabricated.
- Incised wounds are usually superficial, multiple and parallel, and are of equal depth at origin and termination.
- They avoid vital and sensitive areas like the eyes, lips, nose and ears.
- The direction is from behind forwards on the top of the head, from above downwards on the outer side of the upper arm, from below upwards on the front of forearms, variable on the legs and vertical on the abdomen and chest.
- Some mentally disordered persons may inflict hundreds of small wounds upon themselves.
- Paranoid schizophrenics with a strong religious flavour to their delusions may remove penis, scrotum and testes.
- Stab wounds are usually multiple and superficial and seen about the left arm or shoulder and sometimes on the chest.
- Burns are superficial and seen usually on the left upper arm.
- The clothes are not cut and if cuts are seen they are not compatible with the nature of the wounds.

CASE:

A youth alleged that he had been the subject of a murderous attack and had received a number of letters over a long period threatening him with death. He had been placed under police protection. His story was that he had been followed by a man, and when he walked into a stairway he was brutally attacked with a razor. He shouted for help, and his assailant, whom he described in detail, ran away. He was in a weak and frightened state when he reported the matter to the police, and was bleeding from wounds in his back.

On a medical exam the wounds consisted of a number of fine cuts just penetrating the skin between his shoulder-blades, more or less parallel to one another and apparently made from below upward by a right-handed man.

They were undoubtedly self-inflicted, by means of a sharp instrument such as a razor used very carefully. On repeated questioning, he admitted he had made the cuts by fixing a razor-blade on the end of a cleft stick and doing the job by adjusting two mirrors. The various threatening letters were in his own handwriting. Later, he duly confessed to the police.

Therapeutic Wounds :

- These are wounds produced by doctors during the treatment of a patient, such as
  » surgical stab wounds of the chest for insertion of chest tubes,
  » stab wounds of the abdomen for drains,
  » thoracotomy and laparotomy incisions,
  » Incisions on the wrists, antecubital fossa and ankles, and
  » tracheostomy incisions.
- Some of these wounds may be mistaken for traumatic wounds,
  e.g. a surgical stab wound of the chest for putting a drainage tube.
- Sometimes, a traumatic wound may be enlarged and included in the surgical procedure, or a drainage tube may be put in a homicidal stab wound.

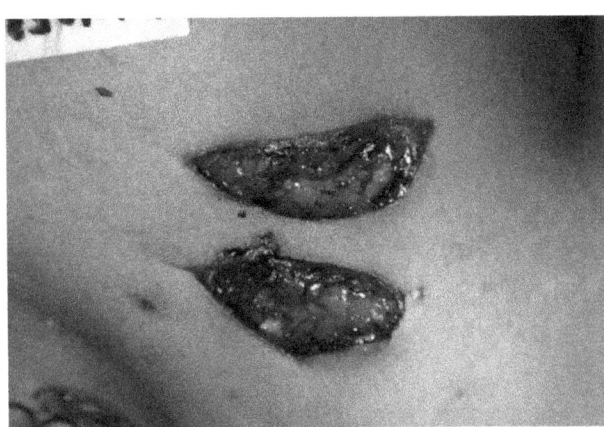

Fig(8.1) Stab wound

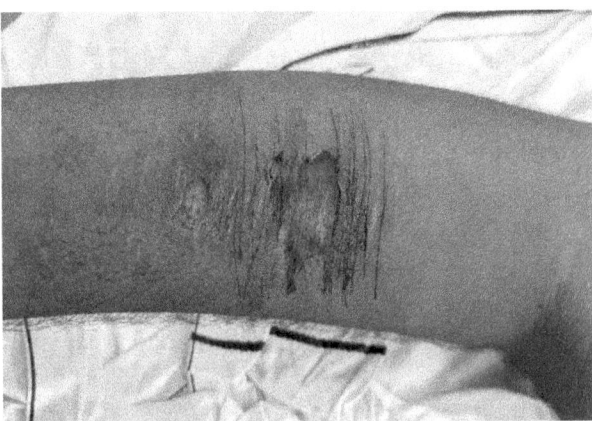

Fig(8.2) Hesitation cuts

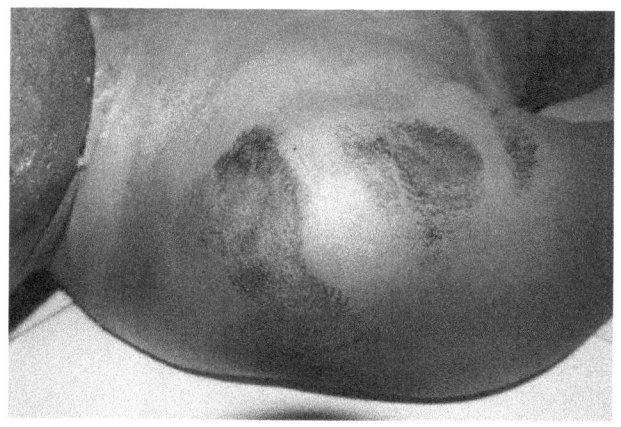
Fig(8.3) Grazed abbrasion

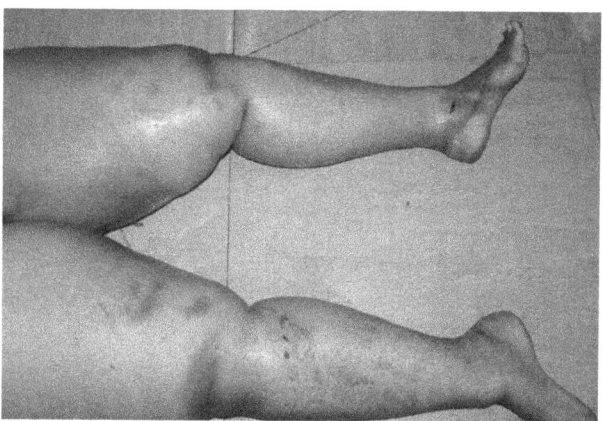
Fig(8.4) Multiple Bruises

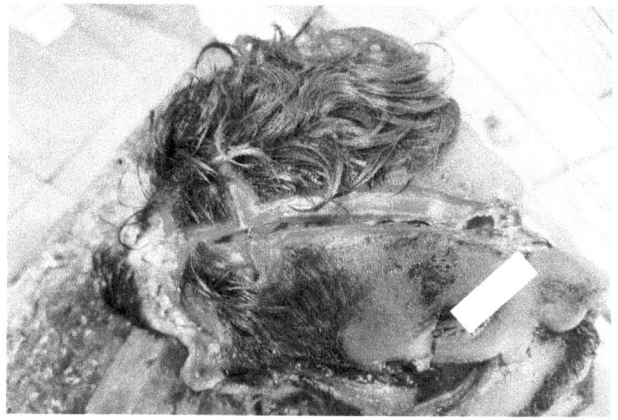
Fig(8.5) Chop wounds

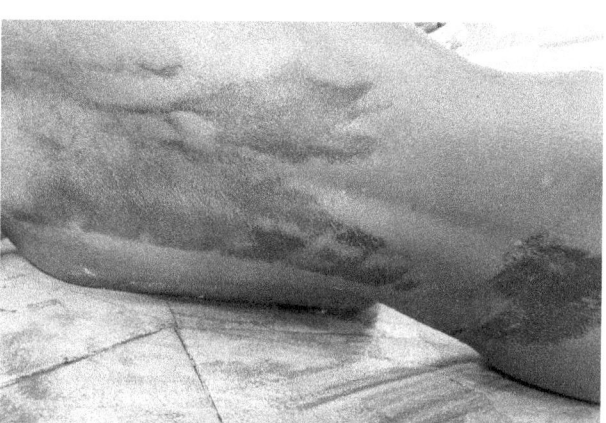
Fig(8.6) Tyre Mark

Courtesy: Professor, Dr. Chandrasekar, MMC, Madurai.
Associate professor, Dr.Sadhasivam, MMC, Madurai.

CHAPTER - 09
FORENSIC BALLISTICS

- A firearm is any weapon which discharges a missile by the expansive force of the gasses produced by burning of an explosive substance.
- Forensic ballistics is the science dealing with the investigation of firearms, ammunition and the problems arising from their use.
(Ammunition-the material fired, scattered, dropped, or detonated from any weapon)
Proximal (internal) ballistics is the study of firearms and projectiles,
Intermediate (exterior) ballistics is the study of the motion of a projectile after it leaves the gun barrel till the time it hits the target.
Terminal ballistics involves the study of behavior of missiles once they penetrate their targets.
Wound ballistics is the study of the effects of missiles on living tissue.

Classification :
According to the condition of barrel :
  I. Rifled weapons:
  1. Rifles:
  a. Air and gas-operated rifles.
  b. 0.22 rifles.
  c. Military and sporting rifles.
  2. Single-shot target-practice pistols.
  3. Revolvers.
  4. Automatic pistols.
  5. True automatic weapons (machine guns).
  II. Smooth-bored weapons (shotgun).
  1. Cylinder bore.
  2. Choke bore.
  3. Paradox (hammered, hammerless).
  4. Breech loader.
  5. Muzzleloader.
  6. Country made.

According to firing action:
  1. Over-bolt action
  2. Under-bolt action.
  3. Lever action.
  4. Pump action or autoloading model.

Rifled Arms :
- The bore is scored internally with a number of shallow spiral "grooves", varying from 2 to more than 20, the most common being 6, which run parallel to each other but twisted spirally, from breech to muzzle.
- These grooves are called "rifling" and the projecting ridges between these grooves are called "lands".
- Rifling is made by a broach.
- Riflings vary in number, direction, depth and width.
- The turning of the spiral groove is called the twist and the angle of turning is called the pitch.

- When the bullet passes through the bore, its surface comes into contact with the projecting spirals which give the bullet a spinning or spiraling motion.
- Rifling gives the bullet a spin, greater power of penetration. a straight course (trajectory) and prevents it from unsteady movement as it travels in the air.

A handgun bullet usually makes a single turn about its longitudinal axis in 25 to 45 cm. of forward motion.

Micro-groove system of rifling consists of 15 to 20 round grooves in the bore of the barrel.

Rifled firearms are divided into :
1. Low velocity (up to 360 meters per second).
2. Medium velocity (360 to 750 m/s).
3. High velocity (750 to 1260 m/s).
4. Very high velocity (above 1260 m/s).
- Small arms include hand arms and shoulder anns.

Caliber or gauge:
- It is measured by the internal dimension of the barrel and is given in decimals of inch or millimeters.
- The dimension of the rifled weapon is measured between a pair of diametrically opposed lands and not grooves.
- In smooth-bored weapons, the bore is measured similarly up to 1.27 cm. (half inch).
- For larger bores, the size is determined by the size of the lead ball which will exactly fit the barrel, and by the number of such balls of equal size and weight as can be made from 454 gm. (one pound) of pure lead.
- Thus the 12 bore gun is one whose diameter is the size of the single ball of lead, when 12 balls are made from 454gm. of lead.
- The smaller the number of gauge, the greater the diameter of the barrel.
- Helixometer is the instrument to examine the interior of the barrel.

Shotgun :
- It may be single-barrelled or double-barrelled, the barrels lying side by side, or occasionally mounted one over the other.
- It is intended for firing a single ball, slug or a charge of shots.
- The barrel varies in length from 55 to 72 cm.
- Shotgun bores vary from 4 to 20.
- The common gauges are 12, 16 and 20.
- The interior of the barrels is smooth .

Cylinder - bore: When the entire barrel from breech to muzzle is of the same diameter,

Choke-bore : the distal 7 to 10 cm. of the barrel is narrow.
- Different degrees are known as full-choke, half-choke and quarter-choke or improved cylinders.
- The choking lessens the rate of spread of shot after it leaves the muzzle, increases the explosive force and increases the velocity.
- There are some shotguns which have ,small portion of their bore near the muzzle end rifled, which are called "paradox guns".

Musket:
- A musket is a military shoulder arm.
- It has a long forestock and usually takes a bayonet (pointed knife-like weapon) at the muzzle.
- It is a smooth-bore weapon, e.g., 0.410 musket.
- The muzzle velocity of the
  - shotgun is about 240 to 300m/s
  - 0.410 musket from 350 to 600 m/s.
- Shotguns are effective up to 30 meters.

The effective range and penetrating power of a shotgun will depend upon the
- quantity of propellent charge,
- size of the shot,
- length of barrel and
- presence or absence of choking .
- Muzzle loading guns are loaded entirely from the muzzle end with the help of a rod using
- gunpowder, pieces of cloth, stones, metal fragments, seeds, bolts, wood, screws, etc.

Other firearms are
- Rifle
- Revolver
- Automatic pistol
- Assault rifles
- Air rifle and air pistol
- Rockets
- Mines
- Grenades
- Electra stun guns
- Humane(veterinary) killers:

CARTRIDGE :

Shotgun Cartridge:
- The shotgun cartridge consists of a case of short metal cylinder which is continuous with a cardboard or plastic cylinder.
- The length of the cartridge varies from 5 to 7 cm.
- Cartridge cases are stamped at the factory to indicate type and make.
- The cartridge case is filled as follows from the base:
  - percussion cap (detonator cap: primer battery cup),
  - gun powder,
  - a thick felt-wad with cardboard discs lying in front and behind it,
  - the shot (charge or load)
  - retaining cardboard disc, over which the edges of the cartridge cylinder walls are pressed .
- The case is rimmed, which helps to keep the cartridge in the correct position in the chamber, and makes extraction easy.
- The case helps to keep the various components in place, prevents the backward escape of the gasses and provides a waterproof container for the gunpowder.
- The powder is protected from the grease wad by a thin grease-proof card wad.
- Wads may be glazed-board. straw-board. plastic, cork, felt, etc. and may be
  - -disc-shaped
  - -cup-shaped,
  - -bizarre-shaped.
- The card -wad behind the shot charge prevents the shot from getting lodged in the feltwad and seals the bore completely.
- Some cartridges contain 'power piston' formed from four leaflets or petals folded so as to produce a cylindrical shape, which holds the shot inside a polythene cup, which may contribute to the wound at short range
- Some cartridges may have brightly coloured plastic granules as a filler between the shot, which may be found inside the wound.

SHOTS (PELLETS)
They are of two types.
1. Soft or drop shot is made of soft lead,
2. Hard or chilled shot is made from lead and hardened by antimony.
    - The shots may also be plated with copper.
    - A rough idea about the number of pellets in a cartridge can be had from the marking on the retaining cardboard disc :
    - **"Buckshot"** is the largest and has a diameter of 6 to 8 mm.
    - Pellets deform easily due to friction as they rub against the inside of the barrel.
    - The heat can cause melting and fusion of pellets.

Rifled slugs
- They are single projectiles, and are used in shotguns for big game hunting.
- They are similar in shape to a blunt bullet with a deep hollow cavity in the base and weigh from 23 to 33 g.
- The sides commonly have angularly inclined fins or ribs that resemble very coarse rifling marks on bullets.
- The slugs are usually a little smaller in diameter than the shotgun bore itself.
- The slugs have much greater range than pellets.
- The spiral grooves on the slugs impart a spinning effect.

Rifled Cartridge:
- It consists of a metal cylinder with a flat base which projects as a rim except in an automatic pistol.
- Rimless cartridge has an extractor groove near the base.
- The primer cup (percussion cap) is fitted in a circular hole, usually in the center of the base and has a flash hole in the center which communicates with the powder space inside.
- The metal cylinder or cartridge case is elongated, and its distal end tightly grips the base of the bullet (projectile or missile).
- The gunpowder lies between the detonator and the bullet.
- Usually there is no wad, but sometimes one piece wad is kept.
- Low-power rim-fire cartridge may not contain gunpowder but only a primer compound in the circumferential hollow rim.
- As such, those cartridges cannot produce the tattooing.
- Many bullets have near the base, a circumferential groove called "cannelure", into which the end of the case is crimped.
- A bullet without cannelure is held in position by stabs on the circumference of the case.

PRIMERS:
- The primer cup contains the priming mixture and an anvil so placed that the blow of firing pin on the primer cup crushes the priming mixture against the anvil center and burns it, which then flashes through the flash hole (fire holes or vents) in the centrefire case head, and ignites the powder charge.
- The primer used in shotgun cartridges is called a primer battery cup.
- The primers which are used nowadays contain compounds of lead, antimony sulfide and barium, instead of mercury fulminate or lead azide.
- These minute particles can travel up to 7.5 to 15 cm.

POWDERS:
1. **BLACK POWDER:**
    - It consists of potassium nitrate 75%; sulphur 10%; and charcoal 15%.
    - It is designated as FG, FFG, FFFG, etc., depending on the size of the grains.
    - The more number of F's, the finer are the grains and the faster in burning.
    - It burns with the production of much heat, flame and smoke.
    - One gram of powder produces 3,000 to 4,500 c.c. of gas.
    - It has largely been replaced by smokeless powder.

2. SMOKELESS POWDER:
- It consists of nitrocellulose (gun cotton), (single-base), or nitroglycerine and nitrocellulose (double-base) or nitrocellulose, nitroglycerine and nitroguanidine (triple base).
- Triple based powder is commonly used.
- They produce much less flame and smoke and are more completely burnt than black powder.
- One gram produces 12,000 to 13,000 c.c. of gasses.

3. SEMI-SMOKELESS POWDER
- It is a mixture of 80% of black and 20% of smokeless type.
  BULLETS (projectiles, missiles),:
- The traditional bullet is made of soft metal and has a rounded nose.
- The metal is lead with varying amounts of antimony added to provide hardness.
- This is known as the round-nose soft bullet, and is usually used in rifles and revolvers.
- The tip of the bullet is called the nose.
- The caliber of a bullet is its cross-sectional diameter.
- In revolver and pistol, the bullet is short and the point is usually round or oval.
- In a rifle, the bullet is elongated with a pointed end.

Variations are:
1. Square-nosed, soft metal bullet, known as "wad-cutter", and used primarily for target shooting.
2. Hollow-point variety has a depression in the nose of the soft metal.
   This bullet is designed to expand or "mushroom" upon impact.
- Mushroom bullets produce more serious wounds.
- Other Types of bullets are
  ○ Short flat point
  ○ Medium flat point
  ○ Medium round nose
  ○ Long round nose
  ○ Medium long sharp point
  ○ Flat base
  ○ Sharp point boat tailed
  ○ Pencil point
  ○ Stream lines with sabot.

FIREARM WOUNDS
- They are usually recognised without difficulty.
- Firearm wounds cause crushing of the tissues and produce an actual hole.
- Wounds produced by rifled weapons may simulate wounds inflicted by a red-hot poker or a burning pointed stick.
- Glancing wounds may simulate incised or lacerated wounds.
- A bullet that passes through glass or some other object, and then strikes the body may produce a wound resembling a laceration.

SHOTGUNS
Shotguns :
- It may be single-barrelled or double-barrelled, the barrels lying side by side, or occasionally mounted one over the other.
- It is intended for firing a single ball, slug or a charge of shots.
- The barrel varies in length from 55 to 72 cm.
- Shotgun bores vary from 4 to 20, The common gauges are 12, 16 and 20.
- The interior of the barrels is smooth.

Cylinder - bore: When the entire barrel from breech to muzzle is of the same diameter,
Choke-bore : the distal 7 to 10 cm. of the barrel is narrow.

- Different degrees are known as full-choke, half-choke and quarter-choke or improved cylinders.
- The choking lessens the rate of spread of shot after it leaves the muzzle, increases the explosive force and increases the velocity.
- There are some shotguns which have ,small portion of their bore near the muzzle end rifled, which are called "paradox guns".

Musket:
- A musket is a military shoulder arm.
- It has a long forestock and usually takes a bayonet (pointed knife-like weapon) at the muzzle.
- It is a smooth-bore weapon, e.g., 0.410 musket.
- The muzzle velocity of the
  ○ shotgun is about 240 to 300m/s
  ○ 0.410 musket from 350 to 600 m/s.
- Shotguns are effective up to 30 meters.
- The effective range and penetrating power of a shotgun will depend upon the
  ○ quantity of propellent charge,
  ○ size of the shot,
  ○ length of barrel and
  ○ presence or absence of choking .
- Muzzle loading guns are loaded entirely from the muzzle end with the help of a rod using gunpowder, pieces of cloth, stones, metal fragments, seeds, bolts, wood, screws, etc.

Wounds From Shotguns:
- The smoke
  ○ extends up to 30 cm.,
  ○ flame up to 15 cm., and
  ○ unburnt and partially burnt powder grains up to 60 to 90 cm.
- The larger the caliber, the greater the distance to watch the powder is discharged.
- The cards travel for two meters, and wad for 2 to 5 meters
- Ammunition plays a great role in the size and pattern of wounding.

The character of a wound depends on.
I. The Distance From which the Weapon is Discharged:
II. The Size of the Shot :
III. The nature of the Explosive:
IV. The Gun itself:

I. The Distance From which the Weapon is Discharged:
- The discharge produces a long,shallow cone with its apex close to the muzzle of the shotgun and the farther along the cone the victim is situated, the larger the wound pattern will be.
- A compact mass of shot emerges from the muzzle and begins to spread , divergence increases progressively as the distance lengthens.

1. Contact and near contact wounds
2. Close Range (up to one meter)
3. Short range (1 to 2 meters)
4. Intermediate range(2 to 4 meters)
5. Long or Distant range (above 4 meters)

1. **Contact and near contact wounds:**
    - They are single, usually round, equal to the bore in size, often ragged because of individual shot and tearing due to gasses.
    - In a tight contact wound, soiling and burning are minimal or absent.
    - As the gasses are blasted within the wounds, the subcutaneous and deeper tissues show severe disruption.
    - The rapid entry of gasses causes a momentary vacuum immediately below the skin, which may cause extrusion of the soft tissues, e.g., fat through the wound.
    - Particles of unburnt powder are driven to some distance through the wound and some of them are found embedded in the wound.
    - These particles cause hemorrhage in deeper tissues and form aggregates of hemorrhages in the margins of the wound.
    - Thus the margins of the wound will be contused.
    - If the contact is tight (hard contact), muzzle impression (copy or recoil abrasion) is seen due to firm mechanical pressure of impact of the metal rim against the skin, and also due to the subcutaneous expansion of gasses lifting the skin forcibly up against the muzzle.
    - The muzzle imprint may be an incomplete, indistinct bruise or rarely may be a perfect imprint of the end of the weapon.
    - Bruising can occur around the muzzle imprint.
    - Muzzle imprint may be lost within the explosive damage associated with the discharge.
    - But, in a double-barrelled shotgun, the unused barrel often leaves a characteristic patterned abrasion.
    - In many cases, muzzle impression is not produced due to rapid removal of the weapon by recoil.
    - In contact shot, the muzzle blast and the negative pressure in the barrel following discharge may suck blood, hair, fragments of tissues and cloth fibers several cm. back inside the barrel called "back spatter".
    - CO in the gasses combines with hemoglobin and myoglobin due to which the wound of entry and the wound track appear pink.
    - This decreases gradually, but may be seen very rarely at an exit wound.
    - Burning, blackening and tattooing of the tissue also takes place in the depths of the wound.
    - The outer shots are deformed by their passage through the bore and choke.
    - Plastic wads retain their shape and diameter within the body, but felt and cardboard wads suck up blood and body fluids and swell.

Contact shot over a bony area:
- Cruciate, stellate or ragged lacerations are seen especially if there is a thick bone immediately under the skin, such as skull due to the extreme force of the blowback phenomenon, as gasses expand beneath the skin and lacerate the margins of the wound, as they exit through the original entry wound.
- The internal damage is diffuse, but there is no cavitation.
- Contact wounds on the head produce greater disruption of the margins, and often show subsidiary linear tears in the skin extending from the margins of the main wound.
- A large irregular hole is produced in the skull, with fissured fractures running from its margins.
- The bone may show burning, blackening and tattooing in the margins.
- The entire contour of the face and head may be destroyed, and the actual point of the muzzle impact of entry wound may be difficult to locate.
- Extreme mutilation is caused due to the explosive effect, because the gasses have restricted space for expansion.

- Comminution of the vault of the skull is usually accompanied by extensive fissured fractures, or 'crazy paving' fracture of the base of the skull, and the roofs of the orbits, and middle ears.
- A large exit wound may be produced with disruption of the cranium and projection of brain tissue for some distance.
- An eye may be blown out of its socket (burst head).

Entrance wound in the mouth or nose
- An entrance wound in the mouth or nose may or may not be accompanied by an exit wound.
- Resistance by the hard palate reduces the power of the shot, and the shot lies mostly in the space between the skull and scalp, at the back or side of the head.
- Here abrasions or bruising of one or both lips with or without laceration is seen.
- Splitting of the angle of mouth may occur due to blast. Shotgun wound in Neck region
- In the neck region a large exit wound or complete destruction may occur. Shotgun wound in Chest region
- On the chest, the skin and subcutaneous tissues may be peeled away from the rib cage to form a pocket which then collapses.
- In contact or near contact wounds on the abdomen, coils of small intestine may lie outside the abdomen due to entry of gas into the peritoneal cavity

LOOSE CONTACT:
- In loose contact or near contact shot, some of the gasses escape with the resulting scattering of the muzzle blast and an unusual arrangement of soot is seen on the skin known as corona, similar to that as seen in rifled weapon wounds.
- In loose contact with skin, the blast effect is less as compared to tight contact, and splitting of the wound margins usually does not occur.

Clothes:
- If the part is clothed, smoke will escape sideways and may be found in each layer of clothing and on the skin.
- The cloth may be slightly burnt at the edge of the hole, and there may be a ring of burning around the skin wound.

2. **Close Range (up to one meter):**
   - Within a distance of about 30 cm., tissues surrounding the wound are
     - slightly burnt by flame
     - blackened by smoke, and
     - tattooed by unburnt or partially burnt powder granules.
   - If the powder is smokeless, there may be greyish or white deposits on the skin around the wound.
   - The deposit of smoke is known as smudging, fouling or blackening.
   - The blackening can be removed by a wet cloth.
   - Unburnt particles of the powder are embedded in the skin producing tattooing (stippling or peppering).
   - The hairs of the trunk and limbs may be completely burnt around the wound.
   - If the distance is greater, the keratin of the hair may melt with the flame, and then solidify on cooling, producing a clubbed appearance of the hairs because of rounded bulges at the tips.
   - Soot soiling diminishes as the distance increases.
   - There may be a wide flare or narrow rim of hyperaemia or even blistering from the flame.
   - If the gun is fired at right angle to the body, the burnt area is circular, and if fired at an angle it is oval, the direction of the firing being indicated by the nearness of the wound to one or other end of the burnt area.
   - The end nearer the wound is the direction towards which the shot traveled.
   - The use of silencers to muffle the sound of discharge, reduce the amount of smoke and powder significantly and cause misinterpretation of the distance from which gun was fired.

- The burnt area darkens and dries after death.
- Blackening and tattooing can be readily demonstrated by infrared photography on both skin and clothing.
- As range becomes greater, the intensity of blackening and tattooing decrease and the spread increases in a fairly regular manner.

Between 30 cm to one meter:
- The tissues up to 30 cm. along the track, and around the wound may be cherry-red due to absorption of CO.
- The wound is single, circular or oval, similar to contact wounds, though the blackening and tattooing are more extensive.
- The margins of the skin wound may be clean-cut or slightly ragged.
- There may be annular bruising around the wound due to tissue damage from the entry of gasses.
- Felt, wads or plastic cups from the cartridge will be found in the depths of the wound.
- The deeper tissues show marked disruption.
- Carbon monoxide may be present in the blood absorbed from the damaged tissues.
- In some cartridges, plastic granules may be used as a filler between the lead pellets, and this coloured material may be found within the wound or on the skin up to 2 to 3 meters and produces very fine, punctate abrasions around the pellet holes.

Important points:
- The plastic cup type wad opens up between 30 to 60 cm. so that four petals stick out, and a circular entrance wound is produced to form a square edged star or capital 'X Shaped Maltese cross pattern of bruising or abrasion encircling it.
- By 90 cm. air resistance folds back the petals and a single hole of entrance will be produced.
- In the 0.410 ammunition, the plastic sleeve expands into only three petals and produces three abrasions.

At a distance of 60 to 90 cm:
- The small shot produces a single circular aperture, 2.5 to 4 cm. in diameter, with singular and lacerated edges.
- There is no burning or blackening.
- Some amount of tattooing is usually seen.
- The tissues within and around the wound are not cheney-red.
- Between 30 cm to one meter, the rim of the wound is irregular and shows some scalloping, often referred to as a "rat-hole".
- There may be annular abrasions and bruising or "rat nibbling".
- At close ranges, when the shots are bunched, they strike one another upon hitting the skin/ clothing and are scattered after entering the body and cause much damage to the internal tissues.
- When a buck shot is fired from close range, the dispersal of the shot through the body may be minimal.
- In the skull, there is less disruption than that at contact range; bursting open of the skull and scattering of its contents is not seen.
- The column of pellets has a cutting action which produces a clean hole.
- Shotgun wounds at contact and close range cause much more destruction of tissues than rifled weapons, due to the greater amount of gas produced, because of larger amounts of gunpowder.

3. **Short range (1 to 2 meters):**
   - A single circular aperture 4 to 5 cm. in diameter, with irregular and lacerated edges are produced.
   - There is no burning, blackening or tattooing.
   - A round hole of 4 to 5 cm. in diameter is produced for all gauges and all chokes.
   - Wads may be found deep inside the wound up to 2 meters.
   - Collect and preserve plastic sleeves, wadding and cardboard.
   - Annular or linear abrasions are caused.
   - Felt, wads or plastic cups from the cartridge will be found in the depths of the wound.

4. **Intermediate Range (2 to 4 meters):**
   - The minimal distance at which shot mass begins to spread is extremely variable.
   - It may be
   - 1 meter with a sawed-off shotgun
   - 2 meters with cylinder bore guns
   - 4 meters with full choke guns.
   - At a distance of two meters, the shot mass begins to spread and individual pellet holes may be detected, which are usually round and show a rim of abrasion at their margins.
   - The wound of entry is irregular.
   - Beyond two meters the wads often strike the body below the shotgun wound.
   - It may penetrate the skin or it may only bruise the skin.
   - The wads found within the wounds are useful to determine the bore of the gun.

At a distance of 3 meters:
   - The central aperture is surrounded by separate openings in an area of about 8 to 10 cm. in diameter.
   - As muzzle-target distance increases, the main entrance defect progressively becomes smaller, and individual pellet wounds increase in number. Occasionally, several individual pellet entrance wounds are in contact producing scalloped defects which are larger than the individual pellet holes.

5. **Long or Distant range (above 4 meters):**
   - Distant wounds are those in which all shots penetrate separately.
   - At a distance of 4 meters, the shots spread widely and enter the body as individual pellets producing separate openings in an area of 10 to 15 cm. in diameter.
   - Each individual pellet reproduces its own track.
   - In the skull, the energy of the shots is greatly reduced, perforating the skin and bone, so that they usually do not travel the entire brain substance.
   - In shotgun discharge, there is no temporary cavitation.
   - The spread of pellets from a fully choked barrel is:
     - 10 meters: 25 cm
     - 15 meters: 35cm
     - 20 meters: 45cm
     - 30 meters: 75cm
   - The spread is almost double from an unchoked barrel.
   - At about 30 meters, the pellets only penetrate the skin or muscle.
   - Death beyond a range of 30 meters is rare, but it is possible for a single pellet or shot to cause death.

Important points to know:
   - For cylindrical barrels about one-third of the spread of shot in cm. roughly equals the range in meters which is very inaccurate.
   - The estimation of range is difficult when replaceable or variable extensions called 'chokes' are used at the end of the muzzle of shotguns.
   - Passage of shotgun pellets through any target before they strike the body, cause the pellets to spread,
     e.g., window glass, screen, or layers of clothing.
   - If a hand is held over the muzzle when discharge occurs, the pattern may be 7-8 cm across as it leaves the hand.
   - Shotgun slugs usually produce large, gaping circular to oval defects with irregular margins.
   - The internal injury is highly destructive and similar to that caused by high velocity rifles.
   - The wound caused by buckshot resembles a bullet wound.

BILLIARD BALL RICHOCHET EFFECT:
- At close range, while the shots are bunched, they strike one another upon impact on the primary target, i.e., the skin or clothes, and spread out in a wide pattern as they pass through the body.
- This causes the shots to spread widely and may suggest a greater range of fire than actually occurred.
- Similar spread is seen if the shots strike any other intermediary object, e.g., door or window, before reaching the victim.
- The phenomenon is termed the billiard ball ricochet effect.
- The final shot spread as seen in X-ray gives a true picture of the range of fire, only when the range of fire is great enough that the shots are spread out, before striking the target.
- In decomposed and burned bodies where the skin pattern cannot be seen, the range of fire can be determined by X-rays.

BALLING OR WELDING OF SHOT:
- Balling of shotgun pellets results in the conversion of shot into a compact mass, which can travel for a few meters in this form.
- In such cases, a circular or oval entrance wound of about 5 to 10 mm. in diameter, and widespread, small, circular punctures are seen, suggesting the use of two different weapons, one a shotgun at distant range and the other a rifle.

II. The Size of the Shot :
- The penetrating power of the large shot is greater than that of the smaller shot
- The smaller the shot, the more minutely irregular are the edges.
- At close range, the wounds produced by shots of various sizes are similar, but small shots usually lodge in the body.

III. The Nature of the Explosive :
- The extent of tattooing depends on
  - the bore of the weapon,
  - the type of powder used,
  - the weapon and
  - the range of blackening.
- The greater the bore of the weapon, the wider the area of blackening.
- With smokeless powder, blackening and tattooing is less marked than with black powder at all ranges.

IV. The Gun itself :
- The pattern of wound depends on
  - the length of the barrel,
  - the bore,
  - absence or degree of the choke present.
- Shorter barrels usually produce greater deposits over larger areas.
- The direction of the fire may be determined from the passage of individual shots through the clothes and tissues, from the grouping of shot marks and the direction of glancing shots.

Exit Wounds :
- Usually shotgun pellets do not exit from the body except :
  - Contact wounds.
  - Tangential wounds where some of the pellets have a very short track through the body
  - Thin part of the body, such as the neck or extremities.
  - Wounds caused by large caliber buckshot or rifled slugs.
- At contact or near range; greater disruption of tissues occurs compared to the entrance wound.

- The margins are everted as the unsupported skin is struck from within, the tissues tend to burst outward, and the skin fragments, but there is no singeing, blackening or tattooing of the margins.
- There may be small, separate wounds made by individual pellets that have become separated from the mass.
- If the skin at the exit of a bullet is well supported, either by belt, corset, etc. or is pressed against a firm surface, e.g., wall, wooden or plaster board, etc. the skin surface will be rigid because of the pressure of the external substance, and the exit wound has clean margins and may be contused.

REVOLVER AND AUTOMATIC PISTOLS:
REVOLVER :
- Revolvers are so-called because the cartridges are put in chambers in a metal cylinder, which revolves or rotates before each shot, to bring the next cartridge opposite the barrel, ready to be fired.
- In the single action type, a bolt had to be moved manually to eject the spent cartridge and to bring a new round into the breach from a magazine cylinder and to bring the cartridge in the proper position for firing.
- In the double action type, the hammer can be cocked by hand, or by a prolonged pull on the trigger.
- The bores vary from 5.6 to 11.25 mm (0.22 to 0.45 inch).
- The muzzle velocity is 150 to 180 meters per second.
- They are low velocity weapons.
- The effective range is 100 meters.

AUTOMATIC PISTOL:
- It is a hand arm in which the cartridge is loaded directly into the chamber of the barrel.
- When a cartridge is fired, the empty cartridge case falls on the ground several meters away, and a new cartridge slips into the breech automatically by spring.
- The cartridges are contained in a vertical magazine in the butt, which can accommodate 6 to 10 cartridges.
- They are really semi-automatic or self-loading, because the trigger has to be pressed each time a round is fired.
- The bores vary from 6.35 to 11.25 mm. (0.25 to 0.45 inch).
- The muzzle velocity is 300 to 360 meters per second or more.
- They are high-velocity weapons.
- Their effective range is about 100 meters.

WOUNDS FROM REVOLVERS AND AUTOMATIC PISTOLS :
- The flame extends up to 8 cm;
- smoke extends up to 15 cm.
- unburnt and partially burnt powder grains and small metallic particles extends
  - up to 40 to 50 cm. with handguns
  - up to 60 to 100 cm. in case of rifle.
- The amount of smoke, flame and powder grains and the distances to which they will be carried will vary depending upon
  - the type of gun powder used,
  - the amount of powder load,
  - the size and weight of the projectile,
  - barrel length,
  - caliber,
  - the tightness of fit between the projectile and gun barrel
  - the type of firearm.

- Silencers will filter out a great proportion of soot and powder particles due to which the range appears greater than it actually was.

Entrance Wound (in-shot wounds):
- They may be classified based on the distance of the muzzle of a firearm from the body;
  - contact shot,
  - close shot,
  - near shot and
  - distant shot.

1. **Contact Shot :**
   - In firm or hard contact (muzzle pushed hard against the skin), the resulting wound is similar to that from a shotgun.
   - In some contact wounds, the imprint of the muzzle of the gun is found as patterned abrasion on the skin around the wound.
   - This results from the great distension of the subcutaneous tissues from the entry of gasses which forces the surface against the muzzle.
   - Many muzzle impressions are not recorded due to the rapid removal of the weapon by recoil.
   - The discharge from the muzzle, i.e. gasses, flame, powder, smoke and metallic particles are blown into the track taken by the bullet through the body.
   - The wound is large and triangular, stellate, cruciate or elliptic, shows cavitation due to the expansion of the liberated gasses in the skin and tissues, which show laceration.
   - The margins are hyperaemic, contused and everted due to gasses coming out of the entering wound under pressure.
   - Singeing of the hair(burns superficially) may be present due to the escape of hot gasses by the sides of the muzzle end.
   - The area immediately around the perforation is abraded, and this thin rim of abrasion is usually covered with powder residue.
   - In firm contact with the skin where the bone is not shallowly situated, the ever expanding gas continues to penetrate deeper, to be scattered in the soft tissues of the body.
   - The wound is not eruptive or explosive in appearance.
   - In contact shot, the muzzle blast and the negative pressure in the barrel following discharge may suck blood, hair, fragments of tissues and cloth fibers several centimeters back inside the barrel called "back spatter".

Note: Back spatter is more common with a shotgun.

Loose contact or near contact:
   - In loose contact or near contact shots, some of the gasses escape with the resulting scattering of the muzzle blast and an unusual arrangement of soot is seen on the skin known as corona.
   - The corona consists of a circular zone of soot deposit surrounding the bullet defect, but separated from it by a band of skin without a deposit of soot.
   - This is due to the gas expanding about the muzzle, first at a velocity too high to allow for the settling out of soot, with a subsequent loss in velocity at a short distance from the muzzle, allowing the soot to finally deposit on the skin.
   Wound has a clear margin, inverted, abraded and surrounded by soot.
   The blast effect is not as marked as in tight contact, and splitting of the wound edges does not occur.
   Evidence of burning is noted on microscopic examination in the edges of the contact and near-contact bullet wounds due to the flame of muzzle blast.

- Singeing of the hair is seen.
- Tattooing begins when the muzzle to target distance exceeds one cm.
- The powder residue is usually grossly visible in the subcutaneous and deeper areas.
- The entrance track is blackened by powder and smoke and seared and changed by flame.
- In loose contact, gas and soot escape from the side of the barrel, causing an eccentric area of burning and blackening.

Contact shot against head:
- Wounds appear as a very large explosive type of injury with bursting fractures.
  the expansion of gasses between the scalp and the skull
  eversion and splitting of the skin at the margins of the entrance wound.
  undermined, ragged, stellate, triradiate or cruciform opening with everted margins from which tears radiate.
  The tearing may be severe, as the gas raises a large dome under the skin which then ruptures.
- Such wounds are usually produced by large caliber pistols.
- Soot may be deposited
  ○ on the bone surrounding the bullet hole
  ○ on the inner surfaces of the skull around the bullet hole and
  ○ on the dura mater
- This should not be mistaken for lead rubbed off on the bone during the passage of the bullet, which is seen only in a localized area.
- Fissured fractures often radiate from the circular defect due to the considerable sudden expansion resulting from the muzzle blast.
- Fractures of the orbital roofs occur due to the same mechanism, but the dura over the orbits is usually not damaged.
- Fractures of the skull radiating from bullet holes are rare.
- A bullet traveling the cranial cavity destroys the structures in its pathway and produces an expansile or explosive effect.
- A bullet fired from a short distance may produce an explosive effect sufficient to burst the scalp, shatter the skull and dislodge the brain.
- In less severe types of injury, a cone of damaged cerebral tissue is seen surrounding the wound track.
- When a bullet moves through the body, a temporary cavity is formed in its path.
- The margins of the wound of entry, subcutaneous tissues and muscles around the track of the bullet may be bright pink due to the presence of CO.
- Abdominal wounds show cavitation because of the blast effect.

When the part is clothed
- The bullet hole in the cloth touching the muzzle is sometimes surrounded by a flat ring corresponding to the outline of the muzzle.
- The loose fibers of the cloth in the center of the bullet hole are often turned outward due to the expanding gasses returning through the defect.
- These fibers are usually blackened by smoke.
- In synthetic fabrics, melting of the ends of these fibers may be observed
- Varying amounts of soot are deposited on the edges of the bullet hole.
- If the clothes are bloodstained, deposits of soot may not be recognised, but the inside of the garment may show large deposits of smoke.
- This is due to the spreading of smoke by the muzzle blast between the skin and the clothing and is seen commonly if the shot passes through several layers of material.

- Each layer is blackened on both sides of the fabric, but the skin wound does not show blackening or tattooing.

2. **Close Shot :**
    - This term is applied when the victim is within the range of the flame, i.e., 5 to 8 cm.
    - The term 'point blank' is used when the range is very close to or in contact with the surface of the skin.
    - The entrance wound is circular with inverted edges, but the rebounding gasses may level up or even evert the margins.
    - The skin is burnt with the singeing(burnt slightly) of the hair.
    - The skin surrounding the wound is
    - hyperaemic
    - shows bruising,
    - burning,
    - blackening and
    - tattooing.
    - The palms and soles are very resistant to powder tattooing.
    - The blackening can be wiped off the skin by a wet cloth, but the tattooing cannot be wiped off.
    - Carboxy-hemoglobin will be present in the wound track in diminishing concentrations up to 30 cm.
    - The length of the barrel of a firearm has considerable effect on the spread of smoke
    - produced on the target,
      e.g., a gun with a 5 cm. barrel will spread the smoke over a much larger area than a weapon having a 15 cm. barrel;fired from the same distance and using the same type of ammunition.
    - Usually, as the distance between the muzzle and the target increases, the pattern of soot or powder on the target increases in diameter and the density of particle deposition decreases.
    - Abraded collar and grease or dirt collar are present.
      Between 30 cm. to 50 cm. There is no burning and blackening, but some amount of tattooing is usually seen.
    - The internal injuries are almost the same as in the case of contact shot.

3. **Near Shot :**
    - This term is applied when the victim is within the range of powder deposition, and outside the range of flame, and smoke, i.e., up to 50 cm.
    - If the discharge occurs at a distance of about 15 cm., the lacerating and burning effects of gasses are usually lost due to the dispersion cooling of the gasses before they reach the skin.
    - The entrance wound is seen as
        - a round hole,
        - slightly smaller than the diameter of the bullet, due to elasticity of the skin,
        - with a bruised and inverted margin and
        - a zone of blackening and tattooing.
    - A small magenta-coloured zone. an actual micro-contusion is seen surrounding each tattoo point.
    - If the bullet strikes the body at an angle, blackening and tattooing has a pear-shaped area, with the larger area on the side nearer the barrel.
    - Abundant gunpowder and a diminishing amount of soot are deposited on the target.

- As the distance increases,
  ○ the intensity decreases and
  ○ blackening and tattooing is spread out over a large area, and
  ○ there is no singeing of the hair and skin.
- Abrasion and grease collar are present.
- Occasionally, when the range of fire is short, small fragments of metal derived from the interior of the barrel of the gun or the bullet itself, are embedded in the skin in the vicinity of the entrance wound.

4. **Distant Shot (Above 50 cm.) :**
   - The entrance wound is
   ○ smaller than the missile due to the elasticity of the skin,
   ○ circular, and
   ○ margins are inverted.
   - Distant entrance wounds of the palms and soles are irregular, often having a stellate appearance, without an abrasion ring, and look like exit wounds.
   - Burning, blackening and tattooing are not seen.
   - The skin adjacent to the hole shows two zones,
   ○ the inner of the grease collar and
   ○ the outer of the abraded collar.
   - In the case of a semi-jacketed bullet, the jacket separates as it goes through the body, and the core mushrooms into small pieces.
   - X-ray gives a picture of "lead snowstorm".
   - The projectile need not strike the bone for this to occur.
   - If a semi-jacketed bullet passes through an intermediary target, the jacket may separate from the core, and both missiles may penetrate the body.
   - When a bullet passes through an intermediary target, such as glass, may cause superficial lacerations around the entry wound and these are referred to as pseudo-tattooing, which are larger and more irregular than that caused by powder.
   - Intermediate targets, such as clothing, jewelry, items in pockets, furniture, doors, windows, walls, etc. modify the appearance of entrance wounds.
   - The caliber of a bullet cannot be determined, if it strikes the skin surface obliquely.
   - Stretching and cavitation and dissipation of kinetic energy are the major causes of the lethal effects of a bullet, together with deformation and fragmentation.

THE ABRASION COLLAR (marginal abrasion):

As the bullet strikes the skin,
it first indents and then stretches the skin surface,
so that perforation takes place through a tense area.
The elasticity of the skin causes the skin defect to contract.

- The skin is abraded (abrasion collar) around the hole due to
○ rubbing of the gyrating body of the bullet against the inverted epidermis and
○ heat of the bullet .
- A black coloured ring "grease or dirt collar" (bullet wipe soiling) is seen as a narrow ring of skin, lining the defect, and is sharply outlined.
- This is caused from the removal of substances from the bullet as it passes through the skin,i.e.,
○ bullet lubrication,
○ gun oil from the interior of the barrel,
○ lead from the surface of the bullet,
○ dirt carried on the surface of the bullet, as it travels through the atmosphere,
○ barrel debris, etc

- It is more marked in a distant shot.
- Dirt collar is less common if the bullet is jacketed.
- Fouling Refers to tiny lesions around the entry wound caused by fragments of metal (from surface of missiles or interior of the barrel) expelled by the discharge.
- Infrared photography clearly indicates the presence of black ring around the bullet hole.
- By contrast, soot is
  ◦ dark in the center and
  ◦ fades towards the periphery.
- The abrasion collar surrounds the dirt collar.
- The abraded collar is reddish at first, but becomes reddish-brown and then brownish-black as it dries.
- Some contusion is present in an abraded collar, and as such, it is also called "contusion collar".
- These two features are proof of an entrance wound.
  ◦ Dirt collar and Abrasion collar
- Abrasion collar may be absent when
  ◦ The tissues are soft and yielding, e.g. in the abdomen or buttocks.
  ◦ where skin is taut, and
  ◦ in some high velocity wounds.
- In these cases, small splits or tears radiating outwards from the edges of the perforation involving a part or complete circumference may be seen.
- In addition to the abrasion collar, there is often a slightly wide circle of peeled keratin, where the stratum corneum of the skin is raised to form a slightly frayed edge around the entry wound.

Skull :
- In the skull, the wound of the entrance shows a punched-in (clean) hole in the outer table.
- The inner table is unsupported and a cone-shaped piece of bone is detached forming a crater that is larger than the hole on the outer table, and shows bevelling (sloping surface).
- Fissured fractures often radiate from the defect.
- As the bone fragments have to pass through the dura before entering the brain, lacerations are usually irregular and involve leptomeninges.
- Pieces of bone from the wound of entrance are often driven into the cranial cavity and may establish the bullet track.
- Pieces of bone may produce short accessory wound tracks.
- At the point of exit, a punched-out opening is produced in the inner table and beveled opening on the outer table.
- The wound is funnel-shaped, with the funnel opening up in the direction in which the bullet is traveling both the entrance and exit wound.
- The exit wound is larger due to the deformity and tumbling of the bullet after entering the skull.
- There are often fissured, sometimes comminuted fractures radiating from the central hole.
- Asymmetry of the bevelling is useful in assessing the angle of fire.
- The same appearance is seen in sternum, pelvis, ribs, dentures and thumbnails.

Puppe's Rule:
- It states that the fractures from the first injury develop normally, while those caused by the subsequent injury are stopped where the structure of the skull has already been deployed.

- It can determine the sequence of shots, when several bullets have struck the cranium.
- This rule is applicable to any multiple blunt force, causing skull fractures.
- This rule has been developed by Madea in relation to bullet injuries.
- The test depends on the observations of the fracture lines either when they intersect each other, or when they intersect a cratered lesion, so that one can determine which crack or defect must have been formed first .

Direction :
If the bullet strikes the body at
- right angle-the abrasion collar is circular and uniform
- at an angle,the wound itself is round, but the marginal abrasion is oval or elliptical,
- The direction of the bullet is from the wide to the narrow side.
- Oblique angle will cause an elliptical mark, the length of which increases as the angle decreases.
- When the bullet enters the body from an oblique angle, one edge of the wound is shelved or undercut, which indicates the direction from which the bullet entered.
- Shelving is usually seen in the deeper layers of the skin rather than in the tissues below.

Clothes :
- If the shot is through a clothed surface, examination of clothing only can indicate its range.
- In a contact shot, the clothing usually shows a cross-shaped perforation and may be singed at the edge of the hole.
- The inner surface of the garment may show an abundant deposit of smoke, even if none is seen on the outside.
- Each layer is blackened on both sides, while skin and wound may not show soot.
- Cotton and polyester shirts allow gunpowder particles to pass freely, causing small holes in the fabric.
- In close shots, the clothing may absorb or filter out all of the products of discharge except the bullet.
- An entrance hole in clothing, if made by a lead or full metal-jacketed bullet, may produce a gray to black rim known as "bullet wipe" (grease, soot or debris from the barrel of the gun).

Exit (outshot) Wounds :
- If the bullet fragments on impact, an exit wound may not occur.
- The bullet may be reduced to granules, and there may be difficulty to remove them from the body, even when identified by X-ray.
- Full metal-jacketed bullets usually exit undeformed.
- Exit wounds may vary considerably in size and shape.
- They may be round, stellate, cruciate, elliptical, crescent-shaped.
- An exit wound produced by a low velocity bullet or a tumbling bullet or a bullet passing side way through the tissues may be elongated or slit-like resembling a stab, incised or lacerated wound.
- The same appearance may be seen in a part of the body in which the skin folds or changes direction,
  e.g . .in the buttock crease, under the arm, or in the groin or umbilical area.
- Exit wounds of the head are usually star-shaped resembling contact entrance wounds.
- The exit wound is of help in determining:
1. the direction of fire,
2. posture of the victim at the time of the shooting, and
3. the number of bullets in the body.

- When the weapon has been fired in contact with the bone or at very close range, the exit wound is usually smaller than the entrance wound
- With increased range the exit wound is larger than the wound of entrance.
- With a high velocity bullet, the two wounds may be of the same size.
- The edges are free from signs of burning, blackening or tattooing and there is no contusion or abrasion collar.

Shored exit wounds:
- If the skin at the exit wound is firmly supported, the exit wound appears as a circular or nearly circular defect surrounded by a margin of abrasion (usually broader than that of entry wound), resembling a wound of entrance (shored or supported exit wound).
- Many shored exit wounds are caused if a firm object, e.g., a belt, the waistband of trousers, etc., brassiere, collar and tie, is pressed against the body at the site of exit wound, or if the body is leaning against a hard surface such as a wall, back of a chair or the floor, door, car seat, mattress, bedding, or if the person was lying down.
- In such cases the skin, crushed by the existing bullet, produces an irregular, lopsided and large abrasion around or adjacent to the wound ("shored" exit wound).
- In a fatty person, the edges of both the wounds of entrance and exit may be everted due to protrusion of fat.
- They may also be everted in decomposed bodies.

Variations in exit wounds:
The variation in the shape and large size of exit wound are due to :
1. The bullet tumbles in the body and fails to exit the nose-end first.
2. The bullet is deformed.
3. The bullet breaks up in the tissues and exits as several pieces.
4. Fragments of the bone may be blown out of the body with the bullet.
5. The unsupported skin at the exit tends to tear and break into pieces.
6. Composition and velocity of missile
- Rarely. slit-like exit wounds are seen probably due to the deformity of the bullet, caused by impact of the bullet on bone during its passage through the body.
  Large entry wounds:
  Entry wound may be larger than exit due to
1. tearing of soft tissues by inrushing gasses,
2. tumbling or yawning of bullet,
3. breaking of bullet with only a portion of it exiting,
4. tangential entry with focal avulsion of tissues,
5. bullets entering through folded or creased skin.
- Revolvers and automatic pistols cause similar wounds, but penetrating power of bullets of pistols is much greater because of the greater velocity and because of their being coated with hard metal.

WOUNDS FROM RIFLE :
- The wounds inflicted on the body are similar to pistol wounds but produce more damage.
- They vary considerably and produce the most unexpected results.
- The flame may extend up to 15 to 20 cm.
- Unburnt powder grains and small metallic particles are not found beyond one meter.
- Smoke is absent beyond 30 cm. from the muzzle.
- In contact wounds, the burning and tattooing is not much.
- The blast effects are also much less and the splitting of the clothes or tissues is the same as that with the revolvers.

- The entrance and exit wounds may be of the same size and shape, if the bullet passes through the body without touching the bone;
- The entrance wound is usually smaller than the diameter of the bullet and looks like a wound made by forcing lead pencil into skin.
- Abrasion collar may not be present .
- Bruising of the deeper tissues around the track of the bullet is seen.
- If the bullet strikes at an angle, the skin may split or be turned up.
- If it strikes a bone, extensive shattering and comminution of bone takes place.
- In such cases, the wound of exit is usually a lacerated hole, varying from about 2.5 cm. to the size of the palm of the hand.
- Bullet fragmentation is much more common in rifle injuries than those due to handguns.
- Between 300 to 1,000 meters, the spin of the bullet becomes regular, and it passes easily through the tissues and cuts a clean hole through the bones.
- Beyond this, it behaves like a low-velocity bullet.

ALTERATION OF GUNSHOT WOUNDS:

The appearance of a gunshot wound can be altered by the following conditions :
1. Drying of margins of the wound opening.
2. Decomposition of the body.
3. Healing of the wound itself.
4. Interference by emergency care personnel.
5. Surgical operation.
6. Interference by non-professional personnel at the scene of death.
7. Washing or cleaning of the wound after death.

X-ray Examination of Gunshot Wound Victims :

It helps to
1. locate the bullet or pellets,
2. locate bullet fragments or jackets,
3. show the track of the bullet. Internal ricochet within the skull may be demonstrated, which helps to determine the direction of the fire,
4. determine the break up pattern of the bullet. This may also indicate the type of ammunition used,
5. determine defects in bone,
6. bullet embolism,
7. locate air embolism accompanying large vessel damage by the missile

YAWNING BULLET -

A bullet traveling in an irregular fashion instead of traveling nose-on is called a yawning bulletYAWNING

TUMBLING BULLET

A bullet that rotates end-on-end during it motion is called a Tumbling bullet.

RICOCHET BULLET :
- A ricochet bullet is one which before striking the object aimed at,strikes some intervening object first, and then after ricocheting and rebounding (glancing) from these, hits the object.
- They are rare, as most bullets on striking a hard surface break up or penetrate the surface.
- The critical angle of impact for ricochet for hard surfaces varies from 10 to 30°.
- Ricocheting of a bullet may occur with inferior firearms and low velocity bullets.
- The bullet may be deformed and flattened before striking the skin.
- The degree of deformity varies depending on the texture of the bullet.
- This produces a large irregularly oval, triangular or cruciate entrance wound with irregular abraded margins.

- As the bullet loses gyrating movements, the abrasion collar is absent.
- Burning, blackening and tattooing are also not seen.
- The path of a ricochet is completely unexpected.
- When the velocity is lost, the bullet only produces an abrasion or contusion.

Internal ricochet:
- Sometimes, after passing through the brain, there is not enough energy left in the bullet to penetrate the skull.
- It may rebound (ricochet) from the inner table of the skull like a billiard ball, producing a second track.
- If it ricochets for a second time, a third wound track is produced.
- A bullet striking at a small angle with the surface may follow the curvature of the skull or a rib and emerge some distance away after having made a track in the subcutaneous tissues.

SINGLE ENTRANCE AND MULTIPLE EXITS

If the bullet splits up within the body and divides itself into 3 or 4 pieces, there will be only one entry hole, but several exits.

BULLET STRIKING THE SKULL BUT NOT ENTERING IT :
- Bullets may graze or rub the top and sides of the cranium without entering it.
- In such cases, entry and exit wounds are found on the scalp about 2 to 3 cm. apart, while the skull between the two wounds shows an oval or elongated gutter-like depression (gutter wound; key-hole defect).

MULTIPLE WOUNDS OF ENTRANCE AND EXIT FROM A SINGLE SHOT :
- A bullet may pass through an arm and the chest so that four wounds result.
- A bullet passing through the chest or abdomen and thigh and lower leg, produces six wounds.
- This occurs when the person is running or sitting in an unusual position.
- When the body surface is irregular, such as the breast or buttocks, several re-entries and exits can take place.

ENTRANCE WOUND IS PRESENT BUT BULLET IS NOT FOUND IN THE BODY:

This occurs when
a. the bullet entering the stomach may be vomited,
b. entering the windpipe may be coughed up,
c. entering the mouth may be spit out,
d. entering the gastrointestinal tract may be passed out in the feces, and
e. when it is so deviated or turned on coming in contact with the bone, that it passes out by the same wound as it entered.

UNEXPLAINED BULLETS IN THE BODY:
- Occasionally, more bullets are found than there are entrance wounds.
- This occurs, due to defect in the weapon, or due to faulty ammunition, or with a loaded firearm unused for several years due to prolonged exposure to high environmental temperature or humidity.
- When such a weapon is fired, the bullet may fail to come out from the muzzle.
- When it is fired again, the second bullet may go off carrying the lodged bullet with it, and both the bullets may enter the body through the same entrance wound.
- This is called a tandem buUet or piggyback bullet (tandem=one behind the other).
- The bullets may separate within the body, or before they hit the target.
- The features caused by flame, smoke and gunpowder may be diminished or absent and the wound may appear as if caused by long-range fire.
- This is because the pushing force of the second bullet is directed backwards due to obstruction caused by the first bullet impacted in the barrel.

Souvenir Bullets :
- If a bullet is present for a long time in the body, there will be no fresh bleeding in the surrounding area.
- A dense fibrous tissue capsule usually surrounds it.
- A small scar indicates the original entrance wound.
- Lead poisoning may occur due to absorption of lead from lead bullets remaining in a body.
- Synovial fluid is capable of dissolving lead.

MEDICOLEGAL QUESTIONS
1. Is the injury caused by discharge of a firearm?
   Firearm wounds are recognised by the appearance of clothing and examination of entrance and exit wounds, the track of the bullet, and the presence of bullet or pellets and residual matter in the clothing or around the entrance wound and in the tissues.
2. What kind of weapon fired the shot?
- The kind of firearm can be determined by the size, shape and composition of the bullet, and examination of cartridge, shots and was left in the body or found at the scene of the crime and the appearances of wounds.
- With the shotgun, the appearances of the wound are characteristic.
- In a muzzle-loading gun, the wad consists of a plug of paper or cloth; in a breech-loading gun of circular discs of felt or cardboard, from which the bore of the gun can be determined.
- Stains on the clothes or skin may show whether black or smokeless powder was used, and microscopic and chemical examination of the stain is helpful in finding out the particular brand of powder.
- Evidence of recent fire can be made out for a few days, by examination of the weapon for mercury vapour.
- Spent cartridge contains residues of primer and detonator.
- In firearm examination, the primary principles of identification are
1. determination of caliber and type;
2. number of rifling grooves;
3. width of rifling grooves;
4. direction (left twist or right twist) of rifling grooves;
5. pitch (angle of the spiral) of rifling.
- These are used to determine whether a bullet could have been fired in a type or model of a gun or specific weapon.
- The bullets expand into the grooves in the rifling, sealing the barrel and preventing excess escape of gasses ahead of the bullet.
- The firearms leave their signature on the cartridge case and on the bullet.
- With all rifled firearms, the bullet is slightly larger than the barrel, and as it passes through the barrel, its sides are marked by the rifling of the barrel (primary markings; class characteristics) and cause the bullet to rotate.
- Class characteristics (bar codes) are determined before manufacture of the gun and result from manufacturing specifications, design and dimensions.
- The class characteristics in fired bullet identifications would be
1. caliber,
2. number of lands and grooves,
3. direction of twist of the rifling,
4. rate of the twist of the rifling, and
5. width of the lands and grooves.

- They are most useful in identifying the make and model of the gun involved.
- The surface of the bullet is also grooved by irregularities on the inner surface of the barrel itself (secondary markings; individual or accidental characteristics), which are specific for that particular weapon.
- These irregularities are produced by the sticking of the particles of the bullet to the bore when shots are fired and is known as 'metallic fouling'.
- Individual characteristics also result accidentally during the manufacturing process, are usually microscopic in nature, and have random distribution.
- These marks are more pronounced on lead bullets where the grooves score the bullet.
- For jacketed bullets, the land markings are more pronounced.
- They are useful to identify one specific gun to the exclusion of all others ("bullet fingerprinting").
- Sometimes, lead bullets may carry a weave pattern of cloth.
- The bullet found in the body known as crime bullet or exhibit bullet is compared under a comparison microscope, with one fired from the suspected weapon known as test bullet.
- The suspected weapon is fired, using the same brand and type of ammunition into a box filled with cotton waste (bullet traps), a bag of rags, a sand bag, oiled saw-dust, blocks of ice, water tanks (bullet recovery tank) or against white blotting paper.
- Fresh pork skins, cleanly shaven are ideal for comparison with patterns on human skin.

3. **From what distance and direction was the shot fired?**
   - The range of fire is determined by the presence or absence of the marks of smoke.flame, tattooing, etc., on or in the body of the victim.
   - When the range is greater, it can be determined only approximately and with difficulty, from the nature of wounds and penetration.
   - Test fire with a suspect weapon using the same at varying distances until a similar spread of pellet markings and other findings is achieved on the target, is useful in estimating the range.
   - The direction of the track depends upon the posture of the body at the time of impact.

4. **If multiple wounds of entrance and exit are present, could they have been produced by a single bullet?** (Already discussed)

5. **If multiple wounds are present, were they produced from the same or different weapons?**
   This is determined by examination of the wound and of the bullet, cartridge, shots, wad, etc.

6. **WHEN WAS THE FIREARM DISCHARGED ?**
   - Tissue reaction to firearm injury is similar as for other types of injury.
   - If black powder has been used hydrogen sulphide may persist in the barrel for a few hours if the breech is closed.
   - The washing from barrels having discharged gunpowder are alkaline, contain nitrite, sulphate and thiosulphate.
   - Smokeless powder leaves a dark grey deposit in the barrel of a recently discharged firearm.
   - It forms a neutral solution with distilled water and contains nitrites and nitrates, but no sulphides.
   - The mixture of gases of explosion has a peculiar smell, which can be noticed prominently up to 4 to 6 hours.
   - After 24 hours no smell is experienced after the discharge of a gun.
   - Due to backward escape of gasses from a fired weapon, the hand of the person that fired the gun sometimes will receive gasses and particles of unburnt powder on index finger, thumb and connecting web area.
   - Rarely smoke deposits are found on both hands.

i. **PARAFFIN TEST OR DERMAL NITRATE TEST:**
    It detects gun powder residue (nitrates and nitrites).
ii. **HARRISON AND GILROY TEST :**
    - This test is not specific for firearm discharge residues, but only for certain elements or compounds to be found in such residues.
    - This detects the presence of antimony, barium and lead.
    - A cotton swab moistened with molar hydrochloric acid is used.
iii. **ATOMIC ABSORPTION SPECTROSCOPY (AAS) AND FLAMELESS ATOMIC ABSORPTION SPECTROSCOPY (F AAS):**
    - It detects antimony, barium and lead from primer and copper vapourised from cartridge case or the bullet jacket.
    - Palms and backs of hands (four surfaces) are swabbed with four cotton swabs moistened with hydrochloric acid.
    - A fifth swab is moistened with acid and used as control.
    - This analytical system utilizes high temperatures to vapourise the metallic elements of the primer residues and to detect and quantitate them.
    - Typically the residue is deposited on the back of the firing hand of the suspect who fired the gun:
    - Detection of primer residue in the palm suggests a defense gesture rather than firing of a gun.
    - In suicide with handgun, primer residue on the palm may be due to cradling the gun with this hand at the time of firing.
    - With rifles and shotguns residue is often detected on the non-firing hand that has been used to steady the muzzle against the body.
    - If the person survives, loss of residue may occur due to washing of hands or rubbing them against different materials.

NAA and AAS can aid in
1. identifying holes in clothing, tissues, wood,etc. as bullet holes, from the presence of lead, antimony, barium and copper,
2. determining range of fire from concentration pattern of antimony around the bullet hole,
3. determining common origin of bullet fragments of shotgun pellets found at different places, from the concentrations of lead, antimony, arsenic, copper and silver in these alloys, and
4. determining from the presence of lead, antimony and barium on hands whether or not a person has fired a gun.

iv. **SCANNING ELECTRON MICROSCOPE-ENERGY DISPERSIVE X-RAY ANALYSIS (SEM-EDXA):**
    - It is the most sophisticated tool which can detect minute traces of gunshot residue (GSR) found on the body of a suspect.
    - As a gun is fired, the GSR comprises chemical substances that burn and produce gasses providing the velocity for the bullet, and metals such as antimony, barium, copper, etc. are also sprayed out and get deposited on the hands, clothes and even on the face of the person.
    - In this gunshot residues are removed from the body using adhesive lifts.
    - The material removed is scanned with SEM for the gunshot residues particles.
    - The X-ray analysis capability is used to identify the chemical elements in each of the particles.
    - The test is positive up to 12 hours after firing.
    - The investigator can conclusively prove if the weapon was used by the suspect with a negligible margin of error.

7. **HOW LONG DID THE VICTIM SURVIVE?**
   It depends on the cause of death, i.e., whether from shock and hemorrhage, injury to a vital organ or septic complications.

8. **HOW MUCH ACTIVITY COULD THE VICTIM PERFORM FOLLOWING THE INJURY?**
   - This varies considerably depending on the site of injury and the organ involved.
   - If the bullet destroys the motor area, brain stem or cervical cord or if a gaping laceration of the heart or aorta is produced, the victim becomes immediately incapacitated.
   - Death is instantaneous if medulla is involved.
   - Sometimes, through-and -through bullet wounds of the brain or heart do not cause immediate disability and the person may be able to carry out voluntary acts.
   - In transection of a major coronary artery, prolonged survival is unlikely.
   - Wounds of the auricles are most rapidly fatal; wounds of the right ventricle come next and the wounds of the left ventricle are the least rapidly fatal.
   - The amount and rapidity of blood loss will also help to form an opinion about the extent of physical activity that would be possible.
   - In any injury to other parts of the body, the victim may be able to walk about.

9. **IS IT A CASE OF HOMICIDE, SUICIDE OR ACCIDENT?**

Trait	Homicide	Suicide	Accident
Site of entrance wounds	Any area	Head or heart	Any area
Shot distance	Any range	Contact or very close range	Close or very close range
Direction	Usually one	Upward or backward	Any direction
Number of wounds	One to many	Usually one	One
Hand pressing trigger	Powder residues absent	Powder residues present.	Powder residues present
Position of the weapon	Not found at the scene	Found at the scene	Found at the scene
Scene	Any place	Usually in his own house	In his house or while hunting, etc.
Sex	Any sex	Usually males	usually males.
Motive	Gang feuds, robbery, revenge, etc.	Insanity, incurable illness, financial loss, etc.	Nil.

BOMB EXPLOSION WOUNDS
- A bomb is a container filled with an explosive mixture and missiles, which is fired either by detonator or a fuse.
- Terrorist bombs often involve only 2 to 10 kg. of explosives.
- When an explosion occurs, the explosive material produces a large volume of gas, and releases a large amount of energy.
- Pressure of up to 1,000 tons per sq. inch. can be generated.
- A minimum pressure of about 700 kilopascals (100 lb/ sq inch) is necessary for tissue damage in humans.

A person can be injured by an explosion in a number of ways.
- Disruptive effects
- Burns
- Air blast
- Flying missiles
- Falling masonry
- Fumes

1. **Disruptive Effects :**
   - If the victim is almost in contact with a large bomb he may be blown to pieces, e.g., when the victim is carrying it.
   - The pieces can be scattered over an area of 200 meters radius.
   - Many parts of the body are never found, having been disrupted into tiny fragments and mixed with the masonry and other debris of the bomb site.
   - A bomb exploding on the ground may cause severe damage or traumatic amputation of the lower legs.
   - A bomb which explodes when the victim is bending over it, may cause severe damage to arms, face and front of the chest.
   - When the victim is a few meters away or with a smaller explosion, disruption is usually limited to mutilation of a localized area.

2. **Burns:**
   - The temperature of the explosive gasses can exceed 2000°C., and the radiated heat can cause flash burns.
   - It burns nearby objects and clothing.
   - The flame causes extensive burns, which involve irregular areas of skin to a different degree.
   - Tight clothing protects, so beneath collars, bras, waist bands, socks and shoes.

3. **Air Blast :**
   - An explosion produces a 'shock wave' which spreads concentrically from the site of explosion at about the speed of sound (1120 ft/sec).
   - This wave of very high pressure is followed by a weak wave of negative pressure (below the atmosphere), a suction which lasts about five times as long.
   - A shock wave exceeding 700 kilopascals (100 lb/sq. inch) pressure is necessary to cause serious damage to the body.
   - The shock wave can throw the victim against a wall or toss him through the air causing blunt force injuries.
   - The clothes may be blown off by the blast.
   - The clothing should be retained for chemical analysis.
   - The shock wave passes through the body.
   - The homogeneous tissues like liver and muscle are not damaged.
   - Blast injury of lungs is seen if the victim is within a few meters of the explosion, and at such a range, the victim usually dies from other injuries.

- Lungs show subpleural patchy hemorrhages, scattered at random, often in the line of ribs.
- Sectioning of lungs shows more discrete scattered areas of hemorrhage, often with a tendency to be more central than periphery.
- Microscopically, alveolar ruptures, thinning of alveolar septae, enlargement of alveolar spaces and circumscribed subpleural, intra-alveolar and perivascular hemorrhages are the main findings.
- Desquamated alveolar and bronchial epithelium is seen lying free.
- This causes reactive pulmonary oedema and blood-stained froth is found in the air-passages, and later bronchopneumonia.
- This specific pulmonary injury of air blast is called 'blast lung'.
- The tympanic membrane most commonly ruptures with hemorrhage in the ear.
- Damage to cochlea is more frequent.
- Subperitoneal hemorrhage and hemorrhages in mesentery and omentum vary in size and laceration of abdominal organs may occur.
- Intracranial hemorrhage, contusion of the brain, injuries of heart and aorta, pneumothorax, ruptured stomach and bowel may occur.
- Death may occur from systemic air embolism, from air which enters the pulmonary veins after blast damage to the lungs.

Underwater blasts:
- When the explosion is in the water, the pressure changes are called underwater blasts.
- The physical changes are similar to those of explosion in air.
- Injuries occur mostly in the gastrointestinal tract and less commonly in the lungs.
- Most of the lung injury is due to pressure transmitted from the abdomen through the diaphragm.
- Solid blast refers to a wave of energy that spreads through a rigid structure when an explosive is detonated near it and people in contact with it can be injured.
- Steel construction of tanks and warships conduct shock waves well and cause solid blast injury.
- The injuries are mostly skeletal.
- The fractures depend on the position of the person.
- Fractures of legs and vertebral columns are more common.
- Gastrointestinal damage is more common than lung damage.
- In some cases, death may occur without any external injury.

4. **Flying Missiles:**
   - The blast may drive multiple fragments of bomb or pieces of nearby objects, e.g., gravel, glass, wood, brick, plaster, etc. through the air into the skin and cause bruises, abrasions and puncture lacerations intimately mixed on the skin.
   - This triad of injury(marshalls triad) is diagnostic.
   - Most of the bruises and abrasions are less than 1 cm. in diameter, although they tend to unite .
   - The puncture-lacerations are also usually of this size.
   - They are ragged, sometimes with soiled margins, and may contain foreign material, such as scraps of clothing, wood or metal.
   - The skin can be darkened by an explosion which drives dust into the skin and causes fairly uniform tattooing.
   - The force of the bomb explosion is extremely directional and the pattern of injury might indicate that the person was carrying the bomb or bending over it or sitting to one side of it.

5. **Falling Masonry :**
   - When a building is destroyed by a bomb blast, the persons inside sustain multiple injuries and die of traumatic asphyxia.
   - Death may be caused due to burns, blunt force injuries, failing debris and rarely from systemic embolism.
6. **Fumes :**
   - If a bomb explodes in a confined space, enough CO is produced to cause asphyxia.
   - In a victim of bomb death, X-rays of tissues should be taken, as pieces of metal, especially the detonating mechanism, may be seen.
   Incendiary bombs
   - Incendiary bombs, e.g., napalm bombs primarily cause burns.
   - A temperature of about 1000° C is produced.
   - In incendiary bombs, usually phosphorus and magnesium are added.
   - The Molotov cocktail is an incendiary bomb which is thrown by hand.
   - In a crude type of this bomb, a bottle is filled with gasoline and a rag to serve as a wick.
   - The wick is lighted and thrown at the target.
   - Various acids and chemicals are sometimes added to increase the destructive effects.

INVESTIGATION OF BOMBING INCIDENTS:
1. Whether the explosion was caused by a bomb ?
   - Dispersed explosion usually occurs in houses when domestic gas leaks into the atmosphere and mixes with the air to form an explosive mixture that then catches fire.
   - A dispersed explosion can blow off clothing and burn the exposed skin.
   - All the exposed parts of the body are affected and all the burns are of the same depth.
   - A bomb explosion (localized explosion) never causes extensive burns.
   - Injuries by blast force, and the fragments are seen on the body.
   - A part of a limb is blown off or a localized area of the body is mutilated.
   - The triad of bruises, abrasions and puncture-lacerations with tattooing of part of the body is diagnostic of bomb explosion.
2. Identification of the dead.
3. Number of dead persons.
4. Cause of Death :
   Death may result from multiple injuries, burns, shock or cerebral air embolism.
5. Circumstances of Death :
   - To differentiate the terrorist from the peaceful citizen, the reconstruction of the scene and the circumstances of the deaths from the autopsy findings are helpful.
   - The injuries on the victims, particularly their type, severity and distribution are of much help.
a. Explosive Force Declines Rapidly:
   - Injury due to the explosive force itself is likely within a few meters of the bomb.
   - With a terrorist bomb, when a person is blown to pieces he must have been in contact with it, i.e., either carrying the bomb, sitting with it or arming it.
   - Persons can be injured by flying fragments and collapsing structures when at considerable distance from a terrorist bomb.
b. Explosive Force is Highly Directional:
   - The parts of the body directly exposed to explosive force only are injured.
   - An explosion at ground level injuries mainly involve lower legs and feet.
   - When a person is in front of a bomb when it blows up, the face, chest, forearms, hands, inner thighs and the legs below the knees are injured, but the back of the body, the lower legs and face escape.

- If a person is bending down over the bomb, the face, chest, lower legs and hands are severely damaged.
- The legs may be blown off or the abdomen disrupted or the hands and arms torn away in the person who was planting the bomb.
- If the thigh, pelvic region and abdomen are damaged, the bomb may have been carried on the lap.
- If a parcel bomb is opened by a person sitting at a desk, his face, chest and hands are injured.
- If a bomb explodes behind a person sitting in a chair, injuries will be produced on the back of the legs below the knee and on the back of the trunk.
- All bodies should be X-rayed before autopsy to identify any radio-opaque objects including those from the bomb mechanism, such as small springs or contacts from the timer or detonator.

DOMESTIC GAS EXPLOSIONS:
- They occur due to leaks in the gas supply.
- Natural gas explodes at concentrations in air between 5 to 15 percent.
- Ignition is usually caused by matches or candles, fires, sparking electric switches.
- The explosion is accompanied by a momentary flame that sets fire to furnishings.
- The air pressure usually rises to less than 10 psi, due to escape through broken windows and doors.
- Deaths are rare.
- The person can be thrown off their feet and injured.
- The damage is haphazard or diffuse.
- The flame singes hair and causes localized superficial burns of exposed surfaces.
- Most deaths occur when the building collapses and the victims are buried in the debris.

Mechanical Explosion :
- Mechanical explosion occurs when a steam boiler bursts due to increased pressure.
- Heat and large volumes of gas are produced.
- The effects are similar to those of chemical explosions

CHAPTER- 10
REGIONAL INJURIES

```
                          Regional injuries
                                 |
        Head injuries      vertebral column        others

Scalp    skull    content of     its parts    spinal cord    chest
                  skull                                      Ribs
                                                             Lung
```

In open type head injuries duramater gets torn and in closed type it remains intact.

Head injury:
- It is a morbid state, resulting from gross structural changes in the scalp, skull & the Contents of the skull.
- The mechanical force may or may not be directly proportional to the amount of injury.

Scalp:
- The thickness of the scalp ranging from few to 15mm
- Most wounds of the scalp are caused by blunt forces eg: fall from height ,blow on the head.
- Scalp wounds presented mostly as contusions or lacerations

Contusions:
In the scalp it may occur in the following areas,
- Superficial fascia(connective tissue)
- Temporalis muscle
- Between the aponeurosis and the Periosteum
- Contusions in the superficial fascia appear as localised swelling and are limited in size because of dense fibro-fatty tissue of fascia.
- Contusions between the Periosteum and the aponeurosis does not show any colour change.

Battle's sign:
- Temporal bruise may appear later behind the ear (echymoses in the mastoid region)
- Bruicing of the scalps can be better felt than seen.
- Multiple contusions in the scalp may join together it is difficult to find out whether there is single blow or multiple blow.

Lacerations:
- Laceration of the scalp resemble the incised wound..
- Blood will be collected out of the vessels due to compression
- Considerable bleeding will occur but the blood will not be projected around the crime scene
- With repeated blows to the scalp, blood will be scattered over the Assailant. By this we can find out the relative position of the victim and assailant.
- We can also find out whether they were inflicted with the right or left hand.
- If the laceration in the right side of the scalp the assailant inflict through left hand & vice versa.
- Blood will be collected out of the vessels due to compression
- Considerable bleeding will occur but the blood will not be projected around the crime scene
- With repeated blows to the scalp, blood will be scattered over the Assailant. By this we can find out the relative position of the victim and assailant.
- We can also find out whether they were inflicted with the right or left hand.
- If the laceration in the right side of the scalp the assailant inflict through left hand & vice versa.

Face:
Bleeding is more in facial wounds due to rich vascularity

Eyes:
Blow on the eye with a blunt weapon may cause Permanent injury to the cornea, Iris, lens or detachment and rupture of the retina and traumatic cataract.

Black eyes:
It is due to Periorbital bruising.
It is caused by
- Direct blow or kick in the anterior aspect of the orbit.
- Injury to the forehead.
- Fracture at the base of the skull in the anterior fossa.
- Fracture of medial wall and orbital floor causes herniation of periorbital fat and inferior rectus muscle into the maxillary sinus.
- X-ray shows a 'tear drop' or polypoid mass in the roof of maxillary sinus.
- It is also known as **Racoon's sign**.

Nose:
Blow on the head may cause bleeding due to partial detachment of mucous membrane without any injury to the nose.

Ears:
Blow to the ear may produce rupture of the tympanum and deafness.

Facial bones:
Softening of the face may result from striking with a heavy stone

Teeth:
A fall or blow with a blunt weapon may cause fracture or dislocation of teeth with contusions and lacerations in lips and gums.

Skull:

fractures

Direct injuries
It occurs in the cases such as:
- Compression or crushing of the head under the wheel vehicle
- An object in motion striking the Head **E.g:bullets, bricks.**
- head in motion striking an object eg:falls & Traffic injuries.

Indirect injuries
- It occur when the person land on the ground with feet or buttocks the pressure is transferred through vertebral column finally to the skull.

Mechanism of fracture of skull
1. Fractures due to local deformation
- If a small mass travelling at great speed sticks the head squarely.
- The affected part of skull bone goes inwards & forms a conical shaped invagination.
- At the apex(centre)of the cone ,the inner part of the skull will be stretched & the outer part gets compressed.
- So the part of the skull gets fracture first ,if the force acts continuously then the outer part of skull also gets fracture.
- Now the fracture line will be completed & runs from the centre part radially.
- At the periphery of the indentation the bone is bent in the opposite direction of the force.
- Convexity of the bandies outwards ,here the outer part of the skull fractures first.
- Here the fractures lines tend to run circularly to in close the base of the indentation.
- If the force act continuously a piece of bone get fragmented the radical fracture lines will be loosed and the depressed to form a comminuted fracture
- Due to the fragments a injury look like it could be a multiple blow to the part skull mistakenly.

Fractures due to general deformation:

When the skull is compressed eg:if application of the injuring force to the lateral part of the skull, the vertical and longitudinal diameters are increased the skull distant from side to side and may fracture by bending.

The skull gets compressed in the following conditions :
1. Between two external objects , Luchas the ground and wheel of a car.
2. Between an external object and spinal column.
3. Body is at rest and heavy abject falls on the top of the head.

Types of skull fractures..
1. Fissured fractures
- It is the most common fracture
- It involves entire thickness of the bone or the inner part or outer part of the skull
- About 70% of skull fractures are linear
- Mostly inner part of the skull gets fracture due to its brittle nature
- Fissured fractures are due to heavy weapon with broad striking surface
- Fall on the feet or buttocks may also causes this type of fracture.
- When a blow is struck on the side and the head is free to move the fracture starts at the point of impact and runs parallel to the direction of the force.
- If the head is supported when struck the fractures start at the opposite side of the impact
- **Example :** In bilateral compression the fractures often starts at the vertex or commonly at the base
- From the hematoma of the scalp we can find out the scale of impact
- Injury of the head due to fall is mostly situated at the level of the hat
- While an injury due to a blow is commonly situated above the hat level
- The fracture line ends to follow an irregular course and is usually not greater than hair's breadth
- The fracture line is often red but usually there no haemorrhage

Multiple blows on the head
- About 20% of the blow are not visible on the x-ray.
- In case of blow and subsequent fall, the fracture lines produced from fall are arrested by the fractures line which are produced by the blow.
- If the two blows are struck the impact may be same but we can differentiate which is the 1st & 2nd blows.
- First blow to the skull will weaken the skull ,the subsequent blows causes a degree of damage out of the proportion of the applied force.
- **Example :** A second blow to the already fractured skull result in the wide spread collapse of the skull and the fragments of bone & the weapon itself go far into the brain.

Different types of blow with respect to the side of impact of skull:
    Anterior blow:
        It produce linear fracture of the orbit, it cross the middle through the cribriform plate
        Pituitary fossa
        Basal part of the occipital bone

Blows to the Anterior parietal bone:
        It produces fracture at the Anterior temporal area
        Vertex
        Anterior & middle cranial fossa

Interparietal blows:
        Fracture running towards the base involving lesser wing of sphenoid and pituitary fossa

Blows to the side of head:
        Here the fracture in middle cranial fossa results in damage to the pituitary gland and the hypothalamus.

Posterior parietal blow:
        Here the fracture lines often cross the petrous temporal bone and extend towards the inner ends of the middle and the posterior cranial fossa.

Blow to the occipital region:
- Here the fracture line crosses the foramen magnum.
- Ocupital buttress petrous temporal bone middle cranial fossa.

Interesting facts:
        Human adult head weighs about 4.5kg, a linear fracture of skull may be produced when the head is hit on the side by a stone weighing 90 to 120g and when a weight of 2.25kg is dropped through a distance of one foot

Puppe's rule:
- The second fracture line will stop at the previous fractures
- New fracture line join the old fracture but didn't cross it
- It helps in sequencing the fracture lines formed due to repeated blows.

2. **Depressed fractures:**
   - They are produced by heavy weapon with small strictly surface.
   - They are also called fractures-a-la signature (signature fracture)
   - Pattern of the fracture resembles the weapon's pattern
   - The part of the skull which got struck first shows maximum depression.
   - Linear fracture may radiate from the depressed fracture indicating the direction of force .

3. **Elevated fracture:**
   - Here one end of fractured segment is elevated over the surface of the skull and other end is depressed into the cranial cavity.
   - This type of fracture is produced by heavy weapon with sharp edge.

4. **Comminuted fracture:**
   - Here there are two or more intersecting lines of fracture which divided the bone into three or more fragments
   - They are caused by heavy weapon with broad area
   - When there is no displacement of the fragment ,It resemble a spider's web or mosaic.

5. **Pond or Indented fractures:**
   - This a simple indent of the skull which results from an obstetric forceps blade ,a blow from a blunt object or forcible impact against some protruding object.
   - It is the variant of depressed fracture .
   - Also known as Ping Pong ball fracture.

6. **Gutter fracture:**
    They are formed when part of the thickness of the bone is removed so as to form a gutter
    E.g: in oblique bullet wounds

7. **Ring or foramen fracture:**
    - It is a type of focussed fracture which encircles the skull here the anterior third is separated at its junction with the middle and posterior third
    - The fracture runs from foramen magnum, it involves middle ear and finally reach deepof the nose
    - As a result the skull is separated from the spine
    - It occurs due to the following situations they are
        i. Falls from a height on to the foot or buttocks
        ii. A severe blow to the vertex
        iii. A forceful blow on the chin in traffic accident
        iv. Sudden violent turn of the head on the spine

8. **Perforating fractures:**
    - These are caused by firearms and pointed sharp weapons like daggers,knives or an axe
    - The weapon pass from one side & leave through other side create a clean cut opening ,which corresponds to the cross section of weapon used

9. **Blow out fracture:**
    Blunt trauma to the eye in which the forces are transmitted via the globe to the bony orbit causing fracture of medical wall and the floor of orbit.

10. **Diastatic or sutural fractures**
    Separation of the sutures occur only in young persons due to blow on head with blunt weapon.
    It is usually seen in sagittal suture.

11. **Expressed fractures**
    These occur as massive fragmentation of skull where some pieces may be found outside the head.

Note : Ossa Triquetra: Sometimes small portions of the brim of skull ossify from irregular independent centres and remain for variable periods of time as small bone. This is called as Ossa Triquetra.

Fracture at base of skull
- It produced in following conditions
- force applied at the level of the base
- General deformation of the skull where ever the forces applied
- Force extension from the vault
- Force applied to the base through the spinal column or face
- Most basal fractures trend to meet &cross the pituitary fossa

Fractures of the base of the skull may be
i. longitudinal - which divide the base in to two halves , it is due to blunt impact on the face and forehead on the back of the head, or in front to back or back to front compression of the head

Ex: run over by a vehicle

ii. Transverse – which divide the base into front & back half, it is due to impact on either side of the head or side to side compression of the head

Ex : run over by a vehicle

iii. Ring fractures
- Anterior cranial fossa fractures are usually seen in direct impact or heavy blow on the chin
- Here blood & csf escape through the nose
- Roof of the orbit get fractured due to fall a back of head
- Middle cranial fossa get fracture due to direct impact behind the ear
- Posterior cranial fossa get fracture due to direct impact on the back of head
- Basal fractures are usually associated with cranial nerve damage
- complications

1. Fracture in anterior cranial fossa
    i. CSF rhinorrhea
    i. Bleeding from nose
    i. Parasthesia is tip of nose
    i. Leptomeningitis
2. Fracture in middle cranial fossa
    i. CSF ottorrhea
    i. Bleeding from ears
    i. Battle's sign
    i. Facial nerve palsy
    i. CSF rhinorrhea
3. Fracture involving paranasal sinuses may cause cranial pneumatocele
4. Direct communication between the cranial cavity and the airway in the sphenoid sinus is produce in fracture of the sella turcia blood escape in to the airway result in instantaneous death
5. Shock
6. Portal entry of bacteria
7. Fat & bone marrow embolism
8. Depressed fracture of the skull pressing the brain may case severe dysfunction coma and death

Age of skull injury
- Healing occurs without the formation of visible callus
- In injury the periosteal blood vessels are damaged delaying the development of external callus
- The edges of fissured fracture stick together within a week
- Fibrous tissue form which 3 to 5 weeks
- If the edges are not in apposition the fibrous tissue from within the months
- If there is much loss of bone the gap is filled only with fibrous tissue

Occurence of brain injury
   i) It occur in
Peneration by a forein object such as kinfe, bullet or fragments of skull in a depressed fracture
   ii) Distortion of the skull.

Contrecoup fracture
Fracture of the skull occurring opposite to the side of force is known as Contrecoup fracture
Usually occur when the head is not supported

Mechanism of cerebral injury:
- Severe brain damage may be caused without actual blow or fall on the head
- Eg: by shaking the infant as in child abuse, may cause subdural haemorrhage
- The brain is easily distorted but is incompressible ,change in velocity either acceleration or deceleration with a rotational element causes brain damage
- In either deceleration or acceleration of the head ,the initial sudden change in velocity would set the head in rotation and this rotational force would transmitted to the brain which would glide, on the duramater.
- The area of the skull beneath the impact get momentarily depressed even without fracture ,may strike the underlying brain causing compression and typical cone shaped contusions are produced on the cortex,
- Other areas of skull like adjacent area of the impact bulge outward simultaneously to accommodate the deformation
- Gliding or shear strains are produced by the angular rotation of the head , which move adjacent strata of tissue laterally
- Sudden arrest of the movement of the skull leads to deceleration of the skull but momentum of the brain will not change, it result in impact of the brain against the wide wall of the skull result in contusion of the cortex &damage to the base of cerebrum ,corpus callosum and brainstem

- As the cerebellum is smaller and lighter it is less liable to damage from rotatory movements of the head
- Holbourn postulates that brain tissues are injured when its constituent particles are pulled so far apart that they do not join up again properly when the blow is over
- In the brain, the amount of this pulling apart is proportional to the shear strains

Contusions of the brain:
- When the head is rotated by an impact, the layers of brain tissue slide over each other at different depths in the cortex.
- Which cause damage to the blood vessels.
- Contusion may occur on surface of cortex or deeper down.

Cerebral contusions:
- They are produced by blunt force and are found in grey and white matter due to injury of blood vessels by mechanical stress
- Contusions are most often found in the frontal and temporal lobes of the brain
- Deeper structures like basal ganglia, midbrain and brain stem are contused especially from impacts to forehead and vertex
- Medulla may be contused in association with fractures which extend into the foremen magnum or involve the atlas and axis
- A larger hematoma may be formed by their union especially in persons with hypertension or in alcoholics

Blows			
Blows to the back of head	Blows to the top of the head	Blows to the side of the head	Blows to the front of the head
It is usually due to falling backwards result in little or no occipital contusion, but it produce sub-frontal & temporal bole contusion and sometimes sub-arachnoid hemorrhage	It produce minimal coup contusion but prominent contre-coup sub temporal or uncal contusion	It produce a lateral coup lesion and more prominent contre coup contusion of the lateral aspect of the opposite hemisphere	It usually do not produce cerebral contusion or laceration. There may be only diffuse subarachnoid haemorrhage. Contusions excite cerebral oedema in the adjacent brain and cause a rise in intracranial pressure. Old contusions appear as shrunken yellowish brown area known as plaque Jaures. The combination of extensive contusion and an associated subdural haematoma is referred to as 'burst lobe' usually seen in frontal or temporal lobe.

```
                        Types of contusion
        ┌──────────────┬──────────────┬──────────────┐
Intermediary coup   Fracture contusions   Gliding contusions   Herniation contusions
   contusions
```

Intermediary coup contusions	Fracture contusions	Gliding contusions	Herniation contusions
Contusions found in deeper structures of the brain, such as white matter, basal ganglia, corpusum and brainstem along the line of impact between the coup and countrecoup points called intermediary coup contusions	Contusions caused by fracture of the skull are called fracture contusions	They are caused by stretching and shearing forces occurring in the region of arachnoid granulations. Eg: falls and motor vehicle accidents Here the contusions are seen in the cortex and white matter of the frontal and central convolutions	Momentary shifting of the brain towards the foremen magnum cause contusions in the cerebellar tonsils and medulla oblongata due to herniation

Age of contusion	
In a hour	– Ischaemic changes occur in neurons
5-12 days	-proliferation of capillaries
First two works	–Macrophages containing fat are present, proliferation of Astrocyte is seen.
2 months	– fullformation of scar is seen. pale or golden yellow in colour.

Lacerations:
- Loss of continuity of the substance of brain is called cerebral lacerations
- Which are mostly due to trauma
- Lacerations are caused by stretching and shearing forces within the tissues produced by blunt force.
- Surface lacerations are accompanied by ruptures of the piamater and subarachnoid haemorrhage.
- Lacerations are usually surrounded by group of contusions
- When the parenchyma is completely disorganized it is called **pulpefaction.**
- Lacerations of the brain mainly seen in depressed fracture of the skull.
- All penetrating injuries produce lacerations of brain.
- Lacerations may also be produced without the fracture of skull.
- They are usually found in regions where the brain is in contact with projecting buttresses and ridges on the inner surface of the skull eg: temporal poles and orbital surface of the frontal lobes.
- In severe hyperextension of the head, as in motor vehicle accidents lacerations may be produced in the pyramids at the junction of the medulla-oblongata and pons.
- These lessons are associated with fracture of the base of the skull and upper cervical vertebrae.
- Healing of surface lacerations cause adhesion between brain and the duramater.
- Healing of deep lacerations involving verntricles may produce large glial cysts filled with CSF.

Contre-coup lesions:
- Coup means that the injury is located beneath the area of impact.
- Contre-coup means that the lesion is present in an area opposite to the side of impact .
- Contre-coup lesions are due to shear strains which generated during sudden rotation of the head.
- Holbourn defines shear strain as a strain produced by applied forces which cause or tend to cause adjoining parts of the body to slide relatively to each other in a direction parallel to their planes of contact.
- A much greater shear strain develops as a result of the rotation of the skull ,because the changes in the rotational velocity are usually greater at the pole opposite to the point of impact, countre-coup injuries are more extensive.
- Contre-coup injuries can also occur when a blow is struck on a fixed head eg: If a person is lying on the ground or against some other surface a heavy blow on the upper temporal or parietal area may cause typical contre-coup injuries either in the contralateral temporal or parietal cortex ,or against the falx on the inner side of the the ipsilateral lobe .There is often coup injury also.

> Contre-coup injury is caused when the moving head is suddenly decelerated by hitting a firm surface eg: striking the head on the ground during a fall usually seen in traffic accidents .Sudden arrest of the head results in the brain which is still in motion ,striking the arrested skull [decelerated injury]

> A blow to the head causes the skull to move forward ,but the brain lags behind for a brief period and the skull strikes the brain [Accelerated injury]

> Formation of a cavity or vacuum in the cranial cavity on the opposite side of impact ,as the brain lags behind the moving skull, the vacuum exerts a suction effect which damages the brain

Brain injures
- Occipital injuries produce severe and extensive contre-coup lesions in the frontal region
- Fall on the frontal region will not produce occipital contre-coup injuries
- In temporal or parietal impacts contre-coup injuries are likely to be diametrically opposite on the contralateral surface of the brain
- A contre-coup lesion may be seen on the opposite side of the same hemisphere eg: a blow on the left parietal area may cause contrecoup lesion on the medial side of the left cerebral hemisphere against the falx

Medicolegal importance:
- A blow to the head produces coup contusions,while contrecoup contusions are either small or absent
- A fall on the head produces contre-coup contusions while coup contusions are small or absent
- Contre-coup injury is seen in skull, brain, liver, heart and lungs.

Concussion of the brain
- Concussion is a state of temporary unconsciousness due to head injury comes on immediately after injury is always followed by amnesia and tends to spontaneous recovery
- True concussion may last for seconds or minutes
- It is due to loss of electrophysiologicdys function of reticular activating system
- **Mechanism** -cerebral concussion occurs due to acceleration /deceleration of the head
- Violent head movement causes shearing or stetching of the nerve fibers and axonal damage
- Severe injuries occur in coronal head motion [left ,right]only
- Sagittal head motion [up & down] produce mild or moderate injury

- At low levels of acceleration/ deceleration ,anatomical damage of the axons does not occur but there is physiological dysfunction the axon may recovery or undergo degeneration.
- With increased physical force ,there is immediate structural damage of axons with immediate stoppage of all activities.
- In mild concussion ,consciousness is not last ,and there is no confusion or disorientation and amnesia may or may not be present
- In severe concussion, there is amnesia and loss of consciousness

Causes
- Cerebral concussion may be produced by direct violence to the head
- Indirect violence as a result of violent fall upon the feet or buttocks or by an unexpected fall on the ground in traffic or industrial accidents

Clinical Features :
1. Flaccid muscles
2. Dilated pupils no response in light reflex
3. Pulse is weak and slow
4. Respiration is shallow
5. Amnesia
6. With severe movement of the head shearing stresses occur in the brain which produce numerous small or punctate haemorrhages throughout the brain called **"commotio cerebri"**

Theories
- The most acceptable hypothesis is "diffuse neuronal injury".
- Experimental evidence suggests that in concussion direct damage occurs to the brainstem reticular formation
- Interference with reticular formation may cause damage to any Part of the brain
- Damage to the Neuron result fromraised intracranialtension ,brainstem deformation or shearing strain but it commonly occurs with acceleration or deceleration injuries
- Death may occur without the patient regaining consciousness or he /she may recover partially and then die suddenly due to concussion of vital cerebral centres.
- In case of recovery ,post concussion syndrome may follow with headache ,dizziness, nausea, vomiting, insomnia and mental irritability.
- The victim may exhibit automatism ,he may commit some violent or criminal act, complete recovery takes place in less than ten days
- Diffuse axonal injury occurs ,when head acceleration occurs over a long time period, as in traffic accidents and falls from a considerable height.

features of diffuse axonal injury:
1) Focal lesion in the corpus callosum and other midline structures like interventricular septum and wall of the third venticle
2) Focal lesion in one or both dorsolateral parts of the rostral brainstem
3) Microscopic evidence of numerous axonal swellings and axonal bulbs

Diffuse axonal injury

	Coma	signs of brainstem dysfunction
Mild	6 to 24 hrs	Absent
Moderate	>24hrs	Absent
Severe	>24hrs	present

Autopsy
- Petechial haemorrhage found in the cortex function of white &grey matter ,roof of the fourth ventricle ,under the piamater of the upper segments of cervical cord.
- Oedema ,foci of myelin degradation may be found
- I mild DAI some axons may be damaged.

Intracranial haemorrhage:
If the bleeding is small and thin layered it is called haemorrhage
If the bleeding is large/more and space occupying it is called haematoma

Types of haemorrhage:
1. Epidural haemorrhage
2. Subdural haemorrhage
3. Subarachnoid haemorrhage

1)Epidural haemorrhage:
Anatomy:
- Duramater is a strong and greyish blue connective tissue membrane
- It has two layers outer and inner layer
- Outer layer is firmly attached to the skull
- Inner layer merges with subarachnoid layer

Control involved in epidural haemorrhage
1. Middle meningeal artery (most common)
2. Anterior ethmoidal artery
3. Transverse sinus
4. Superior sagittal sinus
5. It is seen in young adults (age 20-40 years)
6. It is the **least common intracranial haemorrhage but it has highest chance of fatality.**

Epidural haemorrhage is caused almost exclusively due to trauma Vessel injured depends upon the site of trauma

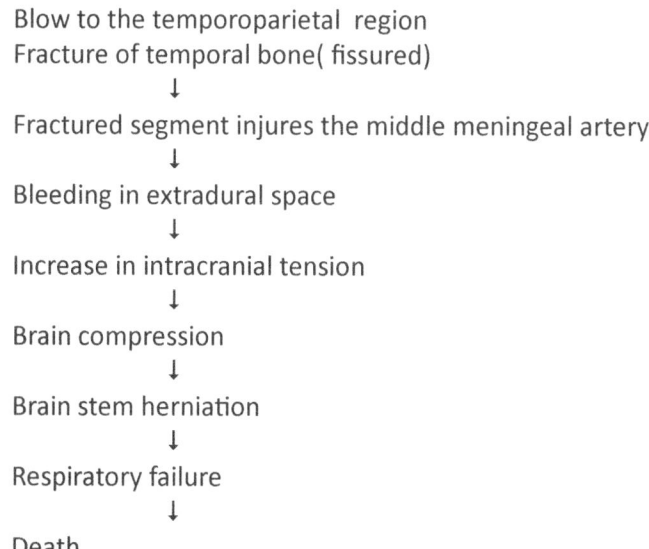

Blow to the temporoparietal region
Fracture of temporal bone(fissured)
↓
Fractured segment injures the middle meningeal artery
↓
Bleeding in extradural space
↓
Increase in intracranial tension
↓
Brain compression
↓
Brain stem herniation
↓
Respiratory failure
↓
Death

1.Blow to the forehead will injure the anterior ethmoidal artery,haemorrhage seen in anterior cranial fossa

2.Blow to the occiput region tear the transverse sinus,here haemorrhage seen in posterior cranial fossa

3.Blow on the vertex may tear the superior sagittal sinus and it cause haemorrhage

4.Various extradural haemorrhage accompanies fracture of skull and is due to bleeding from diploic veins

- In some cases the bleeding is both arterial and venous
- Haemorrhage may occur due to fall from small height ,or on being hit by a moving object or after a minor accident

Facts to know:

- Various bleeding will not produce sufficient pressure to strip duramater from bone
- The formation of the blood clot presses the duramater inward and causes aa localised concavity of the external surface of the brain
- Clots is oval or circular ,rubbery consistency ,reddish purple
- 35 ml of blood is the minimum associated with clinical symptoms
- 100 ml of blood is the minimum associated with fatalities
- Extradural haemorrhage at base of skull is rare
- Extradural haematoma becomes spontaneously small due to escape of blood through a fracture into subcutaneous tissues and scalp
- Phagocytes derived from perivascular cells of duramater which are smaller in size

Subdural haemorrhage

- Subduralspace is very narrow here the bridging veins cross this space to reach the sinuses

Causes:

- Subdural haemorrhage is most common
- It is common in childhood or old age

1. Most cases are due to rupture of bridging veins near sagittal sinus
2. Rupture of inferior cerebral vein
3. Rupture of dural venous sinuses
4. Injury to cortical veins
5. Lacerations or contusions of brain and duramater
6. Rupture of an aneurysm
7. Cerebral tumour ,aneurysm or blood disorders
8. Intake of drugs like Dicoumarol warfarin and heparin

```
                           Mechanism
                               |
           ┌───────────────────┴───────────────────┐
Acceleration-Deceleration injury              Minor trauma (Elderly)
           │                                       │
    Violent shaking                         atrophy of the brain
  (shaken baby syndrome)                          │
                                          Increases in subdural space
                                                   │
                                         bridging veins lose their support
                                                   │
                                             blood accumulates over
                                                   │
                                              prolonged period
                                                   │
                                            chronic subdural
                                          haemorrhage acute type
```

- It arises mostly due to rupture of large bridging veins, rupture of one of the cortical arteries or cerebral lacerations
- Small amounts of subdural haemorrhage are spontaneously absorbed
- Haemorrhage about 100 to 150ml cause death
- In acute type the clinical symptoms & signs look like extradural haemorrhage
- Here lucid interval is greater than 4 hours
- Symptoms are delayed for 24 to 48 hours
- In the early period of haematoma brain compression didn't occur
- After some time secondary changes in the haematoma may increase the size considerably
- Death is common due to secondary pressure upon the brainstem

Subacute type
- This occurs when the bleeding is from smaller bridging veins
- In this type the brain may or may not be damaged
- Here the blood may be thin /watery due to haemolysis or dilution with CSF

Chronic type:
- In this type the colour of the haematoma is very or it may be variegated in colour due to bleeds at different periods
- This type of haemorrhage is known as pachymeningitis haemorrhagica
- In this type the haematoma gets encapsulated by cells from the duramater
- So there is no shifting of the hemisphere toward the other side

Dating of subdural haemorrhage:
- 24 hrs – fibrin is deposited on the duramater
- 36 hrs – fibroblastic activity at the junction of the clot
- 4 to 5 days- 2 to 5 cells thick layer of the fibroblast is seen
- 5-10 days- haematoma is invaded by the caplliaries and fibroblast
- 8th day – haemosiderin laden macrophages seen a membrane of 12-14 cells thick is present
- 14 days – fibroblastic membrane enclosing the arachnoid surface of the haematoma
- 3-4 weeks – haematoma is fully covered by fibrous membrane
- 4-5 weeks- arachnoid membrane has half the thickness of the duramater, the clot is liquefied completely and haemosiderin laden macrophages are present
- 1-3 months- the membrane is hyalinised gold coloured membrane is seen

Subdural hygroma:
- When the arachnoid layers id torn. CSF may pass from the sunarachnoid space into subdural space
- A large collection of fluid may accumulate and cause cerebral compression
- This is called cerebral hygroma

Subarachnoid haemorrhage
- Space between the arachnoid layer and the piamater is called as subarachnoid space.
- This space lies very close to the brain.
- Subarachnoid space consists of cerebro Spinal fluid, circleof willis and portions of cranial nerves.

Causes
- Rupture of berry Aneurysm.
- Arterio venous malformation &rupture.
- Trauma - Lacerations and contusions ofthe brain.
- Stroke
- Asphyxia.
- Blood dyscrasias, leukemias.
- Tears of the ventricular ependyma.
- Rupture of an intracerebral haemorrhage into the Subarachnoid space.
- kick or heavy blow beneath theear can damage the vertebrobasilar vessels & it results in bleeding into the posterior cranial fossa.
- sickle cell disease [Rare cause]

Berry aneurysms
- It is due to developmental defects of the tunica media of the arterial wall.
- Size of aneurysms varies from 3mm to 8 mm or it may be upto several cm.
- It is rare in children and increase in frequency with age.
- Berry aneurysms are most often found at the bifurcation of the middle cerebral, anteroior cerebral and posterior communicating arteries.

Causes for rupture
1. During emotional stress, assault, Sudden exercise, sexual intercourse the level of catecholamines increase which results in high blood pressure, which cause rupture of berry aneurysm.
2. If a person with an already spontaneously leaking aneurysm develops neurological or even behavioural abnormality that leads him/ her into conflict with another person or fall ora traffic accident.
3. Alcohol also results in aggressive behaviour and a fight and fall, resulting in ruptured aneurysm

Vertebral artery
- Injury to the vertebral artery can cause subarachnoid haemorrhage.
- It is injured due the overstretching of atlanto - occipital membrane and impact on muscles overlying the transverse process of upper cervical vertebrae.

Injury to the artery occurs in the following regions
1. Canal of the first cervical vertebrae
2. Just below the axis
3. Just below the foramen magnum,
4. within the subarachnoid space above the foramen magnum

Rupture of the artery occur in following conditions
1. Blows to the neck, motor vehicle accidents, falls and Cervical spine manipulation.
2. Sudden stretching due to partial dislocation of the upper cervical spine or atlanto-occipital joint or a fracture of the tip of transverse process of the atlas.
3. Mechanical forces, especially of a tilting and rotational nature, a blow to side of neck may cause dissection of the wall within the foramina of upper cervical spine.
4. vertebral artery injury commonly occurs when the neuromuscular control of the neck muscle is lowered because the defending mechanical response to the blow by muscle is lost.

Trauma
- Traumatic Subarachnoid haemorrhage over the base of the brain can be caused by lacerations of the internal carotid, vertebral or basal arteries.
- These injuries can be immediately fatal if the haemorrhage is more than 30ml.
- In acute alcoholism, traumatic Subarachnoid haemorrhage is more common due to loss of muscular coordination, resulting in excessive rotational forces within the head.

Points to remember
Subarachnoid blood can be distinguished from subdural blood, because subdural blood will wash away under gently running water, whereas subarachnoid blood imparts a red colour to the brain that does not wash off...

Mechanism
The mechanism of haemorrhage is same as that of for subdural haemorrhage.
Clinical features
. Sudden onset of severe headache
. Nausea & vomiting
. Neck Stiffness / Drowsiness
. Loss of conscious /focal neurologic defects

Autopsy of Subarachnoid haemorrhage

Mild injuries
the subarachnoid haemorrhage is present as splashes of haemorrhage over the areas of contusions.
* In most cases it diffuse overlying the cerebral hemisphere.
*Scarring in Subarachnoid space is rare due to haemorrhage.
* Haemorrhage can be unilateral or bilateral, localized or diffuse.
* Haemorrhage found over the orbital surface, localized or diffuse.
* Haemorrhage found over the orbital Surface of the frontal lobes, parietal lobes and anterior third of the temporal lobes.

Severe injuries
* In severe head injuries, haemorrhage present over the greater part of both hemisphere and is often accompanied by subdural bleeding.
* Blood mixes with CSF and may be distributed over the whole of the brain.
*A slightly yellow discolouration of the leptomeninges is seen as the Subarachnoid haemorrhage becomes older.

ARTEFACT – An object or a thing that is made by a person
- Subarachnoid haemorrhage may be produced as an artefact at autopsy during removal of the brain due to damage to the cerebral veins and the arachnoid.
- It may also be produced in postmortem due to decomposition of lysed blood cells, loss of vascular integrity and leakage of blood into subarachnoid space.

Antemortem subarachnoid haemorrhage:
- In antemortem period of the victim suffered from subarachnoid haemorrhage but survives for few hours, typical Appearances of raised intracranial pressure may be seen at autopsy associated with progressive cerebral oedema.
- In most rapid deaths due to subarachnoid haemorrhage the brainstem and cranial nerve roots are covered by a thick layer of blood clot.
- It affects the vital centres in brainstem & causes death due to cardiorespiratory failure.
- Intracerebral haemorrhage:
- It may be found on the surface or inside the brain.
- Relatively large, deep seated haemorrhage are usually accompanied by other types of brain injury ex:- cortical contusion

Causes

1) Fat embolism
2) Asphyxial states
3) Blood dyscrasias disorder of the blood, bone marrow, clotting proteins or lymph tissue
4) Rupture of lenticulostriate artery
5) Angioma or malignant tumour of the brain
6) Hypertensive cerebral vascular disease
7) Laceration of the brain
8) Blow on the head with or without fracture of the skull
9) Puerperal toxaemia

Traumatic intracerebral haemorrhage

* It follows the mechanism of coup-contrecoup.
* It is mostly seen in the fronto-temporal region and is often associated with fracture of skull
* The patient becomes deeply unconscious from the moment of injury.
* Severe blows on the vertex thrusting the brain down on to the base of the Skull cause large haemorrhage occur in the inferior part of the head of the caudate nucleus and pallidum due to rupture of small branches of the anterior choroid artery.
* Most traumatic haemorrhages occur at the time of accident but bleeding is often due to its nature of oozing from venules or capillaries.
* The continued oozing also be due to damage to further small vessels in the expanding haematoma.
* Clinical signs and symptoms may appear many hours after the injury, in rare cases it may occur several weeks or even months after trauma.

Non traumatic intracerebral haemorrhage

When disease is present, sudden rise of blood pressure due to physical exercise or excitement eg:- Alcohol, scuffle [not very violent fights], assault may rupture and produce haemorrhage.

The commonly found diseases are cerebral aneurysm, degeneration of the cerebral arteries, syphilis, cerebral tumours and hypertension.

The usual source of haemorrhage is rupture of a lenticulostriate branch of the middle cerebral artery, with bleeding into the basal ganglia and adjacent structures.

A single deep – seated haemorrhage in the brain is usually due to some disease.

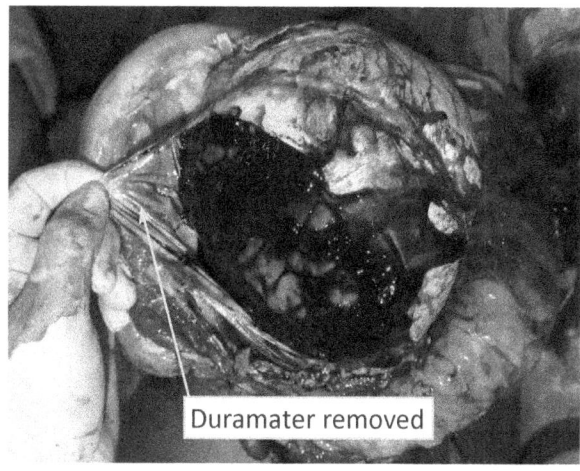

Fig(10.1) Subdural hemorrhage

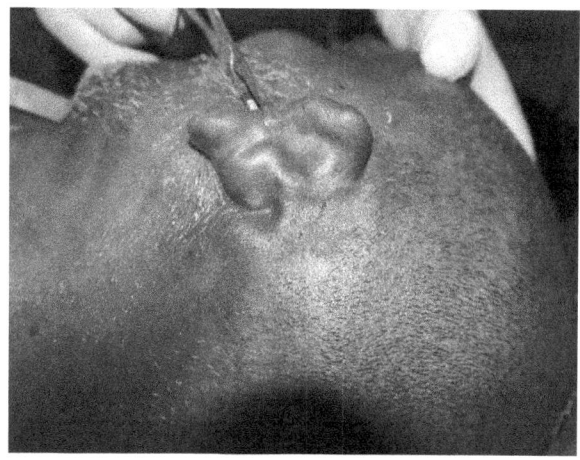

Fig(10.2) Battle sign

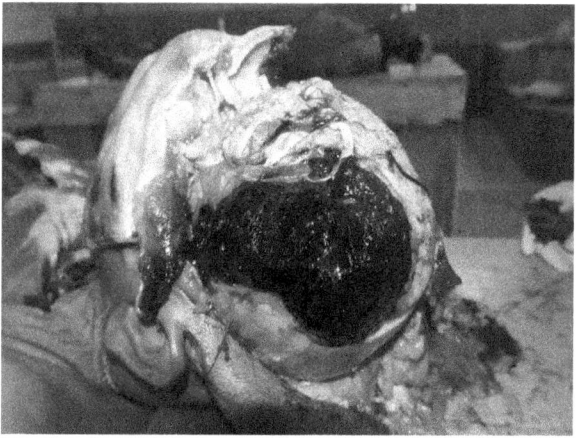

Fig(10.3) Epidural hematoma

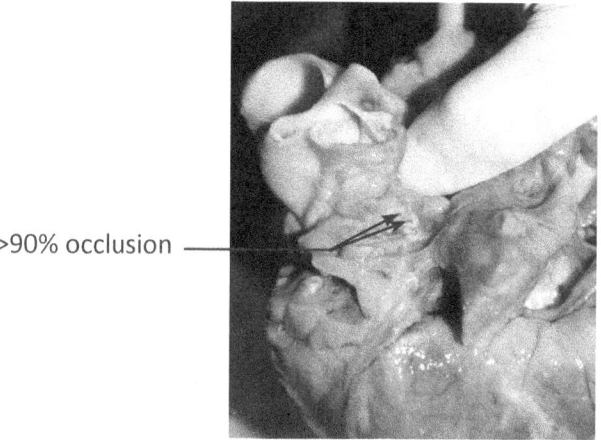

Fig(10.4) Atherosclerotic plug - >90% occlusion in LAD.

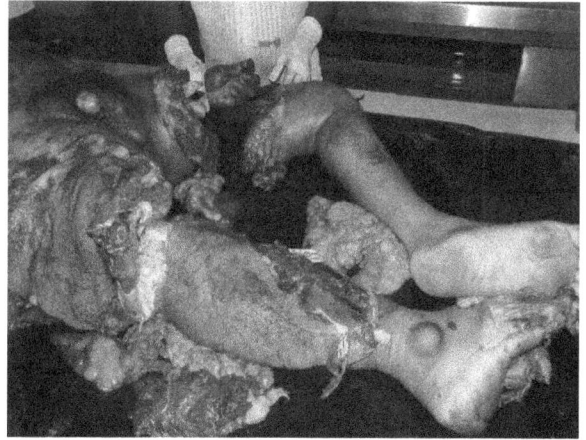

Fig(10.5) Injuries by runover train.

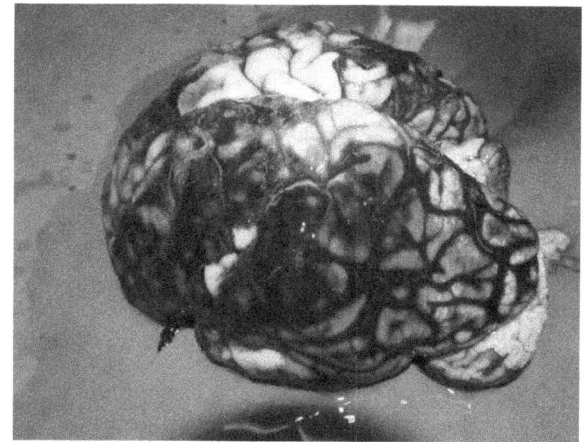

Fig(10.6) Sub arachnoid hemorrhage

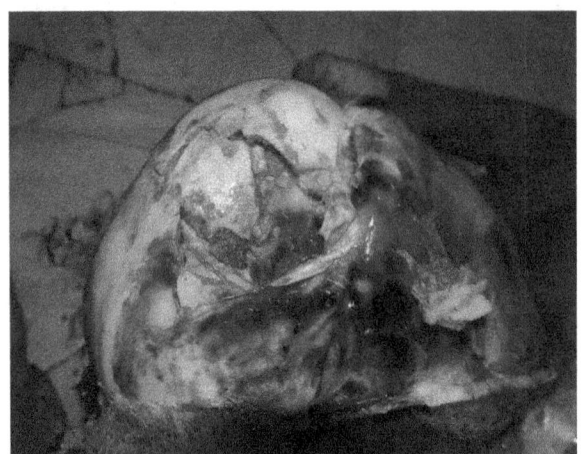

Fig(10.7) Depressed fracture.

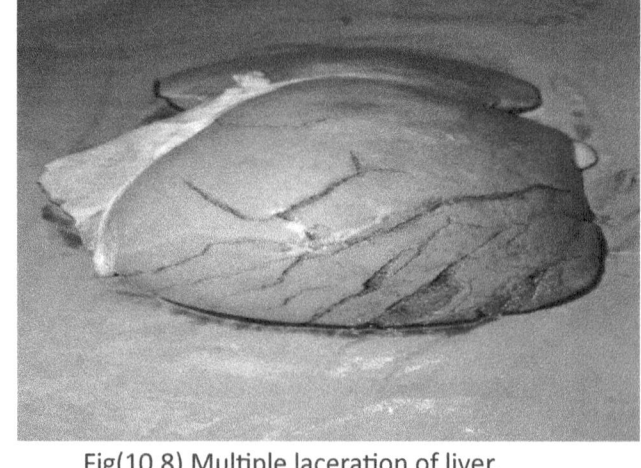

Fig(10.8) Multiple laceration of liver.

Fig(10.9) Fissured fracture of skull

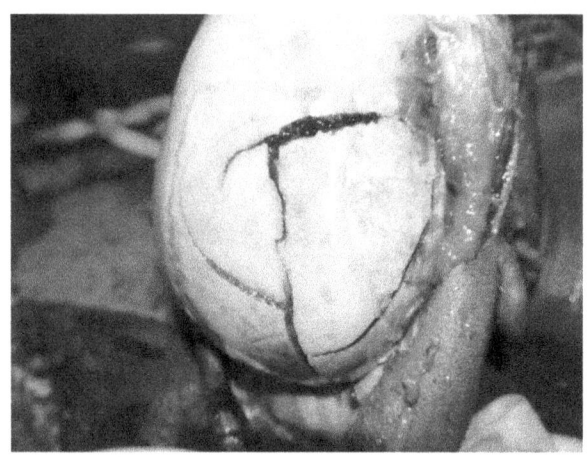

Fig(10.10) Comminuted fracture of skull.

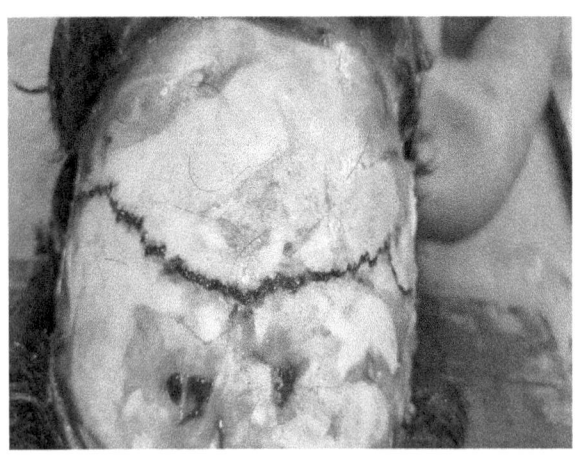

Fig(10.11) Diastatic fracture of skull.

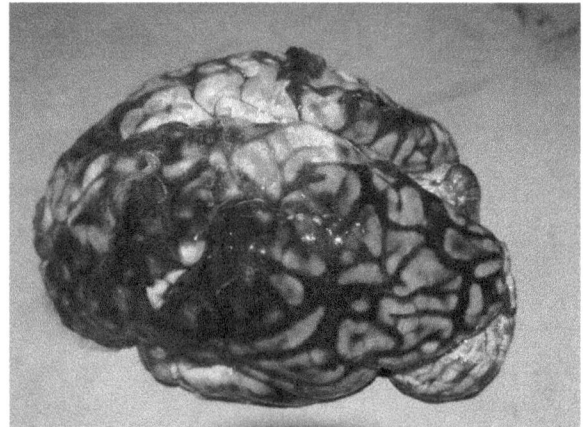

Fig(10.12) Sub dural hemorrhage

Courtesy: Professor, Dr. Chandrasekar, MMC, Madurai.
Associate professor, Dr.Sadhasivam, MMC, Madurai.

CHAPTER - 11
MEDICOLEGAL ASPECTS OF WOUNDS

In this chapter we will discuss about various types of homicide, injuries and wounds from a legal perspective.

Homicide : Killing of a person by another human being.

Types of homicide :

```
                          Homicide
                         /        \
                     Lawful      unlawful
                     /    \      /    \        \
             Justifiable Excusable Justifiable Excusable  Rash/negli-
                                                          gent homicide
                                                          (Sec.106(1), BNS)
                                   |            |
                              Culpable      Culpable homi-
                              homicide Cul-  cide that not
                              pable homicide amount to mur-
                              that amount    der (Sec.105,BNS)
                              to murder
                              (Sec.100,BNS)
```

Lawful homicide :

Death caused by a person but it is considered to be justifiable or excusable as it is unintentional.

Justifiable homicide :

Homicide will be considered to be a justifiable act under these circumstances.
1. Administration of justice – execution of sentence of death.
2. Maintanance of justice – while suppressing riots /executing arrests.
3. Kill in course of violent crimes – eg. A women who kills a person who attempts to rape her

Excusable homicide:

Homicide which is unintentional and done in the thought of good faith.

This may occurs in cases of
1. Killing for self defense – when attacked and no other means of defend.
2. Causing death by accident or misadventure– ex: a car accident or misadventure.
3. Death following a lawful operation.
4. Homicide committed by an insane person.

Note : The term justifiable and excusable homicide are not used in indian law.

Note : The term justifiable and excusable homicide are not used in indian law.

Unlawful homicide :

Homicide which can't be justified or excused by law due to evidence of intension on the part of accused.

- **Culpable homicide :**

Causing death by doing acts.
1. With intension of causing death.
2. ith intension of causing injury that likely to cause death.
3. With the knowledge that such act is likely to cause death (sec.100, BNS).

- **Murder (S.101, BNS):**

Culpable homicide is murder if
1. It is done with intension of causing death.
2. It is done with intension of causing injury, as the offender knows that likely to cause death.
3. It is done with intension of causing injury which is sufficient is the ordinary course of nature to cause death.
4. If person committing the act knows that it will cause death and commits such act without any excuse.

Note : All murders are culpable homicides but not all culpable homicides are murders.

Exceptions :

Culpable homicide does not amount to murder if,
1. It is done under grave and sudden provocation.
2. In order to defend a person or property
3. For carrying out of publice justice.
4. Without any premeditation (prior planning) or "mens rea" (criminal intent).
5) When the person above age of 18 takes risk of death with his own consent.

Note :
The offence is culpable homicide, if the body injury intended to be inflicted is likely to cause death.
It is considered as murder if such injury is sufficient in the ordinary course of nature to cause death.

By considering the nature of weapon, a blow from a fist or stick to vital spot may likely cause death but a wound from a knife to vital spot is sufficient in the ordinary course of nature to cause death.

Some important sections & punishments:

S.103(1), BNS	Punishment for murder	(Death or Imprisonment)+ fine
S.104, BNS	Punishment for murder	Death sentence
S.105, BNS	Punishment for culpable homicide not amounting to murder	(lifetime imprisonment or imprisonment upto 5 years) + fine
S.106(1), BNS	Causing death by negligence	Upto 2 years imprisonment (or) fine (or) both
S.107, BNS	Abetment of suicide of child or insane person	10 years imprisonment
S.108, BNS	Abetment of suicide : Suicide is the act of taking one's own life voluntarily, if a person commit suicide, wherever encourages / intentionally helping such act shall be punished.	Upto 10 years & fine Note: Dyadic death: A person killing someone & then commits suicide.
S.109, BNS	Attempt to murder	Life imprisonment
S.110, BNS	Attempt to commit culpable homicide	Upto 7 years imprisonment (Or) fine (or) both
S.226, BNS	Attempt to commit suicide	Simple imprisonment Upto 1 year (or) fine (or) both

---

Note :
Hardway of committing suicide : shooting, hanging, stabbing are typically a malechoice.
Soft ways of committing suicide : poisoning, drowning.

Increasing gravity of crime Assault
Criminal force
Hurt
Grievous hurt
Culpable Homicide not amounting to murder
Culpable homicide amounting to murder

Injury :
Any harm illegally caused to any person's body, mind reputation or property (S.2(14)BNS)

Infirmity :
- It is any inability of an organ to perform usual function.
- It may be temporary or permanent.
- A temporary mental impairment or terror would constitute infirmity.

Hurt (Sec.114,BNS) :
- Hurt means bodily pain, disease or infirmity caused to any person.
- Hurt does not include mental pain.

Grievous Hurt:
Are following acts such as

1) Emasculation (Means depriving a male of masculin vigour)	Amputation of penis, injuries to genitals, pelvic fracture with injury to parasympathetics. **Note:** If testes are removed before puberty,the person will be impotent.If testes are removed after puberty potency will be retained.
2) Permanent privation (loss) Of sight of either eye	Gouging out of eyes, poking eyes, use of chemicals. Note : Permanent loss doesnot mean that is should be incurable .eg:Asloss of sight due to corneal opacity by cornealinjury may be curable by corneoplasty.
3) Permanent privation of hearing of either ear.	Blow to head or ear that causes injury to tympanum or auditory nerves . Pouring hot liquid into ear.
4) Privation of any member or joints	Term "member" means an organ or a limb being part of man capable of performing a distrinct function. it includes eyes, ears , nose, mouth, hands, feet etc. If any joint becomes permanently stiff, so that normal function is not possible it is grievous injury.

5) Destruction of permanent impairing of the powers of any member or joint	Stricture due to burns, corrossives or any other injury, damage to tendons which leads to permanent impairment of powers of joints, muscles constitutes grievous injury
6) Permanent disfiguration of the head or face	Injuries which cause disfigurement of original appearance. Eg: cutting of nose, ears, injury that leads to scars on cheeks.
7) Fracture or dislocation of a bone or tooth	Note: Here dislocation means displacement mere looseness of teeth will not amount to dislocation.
8) Any hurt which endangers life, or which causes the victim to be in severe bodily pain or unable to follow his ordinary pursuits for a period of 20 days	A wound may cause intense pain, prolonged diseases or lasting injury but does not fall within any of above seven clauses. Under this clause 3 different types of hurt included: 1) Any hurt which endangers life. 2) Any hurt that causes severe bodily pain for a period of 20 days. 3) Any hurt which prevents the victim

Any hurt which endangers life :
Injury that puts the life of injured person in danger.
Any injury to vital parts cannot be called grievous hurt, unless the nature and dimension of injury and its effects are such that the doctors opinion that it actually endanger the life of victim.

Note : Administration of harmfull drug to a person to make him unconscious is not grievous hurt, eventhough in some cases death may be caused if the drug is given in larger dose.

Dangerous injuries :
Injuries that cause imminent danger to life. If no surgical aid is available, it proves to be fatal.
Eg:
- stab on abdomen or head orvital part.
- Hurt that cause rupture of spleen squeezing testicles.
- Injury to large blood vessels etc.,

Any hurt which causes the victim to be in severe bodily pain, or unavailable to follow his ordinary persuits for a period of 20 days.
The extent of hurt and intentions of the offender are considered for giving punishment.

It is difficult to prove that an injured person was in severe bodily pain for 20 days, but it is easier to prove that he was unable to follow his ordinary pursuits due to hurts.

Note :
1. Mere stay of 20 days in hospital does not make injuries grievious (unless he was in severe bodily pain or unable to follow his ordinary pursuits).
2. Ordinary pursuits includes acts of daily routine of person such as eating, taking bath, going to toilet etc, but not refer to duties that constitute the job of person.
3. Dangerous weapons or means : Any instrument for shooting, stabbing, cutting or which can be used as a weapon as a of offense that likely to cause death. Fire or any heated substance, poison or any corrosives. Substance that are harmful to human body to inhale, to swallow (or) to receive into the blood or any means of any animal (using a snake or dog to cause hurt to a person).

Important points:
- In case of hurt, the duty of the medical witness is only to describe the fact.
- It is the court that must decide whether it is simple or grievous.
- The entry made in the wound certificates as simple or grievous is only meant to guide the investigating officer.

Simple Injury :
Injury which is neither extensive nor serious and which heals rapidly.

> **Some important sections :**
> S.115(1),BNS - voluntarily causing hurt
> S.117(1),BNS - voluntarily causing grievous hurt

Some important sections and punishments:

Sections	Acts	Punishments
S.115(2), BNS	Punishments for voluntarily causing hurt.	Imprisonment up to 1 year or fine up to rs 1000 (or) both
S.118(1), BNS	volunteerly causing hurt by dangerous weapons.	3 years Imprisonment (or) with fine (or) both
S.117(2), BNS	Punishment for voluntarily causing grievous hurt.	Imprisonment upto 7 years with fine
S.118(2), BNS	Voluntarily causing grievous hurt by dangerous weapons or means.	Imprisonment upto 10 years with fine.

ASSAULT :
An assault is an offer or threat or attempt to apply force to body of another in a hostile manner. It may be a common assault or with an intent to murder.
- Assault is defined by S.130,BNS
- S.131,BNS : Assault or use of criminal force (imprisonment up to 3 months (or) fine).

ABDUCTION (S.138 ,BNS):
- Whoever by force compels, or by any deceitful means induces , any person to go from any place , is said to abduct that person.
- Intension of the abductor is an important factor in determining guilty of the accused.
- **DOWRY DEATHS:**
The dowry prohibition act of 1961 , defines 'dowry'as any property or valuable security given to or agreed to be given either directly or indirectly.

Note :
1. *Does not include dower or mahr in case of persons whom the muslim personal law applies to.*
2. *It excludes present in form of cloths , ornaments etc,as they are customary at marriages (only total value < rs 2000).*

- Dowry deaths are deaths of young women who are murdered or driven to suicide by continuous harassment and torture by husbands and in-laws in an effort to extort an increased dowry.
- Dowry death occurs either by murder of a married women or she herself commits suicide as she was unable to bear the harassment or cruelty for not giving dowry.
- The usual defence in most dowry cases is that the women commited suicide or death occurred accidentally due to bursting of stove while cooking.

Important points :
- Inquest should be conducted by a magistrate or police officer not below the rank of deputy superintendent of police.
- The postmortem examinations should be carried out by a panel of two doctors preferably.
- In premenstrual and menstrual phase due to hormonal imbalance females become oversensitive and depressive even on trivial issue and commit suicide.
- Hypothyroidism is associated with paranoid and depressive behaviour due to which she may commit suicide.

Legal aspects of dowry death :

Where the death of a women is caused by any burns or bodily injury or occurs otherwise than under normal circumstance within seven years of her marriage and it is shown that soon before she was subjected to cruelty or harrasments by her husband or any relative of her husband for, or in connection with,any demand for dowry to have caused her death.

1. Whoever commits dowry death shall be punished with imprisonment of not less than seven years but can extend to lifetime imprisonment.

WOUND CERTIFICATE:
- The casualty medical officer or any other medical officer may called upon to examine injured person.
- In case of medicolegal injury, examination should be done without delay at any time.
- All details of examination of injured person must be entered in an accident register whether he is admitted into hospital or treated as outpatient.
- be taken at the time of examination.
- The doctor has to fill in the printed form of certificate and has to make 2 copies of it
- One copy sent to the investigating officer in sealed cover
- Other copy is retained for future reference.

Preliminary particulars :

The following should be noted
1. Serial number
2. Name , age and sex of injured person and address
3. Father's / guardian's name
4. Date , time and place of examination.
5. Name and number of accompanying police constable and the police station he belongs to.
6. Names of person who accompanied the injured person with their address.
7. A brief statement of the injured person about nature of Incident, where and when incident took place, details of physical force used in assault .this is recorded as 'alleged by the patient''.
8. Two identification mark.
9. Anthropometry of the victim (ie. ,stature,weight & development)
10. The consent of the person for examination should be recorded.

Various entries in wound certificates:

1.Nature of injury	• All significant injuries should be observed (ie.,abrasion,contusion,location,burns,fractures etc.,) • Multiple injuries can be grouped anatomically. Eg. Injuries of the head , of the trunk or of a limb. • Presence of any foreign body in wound should be noted , preserved and handover to police. E.g: pellets,bullet, hair etc.,
2. Size, shape and direction of each injury	• All injuries should be measured with tape and never guessed. • Photographs showing the position and size of the woundsis desirable. **Shape :** eg: Circular,oval,triangular etc, **Direction :** eg : horizontal, vertical, obliqye etc., • Direction is noted with regard to anatomical position of body. • Pattern of wound should be noted , if present.
3.On what part of body inflicted.	Situation of wound should be noted with reference to some anatomical band mark. Eg: the middle line , a joint or a nipple. Note : technical terms should be avoided as for for as possible.

4. Simple, grievous or dangerous injury	* each injury should to noted whether it is simple, grievous or dangerous. * the injured person must be kept under observation, if the nature of particular injury cannot be made out at the time of examination Eg: abdominal injury with vague symptoms
5. By what weapon inflicted	• Examination of the wound may give fairly definite information about weapon used to inflict it. • In case of wound caused by a broken glass, glass pieces may be inside the wound. Note : if a medical officer is shown a weapon and asked ."were the wounds caused by this weapon?" he should never answer in the direct affirmative, but should state that wounds could be caused by that weapon or were caused by similar weapon. • Any weapon sent by the police, which is alleged to have been used in producing injuries should be examined for marks of blood stains, hair, pieces of cloth etc., adherent to it and should be returned to police after it is sealed.
Whether the weapon was dangerous or not? Remarks	• A dangerous weapon is any instrument for shooting, stabbing or cutting or which can be used as weapon of offense that likely to cause death. • The general condition of the patients should be noted under this column, such as • Conscious or unconscious • Bleeding from any part of body • Paralysis, state of shock • Pulse, Respiration, Temperature etc., • The age of the injury should noted. • The age of the injury is very important for its appearance may or not correspond to the time when it is alleged to have been inflicted, and all the injuries found on a person may not have been inflicted on the same day. • A careful search should be made wounds in concealed parts, E.g., axilla, nape of the neck, rectum etc., Note: 1. When a victim of suicide, homicide or accident dies in the hospital, the medical officer should report the matter to the police immediately. 2. When a dead body is bought to the hospital, do not examine the injuries.

TORTURE:
The world medical associations declaration of TOKYO, 1975:

Defines torture as the deliberate, systematic or wanton infliction of physical or mental suffering by one or more persons acting alone or on the orders of any authority, to force another person to yield information, to make a confession, or for any other reason.

Note:
- *S.120(1),BNS : Voluntarily causing hurt to extract confessions or to compel restoration of property is punishable with imprisonment upto 7 years.*
- *S.120(2), BNS : Voluntarily causing grievous hurt to extract confession or to compel restoration of property is punishable with imprisonment upto 10 years.*

Ethical aspects concerning the doctors with regard to torture are dealt in :
1. Declaration of Geneva, 1948
2. Declaration of TOKYO,1975
3. Principles of medical ethics
4. World conference on human rights, 1993

World conference of human rights, 1993:

Freedom from torture is a right which must be protected under all circumstances, including in times of internal or international disturbance or armed conflicts.

Objects of Torture:
1. To obtain information if a person is suspected to have committed any crime.
2. To sign a document confessing a crime.
3. To take revenge against a person.
4. To obtain testimony incriminating others.
5. To spread terror in the community.
6. To destroy the personality of individuals who raise their voice against dictatorial rule , or oppression in society.

Torture may be carried out by :
1. Criminal and terrorist groups
2. By the police or other security force during the detention and interrogation of prisoners and suspects

Methods of torture:
1. Physical torture
2. Mental torture
3. Sexual torture
4. Pharmacological torture

PHYSICAL TOURTURE/ ABUSE:
- Beating (most common method) – using fist,food , lathi,whips,belts etc.,
- Falanga / bastinado – rods or lathi used to beat on the soles of feet , or rarely on palms.
- Faint red lines may be seen , and often hyper pigment along the injury
- Very painful and debilitating
- A septic necrosis may occurs.
- Telefono – repeated slapping of both sides of the head (over ear) this may cause rupture of eardrums and injury to inner ear.
- Beating on the abdomen while lying down on a table with upper half of body unsupported.
- Finger torture – pencil similar objects are placed in between two fingers and then squeezed hard or twisted.

- Finger nails are pulled out.
- Mutilation – chopping of ears, nose, fingers etc.,
- Dis figuration – throwing corrosives on face or other parts of body.
- Using continuous high pitched sound.
- **Wet submarino** -- forced immersion of head into water, urine etc.,
- **Dry submarino** – tying of plastic bag over the head up to the point of suffocation
  Suspension of body by the wrists, arms or ankles.
- **Parrot's perch** – hanging the victim from a stick between knees and arms bound tightly together.
- **Saw horse** – victim is made to straddle a triangular wooden box which is positions upwards with additional weight suspended from their foot.(scrotal or perineal hematoma may seen in saw horse)
- **Burns** – cigarette burns are most common use of heated solid body, molten rubber dripped on skin.
- **Cold** – victim is made to lie on an ice slab without clothing.
- Electric shock (cattle prod) – main voltage of 110-240 volt may caused burns and death in some cases. electric shock may be inflicted over sensitive parts like genitals, nipples or all over the body.
- **Black slave** – heated metal skewer inserted into the anus.
- Exposure to dogs or other wild animals to inflict bites.
- **Knee capping** – shooting through the knee or lower limbs.
- Disallowing sleep
- **Irritant torture** – irritants like chilli powder, common salt are applied on the delicates parts of the body (eyes,genitals) or open wound.
- **Crushing injuries**–the most common method is with the victim seated or lying on the back and a ghotna (a wooden pole used to pound spices and grains) to be rolled up and down the fronts of the thigh with one or more individuals standing on it.
- Hairs may be plucked or the person may be dragged by the hair.

MENTAL TORTURE:
- Solitary confinement in a dark place.
- Blind folding for a long time or from one place to another blind folded.
- Starving the victim.
- Causing mental anguish to victim by giving false information regarding tragedy involving wife and children.
- Enforced use of psychotropic drugs.

SEXUAL FORTURE :
- Infliction of injuries or insertion of foreign bodies into private parts of victim
- Raping the victim or undressing before others
- Suspension of weights on the penis and scrotum.
- Forced sex with convicts.

Pharmacological Torture:
Using Drugs such as ,
- Muscle Relaxants,
- Pain inducing drugs.
- Psycho-pharmacological drugs to torture Victims.

CONSEQUENCES OF TORTURE:
- Disfigurement of face, Impairment of hearing and Sight, Infections.
- psychic disturbances such as anxiety, depression, Phobias, sleep disturbances, suicidal tendencies etc.
- Death may occurs rarely.

EXAMINATION:
- Torture victims are examined according to Istanbul protocol which set guidelines for documentation of torture and its consequences.
- The Doctors should obtain complete history from the Patient about methods of torture.
- The Injuries should be recorded in detail and marked on body Diagrams.
- Photographs of Injuries should be taken along with Scale placed near Injury.
- All Systems of the body should be examined completely.
- x rays and CT scan done to detect minute Fractures and soft tissue injuries.

TREATMENT:
1. Developing good rapport with the victim.
2. Empathizing with the victim and his family.
3. Avoid Situations that reminds the victim of the torture event.
4. Psychotherapy.
5. Rehabilitation, counselling and re-assurance should be provided.

Note: In India, National Human Rights commission (NHRC), State Human Rights Commission (SHRC) and Human Rights court have been constituted for better protection of human sights and connected and incidental matters thereto.

DEATH IN CUSTODY:

Custody Death: Death occurs during some form of custodial is commoly known as death in custody. It should also Includes death resulting From Police/ Prison officers attempting to,
1. Detain a criminal (or)
2. Person escaping or Attempting to escape From Prison or police custody.
3. During Interrogation.
4. During Third degree torture.

a) During Arrest:
Traumatic asphyxia may occurs to offender while resisting Arrest, As a number of Policeman may fall upon him to overpower. This may cause death.

B) Hog-Tying (total appendage Restrain Procedure):
It is a type of physical restraint in which the Person is Placed in Prone position with his wrists and ankles bound behind his back and secured by a cord. The Person may have difficulty in breathing or may become unresponsive. Death after occurs not during physical restrain but soon following the restrain.

c) choke Holds and carotid sleeper Hold:

Choke hold (bar arm control)	Carotid sleeper hold (lateral vascular neck restraint)
1.) Forearm is placed straight across the neck and then free hand grips the wrist and pulls it back. Causes obstruction of the airway and carotidarteries and immediate unconsciousness.	1. While standing behind a person the arm is placed about the neck with the ante cubetal fossa centered at the mid line of neck. free hand grips thewrist and pulled backward. Causes compression of carotid arteries and jugular veins but not vertebral arteries and the trachea. • Consciousness is lost in 10 to 15 seconds if released victim regains consciousness in 10 to 20 seconds.
Fracture of hyoid bone or larynx may occurs if great force in used .	Neck structures are not damaged.
Rarely death may occurs due to hypoxia and release of catecholamines due to struggle , resulting in fatal cardiac arrhythmia.	Rarely death may occurs due to hypoxia and release of catecholamines.

Death in custody can be due to :
1. Natural Disease: Emotional upset may precipitate an acute Cardiac crisis in Presence of severe diseases. stressful events triggers Diabetes, epilepsy, Asthma etc.,
2. eath immediately After struggle.
3. Death due to injuries sustained during arrest or before arrest.
4. Torture by various methods.
5. Offender may commit suicide.
6. Drug related death: overdose, deprivation, drug carrier through body.

Most common physical sign found in case of custodial torture are :
1. Scars in soles of feet.
2. Muscle and joint disorders.
3. Scars in parts of body.
4. Scars of burns..
5. Chronic pain due to faculty healing of fracture .
6. Broken or missing nails.
7. Broken or missing teeth.
8. Peripheral nerve damage .
9. Loss of hearing .
10. Enlarged feet .
11. Dislocation of shoulder or knee joints .
12. Deviation of nasal septum .

Suicide in custody : they are quite common.

The common method is hanging . sometimes
- Poison may be consumed (or)
- He may jump from a height (or)
- Cut his throat or a large blood vessels .

Investigation is done by a magistrate and postmortem is conducted by a team of doctors.

Autopsy in custodial death;

National Human Right commission (NHRC) has laid down Protocol to be followed in cases of deaths in police action, custodial deaths and death in prison.

All Deaths in police and Judicial custody should be Reported within 24 hours of occurrence to NHRC. While conducting postmortem examination of the deceased, Photographs of the deceased should be taken and Postmortem examination of the Deceased should be Recorded.

- Aim of the video filming and photography of postmortem should be :
1. To record detailed finding of marks of injury and violence which suggest custodial torture.
2. To act as video graphic evidence so as to rule out any influence or suppression of material information.
3. To facilitate an independent postmortem examination report at later stage if required.

Protocol for video filming and photography of postmortem examination:
1. The doctor should narrate his observations while conducting the postmortem examination.
2. A total of 20-25 coloured photographs covering the whole body should be taken (some photographs should be taken without removing cloths)
3. Photographs should include ,

a. Profile photo – face (from ,right lateral , left lateral)
b. Front and back of body (upto torso-chest and abdomen)
c. Upper extremity (front and back)
d. Lower extremity (front and back)
e. Focusing on injuries (after properly numbered)
f. Internal examination findings

4. While taking photographs the camera should be held at right angle to the objects.

5. Video filming and photography should be done by a person trained in forensic photography and videography (good quality camera with 10 X optical zoom and minimum 10 mega pixel should be used).

SUDDEN DEATH DURING OR IMMEDIATELY AFTER A VIOLENT STRUGGLE OR DURING EXERCISE:

Sympathetic stimulation causes an increase in heart rate, force of myocardial contraction and blood pressure.

During heavy exercise there will be progressive rise in systolic pressure with little change in diastolic pressure. serum potassium level will increase during exercise

POST EXERCISE PERIL :

Sudden death occurs not only during exercise , but often during first few minutes after cessation of strenuous exercise .

Strenuous exercise

- Increase in serum potassium level
  - Post exercise within 1 to 2 minutes.
  - Sudden decrease in potassium level(hypokalemic state)

- at first 3 minutes after cessation of exercise
  - catecholamines reaches its highest level.
  - increase in nor-epinephrine (7 to 10 times) increase in epinephrine (3 to 8 time)
  - Nor-epinephrine interacts with alpa-1 receptors
  - Vasoconstriction of of coronary arteries
  - Cardiac ishremia
  - May cause post exercise arrhythmia (post exercise peril)

1. Intense struggle with police or others	Struggle often arises when agitated,excited, psychotic or otherwise hyperactive person struggle commonly due to toxic effects of cocaine and /or amphetamine abuse.
2. High intensity exercise	Increase blood pressure and heart rate , precipitates an actuate cardiac crisis in presence of preexisting disease
3. Anatomically nondiagnosible natural diseases	Ex: wolf Parkinson white syndrome, prolonged Q-T syndrome etc.,
4. Alcohol abuse	Chronic alcoholics may have prolonged Q-T interval which is associated with sudden death and increase in level of nor-epinephrine which can aggravatearrhythmia during violent struggle which can be fatal .
5. High intensity emotions ,psychological stress , potentially fatal cardiac arrhythmia with or without underlying heart disease. Note : the stress associated with assault or simple fear of severe injury may precipitate catecholamine release and stress the myocardium into fatal dysrhythmia.	

Cocaine causes increased release of catecholamines from the adrenals and inhibits nor-epinephrine-re-uptake due to which coronary arteries contract, reducing myocardial perfusion which can be potentially fatal with or without underlying disease.

CAUSES OF DEATH FROM WOUNDS:

Death from wounds

Immediate / direct causes
1. Haemorrhage
2. Shock
3. Mechanical injury to vital organ.

remote / delayed / indirect causes
1. Infection / septic shock
2. Gangrene or necrosis
3. Crush syndrome / acute tubular necrosis.
4. Thrombo embolism
5. fact embolism
6. acute respiratory distress syndrome (ARDS)
7. suprarenal haemorrhage.
8. other cause :
* neglect of injured person.
* surgical operation.
* Natural disease.

IMMEDIATE CAUSES :
1. Haemorrhage : escape of blood from the cardiovascular system.

Haemorrhage can be external or internal.
- Traumatic hemorrhage – bleeding due to various types of wound.
- Spontaneous haemorrhage – bleeding occurs in absence of trauma.
- Petechiae – minute haemorrhagic spots (usually capillary or venular origin).
- Ecchymoses – (1 to 2 mm) large areas of extravasated blood.
- Haematoma – localized collection of blood (usually clotted).
- Apoplexy – large effusion of blood into an organ (term commonly used for cerebral haemorrhage)

Haemorrhage can be classified into two types according to time it occurs:
1. Primary haemorrhage – occurs at the time of injury.
2. Secondary haemorrhage – occurs from same site as primary haemorrhage but is usually delayed for several hours after injury (upto 24 hrs or more).

Difference between external and internal hemorrhage

External hemorrhage	Internal haemorrhage
• It may produce syncope and death either rapidly, if a large vessel has be injured (or) – slowly if a number of small vessels have be damaged. • Minor injury may be produce death from haemorrhage in persons with haemophilia. • Approx amount of blood last can be calculated by seeing blood shocked cloths and surrounding of victim.	• It may occur in penetrating wound, gun shot wound and due to rupture of organ or vessels. • Wounds can continue to blood copiously after death due to passive leakage, especially if the injured part of the body is dependent. • ie., lower than rest of the body
Note : the sudden loss of blood is more dangerous than the same quantity of blood last slowly as when leakage is slow, body can compensate by adjusting vascular bed and restoration of blood volume by transfer from other aqueous compartment.	**Note :** blood can also accumulate in large quantity within the pleural and peritoneal cavities after death.

Mechanism of death:
1. Rapid loss of 1/3 rd or blood from body causes death due to irreversible hypovolaemic shock (death from cerebral anoxia).
2. Haemorrhage creating increased pressure on a vital organ can cause death .
Eg :
a. effusion of 300 to 400 ml of blood into pericardial sac interferes with heart's action (cardiac tamponade).
b. intracranial haemorrhage may cause death from cerebral compression.
c. bleeding into the trachea or bronchi can cause rapid death from asphyxia.

2. SHOCK :

Shock is a circulatory disturbance characterized by hypoperfusion of cells and tissues due to reduction in the volume of blood or cardiac output , or redistribution of blood resulting in a decrease of effective circulating volume.

Primary shock:
- Also as neurogenic shock / vaso – vagal shock/ reflex cardiac arrest.
- It results from a sudden reduction of venous return to the heart due to neurogenic vasodilation with pooling of blood in peripheral vascular bed, especially in the splanchnic area.

Causes :
- Psychological factors like fear, pain,anxiety and emotions play a major role.
- Sympathetic outflow is disrupted resulting in unopposed vagal tone.

Secondary shock :
Progressive circulatory failure and damage to tissues.
- Also known as delayed shock , because the circulatory disturbance usually develops gradually or after a latent period following injury.

Stages of shock :
1. Non progressive phase : in this reflex compensatory mechanisms are activated and perfusion of vital organs is not affected.
2. Progressive state : in this tissue perfusion is reduced with increasing circulatory and metabolic imbalances.
3. Irreversible stage : this occurs after severe injury to cells and tissues.

Types of shock based on the stressful circumstances under which occurs
1. Haemorrhagic shock / hypovoleamic shock
2. Traumatic ./ wound shock
3. Burn shock
4. Surgical shock
5. Cardiac / cardiogenic shock
6. Septic shock
7. Endotoxic shock

Postmortem appearances:
The findings is secondary shock are circulatory changes , and degeneration and necrosis in various organs, the circulatory changes include congestion of all the internal organs , petechial haemorrhage in serious cavities and oedema of the viscera.

Types of shock	Clinical examples	Principal mechanisms
Cardiogenic shock	Myocardial infection, rupture of heart, cardiac tamponade, arrhythmia, pulmonary embolism.	Failure of myocardial pump due to intrinsic myocardial damage or extrinsic pressure to outflow.
Hypovoleamic shock	Haemorrhage, fluidloss (eg, diarrhea, burns, vomiting)	Inadequate blood or plasma volume
Septicshock	Gram – negative septicaemia (endotoxic shock) or gram – positive septicaemia	Peripheral vasodilation and pooling of blood; endothelial cell injury withDIC.
Neurogenic shock	Anaesthesia, spinal cord injury	Peripheral vasodilation with pooling of blood

3. MECHANICAL INJURY TO A VITAL OPRGAN:

severe injury to vital organ, such as crushing of brain, heart etc, is rapidly fatal.

Remote / delayed causes :

1. infection :

wound infection may caused by streptococci, staphylococci,

b. Coliform bacilli, Clostridium welchii and Clostridium tetani etc.,

a. primary wound infection : caused by organisms, which are carried into wound at the time of injury.

eg: from the skin, clothing, dirt etc.,

b. secondary wound infection : caused by organisms which invade the wound after injury.

eg : by airborne droplet infection, contaminated dressing etc.,

Direct infection: Infection actuate site of an open wound such as state wound, a gun short wound and fracture of anterior cranial fossa communicating with an air since may cause meningitis.

Remote infection : uterine infection following upon criminal abortion may cause meningitis.

Note :

- staphylococcal infection – may produce localized abscess.
- streptococcal infection – may produce diffuse spreadin gcellulities.
- Clostridium perfringens – may cause gas gangrene.

	Important conditions
1. septicemia	Presence or rapidly multiplying highly pathogenic bacteria in the blood. (there may be enlargement of spleen, and non specific toxic signs in other organs)
2. pyaemia	Dissemination of small septic thrombi in the blood which causes effects at the site where they lodged.
3. bacteraemia	Presence of small number of bacteria in the blood which do not multiply significantly.

2.GANGRENE OR NECROSIS :

- gangrene is death of a part accompanied by putrefaction
- it results from severe crushing of a part and tearing of blood vessels.

3. RENAL FAILURE FOLLOWING TRAUMA : (acute tubular necrosis ;crush syndrome)

The cause may not well known, but may involve the juxata glomerular apparatus and the rennin-angiotensin system and DIC effects on the glomeruli.

- Crush syndrome may also called as rhabdomyolysis or Bywater's syndrome.
- This condition characterized by major shock and renal failure after a crushing injury to skeletal muscle of limbs.

This causes occurs commonly is catastrophes such as earthquakes , to victim's that have be trapped under fallen masonry or vehicular run over injury.

- Non traumatic causes – severe burns, mercury poisoning, sea snake bite etc.,
- There will be no specific gross changes in the kidney.
- Cellular infiltration is seen in the interstitial tissues around the degenerated and necrosis tubules. The distal tubular segments and the collecting tubules contain casts of heme compartment.

4. THROMBOEMBOLISM:

- Injury to endothelium of vessels results in thrombus formation.
- Detached thrombi result in embolism which can enter the right ventricle , pulmonary infarction , acute circulation . it may result in pulmonary infraction , acute pulmonary edema and death.
- Most common site of thrombosis : deep femoral , the popliteal and posterior tibial veins.
- Usually occurs due to traumatic lesions of lower extremities , especially fracture of bones .

Economy class syndrome :

leg vein thrombosis may occurs after any period of stagnation or pressure on the legs and has be reported in long distance air passengers.

Note : foreign bodies may enter veins or arteries and are transported as emboli.
Eg: bullets and pellets

5. FAT EMBOLISM:

Causes:
1. Fracture of long bone or pelvis (incidence is up to 2 to 10% in multiple fracture)
2. Blunt trauma
3. Sickle cell anemia
4. Burns
5. Joint reconstruction
6. Liposuction
7. Cardiopulmonary bypass
8. Decompression sickness
9. Parenteral lipid infusion
10. Sickle cell crisis
11. Pathological fractures

The presence of fat droplets in the blood stream indicates that injury was produced during life , except in case of burning and advanced putrefaction.

Clinical features:

The emboli enters the pulmonary vessels and obstructs the flow of blood through the lungs

Signs & symptoms:

- Cyanosis , precordial pain, rapid pulse and respiration , hyperpyrexia and petechial haemorrhage caused by impaction of fat droplets in small venules of any part of body.
- Reddish brown non palpale petechiae, particularly in the axillae, with 24.36 hours of injury.
- Subconjectival and oral hemorrhages and petechiae.
- Retinal hemorrhages with intra-arterial fat globules are visible upon fundus examination.

Autopsy :
- Death usually occurs about the tenth day, but may be delayed up to three weeks.
- The pulmonary vessels, arterioles and capillaries are seen filled with globular fat emboli. The lungs show congestion, oedema and sight hypostastic pneumonia. the brain, heart and kidneys may show scattered emboli.

Note : bone narrow fat is scanty in children, due to which fat embolism is rare.

Air embolism: Air embolism is an uncommon, but potentially catastrophic event that occurs as consequence of entry of air into vascular.
1. Incised wounds of the lower cervival regions involving the jugular or subclavian veins
2. A wound of the sagittal sinuses inside the skull
3. Faculty technique while giving IV injection
4. Crush injuries to chest
5. Positive pressure ventilation in newborn infant
6. Faculty technique during abortion (illegal abortion)
7. Caisson's disease.
8. Artificial pneumothorax and pneumo peritoneum.

Note : penetration wound by bullet does not usually produce air embolism.
- 2ml of air in the cerebral circulation can be fatal.
- 0.5 ml of air into a coronal artery can cause cardiac arrest.
- Injecting more than 100 ml of air into the venous system at rates greater than 100 1/s can be fatal.
- Air injected into a limb artery is not harmful, as most of the gas is absorbed rapidly.

Demonstration of air embolism:
- X ray examination of the whole body may detect large quantities of air.
- Ophthalmoscope – air bubbles in the retinal arteries can be demonstrated with an ophthalmoscope.
- Pyrogallol test : the gas is collected from the heart and bought into contact with alkaline pyrogallol solution, which terms brown in presence of free oxygen and indicates antemortem air embolism.

Autopsy :
The head should be dissected first, to look for air in cerebral arteries.
In air embolism, right ventricle is distended with air under pressure and bright-red forthy blood is found in the right side of the heart, venacava, pulmonary arteries and coronary veins.
- Before dissection of other thoracic organs, the pericardium is opened, heart is lifted upwards, and apex is wet with knife.

6. Acute respiratory distress syndrome (ARDS)
Sudden and progressive from of acute respiratory failure in which the alveolar capillary membrane becomes damaged and more permeable to intravascular fluid (diffuse alveolar damage).

Causes :
- Heavy impacts on the thorax
- Blast injuries to chest
- Pulmonary infections,
- Toxins
- Systemic shock
- Irritant gases
- Aspiration of gastric contents
- Near drowning etc.,

The victim may suffer from severe dyspnoea progressive respiratory failure due to poor exchange of gases. Diminished tidal volume.

The lungs are retain their shape after removes and may be double in weights

Note : lungs becomes fibrotic in 50% of persons who survive.

7. Disseminated intravascular coagulation (DIC):

Activation of coagulation sequence that leads to microthrombi formation throughout the microcirculation.

There is consumption of platelets, fibrin and coagulation factors and secondarily activation of fibrinolytic mechanisms (consumption coagulopathy).

Causes:
- Trauma.
- Sepsis and severe infections.
- Shock and burns.
- Malignancy
- Severe transfusion reactions
- Snake envenomation
- Obstetric complications – amniotic fluid embolism; abruption placenta; HELLP syndrome and eclampsia.
- Heat stroke and hyperthermia.
- Severe non specific stress.

Autopsy : DIC is confirmed at autopsy by the casual amount and distribution of bleeding in the body and by the finding of fibrin cloths and signs of ischaemia, of infraction of many organs on microscopy.

ANTEMORTEM AND POSTMORTEM INJURIES :

- Antemortem injuries can be distinguished by some features are very important medicolegally.

Difference Between Antemortem and Postmortem injuries.

S.NO	FEATURE	ANTERMORTEM WOUNDS	POSTMORTEM WOUNDS
1	Edges	Swollen, everted, retracted	No swelling
2	Gaping	Present in incised and lacerated wounds	No gaping, but are closely approximated
3	Bleeding	Severe bleeding, usually arterial	Little or no bleeding
4	Spurting	Present	Absent
5	Extravasation of blood	Blood extravasated in the subcutaneous tissue	No extravasation of blood
6	Staining of tissues	Adjacent tissues are stained which cannot be removed by washing	Easily wasted away
7	Vital reaction	Present, ie, inflammation and repair	Absent
8	Histology	Infiltration of leukocytes, macrophages etc.,	Absent
9	Enzymatic activity	Increased activity of esterase adenosine triphosphate aminopeptidase, acid and alkaline phosphatase	Diminished or no enzyme activity.

Note : injuries inflicted shortly before death cannot be distinguished from those inflicted shortly after death.

Features with doubtful reliability:
- Wounds produced shortly before death are not always associated with thrombosis and fibrin deposition .Absence of swelling does not exclude antemortem injury.
- While blood cells , are capable of movements for few hours cardiac arrest . this makes a " **vital reaction** " to injury of doubtful reliability.

Physically components of vital reaction :
Swelling , effusion of lymph, leucocytic infiltration , pus formation or evidence or evidence of repair

Time of infliction of the wound :
- The changes vary according to the size of a wound , the type of wound , the tissue and the age and health of the victim.
- Only an approximate time can be determined.
- Healing by first intention – union in a clean incised wound with opposition of the edges.
- Healing by second intention – granulation tissue is formed.
- Enzyme histochemistry contributes to the timing of wounds inflicted 1 to 8 hours before death . the biochemical methods are most useful for the timing of wounds , inflicted during the last hour before death.

CHAPTER - 12
THERMAL DEATHS

Definitions:
Thermal injury is tissue injury due to application of heat or cold in any form to the external or internal body surface.

Cold injury:
Hypothermia: Exposure to cold produces hypothermia which is defined as core temperature below 35°C (i.e. Oral or Axillary temperature).
Temperature regulation centre is in Hypothalamus.

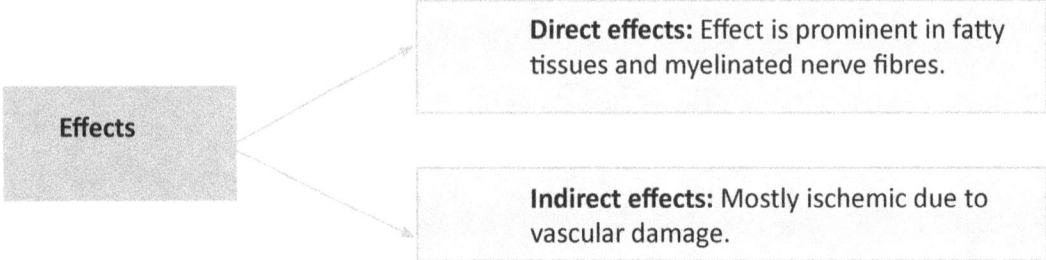

Note:
- *Body can tolerate dry cold than wet cold*
- *Fat person and women can tolerate cold than lean person and men*

Local effects of hypothermia:
- Skin becomes pale due to vascular spasm.
- Followed by erythema, edema due to vascular dilation, paralysis and increased capillary permeability.
- Blister formation in skin subcutaneous muscles and nerve.
- Tissues become firm, hard and necrotic. Followed by vascular occlusion, thrombosis.
- Inflammation and infection may be seen in tissues.

Localized effects of hypothermia:
- Trench/immersion foot:
- Trench foot and trench hand are types of immersion injuries
- Formation of ice crystals and obstruction of blood supply commonly occurs.
- Typical evidence is blue-black discoloration of fingers, toes or nose, ear & face.
- In mild cases numbness, prickling & itching of skin and subcutaneous tissue.
- In deep frostbite-skin becomes white or yellow immobile, edema, blisters, necrosis and gangrene beyond the line of demarcation.

General effects:
3 stages:
First stage: Patient feels cold, shivering and the body temperature falls
Second stage: Shivering stops (temperature is at or below 35° C), Patient depressed, lethargy, stupor and coma on further cooling
- Muscle become stiff and impaired joint movements seen.
- Respiration, Circulation & Metabolic process are slowed down.
- Oxygenation to cells gets deprived.

Third stage: If the temperature becomes less than 27°C then death results due to failure of hypothalamic centre which may leads to anoxia.

Postmortem finding:
External:

Pink or brownish area seen on the extensor surfaces, mostly present on knee, elbow, hip joints.
- Postmortem staining in pink.
- The extremity is cyanosed.
- Edema and blistering of skin seen.
- Blood -Bright red in colour
- Lungs -Congested, edematous, hemorrhagic
- Stomach-Brownish black area in the gastric mucosa

Internal:
- Blood -Bright red in colour
- Lungs -Congested, edematous, hemorrhagic
- Stomach-Brownish black area in the gastric mucosa
- Heart -Dilation of atrium & ventricles
- Liver and spleen-Congested
- Intestine-ulceration

Medicolegal importance:

Accidental - Drunkenness, mountaineering or person immersed in ice cold.
Homicidal - Infanticide.

Paradoxical undressing:
- In hypothermic deaths body is found partially or fully undressed.
- At the stage of failure of thermal regulatory system, vasoconstriction of blood vessels of skin doesn't occur. This pools the blood from core to periphery which increases body temperature.
- This increase in body temperature makes the person feels irritation. It forces the person to remove clothes.
- During hypothermia, the person becomes disoriented, removes clothes which in turn decreases temperature of the body.
- This may be misinterpreted as murder followed by rape.

Hide & die syndromes:
- In hypothermic deaths, bodies are found in places like bed or bench or beneath the shelf in order to prevent from cold.
- At terminal stage of life, hallucinations and mental confusions may occur due to hypothermia.
- Alternatively, the person may pull down the house hold articles from top which may give attempt to hide.
- This may lead to misinterpretation of robbery.

Neonatal cold injury:
- Fall in temperature due to failure of metabolism (Core temperature below 32°C)
- Child becomes lethargic, drowsy, refusal of food is common.

External features:
- Swelling & pitting edema of extremities.
- Skin & subcutaneous tissues are edematous which starts from distal part of leg trunk.
- Pulse is absent, respiration rate is slow and irregular.

Internal features: Gastrointestinal bleeding petechial hemorrhage oozing of blood in injection site or scratches.

Diagnosis:

Massive pulmonary hemorrhage without infection.
Frothy, blood stained secretion in mouth.
Mild ascites edema and cyanosis of extremity.

Medicolegal importance:

This is the common method of killing unwanted and illegitimate child.

Heat injury:

Heat injury includes
- Heat cramps
- Heat hyperpyrexia
- Heat prostration

Heatcramps: [Miner's /stoker's / Fireman's Cramps]
- Occurs due to fluid & electrolyte depletion.
- Usually seen it workers works in high temperature which causes profuse sweating.
- Sudden in onset.
- Severe& painful muscle cramps & spasm involved in muscle groups which are hard lumpy and tender.
- Face in flushed, Pupils are dilated.
- Patient complains of dizziness, tinnitus, headache and vomiting
- Skin is moist and cool.

Head prostration: [Head Syncope/collapse]
- Results from salt depletion and dehydration due to excessive sweating and vasodilation.
- Condition usually seen in tropics & desert.
- Patients suddenly feels weak, giddy, nausea, dizziness, throbbing headache.
- Systolic BP is <100mmHg.
- Face is pale, pulse is weak.
- Skin is moist & cool.

Head stroke: [Heat hyperpyrexia]
It is a life-threatening medical emergency resulting from failure of thermal regulatory mechanism
It is characterized by cerebral dysfunction with impaired consciousness, hyperthermia (temperature >40°C) and absence of sweating.

Classification:
- **Classic** – Seen in patient with immunocompromised homeostatic mechanism.
- **Exertional** – Person with strenuous environment in thermally stressful condition.

Predisposing factors:
- » Environmental factors – High temperature, increased humidity
- » Non-environmental factors – Extreme of age (Infants and >65yr), Malignant hyperthermia, thyrotoxicosis, Medication like anticholinergics, antihistamines and Phenothiazines.

Clinical features:
- Prodromal symptoms like dizziness, nausea, vomiting, confusion, unwanted movements, disorientation, drowsiness
- Skin is hot, tachycardia, hypoventilation
- Pupil is constricted
- BP is elevated in early, later it decreased
- Delirium, Blurredvision, Disorientation collapse &unconsciousness

Postmortem findings

External:
 Early occurrence & rapid development of Post mortem changes (due to high temperature)

Internal:
 Lung is congested and edematous
 Heart -Dilation of right-side area
 Subendocardial hemmorrhage
 Brain -Congested &edematous

Heat exhaustion/ Hyperthermic anhydrosis / Desert Syndrome
- Prolonged strenuous activity with inadequate water or salt intake in a hot environment
- Symptoms associated with heat syncope and heat cramps
- Nausea, vomiting, malaise, myalgia
- Headache, dizziness, fatigue
- Anxiety, impaired judgement

Burns:
- Burn is a heat injury caused due to an application of heat or chemical substances to external or internal surfaces of body.
- The minimum temperature required to produce burn is about 44°C for about 5 to 6 hours.

Varieties of burns

Burns due to solid object:	It causes destruction of the tissues, epidermis may be blackened, hair become blackened curled, breaks off totally when it is in contact with flame.
Burns due to kerosene, oil & petrol:	Sooty blackening of the parts and have a characteristic odour
Burns due to explosion:	Blackening and tattooing of skin
Burns due to x ray and Radium	Redness of skin to dermatitis with hair removal and pigmentation around the skin. Several exposures lead to redness, dermatitis or fingernail slow wart like growth
Burns due to UV rays (sun, mercury, infrared rays)	Redness and dermatitis
Radiant heat burns	Exposure of heat source (i.e. sun burn)
Microwave burns	Well demarcated, full thickness burn
Burns due to corrosive substance	Ulcerated patches, usually form blisters, hair is not burnt and line of demarcation is absent. **Strong acid** - leathery burn **Alkalies** - peeling of skin, moist, greyish area

Degree of burns

Dupytren classified burns into 6 types but they were merged in 3 degrees by Wilson.

Epidermal:(1st and 2nd degree Dupytren) • Affected part is erythematous • Swelling due to capillary dilation & fluid exchange. • There is split in the epidermis or at the junction, epidermal-dermal junction.	**Features :** • Formation of blister (vesicle or bulla) Which covered by while, avascular epidermis the border is red usually 5 to 20 cm. • Base is red in colour, and it is painful. If epidermis is lost, the dermis is red, inflamed and tissue fluid is present • If repair complete there is no scar formtion.
Dermo epidermal (3rd & 4th degree Dupytrens) • Whole thickness of skin is destroyed with destruction of skin appendages. • First degree burns central zone necrosis or zone of redness of skin.	**Features:** skin become smaller in size, depressed area of tissues seen • Colour of lesion is brown or black. • Necrotic tissue is peeled off within a week and it heals by Scar formation. • Contraction of the tissue at the site of scar leads to impaired function and are painless. • Pain and shock is greater than in first degree burn.
Deep(5th & 6th degree dupytrens) • Destruction not only upto skin & subcutaneous tissue but also reach bone, muscles and nerves are also involved.	**Features:** • Similar to the second degree but all parts of skin, subcutaneous tissue, fascia, muscle, nerve, bones are completely burnt.

Duputrens & wilson classification

Degree of damage	Dupytren's	Wilson's
Erythema	1	Epidermal
Vesication with blister formation	2	epidermal
Destruction of superficial skin	3	Dermo epidermal
Destruction of whole skin	4	Dermo epidermal
Destruction of deep fascia & muscle	5	Deep
Involvement of Vessels, fascia and bones	6	Deep

Effects:
1. The degree of heat
   - If the heat is high the effect is secure for purpose of burning of a dead body
   - For complete incineration human body must be burned for one and half hour at 1000°C

   - The ashes weights about 2 to 3 kg and it contain bone fragment which is the clue for identification as human ash.
2. Duration of exposure:
   - If duration of heat applied is greater then the symptoms are. severe
3. The extent of burn
   - It is estimated by rule of nine or

Rule of Wallace
9% to heat & neck (7% of heat &2%of neck)
9% of each of upper limb (4% of arm,3% of forearm,2% of hand)
9% of front of each lower limbs
9% of front of each lower limbs
9% of back of each lower limb (10% of thigh 5% of leg, 3% of foot)
9% of front of chest
9% of back of chest
9% of front of abdomen
9% of back of abdomen

Note:Palmar aspect of patients hand is about one present of body surface area Involvement of 50% of body surface will prove as fatal

1. Site-burns of head, trunk or the anterior abdominal wall are more dangerous
2. Age-children are more susceptible than old people
3. Sex-women are more susceptible

Local effects
- Vascular thrombosis
- Tissue necrosis
- Increase in evaporation of water from burnt surface & local heat loss

Causes of death
- Primary (neurogenic) shock due to pain
- Death burns occur within first 48hrs due to fluid loss from burnt surface
- Insmoke- inhalation of carbon monoxide, carbon dioxide or cyanide may lead death due to O2 deprivation &non-specific toxic substances.
- Toxemia- due to absorption of various metabolites from the burnt tissues
- Sepsis
- Biochemical disturbances – fluid loss and destruction of tissue leads to hypokalemia
- Gastrointestinal disturbances such as peptic hemorrhage in the intestine and stomach
- Pulmonary edema due to inhalation of carbon monoxide and carbon dioxide
- Gangrene tetanus.

- Accidental falling in the burnt houses
- Pulmonary embolism
- In sure burns- respiratory distress, pulmonaryedema, pulmonary embolism
- Death may also occur due to malignant transformation of burn scar after recovery.

Estimation of percentage of body surface area

Area of body	1 to 4	5 to 9	10 to 4	Adult
Head &neck	19	15	14	9
Front of trunk	16	16	16	18
Back of trunk	16	16	16	18
Upper limb	19	19	19	36
Lower limb	30	34	34	1
genitalia	0		1	1

Post-mortem appearances

Clothes- If clothes are burned it indicates both flame& flash burn occur
- Pure cotton fabrics transmit more thermal energy than polyester cotton.
- As fabric weight increases intensity of burn decreases.
- Loose garment catch fire easily & more dangerous than tight fitting clothes.
- Nylon and Polyester produces serious burn .
- For purpose of analysis of volatile substances.

A piece of clothes should be placed in a glass container with screw tap lid On preserving in a plastic bag volatile gas will escape so it will not be used.

External
- Heat rigor may be observed in the muscle.
- It is difficult to determine the time of death as body temperature, postmortemhypostasis and rigor mortis cannot be assessed.
- Decomposition is fast in body which burns partially and greatly reduced in severe burns.
- Hair gets completely burnt.
- Portion of body where the clothing is tight becomes less affected(i.e. skin under belt, shocks etc.)
- Dry leather skin appearance gives the clue for presence of residual accelerants.
- Tongue protrudes due to contraction of tissues in neck and face.
- Froth may appear at the mouth & nose due to pulmonary edema caused due to heat irritation of air passages.
- **Hands**:Skin can be removed as glove. By removal of superficial layer of skin by wiping, tattoo marks are visible.
- Blister formation due to increased permeability of superficial blood vessel due to heat and it contains serous fluid contain albumen &Chlorides.
- Blisters of second-degree burns cannot be distinguished from blister seen in carbon monoxide poisoning, coma and gasoline exposure.
- Various types of blister burst they leave a pale moist, raw surface with yellow, tan, dark brown & leathery as it dries.

Pugilistic attitude:

(boxing, fencing or defense attitude)
- The legs are flexed at the hips & knee .
- Arms are flexed at elbows & wrist & held in front of body.
- Heat is slightly extended, finger nails as like of claws.
- Contraction of paraspinal muscle leads to opisthotonos.
- Degree & severity position depends on heat intensity & duration of heat.

Mechanism
- This stiffening occurs due to coagulation of muscle protein and muscle contraction is due to dehydration.
- Flexor muscle are usually bulkier than the extensor muscle, so flexion is common.
- It occurs whether the person is alive or dead at time of burning

Heat rupture
- In severe burning there is a splitting up of skin or soft parts of body
- It occurs anywhere in the body usually seen in areas such as calves, thighs, Extensor surfaces and joints
- Superficially it resembles as incised or lacerated wound.

Difference between Incised and lacerated wounds

	Incised	lacerated
Cause	Exposure of heat	Blunt force
Site	Fatty tissue	Anywhere
Bruising	absent	present

Flash burns
- It is variant of flame burn.
- It refers to sudden burning or explosion of gases or particulate material for example explosion of inflammable gases.
- Produce uniform first degree burn and if heat exposure is intense it produces second degree burn any where

Other effects:
- Obesity & clothes will determine how faster burn occurs
- If adipose tissue is burned then it leads to skeletal muscle damage & amputation
- Human body burn fast when the subcutaneous fat is burned
- Some other parts are preserved
- In sitting person, buttocks may get preserved and hands & feet may drop in severe burning.
- flame burns usually have patchy distribution & different in size & shape.

In severe burns skin may be stiffened & yellow brown leathery, muscles become small.

Muscle under the burnt area are pale

Burnt bone is gray white in colour.

In a burned body
- Cornea is white & transparent.
- Lens is opaque.
- Teeth are deranged.
- Rarely body cavity may be opened by partial destruction of walls of abdomen.

Internal

Heat hematoma: It occurs when the head is exposed to an intense heat, cause burning of skull and it resembles extradural hemorrhage.

Appearance: It is soft, chocolate coloured, if the blood contain carbon monoxide then the clot is pink in color.

clots gives the appearance of honey comb.

Thickness of the clots is from 1.5 to 13mm.

Common site: parieto-temporal region, sometimes occipital and frontal region

Mechanism: Blood being boiled from the diploic layer of bone through emissary vein and venous system

---

Note: Heat hematoma contain carboxyhemoglobin but extradural hemorrhage occur by injury before the fire doesn't contain carboxy hemoglobin

Heat hematoma is shrunken and compresses the brain tissue, adjacent brain shows hardening & discoloration

---

Thermal fractures of the skull

Two types of skull fractures:
1. Due to increase pressure of steam in the intracranium causes separation of suture which leads to fracture
2. Fracture occurs due to rapid drying of bone with contraction

- Only outer table of skull gets involved.
- Displacement is not seen
- It is usually above the area of temple and sometimes bilateral

- Heat fracture may cross the suture line
- Prolonged exposure of heat may break the hyoid bone

Carbon monoxide levels:

In burns
- Carbon monoxide levels in blood will more than 10% and it may reach upto 70 to 80%.
- Even 30 to 40% of levels of carbon monoxide in children and old age causes death.
- The blood is cherry red in colour and may becomes brownish due to heat
- The level of carbon monoxide saturation depends on amount of carbon monoxide inhaled and duration of exposure.

Absence of carbon monoxide seen in
1. Rapid death
2. Flash fire
3. Death by suffocation
4. Low production of carbon monoxide in heart and lung disease

Death from suffocation:
- Death occurred because of aspiration & suffocation of coal particles
- Which is commonly seen in nose,mouth,larynx,trachea,bronchi, oesophagus and stomach
- Blood is cherry red in colour
- Absolute proof forpresence of carbon particles in terminal bronchioles on histological examination.
- Presence of carbon particles and elevated carbon monoxide saturation is proof that the person remains alive during fire.
- The amount of soot particles depends on type of fire and duration of inhalation of smoke

Inhalation of flame (OR) Superheated air

If person inhales flame then burns are observed in interior of mouth,tongue,fauces, nasal passage, larynx with destruction of vocal edema & acute edema of larynx and lungs

Heat effects on the pharynx,epiglottis in post-mortem

Dry heat is limited upto oropharynx and upper airway

Appearance

Interior of larynx, Trachea and bronchi are thickened & red

If the temperature is low
- Mucosa shed into the lumen and smaller airways
- Sometimes inhalation of flame causes vomiting

Inhalation of poisonous gas such as cyanides and oxides of nitrogen causes pulmonary edema.
- It can also cause alveolar collapse due to decreased surfactant production, &bronchociliary injury.

Note:In blood, cyanide level is <0.3mg %.Cyanide is produced insignificant in concertation while decomposition.

Viscera:
- Hemorrhage seen in tongue root and neck muscle.
- Petechial hemmorrhage seen in pleura, pericardium and endocardium.
- Tissue edema.
- Brain and liver are hardened and discoloured.
  (Brain gets shorten, firm, yellow to brown in color)
- Brain tissue gets oozed out.
- Inflammation & ulceration of payer's patches seen.
- Petechial hemmorrhages of stomach & duodenum is common.
  Curling refers to sharp punched out mucosal defects which may be superficial or deep commonly seen in skin and in first part of duodenum.
- Erosion of larger vessels produce hemmorrhage.
- Spleen is enlarged & softened.
- Jaundice may occur.
- Presence of heme cast in medullary tubules are common.

Laryngeal edema:
- Caused by allergic reaction, infections, tumors, flame inhalation.
- It causes; laryngeal, tracheal, respiratory burns which may leads toadult respiratory distress.
- Amount of edema decrease with increase in postmortem interval.

Collection of blood:
- Blood should be collected from heart or the major vessels in a tight container
- If clotted, clot is preserved
- If blood is absent it can be obtained from spleen, narrow liver or muscle

Age of burns:
» Redness is immediate response
» Vesication seen in 1-2 hours
» Exudates becomes dry in 12-24 hours
» Dry brown crust in 48 -72 hours
» Superficial slough separates in 4-6 days
» Deep slough separates in 15 days
» Granulation tissue seen in >15 days
» Formation of deformity occurs in several weeks

Marjolijn Ulcer:
Malignant transformation of untreated or non-healing wounds leads to chronic ulceration is called Marjolijn ulcer(squamous cell carcinoma).

Antemortem & post-mortem burns

Triad	Antemortem burns	Post-mortem burns
Line of redness	Present	Absent
Blister	Contain serous fluid, protein& chlorides	Air and thin clear fluid
Base	Red and inflamed	Dry, hard& yellow
Vital reaction	Cellular exudation Reactive changes in the tissue	Absent
Enzymes	Increase in enzyme seen in peripheral zones.	No such increase in enzyme level.

Post-mortem blisters
- Sometimes blisters with redness is seen in postmortem burns due to contraction of dermal capillary
- Protein content of serous fluid doesnot have much difference in antemortem and Postmortem blisters
- Burns produced seen in naked eye before or after death or by microscopic examination

Medicolegal importance

Suicidal:

Common in India and among women due to pour of kerosene over the heads and clothes
- Burns are usually not seen in the feet and lower legs.

Accidental
- Common in children & elderly.
- Accident result from smoking in beds.
- Faulty use of equipment.

Homicidal
- Quite common in India.
- Dowry encourages young women to pour kerosene on them and set fire.
- In case of traumatic epidural hematoma (EDH) which produced before fire contain carboxyhemoglobin.
- Self inflicted burns

SCALDS
- It is a injury due to hot liquid (>60°C) or from steam.
- water at > 70°C causes full thickness of scald of the skin within 1 seconds of contact.
- severity of burn depends on duration of contact with skin & temperature of the fluid.
- Redness appears at once & blistering will takesplace within few minutes, blister fluid contain white & red cell Papillae in the floor of the blister.

Difference between Epidural hematoma due to burns and Epidural hematoma due to blunt force.

	Due to burns	Due to blunt force
causes	Burning of skull due to prolonged heat	Blunt force in the head
Situation	Anywhere	Adjacent to sylvian fissure
Position	Bilateral	Unilateral
Distribution	Diffused	Localized
Origin	Dural venous sinus vein	Middle meningeal artery
Characteristics	Honey comb appearances	Disc shaped
Crossing the suture line	Present	Absent
Injury to brain	present	absent

Degrees of scalds
- Erythema by vasoparalysis.
- Blister formation due to increased permeability of capillaries.
- Necrosis of dermis.
- scalds show soaked liquid appearance & white colour of skin.

Features:
- The injury is limited to the area of contact
- scalding occurs only through clothes.
- Scald are usually large but small while splashing.
- Streak lines of liquid runs downwards from main lines causes line of blister eg: oil.
- Scald usually have sharply, demarcated edges, corresponding to the liquid & produce a offensive smell.
- Scars of scald usually thinner than deeper burns.

If inflammable fluids are used there is signs of burning marks seen on some parts of body
Toxic epidermal necrosis are due to disease or drug cause redness and separation of superficial skin layers that gives similar appearance of scalds.

Note:
- *At postmortem examination blister doesn't show hyperemia (no blood flow) at the surroundings.*
- *Clothes worsen the damage of body by increasing the contact with hot liquid and reducing the effect of cooling*

Occurrence
- » Accidental bursting of hot bottles bursting, splashing of fluid while cooking.
- » Occasionally children drink the hot water containing bottles caused severe steam of the mouth causes edema of the glottis .
- » suicidal is rare.
- » throwing of boiling water cause injury.
- » murder and steam burns in rare.
- » Spontaneous human combustion (Preternatural combustion)
- » It is rare.
- » During putrefactionMicroorganism action produces aninflammable gas in the abdomen upon Organic matter.
- Mostly occur in hot fire area.

For example:
- If the person is alcoholic confused, instable and lack of judgement .
- It usually appears in elderly women and she collapses, falls and part of body with contact catches fire and burns by the action of limited oxygen in the room.
- The process continues the adjacent body fat melts and repeated along the knee joint and burning stops with less fat.
- The only part remained undamaged are one or both .

Difference between burns due to Dry heat, Moist heat and Chemicals.

	Dry heat	Moist heat	Chemical
cause	Flame, solid body, x ray	Steam or liquid >60 C	Corrosive chemicals
site	At & above of contact	At & below of contact	At & below of contact
skin	Dry & wrinkled	Sudden & bleached	Destroyed -may be
Redline	present	present	absent
Colour	black	bleached	Distinctive
Ulceration	absent	Absent	present
Scar	Thick & contracted	Thin & less contracted	Thick & contracted
Splashing	Absent	present	Present
clothes	burnt	Wet not burnt	May be burnt

ELECTRICAL INJURIES

Alternating current is dangerous than direct current.

Amount of current

In India – voltage of domestic supply is usually 220 to 240 volts.

10 mA of current causes pain & muscle contraction 60mA of current is dangerous.

100 mA of current is lethal.

Path of current
> Death is more likely if the brain stem or heart is the direct path.

Duration of current flow
> Increase in the current flow will increase the severity.
> Electrocution refers to death caused by passage of electric current.

Electrical injuries consist of
- Fatal Electrocution – death caused due to passage of high current is body.
- Electric shock & burns.
- Note: fatal Electrocution is common.
- The effect of electricity depends on voltage & resistance offered
- If the body is well insulated it doesn't conduct the current
- Dry skin offers more resistance, resistance is low when the skin is covered with sweat

Local effects
- Passage of current through skin produces heat.
- Cause boiling & splitting of tissue fluids
- A wet skin may not show electrical burn
- Dry skin shows an electrical burn

Electrical mark (joule burn)
- It is a specific & diagnostic mark of electricity contact
- It is usually found at point of entry of current and it is usually seen in high tension electric current.

Characterestics of joule burn.
1. This mark is usually round or oval, one to 3mm in diameter around some part or whole skin
2. Some marks the skin breaks at or near the margin of floor which resembling as a broken blister
3. If the contact duration is long then skin looks brown & at last skin is burnt as contact is prolonged
   Shape of mark resembles that of linear wire

   Pathognomic features:
   Areola of pale skin (blanched) seen at the periphery of electrical mark.
   Commonly found in exposed part of body especially in palmaraspect of hand

Histological examination
Electric marks usually show:
» Coagulation of dermis with separation of epidermis in some areas
» In other areas, cells are elongated arranged in parallel rows or almost right angle to the dermis

Flash burns or spark burns:
» Very high heat results from flash over the burns which resemble that of thermal heat
» In spark burn there is a gap between metal & the skin and conduction done through air.
» In spark burn there is a gap between metal & the skin and conduction done through air.
» In flash burns central nodules of fused keratin is brown or yellow in colour and is surrounded by areola of skin.
» Usually this burn leads to pin point contraction, if the contact is prolonged.

High voltage burns
- It is associated with third degree burn.
- Soft tissues are destroyed over a wide area.
- About 1000 volts will produce burn for severalmm, and 100 kilo volts will produce burn over 35cm.
- Very high voltage current produce massive destruction of tissue, loss of extremity & rupture of organ.

For example
> If bone gets involved:
> 1. Periosteum is elevated.
> 2. Superficial layers of bone is fractured.
>
> Note: High tension electric current produce multiple small, pitted burns
> Skin becomes brown or greyish.
> Multiple burnt are punched out lesion produce crocodile flash burn due to arc dancing over body surface.
> Punched lesion commonly presented as seen in injuries of bullet, stab (or)incised wound.

Absence of burns seenin the following conditions
> voltage is low and the area of contact is large (ie hot wire is touched with the wet hand).
> Area of contact is small in voltage is low.
> Brief contact in line wire doesn't produce burn.

Electric burn or split
- » Bare wire pressed against the skin and the burn is linear, areola has a pale zone parallel to the central.
- » If the tip of the rod at right angle of skin the burn is present as circular hole which penetration into the skin, muscle& bone.
- » If the metallic current is passed, their impression of the metal in the skin & subcutaneous tissue.

Appearance:
- » Dry, hard, firm, blackened with irregular edges that gives various types of burn oval round heat or depth of lesion in greater than appears on skin.
- » Peeling of skin is commonly seen, wrinkling of skin, localized edema of the limb and at last may be development of aseptic necrosis.

Histopathology
- Blister formation in the squamous epithelium and the external horny layer.
- Large vacuoles are produced with in the epidermal cells.
- Nuclei is fusiform, hyperchromic (peculiar formation of nuclear contour is palisade type appearance).
- This change is called streaming of nuclei.
- These flattened cells are darkly stained than the normal cells (i.e.hematoxylin eosin stain).
- Nuclei in the vascular media is spiral in shape.
- Localized degeneration media is spiral in shape.
- Tearing of elastic fibres.

Exit marks
> Variable in appearance but some features are those of entry mark.
> There may be mark damage of tissue.
> Split in the skin at point where the edges areraised into ridges by the passage of current.

Postmortem appearances
> Scene and site are more important than the postmortem examination.
> Clothing including shoe, gloves should be examined.

Note:
- *In cardiac arrhythmia person is pale and.*
- *In respiratory failure cyanosis is seen.*
- *Rigor mortis developed early & postmortem lividity is well developed .*

External
- » Eyes are congested & pupil is dilated.
- » Rigor mortis developed early & postmortem lividity is well developed.
- » In about 50-60 case of electrical burn marks contusion & laceration at the entrance & exit point occasionally the lesion may extend subcutaneous tissue, bone & muscle.
- » Greyish circular spots which firm to touch, no inflammation at the site of entrance & exit points.
- » Convulsion caused electric discharge may cause spine & limb fracture.
- » Discolouration of skin seen in face & the trunk.
- » In some case the entrance & exit mark cannot be determined in that situation determined histological method or electron microscopy is used.

Internal
- » Lungs are edematous & congested.
- » Petechial hemerrhages may found along in passage of the current under the endocardium, pericardium, pleura & the spinal.
- » Brain meninges & parenchymatous organ are congested.
- » Vascular thrombosis.
- » Skeletal muscle in the pathway of current may show Zener's degeneration.
- » Bone nerves, zig zag fractures.

Note:
- *Heat generated by the current may melt the calcium phosphate with show is radiographical findings as round dense foci which is called bone pearls or wax drippings.*
- *Explosive effect of high ampere current may produce injures like bullet, stab or cut wounds. small metals balls derived from metal contacting the electrode is called as current pears*

Cause of death
Paralysis of medullary centre circuit from any of limb is connected to head brain stem & upper cervical lord

Circuit involving the heart & death occurs from ventricular fibrillation.

Secondary cause infection or from the hemorrhage damage do the vessels.

Medicolegal aspect
Accidental defective electrical appliances or negligence in use of equipment.

Traumatic injury the electric shock during electroconvulsive therapy in treatmentof mental disorder patients.

Suicidal cause is rare.

Homicidal-drop of plugged circuit in a electrical circuit in to bucket while taking a bath.

Treatment
If person is contact with the electricity he should pulled with the bare hard the current is switched off.

Person marked with stick or dry cloth or newspaper or rubber gloves.

Artificial respiration & closed cardiac massage is principle treatment.

Judicial electrocution
Death penalty carried out using the electric chair is some states of USA.

The person is forced to sit in electric chair & one electrode is connected to scalp & other in right lower leg by another electrode.

The voltage various in power from state to state current of 20000 volts & ampere passed from one minute

After spasm &unconsciousness the same of current is passed.

Appearance
- Third degree burn.
- site of contact – scalp & skin.

LIGHTNING STROKE

- It is due to electrical discharge from the cloud to earth. The electrical current is about 20,000 amperes & 1000 to 1000 million volts.
- A Single flash of lighting stroke lasts about 1/1000 second due to which no burns, or only minor burns & blackening of hair.
- Dry skin & dry clothes are bad conductors.

  - Dry skin & dry clothes are bad conductors.
  - Wet skin & Wet clothes are good conductors.
  - The effects of lighting seen for about 30 metre.
  - Direct strike the current enters & spread to all over the body.
  - Side strike it hits the object (i.e.) tree & jumping from it strikes the person.
  - Study of Lighting pathology is keraunopathology.

Influencing Factors:
- Electricity passing from earth.
- Flash burns.
- Fore produced by displaced air.
- Air movement.

Clothes:
- It is usually burnt or torn.

In some cases, clothes are thrown out from the body.

In exceptional cases – clothes are not damaged even though person in killed by lighting.

Postmortem appearances:
- External.
- It causes contusion, fractures, ruptures, variety of burns in various site.
- Discolouration of skin.
- Internal.
- Rigor mortis appears soon and passed off quickly.
- Intense edema of skin develops at the point of entry due to paralysis of local capillary & lymphatic Vessels.
- Internal organ shows presence of clots &thrombi.
- Signs of asphyxia is present.
- Meningesgetscongested& Lacerated.
- Subarachnoid & intracerebral bleeding.
- Haemorrhagein pleura & pericardium.
- Lungs are congested.
- Blood vessels gets thrombosed.
- Eardrum are ruptured.
- Hemorrhage in ear drum.
- burns may be.

Linear:
- Very from 0.3 to 2.5 cm in length.
- Areas are of tenincreases, folds of skin Irregular, linear, first degree burns may follow skin creases.

Arborescent(or) filigree burns:
- Burns are superficial,thin,irregular& Irregular margins on skin.
- It resembles the branching of tree.
- Fern like pattern is mostly found in shoulders & flanks.

Mechanism
- Caused due to staining of the tissue by haemoglobin from the lysed RBC along the way of passage of electric current which gives redness.
- It appears within few minutes to one hour of accident.
- Important features -Red streaks following the skin crease.

Surface burns
- It is true burns occur beneath the object carried by the person with flash.

Causes of death
- Involvement of central nervous system with paralysis of heart & respiratory center.

Medicolegal importance
- Mostly death occurs in open area like under the tree.
- Less than half of person is killed by lighting.
- This death is always accidental.
- Sometimes person may be dead in open field or highway it shows contusion & fracture.

Radiation
It causes damage through infrared frequency.
Uses: industrial application
Medical application
External therapeutic techniques
Internal therapeutic agents.

Delayed effects
- Malignant tumors.
- Leukemia.
- Ulceration.
- Gangrene.
- Cataract.
- Sterility in both sexes.
- Osteosarcoma.
- Mental defects, stillbirth

Radiation syndrome.
200-500 rods produce a radiation illness
Radiation syndrome is associated with nausea, vomiting, electrolyteimbalance and circulatory failure.

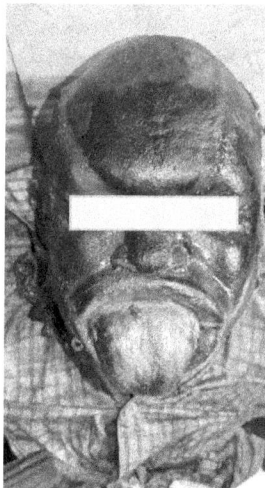

Fig(12.1) Tette de negre.

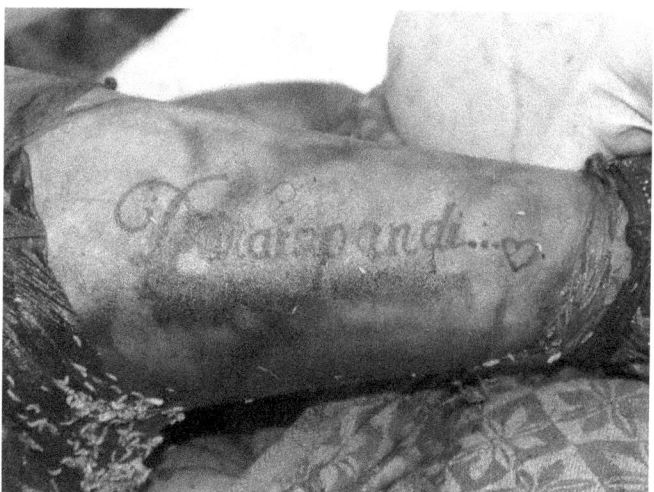

Fig(12.2) Tattoo marks in burns.

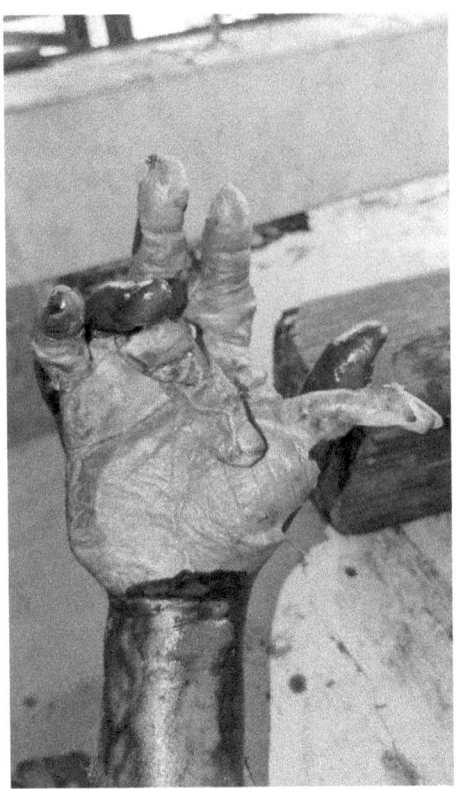
Fig(12.3) Degloving of hand.

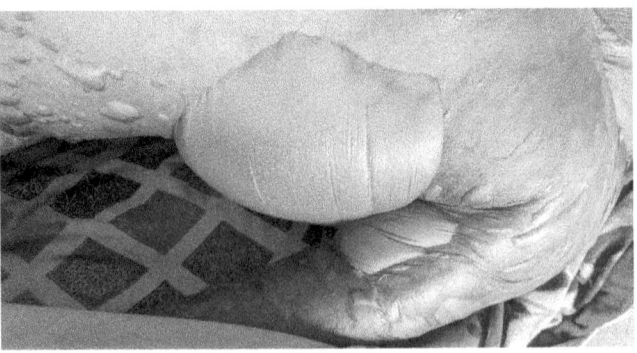
Fig(12.4) Blister formation.

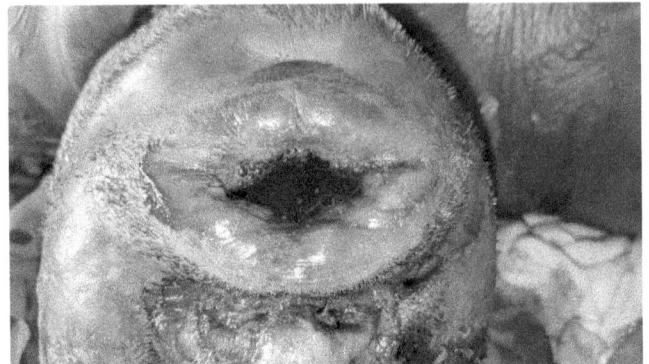
Fig(12.5) Fish mouth appearance in a burnt face.

Fig(12.6) Puglistic attitude.

Courtesy: Professor, Dr. Chandrasekar, MMC, Madurai.
Associate professor, Dr.Sadhasivam, MMC, Madurai.

CHAPTER - 13
STARVATION

It refers to suffering or death due to actual withholding of food or due to administration of unsuitable food.

Types
1. Acute starvation
2. Chronic starvation

Acute starvation	Chronic Starvation
Occurs due to sudden and complete stoppage of food	Occurs due to gradual deficiency in supply of food In chronic starvation changes are gradual Hunger & hunger pains
In Acute starvation Feeling of hunger for initial 30 to 48 hours	Lethargic both mentally & physically
Pain in epigastrium relieved by pressure	Rapid weight loss in initial 6 months
Emaciation, Depletion of subcutaneous fat	Cachexia (weakness & wasting of body)
Progression of muscle weakness	Anaemia
Cardiovascular changes	Hypotension, Hypothermia and vascular stasis
Extreme state of emaciation reached	Mental disturbance (lethargy, gross mental retardation)
Death after reaching 40% of original body weight	Pedal oedema
	Death by infections, circulatory failure and dehydration due to diarrhoeal episodes

Symptoms of acute starvation:
1. Sunken eyes and dilated pupils
2. Bony prominences visible due to extreme emaciation.
3. Lips becomes dry and cracked.
4. Extreme thirst, scanty secretion of saliva and saliva turns thick
5. Skin becomes dry, wrinkled and pigmented
6. At rest, pulse rate is low and paroxysmal tachycardia occurs as an interruption during excertion
7. Temperature becomes subnormal
8. Initially constipation occurs and diarrhea, dysenty are common as the person progresses to death.
9. Scanty, turbid and concentrated urine is excreted
10. Ketoacidosis seen due to extrme fatty acid metabolism
11. On severe emaciation the following are seen
    - Concavities of intercostals space
    - Concavities of supraclavicular fossae
    - Prominent ribcage

In chronic starvation blood sugar, proteins, chlorides and cholesterol gets lowered.
Raise in levels of ketone bodies, urea and non protein nitrogen (creatine, creatinine, uric acid etc..) are seen in blood

Nutritional utilization during starvation and its mechanism

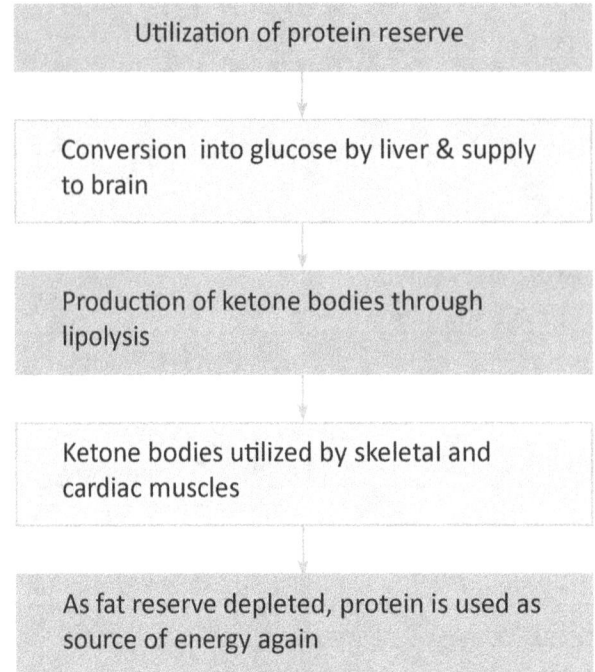

Note :
The main cause of death in case of starvation is
1. Circulatory failure due to brown atrophy of heart
2. Intercurrent infection which leads to multi organ failure
3. Ventricular fibrillation
4. Dehydration and hypothermia

Fatal period:
The time in which a person dies after fatal dose is given (or) after withdrawal of food

S.No	Conditions	Fatal period
1)	Both food & water withdrawn	10 - 12 days
2)	If food alone withdrawn	6 - 8 weeks
3)	Newborns without food (or) water	7 - 10 days

Note :
The main cause of death in case of starvation is
1. *Circulatory failure due to brown atrophy of heart*
2. *Intercurrent infection which leads to multi organ failure*
3. *Ventricular fibrillation*
4. *Dehydration and hypothermia*

Points to remember:
If 70 to 90 % of body fat and 20% of body protein are lost, it leads to death.

Factors influencing fatal period:

Age : Both extremities of age suffers a lot
Sex : Females can withstand for longer period
Condition of body : Fatty healthy people withstand better
Temperature : exposure to cold (or) heat hastens death Physical exertion hastens death

Postmortem appearance in case of starvation	
External appearance	Internal appearance
Skin is pale, elastic and pigmented	Complete depletion of fat even in omenum, mesentry and internal organs
Follicular hyperkeratosis may be seen	Female breast and bichats buccal pad are the last site where fat disappears and sub epicardial fat is replaced by watery gelatinous material
Patches of subcutaneous oedema around ankle & medial thigh	Progressive demineralization followed by osteomalacia, rickets, dental defects are seen
Pressure sores on buttocks, heels & spine may be seen	Reduction in size and weight of all organ except brain.
Dry and brittle hair & nail also becomes brittle	Brain becomes pale and soft.

Marked oedema of face trunk and limbs with ascites and pleural effusions seen in wet type	Decrease in blood volume seen and urinary bladder is empty.
	Muscle & muscle fibres :
	  Muscle gets atrophied and darker due to deposition of lipochrome
	  Fibres lose striations

Fig(13.1) Starvation. Courtesy: Professor, Dr. Chandrasekar, MMC, Madurai. Associate professor, Dr.Sadhasivam, MMC, Madurai.	**Lungs :** Pale & collapsed
	Heart : Brown atrophy seen & chambers are empty.
	Stomach & intestine: • Mucosa stained with bile • Mucosal atrophy seen • Bowel filled with offensive watery fluid and gas
	Liver & kidney: Atrophied and necrosis seen.
	Spleen: Shrunken
	Gall bladder: Distended with bile.

Medicolegal aspects :-
1. Exclusion of disease which may cause loss of weight.
2. Ex: malignancy, progressive muscular atrophy, Addissions disease, diabetes mellitus, pernicious anaemia, tuberculosis & chronic diarrhoea may cause loss of weight
3. In case of disease like tuberculosis, it is difficult to find whether the disease is a result of cause or effect.
4. Marked loss of weight and depletion of fat on autopsy indicates that the death is due to starvation.

Important point :

When a person going on hunger strike is found to have weight loss and ketoacidosis in urine then forcible feeding by arrest is considered to be a lawful act.

CHAPTER- 14
MECHANICAL ASPHYXIA

- Asphyxia is the interference of respiration due to any cause, i.e. mechanical, environmental or toxic, resulting in failure of intake of oxygen by the tissues together with failure to eliminate carbondioxide.
- Asphyxia literally means pulselessness. But in forensic context and everywhere in medical science, asphyxia means lack of oxygen.

Causes of asphyxia

There are various ways which result in asphyxia; they are grouped according to their mode of causation.

I. Closure of external orifices: Smothering.
II. Compression of neck: Hanging, strangulation, throttling, bansdola, mugging and autoerotic asphyxia.
III. Occlusion of air passage from within: Gagging, choking and café coronary.
IV. Lack of oxygen in the atmosphere, or inhalation of irrespirable gases: Suffocation.
V. Restriction of movement of the chest or abdomen: Traumatic asphyxia, burking and overlaying.
VI. Prevention of gas exchange in the lung by fluids: Drowning.
VII. IInability to utilize oxygen by peripheral tissues: Cyanide poisoning.

Mechanical asphyxia:

Asphyxia due to mechanical force. The causes of mechanical asphyxia are classified into:

Obstructive causes	Smothering, gagging, choking and café coronary.
Constrictive causes	Hanging, strangulation, throttling, lynching, bansdola, mugging and garroting.
Restrictive causes	Traumatic asphyxia, burking and overlaying.
Replacement causes	Drowning.
Chemical asphyxiants	Carbon monoxide and cyanide poisoning

Classical signs of asphyxia:

Any way be the causation of asphyxia, it leaves certain signs on thebody. They are not specific to asphyxial deaths alone, but invariably present is most cases of asphyxia and are hence calledas the classical signs of asphyxia. They are also commonly referred to as "asphyxial triad" and these are:

I. Cyanosis
II. Congestion of organs
III. Petechial Hemorrhages.

Non-specific signs:
- Abnormal fluidity of blood
- Dilatation of right chambers of heart.

Specific sign:

Specific sign indicates the exact way in which the fatal chains of events were initiated.

Example:

I. Ligature mark on the neck in hanging and ligature strangulation,
II. Finger nails abrasions on the neck in manual strangulation (throttling),
III. Fluid in the air passage in drowning,
IV. Food bolus in the larynx in café coronary, etc.

Classical signs of asphyxia:

i. **Cyanosis**
   - The color of oxygenated blood is scarlet red. When the hemoglobin is not fully saturated with oxygen, then it is said to be reduced and the blood assumes a blue color, which is termed as "cyansis".
   - For cyanosis to be evident externally, there should be at least 5 g of reduced hemoglobin per 100 mL of blood. Cyanosis is well-appreciated in the peripheries like fingernails, lips and tongue and hence it iscommon use to say "peripheral cyanosis."

ii. **Congestion**
   - Collection and stasis of blood due to obstruction of venous return is called as congestion. When the neck is compressed as in hanging, due to defective venous return, there is congestion of the face, as well as in all the internal organs.
   - Congestion is associated with tissue swelling, if there is continued venous obstruction. Prolonged congestion leads to edema of the visceral organs.
   - When circulation stops completely, the walls of the capillaries become permeable resulting in exudation of fluid from the capillaries into the neighboring tissues leading toedema.

iii. **Petechial hemorrhages**
   - Progressive increase in the venous pressure will lead to rupture of post-capillary venules. This leads to escape of blood producing small bleeding points, varying from pinpoint to pinhead size. They are called as petechial hemorrhages.
   - They are readily appreciated on the serous membranes such as sclera, conjunctiva, pleura and the pericardium.

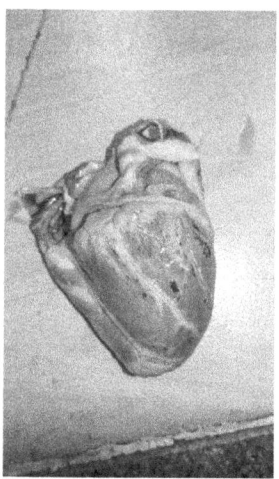
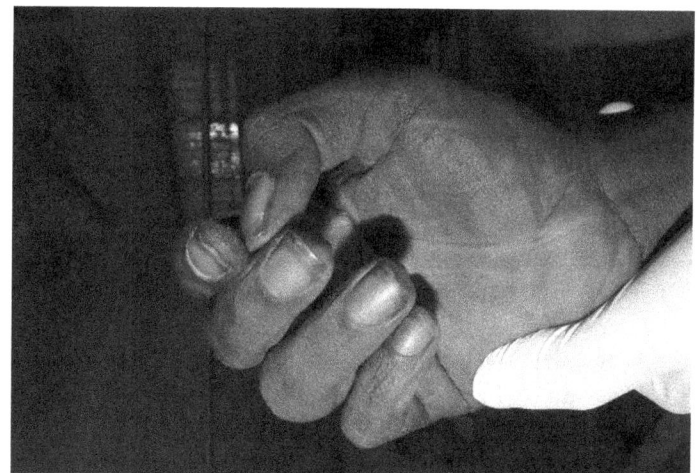

Fig(14.1) Petechial hemorrhage of pericardium.

Fig(14.2) Cyanosed hand due to asphyxia

Courtesy: Professor, Dr. Chandrasekar, MMC, Madurai.
Associate professor, Dr.Sadhasivam, MMC, Madurai.

HANGING

- **Hanging** is a form of asphyxia caused by suspension of the body by a ligature around the neck. The constricting force being his own body weight.
- Hanging is the preferred method of choice for committing suicide and is said to be a relatively painless form of death. **Hanging is almost always suicidal, unless proved otherwise.**
- **Note:** Suicide note is present in many situations and in some female cases, a note regarding the reason for committing suicide and details of individuals who were responsible in forcing her to commit suicide may be hidden inside the inner garments and are recovered during autopsy. If any such documents are recovered, they are handed over to the police with acknowledgement after retaining a copy of those recovered documents.

Types of hanging

Depending on the degree of suspension

(i) Complete hanging:	The entire body is suspended and no part of the body touches the ground. Hence, the whole of the body weight acts as the constricting force.
(ii) Partial hanging:	The whole body is not suspended and some part of the body is in contact with the ground and the constricting force is only part of the body weight. **Ex:** The feet are in contact with the ground; the individual is in kneeling position or in lying position with only the head hanging out.

Depending on the position of the knot

(i) Typical hanging:	The ligature passes symmetrically on both sides of the neck toward the point of suspension and the knot is at the nape of the neck. The head will be flexed and bent forward. The maximum pressure exerted by the ligature is directly opposite to the point of suspension and death is presumed to be purely due to asphyxia, and hence called as typical hanging.
(ii) Atypical hanging:	The whole body is not suspended and some part of the body is in contact with the ground and the constricting force is only part of the body weight. Example: The feet are in contact with theground; the individual is in kneeling position or in lying position with only the head hanging out.

Causes of death in hanging
i. **Asphyxia:** Due to constriction of the trachea.
ii. **Venous congestion:** Due to occlusion of jugular veins.
iii. **Combined Combination asphyxia and venous congestion:** of the above two. Combined asphyxia and venous congestion is the cause of death in 90% cases.
iv. **Cerebral Anemia:** Due to constriction of carotid and vertebral arteries.
v. **Reflux vagal inhibition:** When the ligature material rubs over the carotid sheath, there is stimulation of carotid body which leads to reflux vagal inhibition, resulting in sudden stoppage of heart.
vi. **Fracture dislocation of cervical vertebra:** Occurs only in judicial hanging or hanging accompanied with a long drop (6 to 8 meters) and the knot is below the chin. Here the maximum pressure is exerted on the cervical vertebrae as a result of sudden drop accompanied by the weight of the body. This leads to dislocation and instantaneous fracture at the level of C2, C3 cervical vertebrae, with-corresponding injury to the spinal column. In this condition, death is instantaneous.

Delayed deaths in hanging:
When hanging attempt is foiled by timely intervention andresuscitation, the hypoxic and ischemic effects to the brain andbrainstem will lead to delayed deaths of the individual. In such cases, death is due to:
i. Infection
ii. Edema of larynx and lungs
iii. Hypoxic ischemic encephalopathy
iv. Infarction of brain
v. Brain abscess
vi. Cerebral softening and liquefaction.

Postmortem appearance

All the classical signs of asphyxia namely, peripheral cyanosis, visceral congestion and petechial hemorrhages are present in most of the cases of death due to asphyxia.

Ligature mark:
- The compressing force of the ligature material results in the production of an injury around the neck in the form of a pressure abrasion.
- The ligature leaves a furrow of its own width and pattern. It develops due to the pressure exerted by the ligature material on the skin surface.
- The bed of the ligature mark is pale and dry; pressure exerted by the ligature material pushes the blood from the underneath skin surface and the tissues become pale. Later on with the passage of time, it becomes
- parchmentized due to the effect of drying.
- The edges are abraded (reddish-brown): Due to the frictional force between the skin and the ligature material. Ecchymosis and congestion of adjacent skin may be seen.
- The pattern of the ligature material often gets imprinted on the skin surface as a pressure abrasion/imprint abrasion
- The ligature mark is usually situated at the upper border of the neck, above the thyroid cartilage, just below the chin. Itruns obliquely upward and backward, symmetrically on both sides of the neck, toward the point of suspension/the knot.
- **Microscopically**, the ligature mark displays the usual characteristics of abrasion, showing desquamation and flattening of cells of the epidermis.
- If death has occurred quickly, evidence of vital reactions at the margins of the ligature mark may be difficult to demonstrate even by microscopy.

Other external findings
- Face is congested, with cyanosis of lips and nail beds.
- Post-mortem staining will be seen over the distal part of both upper and lower limbsof the body. This can be appreciated only if the body was in the suspended position for a minimum period of 4 to 6 hours. This type of distribution of postmortem staining is called "glove and stockings fashion" of postmortem hypostasis. Petechiae in the lower limbs, if the body is suspended for a long time (8 to 12 hours).
- Neck is elongated and the head is tilted toward one side away from the knot.
- Tongue may be protruded and bitten.
- **Salivary stains** at the angle of mouth: Diagnostic of antemortem hanging and could be present in 40 to 60% cases. When the ligature material rubs over the sub-mandibular salivary glands, there is increased salivary secretion, which could be found dribbled and dried along the angle of mouth of one side, when the head is tilted opposite to the point of suspension.
- In my postgraduate dissertation study and further experience (nearly 1000 cases of hanging), the salivary stains were present in nearly 40% cases. Author has seen many cases where there were ants crawling along a line on the front of chest, after washing the body, we could notice the underlying dried salivary stains could be, dribbled from the angle of mouth. Hence, a careful search for this finding of dried salivary stains will help to confirm a large number of cases as antemortemhanging.
- **Le facies sympathique:** If the knot presses on the cervical sympathetic ganglia, the eye on that side may remain open and the pupil dilated; the eyes on the other side will remain partially open or closed.This is very rare and observed in less than 1% cases, but if present it is also a surest antemortem sign of hanging.

Neck dissection
- Neck is examined after removal of the brain, thoracic and abdominal contents (bloodless field of dissection).
- Superficial incisions of the ligature grooves may show smallhemorrhages in theunderlying layers of the skin, caused by directtrauma.
- Extravasation and bruising of the muscles of the neck may be present, especially over the sternocleidomastoid and platysma. The intima of the carotid arteries may show transverse tears (splits) with extravasation of blood in their walls. These changes are due to thetraction effect of the body with the ligature material.
- The subcutaneous tissues immediately above and below the ligature mark are congested.
- The tissues underneath the ligature mark are pale and parchment-like.
- The lymph nodes of the neck above and below the ligature mark show evidence of congestion, stasis and hemorrhage. This is also a useful finding of antemortem hanging.

Hyoid bone
- The relevance of fracture of the hyoid bone in hanging is minimal. It only signifies that there was external compression over the hyoid bone.
- Hyoid bone is a highly compressible bone and hence fracture occurs only occasionally; fracture is more common above the age of 40 years as the bone gets calcified in old age and the flexibility is restricted.
- The commonest pattern of fracture is outward fracture (abduction fracture) which is due to antero-posterior compression. The broken piece of bone has an outward angulation.
- Case studies have shown that the incidence of hyoid bone fracture is relatively high when:
  i. the ligature material is a hard material like rope or string
  ii. the ligature material should directly compress the hyoid bone, and
  iii. The longer the period of suspension of the body, the chances of fracture is increased. From this it is evident that the hyoid bone fracture should not be given much importance, it only indicates thatthere has been some pressure over the hyoid bone and no information regarding whether death is due to hanging could be made out from the fracture of hyoid bone. But the fracture of hyoid bone is more common in throttling, as there is direct pressure over the hyoid bone. In any fracture, theantemortem nature should be checked; extravasation of blood and if necessary benzidine test and histopathology.

Effects of decomposition on ligature mark:
- In any case, decomposition alters the findings, mainly the external injuries; but though ligature abrasion is a superficial injury fortunately resists putrefaction for a reasonable period of time. During the process of compression of the neck, the blood underneath the ligature abrasion is pushed away from those areas and hence putrefaction is markedly delayed on the ligature abrasion.

Lynching:
- Homicidal hanging of a person by the mob in the public is called as lynching.
- The person who is suspected to be involved in heinous crimes like dacoity, murder, or sexual assault (especially on the white people) is over powered by the mob, and hanged forcefully in the public to raise fear among the public. This was in practice in the ancient period and the aim of committing lynching is to raise fear among the public and as a deterrent to the society in committing such grave crimes.

Postmortem hanging: (Postmortem Suspension)
- Occasionally, after a victim has been murdered by some other means the body may be suspended to simulate suicidal hanging.
- Findings of asphyxia will not be evident and the actual cause of death may be easily madeout during autopsy. Postmortem nature of ligature abrasion has to be differentiated and confirmed by the presence of vital reactions and HPE, if necessary.
- When the victim is killed by throttling or ligature strangulation and then suspended; signs of asphyxia will be present and hence difficulties do arise. But a careful observation may reveal fingernail abrasions in throttling and horizontal complete encircling ligature abrasion in cases of ligature strangulation. Also, internal neck dissection (bloodless field) will be highly rewarding and most cases could be solved on the autopsy table itself.

Fibers of ligature material:
- Presence of fibers of ligature material in the hands of the victim indicates that the victim has handled the material either while committing suicide or by struggle to get rid of the constricting force during the process of death in hanging or strangulation. Absence of such fibers in the hands of the victim indicates that the victim has not touched the material at all, thus indicating postmortem hanging(especially when the material is a rope or clothing).
- In case of postmortem suspension, examination of the upper surface of the branch of the tree or beam (point of suspension) will indicate the direction of traction force. In such situation, the ligature material is first tied around the neck and is pulled from the opposite side to suspend the body. The direction of markings made by the fibers of the ligature material at the point of suspension will be away from the body (anti-clockwise). Whereas, if it is a case of suicidal hanging, the markings will be in a clockwise direction. This finding may occasionally be helpful in postmortem hanging.

STRANGULATION

- It is a form of violent asphyxial death accomplished by application of external force to constrict the neck, either by hands (**manual strangulation/throttling**) or by a ligature material (**ligature strangulation**) or by any other means.
- There is no suspension of the body in strangulation and hence the constricting force is not the victim's own body weight rather external compression by an assailant.
- Ligature strangulation is mostly homicidal, occasionally accidental and rarely suicidal (but a person cannot successfully commit suicide by throttling).
- Sometimes, death may occur due to sudden vagal inhibition without leaving any signs of asphyxia on the body.
- Symptoms of ligature **strangulation:**
- There is complete occlusion of air passage due to sudden compression of the neck. Unconsciousness develops very quickly and instant death is common, since the victimis overpowered by the perpetrator and evidence of struggle may or may not be present.
- In incomplete occlusion for a longer duration, there will be intense cyanosis and congestion of the face, bleeding from the mouth, nostrils and ears may be seen.

Causes of death
- Asphyxia
- Cerebral ischemia
- Vagal inhibition: If death is due to vagal inhibition, evidence of asphyxia will not be present on the body.

Postmortem appearance in ligature strangulation
External appearance:
Ligature mark:
- The ligature mark is well-defined and grooved. The intensity and the pattern depend on the amount of force exerted by external compression and the ligature material used.
- It is usually situated at or below the level of the thyroid cartilage.

- It completely encircles the neck, without any discontinuity.
- The direction of the ligature is horizontal or horizontally oblique, with crossing over to the opposite side. In some cases, the ligature material will be encircling the neck several times producing more number of markings and many a times there may be evidence of more than one knot.
- The direction of the ligature mark depends on the relative position of the assailant and the victim at that time of strangulation.

i. It will be horizontally oblique, if the victim was in lying position
ii. horizontal, when both the victim and the assailant are in standing posture
iii. oblique if the victim was sitting and the assailant standing behind and also when the victim is dragged from behind.

- The margins of the ligature mark will be reddish, ecchymosed and the base will be pale. With passage of time, the ligature abrasion becomes dry, hard, parchment-like.
- The pressure exerted on the neck by the ligature material produces an imprint abrasion.
- Abrasions and ecchymosis of adjacent skin will be more evident than in hanging.
- If the ligature material is soft and yielding or if it is removed soon after death, then the ligature mark may not be visible over the skin surface. In such situations, a second examination of the neck after several hours may show the presence of a faint pressure abrasion.
- If the ligature material is not present in situ and recovered later, the presence or absence of fibers from the ligature material over the ligature mark can be identified by application of adhesive cello tape and examination under the microscope for comparison.
- Accidental ligature strangulation: A scarf or dupatta may be caught in a moving fan, vehicle, machinery belt, etc. and can result in severe constriction of the neck and produce instantaneous death by ligature strangulation.

Asphyxial signs:
- All the classical signs of asphyxia will be more marked than in hanging.
- Eye balls may be open, prominent and congested with dilated pupils.
- Discharge of blood stained fluid may be seen over the mouth and nostrils.
- Intense congestion of face is usually present and multiple petechial hemorrhages over the forehead are a common finding.
- Tongue will be protruding, bitten by teeth, bruised, swollen and deeply cyanosed.
- Hands may be clenched. While the victim attempts to defend him by inserting his fingers in between the neck and the ligature material, nail scratch marks in the form of linear or crescentic abrasions can be seen over the neck and rarely cadaveric spasm may occur instantaneously at that moment.

Internal appearance:
- Excluding the neck, all the body cavities and visceral organs are examined first in order to get a bloodless neck field. This will also avoid introduction of artefacts in the neck field and the resultant misinterpretations.
- In case of ligature strangulation, evidence of bruising will be present on all the underlying layers of tissues; namely, the subcutaneous layer, muscles of the neck, tracheal rings and also on the posterior pharyngeal wall
- Since the pressure exerted by the ligature material is over the surface of the thyroid cartilage, fracture of the superior cornua of thyroid cartilage is relatively common in strangulation, with extravasation of blood in the surrounding soft tissues.
- Other internal organs like larynx and trachea show intense congestion, with frothy mucus and also petechial hemorrhages.
- Lungs show multiple hemorrhagic patches and petechiae over the surface, with marked congestion and emphysematous bullae. Presence of emphysematous bullae associated with congestion and petechiae indicates the agonal struggle of the victim.
- All the other internal organs will be congested and petechiae may be present.
- Involuntary discharge of urine and fecal matter may be seen in many cases.

- Since, ligature abrasion resists decomposition for relative period of time, cases of ligature strangulation can be positively solved even if the bodies are recovered a few days later.

THROTTLING

- Throttling (manual strangulation) is a form of violent asphyxial death, in which the assailant uses his hands to produce compression of the neck of the victim.

Autopsy findings:
- All the classical signs of asphyxia will be markedly evident.
- Petechial hemorrhages on the forehead are a frequent finding, indicative of more severe forms of violent asphyxia than hanging.
- Multiple pressure spots of bruising will be seen over the neck due to assailant gripping the neck with fingers.
- The fingernails of the assailant produce crescentic and linear abrasions on both sides of the neck. The victim also produces certain nail marks by himself during the attempt of struggle to relieve the assailant's hands from causing compression.
- **Bruises:** Usually circular, dark red or purple in color 1–2 cm size, resembling the shape of the finger tips. If fingers slide over neck then it can produce elongated bruises.
- **In case of throttling by one hand:** There will be bruise mark by thumb on one side and bruise marks of four fingertips on the other side. These bruise marks which are red or purple in the beginning may turn brown later on This way of using one hand is common when the victim is an infant.
- **When both hands used for throttling:** Corresponding thumb mark of one hand and four fingers of the other hand will be seen on either side of the neck.
- On dissection of neck, evidence of bruising on the underlying subcutaneous soft tissues and neck muscles are seen, which correspond to the pressure abrasions present on the external skin surface (specific finding of death due to throttling).
- Signs of extravasation and bruising will be present over the tracheal rings and also on the posterior pharyngeal wall (as the posterior pharyngeal wall gets compressed over the hard vertebral column).

When some intervening soft material is used between the hands and the neck:
- External signs such as fingernail scratches and pressure abrasion exerted by the bulb of the fingers would be absent. Even then, signs of asphyxia would help to group the death as asphyxial death, followed by dissection of the skin and subcutaneous tissues layer by layer will reveal bruising of underlying layers of skin and bruising of the neck muscles. Also, fracture of hyoid bone and contusion of tracheal rings and posterior pharyngeal wall would be present to confirm death was due to throttling.

Hyoid bone:
- Hyoid bone fracture is relatively more common in throttling. There is inward compression fracture (adduction fracture) and the broken fragment of bone has an inward angulation, with extravasation of blood into the surrounding soft tissues.
- Evidence of struggle in the form of abrasions and bruises may be seen over the mouth, nose, cheeks and forehead, lower jaw, back of shoulders or any other part of the body.
- Sometimes fracture of the ribs and injuries to organs inside the chest and abdomen may be present, when assailant kneels or sits over chest.

Types of hyoid bone fractures:

i. Adduction fracture:
- It occurs in throttling; the broken fragment has an inward angulation due to the force exerted by the fingers of the assailant

ii. Abduction fracture:
- In cases of hanging and ligature strangulation, there is outward angulation fracture (abduction fracture) of the hyoid bone.
- This is due to anteroposterior compression exerted by the ligature material.
- The broken piece of bone has an outward angulation.

Antemortem nature of fracture:
- In any case of hyoid bone fracture, the antemortem nature of the fracture is confirmed by the extravasation of blood at the fractured site and into the surrounding soft tissues.

Smothering:
Smothering is closure of the external orifices of respiration, namely the mouth and the nostrils with the help of hands or other objects like pillows, bed sheets and soft materials, etc. resulting in death due to asphyxia. The victim is usually an infant or intoxicated individual.

Autopsy findings:
- If bare hands are used for smothering, an area of paleness around the mouth and the tip of the nose will be present, with scratch abrasions on the nose and mouth. Evidence of nail markings can also be made out around the site of compression.
- These external signs may be absent if soft intervening materials such as a cloth or pillow are used to cause smothering. However, the internal findings of asphyxia will be evident irrespective of the method of smothering.
- All the classical signs of asphyxia like congestion, cyanosis and petechial hemorrhages will be present.
- In addition to these external signs, examination of the oral cavity will reveal bruising andlacerations on the inner surface of the lips, even if soft intervening materials were used. These injuries are a result of the counter pressure exerted by the teeth. Bleeding gums, bruising of the gingival surface and injury to the tongue are commonly encountered.

BURKING

- Burking is a form of homicidal asphyxial death brought about by combination of smothering and traumatic asphyxia.
- It is named after William Burke and Hare, who used to murder the beggars by this method to supply dead bodies to the department of anatomy in a medical school.
- **Method:** In a grossly intoxicated individual, one will sit on the chest and hold the hands tightly by the side, while the other will firmly press over the mouth and nostrils and the result would be rapid asphyxia. Death is due to combined effects of traumatic asphyxia and smothering.

Autopsy findings:
- Signs of asphyxia namely cyanosis, congestion and petechial hemorrhages are present.
- Evidence of smothering mainly, bruising on inner surface of lips with lacerations due to counter pressure offered by the teeth will be
- evident.
- There may be fracture of ribs caused by the weight of the person sitting on the chest.
- Signs of resistance are minimal and drag marks in the form of abrasions over the back of shoulders and bony prominences may be present.

Mugging:
> Mugging is a homicidal form asphyxia brought about by compression of the neck by the angle of the elbow orthe knee, also by the pressure exerted by the foot of the assailant.

Bansdola:
> It is a method of homicide, using bamboo sticks to bring about asphyxia. Two bamboo sticks are placed, one on the front of neck and the other on the back; one end is fixed by tying the two bamboo sticks together and the other end is slowly tightened with a rope, resulting in effective compression of the neck.

Garroting:
- Garroting is homicidal form of asphyxia by applying a ligature around the neck, from behind the victim, when he is unaware.
- Hence, the victim is stunned followed by imminent loss of consciousness due to twisting the material quickly from behind.
- Since the victim is unaware, there is no evidence of any struggle as all the events unfold so quickly.
- By this way, it is possible to overpower even a healthy strongindividual and kill him.

Accidental forms of death due to asphyxia:

Suffocation:
- It is a form of asphyxia which is produced by inhalation of irrespirable gases. The common gases involved are hydrogen sulfide, methane, carbon monoxide, carbon dioxide, etc.
- Suffocation can also occur in high altitudes and decompression sickness.
- In suffocation the respired air contains very low concentration of oxygen, resulting in breathlessness and asphyxia.

Café coronary:
- It is a misnomer; a grossly intoxicated individual while trying to eat a big bolus of food (meat) tries to speak or laugh and suddenly becomes pale, followed by unconscious and death.
- Due to gross intoxication, there is absence of gag reflux resulting in failure to swallow or cough out the bolus of food and the result is
- It choking. appears as if the person died due to sudden cardiac arrest and hence the name "café coronary".

Autopsy findings:
> The coronaries will be patent; signs of asphyxia will be evident and the bolus of food will be found impacted on the larynx resulting in choking of the respiratory passage.

Traumatic asphyxia:
- Asphyxia produced as a result of restriction of movements of the chest and abdomen, as v b consequence of trauma is called as traumatic asphyxia.
- Examples of such incidence of traumatic asphyxia are:
  - Steering wheel impact in road traffic accidents: The steering wheel may get impacted over the abdomen, resulting in inability of movement of abdomen and chest. There is pronounced congestion above the levelof impact and paleness below the level.
  - Stampede: In this, the individual gets trapped in a crowded place or falls down and the crowd of people stamps him, where it becomes improbable for the individual to breath with the weight of these individuals.
  - Fallen masonry: Falling of heavy objects like bricks, concrete slabs and other construction material on the chest and abdomen.
  - Falling of sand/rice bags on an individual.
  - Individual trapped in between two hard objects like heavy vehicles, heavy weight objects or machineries and in cases of collapsed buildings, where the individual gets trapped in between the two hard objects whichprevent the movement of chest and abdomen.
  - An intoxicated well built adult over lies on an infant during sleep (overlaying)

- In all these circumstances, there is restricted respiratory movement due to external compression on the chest and abdomen.
- Signs of asphyxia will be markedly evident.
- There will be intense congestion mainly above the level of compression, cyanosis and multiple petechial hemorrhages seen both externally and internally.
- Injuries may or may not be noticeable.

Sexual asphyxia: Auto-erotic asphyxia:
- It is presumed that the lowering of consciousness due to any cause such as drugs or partial compression of neck results in increased sexual pleasure by prolonging the time orgasm.
- People with perverted sexual behavior (masochist) partially asphyxiate themselves by compression of the neck, usually by hanging to go in for a transient period of unconsciousness to accomplish their aim of in creased sexual pleasure by prolonging the time period of erection.

Method:
- In this method, a thick soft material is used as a pad to protect the neck. Then a ligature is applied over the pad, around the neck in the form of running noose, with one free end tied to the limb (elbow, wrist or ankle) after passing through some mechanical device like a pulley.
- The noose can be tightened by extending the arms or legs, and when consciousness is lost, the relaxation of the limb releases the pressure on the neck and the individual regains consciousness after a brief period of time.
- Occasionally the constriction may not get relieved; due to faulty function of the mechanical device or the noose getting entangled. In such a situation, death results due to asphyxia as a result of accidental hanging.
- Death is unintentional as indicated by the scene and the devices used.
- The diagnosis of sexual asphyxia can be made by examination of the scene of crime, which will show the presence of pornographic materials or literature near the body. The dead body may be partly or fully naked with female garments and costumes found nearby.
- The person may blindfold himself or stand infront of a mirror to watch the events. There may be evidence of recent seminal ejaculation.
- Old scars around the neck may be present, as evidence of previous episodes.
- These cases may be misdiagnosed as cases of suicidal hanging. Examination of the scene will reveal evidence of abnormal sexual behavior and evidence of such act practiced previously like grooves in rafter or doors.
- Findings consistent with suicidal hanging will be totally absent.

CHAPTER - 15
DROWNING

Definition

Drowning is a form of asphyxial death in which there is replacement of air passages by any fluid usually water, resulting in displacement of air from the lungs.

- For drowning to occur, complete submersion of the body is not necessary. If the mouth and nose are submerged, it can cause drowning and result in death.
- A person who does not know swimming when enters into water, sinks in water as the specific gravity of the body is higherthan that of water.
- He raises up on to the surface of water due to buoyancy of the body, air trapped inside the clothing and by the struggling movements made by him.
- When the mouth and nose come above the water level, he expire the air from the lungs to inhale fresh air, during this process he inhales more of water than air, and also swallows some amount of water. This process may continue two or three times and he finally sinks into water once he has inhaled enough of water.

Types of drowning:

Drowning is classified into

Three types:
i. Wet drowning.
ii. Dry drowning.
iii. Hydrocution (Immersion syndrome):
- With respect to presence or absence of water in the lungs, drowning is divided into **wet drowning** and **dry drowning** respectively.
- **Wet Drowning** is further subdivided into two types, according to the

Type of water:
1. fresh water drowning
2. sea or salt water drowning

According to the period of survival drowning may be labeled as:
- Immediate drowning
- Near drowning: Rescued but died within 24 hours
- Secondary drowning: Death after 24 hours due to complications of drowning like infections, encephalopathy, hypoxia, etc.

Wet drowning:

Water enters into the lungs and the air present in the air passages is displaced. This water mixes with the residual air present in the lungs and forms a fine white froth, which is evident by dissection of the bronchioles during autopsy.

Mechanism of death:

- The mechanism of death in drowning and the patho-physiology involved in the process of drowning depends on whether the medium of drowning is fresh water or salt water.
- Once water enters into the lungs, it gets absorbed into the circulation, resulting in haemodilution. This in turn leads to cardiac overload and acute pulmonary oedema. During this process, there is lysis of the RBCs and release of potassium, leading to ventricular fibrillation. Death may take place in 5 to 8 minutes.
- When water with high salinity (sea water) enters into the lungs, water is imbibed from the circulation into the lungs, resulting in hemoconcentration and death is due to massive pulmonary edema. The individual may survive for 8 to 12 minutes in sea water drowning.

Dry drowning:
>In this type of drowning, water does not enter into the respiratory passages at all.
- When the person drowns, he may try to with hold his breath to prevent water entering into the lungs which result in intense acute laryngeal spasm.
- This intense laryngeal spasm prevents neither water nor airto enterinto the respiratory tract; and the result is death by asphyxia due to drowning.

Hydrocution/Immersion Syndrome:
- In some cases, when the cold water strikes over the epigastrium, it may result in vagalinhibition leading to reflex cardiac arrest.
- Even in people who know swimming, while they dive into the water, hyperstimulation of nerve endings all overthe body by cold water leads to "hydrocution" and ventricular fibrillation.
- This form of drowning is very difficult to diagnose at autopsy, since the victim knows swimming. There is absence of any signs of asphyxia, no pathological evidence of any fatal disease and the chemical analysis report is negative.
- Arriving at the cause of death is by ruling out, since vagal inhibition does not leave any specific autopsy findings. Hydrocution is one of the causes of negative autopsy.
- Opinion is based on the circumstantial evidences.
- Other causes of death in drowning:
- Injuries sustained by the victim, by hitting over some hard protruding objects inside the water medium.
- Shock due to pre-existing heart disease.
- Exhaustion: Due to prolonged swimming.

Postmortem findings:

A. Non-specific signs: External:

The external signs in drowning are:
1. The clothes and the hair will be wet.
2. Sand, mud and weed particles will be found adherent overthe skin surface and on the clothing.
3. **Washer women hand:** The skin surface over the palm and soles become wrinkled, soddened and bleached. This isnot an antemortem sign of drowning. It indicates the period of immersion of the body in water. Prolonged period of exposure with water increases the intensity of "washer women hand"
4. Cutis anserina (**Goose skin**): It is due to contraction of the erector pillori muscle, which leads to puckered appearance of the hair follicle.
5. Cyanosis, external injuries including broken nails and bleeding from ear can be seen. The injuries may be abrasions, lacerations or contusions and it has to be differentiated from the postmortem injuries caused by aquatic animals.
- In drowning, the body floats over the water surface with face down position and hence postmortem hypostasis will be prominent over the face, front of chest and limbs.

B. Specific signs:
- The presence of fine, tenacious, white or blood-tinged froth around the mouth and nostrils are an important finding in drowning. This froth reappears even if it is wiped off and if pressure is applied over the chest. This is an important antemortem sign of drowning and is called "**the sign of drowning**"
- **Mechanism of formation of froth:** Water enters the lungs and damages the bronchial epithelium and the surfactant, there is residual air present in the bronchioles with all these there are violent respiratory movements by the efforts of the victim for survival; all these result in chirring effect and result in the formation of the fine tenacious froth
- **Cadaveric spasm:** While attempting to save oneself, the individual may tightly grasp the weeds and plants present in the drowning medium. During this process, the individual develops sudden spasm due to development of instantaneous rigor. It indicates that the victim was alive when he entered into the water.

Non-specific internal signs:
- All the internal organs will be congested.
- Edema easily appreciable in lungs.
- The chambers of the heart may contain fluid blood
- There will be multiple petechial hemorrhages (Tardieu spots) over pleura and pericardium.
- Sand and mud particles can be seen in the nose, mouth or inoropharynx.
- Large quantity of water may be swallowed during the process of drowning, which will be detected in the stomach.

Specific internal signs:
- Emphysema aquosum: Lungs are heavy and voluminous, water logged with prominent rib indentations on the surface. Multiple petechial hemorrhages on the subpleural surface and the intestinal spaces of the lung and are known as "Paltauf's hemorrhages."
- Cut-section of the lungs will demonstrate frothy exudation. This lung picture of drowning is called emphysema aquosum.
- Dissection of the bronchial tree: It is always preferable to dissect the lung along the bronchial tree, which shows fine, leathery, tenacious white or blood stained froth in trachea and bronchi upto the terminal bronchiole. Sand, mud or sludge particles may be seen in the trachea, bronchi or primary and secondary bronchioles.

Floatation of the body:
- Floatation in water takes its own time and is mainly dependent on the temperature of the environment, as temperature directly influences the rate of decomposition.
- Once the body sinks under the water, it remains on the undersurface till enough gas es accumulate inside the body, then the body comes back tothe surface of water and float.
- Floatation of the body usually takes 18 to 24 hours in summer and 24–48 hours in winter.
- Rarely, drowned bodies may get entangled in the aquatic vegetations and may not come to the surface in a few days and may come out to surface after weeks in a bloated stage.
  Bodies drowned in deep lakes at hill stations may not come up to the surface for a long period of time, as the extreme cold temperature markedly delays putrefaction.

Decomposition: A challenge to the autopsy surgeon:
- When the body is fresh, the lung findings are easily appreciated in most cases and hence there exists no difficulty in finding out the cause of death in cases of drowning.
- But, it is unfortunate that many of the victim persons drown when nobody observes them and noticed only when the body comes to The surface of water after a reasonable period of time in a decomposed state.
- All the lung findings may disappear when the body is moderately decomposed. This is due to passive diffusion of water from the lungs Into the body and decomposition of the lung parenchyma. Such cases are really a challenge to the forensic pathologist. However, a meticulous dissection of the bronchial tree for search of any minute foreign particles like mud, sand or any other materials which are suspended in thedrowning medium, will help to ascertain the cause of death.

Shallow water drowning
- An intoxicated person may fall conscious by the side of a drainage channel and accidentally dip his head into water and death may result due to aspiration . At autopsy, the sewage material may be found in the respiratory tract indicating death due to drowning, this is also called as "shallow water drowning."
- It is always difficult to opine about the manner of death in drowning, as the postmortem findings may be similar in all the cases of accidental, suicidal or homicidal drowning. There may be some signs of resistance in case of homicidal drowning and these signs of struggle will be absent when the victim is unaware. Hence, opining about the manner of death in drowning is much of uncertainty.

Laboratory tests used in cases of drowning:
Laboratory tests:
  i. Diatoms test
  ii. Gettler's test
  iii. Serum magnesium
  iv. Serum strontium

In this, Gettler's test and diatoms tests are important.

Diatoms test :	
	• Diatoms are unicellular algae with their cell wall made of silica. Itresists acid digestion.
	• They are present in all types of water fresh, marine, river and lake water.
	• There are more than 15 thousand species of diatoms; they are of different shapes and sizes.
	• When an individual dies due to drowning; these diatoms enter the lung, carried into circulation to different parts of the body, including the bone marrow.
Gettler's test:	• This test is used to find out the chloride concentration from the right and left ventricular chambers of the heart.
	• Normally concentration of chloride will be equal in both right and left side chambers of the heart.
	• In case of fresh water drowning, the chloride content will be low in the left ventricle due to hemodilution. In sea water drowning, the chloride concentration will increase by 40% due to hemoconcentration.
	• This test is useful to differentiate sea water drowning from fresh water drowning. The significance of this test is highly doubtful and has less practical application.

Isolation of diatoms from bones:

When decomposed bodies recovered from water are brought for autopsy, any of the long bones or sternum is isolated and sent to the *FSL*.

These bones are subjected to acid digestion and then centrifuged. The sediments are then examined under microscope for diatoms. Diatoms resist acid digestion, as they have a protective silica cell wall.

Medicolegal Importance of diatoms:
- Cause of death can be ascertained when decomposed or partially skeletonized bodies are recovered from water.
- Place of drowning: Comparison of diatoms present in the body with that of the diatomspresent in the alleged drowning medium helps in concluding the place of drowning. Especially useful in cases of drowning in fast flowing water and in bodies recovered from ditches (diatoms help to find out antemortem drowning and place of drowning).
- While comparing the diatoms, the number, size, shape and percentage of the diatoms are all taken into consideration.
- Diatoms test has got its own limitations of application and hence cannot be considered as a concrete proof of antemortem drowning.
- However, negative results may sometimes be helpful in ruling out the possibility of drowning.

Medicolegal aspects encountered in cases of drowning:
- Drowning is usually accidental, sometimes suicidal and rarely homicidal.
- But it is not uncommon to kill the person by some other method and submerge the body in water, to simulate death due to suicidal drowning.

CHAPTER - 16
IMPOTENCE AND STERILITY

Some important definitions:
1. **Impotence:**
   Inability of a person to perform sexual intercourse.
2. **Sterility:**
   - Otherwise called as infertility.
   - It can be defined as inability of the male to beget children and in case of female it is the inability to conceive children.
3. **Frigidity:**
   It is the inability of female to initiate or maintain sexual arousal pattern.
4. **Premature ejaculation:**
   Ejaculation occurs immediately before or immediately after penetration into vagina.
5. **Sexual dysfunction:**
   Impairment either in desire or in the ability to achieve sexual gratification.

Legal issues related to impotence and sterility:

Civil issues:	Criminal issues:
1. Voidable marriage	1. Rape
2. Adultery	2. Unnatural offenses
3. Disputed paternity	
4. Legitimacy	
5. Claim for damages When sexual function is lost as a result of an assault or accident.	

Examination of a person for impotence & sterility
It includes:
1. Examination of central nervous system.
2. Look for pulsation of peripheral arteries.
3. Examination of condition of testes, epididymis, spermatic cord and penis.
4. Test for sensation of private parts.

Note: Blood pressure and pulse rate should be measured.

Nerve supply and blood supply:

Penis	nerves from 2nd, 3rd and 4th sacral segments via pudental nerve and Pelvic plexus
Glans penis (sensory supply)	dorsal nerve branch of pudental nerve
Corpora cavernosa	excitatory (parasympathetic supply) by erigentes nerve Inhibitory (sympathetic supply) by thoracolumbar plexus
Arterial supply	glans penis and shaft supplied by deep pudental artery
Venous supply	penile veins

Size of penis:
    Flaccid- 2.5 to 4 cm during infancy
            5cm in children till puberty
            6 to 7 cm at puberty
    Erect- 13 to 15cm in adults

Palpation of seminal vesicles and prostate done through per rectum
    To rule out sterility, examination of seminal fluid must be done

> **Bulbocavernous reflex test:**
> On adequate nerve sensation in penis squeezing of glans immediately causes contraction of anus.

Causes of impotence in males:

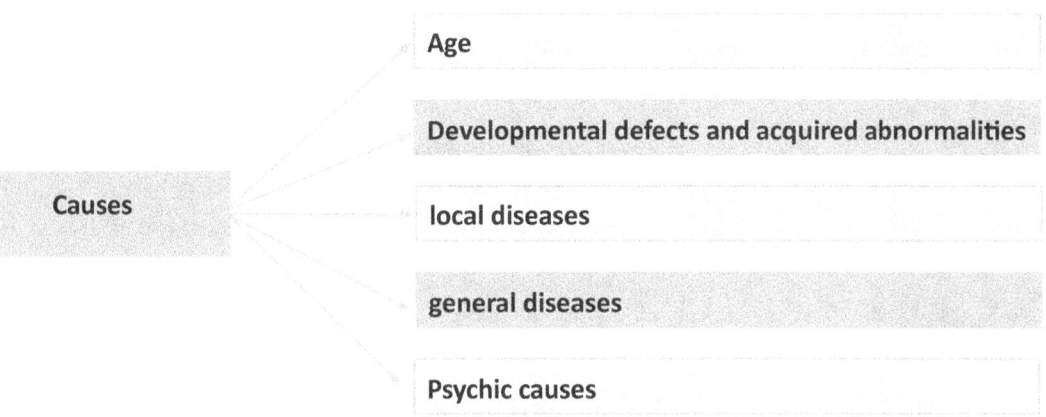

1. **Age:**
   - Irrespective of age poor physical development of penis is the common cause of impotence.
   - Precocious development seen in cases such as
   » gonadal or adrenal tumors
   » MCcune Albright syndrome

   On aging the power of erection diminish but cases were recorded that even 94 years old men having children indicates that fertility can lasts till end of life.

2. **Developmental defects and acquired abnormalities**
   In cases such as
   - Non development of penis
   - Intersexuality
   - Hypospadiasis
   - Epispadiasis
   - Double penis

Note:
- *If the testes are removed before puberty then both impotence and sterility results, but if it is removed after puberty then potency retained.*
- *X rays causes temporary azoospermia.*
- *disease related with endocrine system may produce impotence but occasionally the reverse effects of excessive sexual desire may be seen(satyriasis)*
- *Alcoholism, anabolic steroids, heroin and cannabis causes erectile dysfunction*
- *Heavy smoking causes thrombosis of penile arteries which leads to impotency*

---

3. **Local diseases:**
    In cases such as large hernias elephantiasis ,phimosis ,hydroceles,paraphimosis and adherent prepuce temporary impotency occurs due to mechanical obstruction
    Diseases such as gonorrhoea,sores on the glans sarcoma,tuberculosis ,syphilis may cause impotence or sterility or both
    - Pubic bone fracture may causes injury to parasympathetics and fracture of spine at L4 - L5 level injuries local segments and may leads to impotency.
4. **General diseases:**
    - Mostly general diseases causes temporary impotence and normal function will be rapidly regained
    Ex: diabetes , pulmonary tuberculosis ,chronic nephritis.
5. **Psychic causes:**
    - Temporary impotence may be due to emotional disturbance.
    - First night impotence or honeymoon impotence are common causes of temporary impotence which is due to fear and it can be overcome soon.
    - Disgust of sexual act and dislike of partner may causes temporary or permanent impotence.

Causes of erectile dysfunction

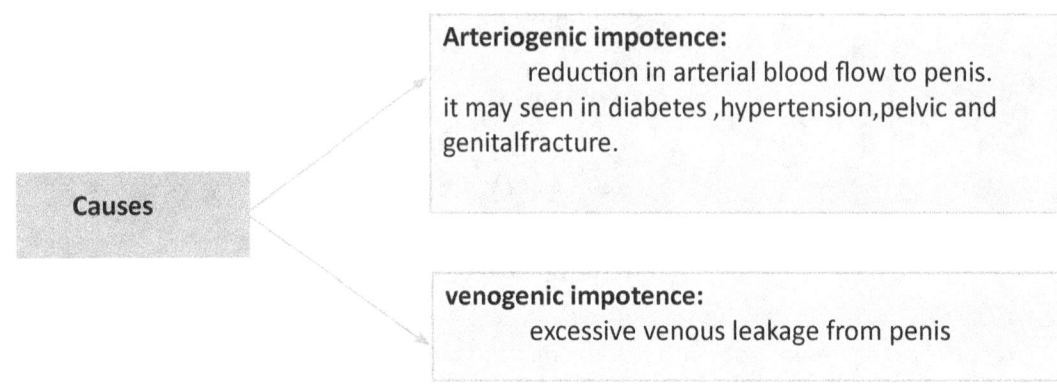

Note:

Erectile dysfunction may also seen in endocrine defects such as testosterone deficiency ,LH and prolactin ,hypothyroidism,Cushings syndrome etc..

Diagnosis of erectile dysfunction:
1. Papaverine 15mg and phentolamine 0.5 mg i.v is given at lateral sides of penis
2. Ask the person to stand for 2mins after injection
3. Observe for 30mins for degree of erection

Observation:
- Early response seen in psychogenic case
- Arteriogenic or cavernogenic case requires 0.5 mg papaverine and 3ml phentolamine

---

Note:

Sildenafil 50mgis commonly used now a days to test potency.

Treatment:
    Ultrasonogram followed by penile angiogram used to study penile blood supply.
- Microvascular surgery and epigastric dorsal artery bypass grafting cure vascular problems.
- Venous leakage can be corrected by tying and removing deep dorsal vein of penis.

Causes of impotence and sterility in female:
1. **Age:**
    - Age has no effect on potency in female.
    - Sexual desire is not completely lost in old age.
    - Fertility lasts till menopause from puberty.
2. **Developmental defects and acquired abnormalities:**
    In malformed females, turners and intersexuals vagina is sometimes absent which causes permanent impotence and sterility.
    Defects such as a total occlusion of vagina adhesion of labia & tough imperforate hymen can be cured by surgery.
    Conical cervix and absence of uterus, ovary or fallopian tubes produce sterility but not impotence.
3. **Local diseases:**
    If doesnot cause impotence but may cause sterility
    Temporary impotence may be due to hyperaesthesia of vagina, prolapse of uterus, elephantiasis etc...
4. **General diseases:**
    - Usually it doesn't cause impotence in female
    - Exposure to lead or X ray may causes sterility.
5. **Psychic causes:**
    In males- non erection
    In females- vaginismus

Vaginismus:
- Spasmodic contraction of vagina due to hyperaesthesia.
- It is a classical example of psychosomatic illness.
- It involves muscles such as levatorani and adductor muscles.
- In fully developed state of vaginismus constriction of vaginal outlet is so severe and penetration by penis is impossible

Aetiology:
1. Male sexual dysfunction (wife's high levels of sexual frustration developing secondary to husband's impotence).
2. Psychosexually inhibiting influence of excessively severe control of social conduct due to religious orthodoxy.
3. Specific incidents of prior sexual trauma.
4. Stimulus derived from attempted heterosexual function by a woman with prior homosexual practice.
5. Secondary to dyspareunia. Severe laceration of the broad ligament, pelvic endometriosis, ulceration or fissures in the vagina, if untreated may lead to increasingly painful coitus and vaginismus.
6. Rarely, personal dislike or a general feeling of disgust at the idea of coitus. Anxiety, stress, fear of pain, guilt complex, etc. can cause strong contractions of paravaginal muscles at the time of intercourse.

Note:
- *Psychotherapy is beneficial.*
- *Psychological causes affect fertility adversely.*
- *A woman may be sterile or impotent with a particular man but not with another.*
- *Both environment and nutrition have some influence upon conception.*
    " fecundation ab extra":
    Insemination occurring due to passage of spermatozoa from external genitalia to uterus.

STERILISATION
- It is a procedure of making male or female person sterile without interface with potency.
- It may be direct or indirect.

Direct:
- Intentional sterilisation by surgery.

Indirect:
- It is unintentional.
- Sterilisation occurs as an accidental act while performing surgery for some other purpose.

Types

Compulsory
Carried out on mental defectives or as a punishment Sexual criminals.

Voluntary

Therapeutic
performed to prevent life of women from danger on further pregnancy.

Contraceptive
- Surgical
- Radiological
- Chemical
- Mechanical

Eugenic
In order to prevent conception Of physically & mentally defective children.

Principles to guide person about sterilization:

To avoid legal complications, the following precautions should be taken.
1. The written consent of both wife and husband should be obtained for contraceptive sterilisation.
2. It is not unlawful if performed on therapeutic or eugenic grounds after obtaining true and valid consent.
3. It is preferable to have a check up after vasectomy. The person should be advised to abstain from sexual intercourse for about three months or until the seminal examination shows absence of spermatozoa on two successive occasions.
4. The pills containing hormonal substances may be harmful rarely, and so necessary precautions have to be taken to avoid any complications.

ARTIFICIAL INSEMINATION

In order to produce pregnancy, semen is introduced artificially into vagina, cervix or uterus. It is called as Artificial insemaination.

Types

A.I.H
Semen of women's husband is used
Also called artificial insemination homologous or artificial insemination husband

A.I.D
- semen of some person other than husband is used
- artificial insemination donor

A.I.H.D
Pooled semen of donor and husband together is used

311

Semen is obtained by masturbation and one ml is deposited by means of a syringe in or near the cervix The timing of insemination is important as the life span of the spermatozoa in the female reproductive tract is short. The time of maximum fertility coincides with ovulation. The ovum can survive in a fertile state for 12 to 24 hours after it leaves ovary. The usual time taken by sperms to travel from vagina to tubes is 6 to 24 hours. The power of sperms to fertilize is usually retained for about 48 hours. Because of the problem of timing, insemination on several successive days in the month increases the chances of pregnancy. The success rate is 30 to 40% pregnancies within three to four months of the start of treatment. The use of frozen semen for AI.D. is becoming increasingly common. This is done by addition of glycerol, slow cooling, rapid freezing and storage at minus 196°C.

Indications:
(1) When the husband is impotent.
(2) When the husband is unable to deposit the semen in vagina due to hypospadiasis, epispadiasis, etc.
(3) When the husband is sterile.
(4) When there is Rh incompatibility between the husband and wife.
(5) When the husband is suffering from hereditary disease.

Precautions: Certain recommendations have been made when a donor is used. They are:
1. Consent of the donor and is wife is essential.
2. The identity of the donor must remain secret.
3. The donor should not know to whom the semen is donated and the result of insemination.
4. The donor must be mentally and physically healthy and should not be suffering from any hereditary or familial disease. He should be screened with all available tests including chromosomal studies for possible genetic defects.
5. The donor must not be a relative of either spouse; he should have had children of his own.
6. The race and characteristics of the donor should resemble those of the husband of the woman as closely as possible.
7. The donor should be of the same blood group as, that of the husband.
8. There should not be any Rh incompatibility between the donor and recipient.
9. The physician should have permission to use his own best judgement in selecting the donor.
10. The couple should be psychologically fit and emotionally stable.
11. The woman to be inseminated and her husband must give consent in writing that an unknown donor should be used.
12. A witness must be present, when insemination is done.
13. It is usually wise to use"pooled" semen. When husband's semen is mixed with that of a donor, there is the technical possibility that the husband may, in fact be the father of the child.
14. The physician who administers the artificial insemination should avoid delivering the child. This will avoid the necessity of either falsifying the birth records or disclosing the true paternity in those records.
15. Usually, a single donor's semen is not used to produce more than ten children.

Legal problems:
1. **Adultery:**
    S.497.I.P.C explains sexual intercourse as necessary part of adultery
    So person undergone artificial insemination need not be feel guilty
2. **Legitimacy:**
    The child born as a result of artificial insemination is illegitimate and cannot inherit property
3. **Nullity of marriage and divorce:**
    If A.I is adopted due to sterility ,then it cant laid a ground for divorce
    But if A.I adopted is due to impotence ,then it is a ground
    A child born naturally after the birth of child by A.I
    The status of child born by A.I remains illegitimate untill it is adopted.
    The status of naturally born child is legitimate.
    An unmarried woman of widow may have a child from A.I but it remains illegitimate.

CHAPTER- 17
VIRGINITY, PREGNANCY AND DELIVERY

Virginity:
- A female who has not experienced sexual intercourse is said to be virgin
- The term 'Defloration' indicates loss of virginity

Note:

Defamation and rape are the legal issues regarding virginity.

Anatomy of female genitals:
- Two lips of labiamajora meet in front as the anterior commissure and in back as the posterior commissure in front of the anus.
- Virgin have thick, firm, elastic and rounded labiamajora
- Just within labia majora two thin folds of soft, small, pink and sensitive structure seen called labia minora
- Fusion of lower portions of labia minora forms a fold called fourchette.
- This fourchette divides anteriorly to enclose clitoris
- Anterior to clitoris, fourchette fuses to form prepuce and posterior fusion forms frenulum.
- Fossa navicularis:
- It is the depression between fourchette and the vaginal orifice
- Mons veneris, clitoris, libiamajora, labia minora, vestibule, hymen and urethral opening constitutes vulva.

Vaginal passage:
- 7.5 cm long
- Anterior wall is shorter(6cm)
- Posterior wall is longer(9cm)
    » In nulliparous women width of upper end is 3 to 4 cm
    » In parous women it is 6 to 7 cm
- Vagina is narrow and tight structure with rugae in the mucosa
- After frequent sexual intercource of about 15 to 20 sexual acts, rugae becomes less prominent and vagina lengthens into posterior fornix and full length of examining finger can be inserted
- Rugosity disappears after first birth but rarely may also be absent in a virgin.
- In virgin both fourchette and posterior commissure are intact.
- Repeated intercource made fourchette as a irregular thickened scar
- During child birth fourchette gets lacerated.

Hymen:
- It is a thick fold of mucous membrane and is about 1mm
- In children it grows 1mm diametrically per year and reaches about 10mm in pubertal girl
- At the time of puberty its diameter is nearly 1.2 cm and appears as series of folds
- More than 1cm diameter in pubertal girls indicates sexual abuse

Types of hymen:
1. **Semilunar or crescentic:** (commonest type) at 10 and 11 clock position, which may be equal in size or more prominent on one side
2. **Annular:** opening is oval and situated near the centre of the membrane
3. **Infantile:** a small linear opening in the middle
4. **Cribriform:** several opening

5. **Vertical:** the opening is vertical
6. **Septate:** two lateral openings occurs side by side, separated partially or completely by thin strip of tissue
7. **Microperforate:** Tiny opening with large posterior component
8. **Fimbriated**
9. **Imperforate:** no opening
10. **Denticular:** look like a set of teeth surrounding vaginal opening.

Note:
- *Sometimes the margin of hymen is fimbriated with multinodular appearances and may be mistaken as artificial tears*
- *Natural notches are symmetrical, occur anteriorly and do not extend to vaginal wall*
- *Artificial tears usually occurs posteriorly on one or both sides*

Principal signs of virginity:

Triad →
- Intact hymen
- Normal fourchette and posterior commissure
- Narrow vagina with rugose walls

Difference between virginity and defloration.

Trait	Virginity	Defloration
hymen	It is intact, rigid and inelastic: the edges are distinct, smooth and regular with a narrow opening hardly allowing a small finger to pass	It may be torn or intact: in the latter case it is loose, elastic, with a wide opening allowing passage of two or more fingers
Labia majora	They are apposed to each other, fully developed and completely close the vaginal orifice	They are not apposed to each other, not prominent and at the lower end vaginal orifice may be seen
Labia minora	They are in contact and are covered by labia majora	They are not in contact and are exposed and separated from labia majora
Fourchette	Intact	Torn or intact
Fossa navicularis	Intact	Disappears
Vestibule	narrow	wide
vagina	It is narrow, the rugae more folded, and the vault more concial	After repeated intercourse is usually grows in length, and the rugae are less obvious

Medicolegal aspects:
    Unruptured hymen is not an absolute proof of virginity
    With intact hymen there are true virgin and false virgins

Causes of rupture of hymen:
1. An accident , a fall on a projecting substance or by slipping on the furniture or fence or while playing at seesaw . in these cases tearing takes place through the lateral margins of the labia into the vaginal wall, perineum ,perineal body and hymen ,and usually injuries on other parts of the body will be seen. Such hymen tears are never associated with abrasion and bruising of the margins .hymen does not rupture by riding ,jumping ,dancing ,etc
2. Masturbation,hymen is not injured in mist cases because manipulation is usually limited to the parts anterior to the hymen .Labia minora and clitoris are enlarged in such cases .the vaginal orifice may be dilated and edges of the hymen may show scratches
3. Surgical operation
4. Foreign body e.g,, sola pith introduced into vagina for rending very young girls fit for sexual intercource (aptae viris)
5. Ulceration from diphtheria fungus or other diseases
6. Scratching
7. Sanitary tampon sometimes rupture the hymen

Breasts:
- In a virgin the breasts are firm ,elastic and hemispherical with areola which is pink in fair complexioned women and dark brown in dark women.
- Breasts become large and flabby by frequent handling, ,milk may be found in the breasts of virgins
- If hymen is loose or lax then it may not be rupture even after repeated act of coitus
- But hymen is always present in a virgin in some or other form

Caruncule hymenales:
    If women who have experienced sexual intercource and in those who delivered a child hymen gets destroyed and shows fleshy ,round projections know as carunculaehymenales
    Also called as myrtiforms

PREGNANCY:

Diagnosis of Pregnancy

Positive signs:	Probable signs	Presumptive signs
1.Foetal parts & movement	1.enlargement of abdomen	1. Amenorrhoea
2.Foetal heart sounds	2.changes in uterus & cervix	2.changes in breasts
3.Placental and umbilical soufflé	3.intermittent uterine contraction	3.morning sickness
4.USG & radiological examination		4.quickening
5.ballotment		5.changes in vagina & skin
6.uterinesoufle		6.urinary& sympathetic disturbances
		7.fatigueability

Presumptive signs of pregnancy:

1.Amenorrhoea:
- Menstruation may occur for first 2 to 3 months after conception until decidua vera and decidua reflexa fused
- After 2 to 3 months there is lag of menstruation in case of pregnancy
- It may also occurs in women with intense desire for pregnancy

2. Changes in breast and skin
- significant in primigravidas and less marked in multiparas

Usual signs:
- After 2nd month- increase in size ,becomes nodular
- Further enlargement exposes enlarged superficial veins
- Nipples deeply pigmented and more erectile
- Areola becomes dark brown
- 3rd month- colostrum secreted
- After 6 months striae are seen in primigravida
- Skin becomes pigmented and linea nigra appears

3.Montgomery's tubercles:
Sebaceous glands around nipples gets enlarged and form small rounded dark coloured tubercles at the end of 2nd month

4. Morning sickness:
Appears at the end of first month and disappears 6 to 8 weeks later

5.Quickening:
The first eppearence of movement of foetus felt by pregnant women is called quickening.
Usually occurs about 16 to 20th week

6.Changes in the vagina:
The mucous membrane of the vagina changes from pink to violet ,deepening to blue as a result of venous obstruction ,after the fourth week . This is known as **Jackquemier's sign** or **Chadwick's sign**.

7.Fatigue:
Easy fatigue is very frequent

9.Sympathetic disturbances:
Salivation ,perverted appetite and irritable temper are common

II .PROBABLE SIGNS OF PREGNANCY:

1.Enlargement of the abdomen:
During pregnancy ,abdomen gradually enlarges in size after the twelfth week. End of third month ,the uterus fills the pelvis ,and between third and fourth months appears over the brim. At fifth month,it is midway between the symphysis and umbilicus .End of sixth month,it is at the level of the umbilicus. At the seventh month it is midway between the umbilicus and the xiphisternum and the end of the eight month and early ninth month it reaches the xiphoid cartilage.

The umbilicus becomes level with the skin by about the seventh month.

Striae gravidarum seen in late pregnancy 96th to 7th month) and around the time of delivery ,become paler with time ,and after a year or so appear as white scars (lineaalbicantes).

2.Uterus:
Hegar's sign: If one hand is placed on the abdomen and two fingers of other hand in the vagina ,the firm hard cervix is felt and above it the elastic body of the uterus ,while between the two the isthmus is felt as a soft compressible area. This is the most valuable physical sign of early pregnancy.

3.Cervix:
Goodell's sign:
From the second month,the cervix progressively softens from below upward, which is well marked by fourth month.

4. Intermittent uterine contractions:
   Braxton Hick's sign : Each contraction lasts about a minute and relaxation for about two to three minutes .they are present even when the foetus is dead

5. Ballottement:
   It means to toss up like a ball. This is positive during the fourth and fifth months of pregnancy as the foetus is small in relation to the amount of amniotic fluid present. to obtain vaginal ballottement, two fingers are inserted into the anterior fornix and a sudden upward motion given. This causes the foetus to move up in the liquor amnii and after a moment ,the foetus drops down on the fingers like a ball bouncing back. External ballottement can be obtained by imparting a sudden motion to the abdominal wall covering the uterus; in a few seconds the rebound of the foetus can be felt .this can be negative if the amniotic fluid is scanty

6. Uterine souffle:
   This is a soft blowing murmur.
   Synchronous with the mother's pulse
   It is heard by auscultation on either; side of the uterus just above inguinal ligament towards the end of fourth month due to increase of blood flow through the uterine vessels.

7. Biological tests:
   They are based on the reaction of test animals to chorionic gonadotropins contained in the pregnant woman's blood or urine .

POSITIVE SIGNS OF PREGNANCY:

1. Foetal parts and movements:
   Active foetal movements are felt by placing the hands on the uterus from 16 to 18 weeks foetal parts such as head and limbs can be distinctly felt after 24 weeks of gestation.

2. Foetal heart sounds:
   Important and definite sign of pregnancy .
   They are heard between 18 to 20 weeks for the first time .
   The sounds are like the ticking of a watch placed under a pillow .
   They can be monitored and recorded accurately by an electronic foetal monitor.
   Their rate is usually about 160 at fifth and 120 at the ninth month.
   They are not synchronous with the mother's pulse
   Foetal heart sounds are not heard:
   1. When the foetus is dead
   2. When there is excessive quantity of liquor amnii
   3. When abdominal wall is very fat
   4. When examination is made before 18 weeks of pregnancy

3. Placental souffle:
   This is a soft murmur heard over the placental site, the rate of which corresponds to that of foetal heart sounds

4. Funic or umbilical souffle:
   This is a blowing murmur synchronous with foetal heart sounds and supposed to be produced in the umbilical cord

5. Radiological examination:
   At about fifteen to sixteen weeks, foetal parts can be detected
   shadows to be searched in the pelvis of the mother are
   - Crescentic or annular shadows of the skull
   - A series of small dots in a linear arrangement of the vertebra column
   - A series of fine curved parallel lines of the ribs ,and
   - Linear shadows of the limbs .usually the skull and spine are seen at fifteenth to sixteen weeks
     Later stage x ray examination may be of value in the diagnosis of a twin pregnancy ,fortal death or abnormality ,hydatidiform mole etc..

6. **Ultrasonography;**

Scanning of abdomen and infant brain will reveal 1. Intracranial haemorrhage and damage to brain ,2. Bony injuries ,periostitis and osteomyelitis ,3. Cerebral oedema .the sex of the unborn should not be disclosed.

SIGNS OF PREGNANCY IN DEAD:

- Presence of embryo, foetus, placental tissue, products of conception indicates pregnancy.
  Uterus:
- Appears thickened and larger
  Ovaries:
- Corpus luteum found in one or both ovaries.
  Even in exhumated bodies foetal bones will be found as remnants.
- All external signs and local signs seen in living persons can be made out. In addition to that, on internal examination, the uterine wall appears 4 to 5 cm thickness.
- Uterine cavity is obliterated by apposition of anterior and posterior walls.
- After 6 weeks, thickness of the uterus is about 1 to 2 cm.
  1) Perineum tear — sign of recent delivery
  2) Extensive caput — a sign of prolonged/ obstructed labor
  3) Inner surface of uterus with blood clots and bits of placenta
- Bladder is hyperemic and sub-mucosal hemorrhages may be present.

- Perineum shows old tears and healed scars.

Posthumous child:

- If the women being conceived and then the husband died, the child born to this women is said to be posthumous.
- It is the child born after death of father.

SUPERFECUNDATION:

It refers to fertilization of two ova at the same period of menstruation by two separate actions of coitus.

This leads to twin pregnancy.

In the case of twin pregnancy development of foetus is parallel but not equal.

The development of foetus in case of twin pregnancy depends on relative supply of nutrients.

In most of the cases one of the fertilized ovum gets restricted from development and expelled out during labor as a unrecognizable flattened structure called foetus compressus or foetus papyraceous.

SUPERFOETATION:

It refers to fertilization of second ovum in a women who is already pregnant.

Sometime fertilization may occurs during first trimester as decidual cavity gets obliterated only at the end of first trimester.

Two foetus may born together or else the second foetus may born after its full development.

Superfoetation commonly occurs in biparous women and women with double uterus.

PSEUDOCYESIS:

It is otherwise called as phantom or spurious pregnancy.

Commonly occurs in person nearer menopause or in women who have intense desire of being pregnant.

All symptoms of pregnancy is experienced by the women in this case. Considerable increase in size of abdomen is seen as deposition of fat, tympanites or contraction of diaphragm pushing forward the entire abdominal wall.

Radiologic examination will be helpful in earlier detection as many cases remains unknown till full term.

Ectopic pregnancy:

Complications of ectopic pregnancies include:

1) Hemorrhagic shock
2) Hemorrhage into broad ligament causes sepsis.
3) Air embolism

MATERNAL DEATHS:

A WOMEN MAY DIE DURING PREGNANCY OR DURING DELIVERY BECAUSE OF THE FOLLOWING CAUSES.

Air embolism within large veins and heart

Lethal amniotic fluid embolism is most commonly associated with relatively small tears in the uterus, cervix er vagina.

Abnormal placentation is important factor which causes hemorrhage. Placenta weighs less than 350g has adverse effects on pregnancy.

Pre-eclampsia related with toxemia

DELIVERY:

Delivery is defined as a process by which there is expulsion or extraction of the child from theuterus, with or without external help. It may be spontaneous or induced.

Medicolegal aspects of delivery:

The question of delivery arises in situations like:

– Abortion

– Infanticide

– Concealment of birth (Infanticide section 94 BNS)

– Divorce and nullity of marriage.

– Delivery is considered as a valid ground for delayed execution of judicial death sentence upto 6 months.

Signs of recent delivery in living:
General appearance of indisposition:

- The woman looks pale and sick, with shrunken eyes for the first 2 to 3 days.
- Presence of dark colored pigmentation over the lower eyelids.
- Pulse andbody temperature are slightly raised.

Changes in the breast:

- Breasts are full and prominent, having a knotty or nodular feeling and tender.
- Nipples: Enlarged, surrounded by darkened areola and Montgomery's tubercles.
- Nipples on squeezing yield milk.

Abdominal changes:
- Abdomen is lax, flabby and the skin over the abdomen appears wrinkled.
- Striae gravidarum, linea albicantes and linea nigra are seen due to over stretching of the skin over the abdomen during pregnancy.
- Intermittent painful uterine contractions are felt by the patient for 4 to 5 days
- The uterus gradually diminishes in size at the rate of 1.5 cm/day.
- On 6th day, the height of the uterus is midway between umbilicus and the pubis; on 14th day, fundus is at the level of pubic symphysis. The uterus comes back to normal position by 9 weeks.

Labia majora and labia minora:
- Swollen, tender, bruising and laceration of the labia may be present.

Fossa navicularis and posterior commisure:
- Shows tears which may extend upto perineum in Primigravida

Changes in the vagina:
- Vagina is spacious with loss of rugosity and the walls are relaxed.
- May show recent tears which heal by 7th day and the rugae reappear in about 3 weeks.

Changes in the cervix:
- Cervix is soft and patulous.
- Internal Os closes by 24 hrs and the external Os appears soft and admits two fingers.
- After 1 week, the external Os admits one fingerwithdifficulty andit closesby 2ndweek.

Lochia:
- It is a discharge from the vagina, which is present for a period of 2 to 3 weeks after delivery. It has peculiar disagreeable odor; it gradually changes in color and consistency. Lochia is of three types depending on its color.
- Lochia rubra: It is bright red containing blood clots; it is thick in consistency and is present for the first 4 to 5 days after delivery.
- Lochia serosa: During the next 4 to 5 days, the lochia changes in color and appears serous. The consistency becomes gradually thin and pale.
- Lochia alba: From the 9th day onwards, the color is yellowish gray which becomes white and turbid and finally disappears in two weeks.
- Laboratory findings: Urine shows presence of hCG even after delivery. It can be detected in traces upto two weeks after delivery

SIGNS OF PREGNANCY IN DEAD:
All external signs and local signs seen in living persons can be made out. In addition to that, on internal examination, the uterine wall appears 4 to 5 cm thickness.
- Uterine cavity is obliterated by apposition of anterior and posterior walls.
- After 6 weeks, thickness of the uterus is about 1 to 2 cm.

On dissection of the uterine cavity:
- The area of the placental attachment shows irregular, nodular, and elevated raw surface ofabout 15 cm in diameter. It gradually diminishes in size when the uterus contracts. By end of 2nd week, its 3 to 4 cm in diameter and by 6th week,

it is 1 to 2 cm in diameter.
- Peritoneum covering the lower part of uterus is arranged in folds
- Bladder is hyperemic and sub-mucosal hemorrhages may be present.
- The changes in the labia and vagina are similar to that of in the living.
- Perineum shows old tears and healed scars.

SIGNS OF REMOTE DELIVERY IN LIVING:
Externally abdomen lax and flabby.
- Lineae albicantes present in all the cases and striae gravidarum may be seen in some cases.

Breast:
- Breast will be soft and pendulous. Nipples are larger, darker and appear raised.
- Areola is dark with Montgomery's tubercles.
- On palpation, the breasts are nodular in consistency and in some multipara, striae may be present on the surface of the breasts.

External genitalia:
- Labia majora is dark and are not in close apposition with each other.
- Labia minora is pigmented, dark and protrude out through the gap in between the two sides of labia majora.
- Fourchette and posterior commissure may show lacerations.
- Vagina: Looks capacious, dilated and the walls appear relaxed.
- Hymen: Absent and represented by carunculae myritiformis.

IMPORTANT POINTS:
SUPPOSITIOUS CHILD:
- A woman presents a child, as she is said to have delivered the child; but the fact is that she has not delivered any such child.
- Examination of the female for signs of recent delivery and DNA analysis will be helpful to sort out the issue.

- **LEGAL ISSUES RELATED TO SUPPOSITIOUS CHILD:**
» Inheritance of property.
» Blackmailing a male.
» When a widow claims higher compensation from her husband's employer.
» Bringing a charge of breach of promise of marriage against a man, who is alleged to be the father of that child.

Note:
Section 93 BNS: Abandoning a child of less than twelve years by the father, mother or caretaker, shall be punished with imprisonment upto 7 years.
Section 94 BNS: Whoever intentionally conceals the birth of a child; either dead born or still born and buries or disposes by other means, shall be punished with imprisonment upto two years.

CHAPTER - 18
ABORTION

- Abortion is a process by which the products of conception are expelled either spontaneously or by induction, before the foetus reaches the viability (28 weeks of gestation).
- It legally defined as the expulsion of products of conception at any time priorto full-term normal delivery.

Premature labor:
Delivery of fetus after reaching viabilitybut before full term.
- 1st trimester termination of pregnancy is called abortion.
- 2nd trimester termination of pregnancy is called miscarriage.
- 3rd trimester termination of pregnancy is called premature labor.

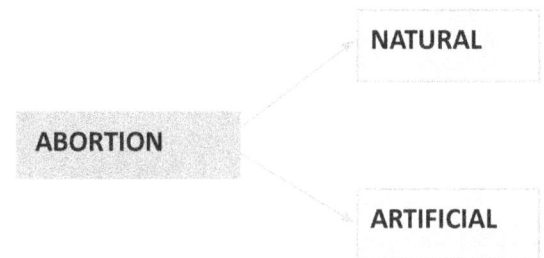

- Natural Abortion may be spontaneous or accidental.
- Artificial abortion may either be:
  1. Legal, justifiable or therapeutic abortion
  2. Criminal abortion.
- Natural abortions usually occur by 2nd or 3rd months of pregnancy and the incidence is about 10%.

Causes of natural abortion:
- **Maternal causes:**
- Acute and chronic infections of genital tract; Rh incompatibility, congenital defects of the uterus; poisons like phosphorus, lead, quinine and mercury; accidental injuries and metabolic disorders like diabetes and thyrotoxicosis.
- **Placental causes:**
- Acute hydramnios, hydatidiform degeneration of the placenta and other diseases related to decidua or placenta.
- **Foetal causes:**
- Developmental defects of the foetus, and intra uterine death of the fetus due to various reasons.
- Exposure to radiation may leads to abortion.

Criminal abortion:
- It is unlawful destruction or expulsion of the fetus or products of conception from the mother's womb, without any considerable therapeutic indication.
- It is usually adopted by
  Unmarried girls.
  Widows planning for remarriage.
  Female infanticide.

Causes of death in criminal abortions:
  i. **Immediate/Rapid death:** Hemorrhage, perforation, vasovagal shock and fat/air embolism.
  ii. **Delayed death:** Generalized peritonitis, complication of local infection, tetanus, septicemia and toxemia.
  iii. **Remote causes of death:** Jaundice and renal suppression, bacterial endocarditis, pneumonia, pulmonary embolism, emphysema and meningitis; sometimes, death is also due to the poisonous effect of the drugs used to procure abortion.

Complications of criminal abortions:
- Endotoxemia, septic shock and death.
- Fatal hemorrhages.
- Necrosis of cervical canal.
- Delayed air embolism.

Amniotic fluid embolism:
  It mostly occurs during the phase of active labor and rarely in 1st or 2nd trimester abortions following trauma and amniocentesis.
- The amniotic fluid enters the maternal venous circulation and results in pulmonary microvascular obstruction and results in severe vasospasm of pulmonary vasculature and hypoxia; usually death occurs in the 1st hour.
- If death is not immediate, then disseminated intravascular coagulation and fibrin deposition occurs in most internal organs.
- Diagnosis is by demonstration of fetal squamous cells, meconium, lanugo hair, fat globules, chorionic and amniotic cells in the lung by HPE.

Difference between natural and criminal abortion

Trait	Natural abortion	criminal abortion
Cause	Predisposing diseases	Pregnancy in unmarried women or widow.
Infection	Rare.	Frequent
Marks of violence	Not present on the abdomen	May be present on abdomen.
Genital organs	Injuries are not present	Injuries such as contusions, lacerations, perforations, etc., may be seen in uterus or its contents and vagina.
Toxic effect of drugs	Absent	Erosions and inflammation of vagina and cervix due to local application of irritant and caustic substances may be present. GI (or) urinary tract may show signs of irritation
Foreign bodies	Not present in genital tract	May be present in genital tract
foetus	Wounds absent	Rarely wounds may be present

TYPES OF ABORTIONISTS

- **Medical expert (or)** qualified professionals
- **semiskilled abortio** (Midwives, nurses, chemists)
- **Unskilled abortionists** (Quacks, untrained persons)

Methods adopted:
    Mechanical violence: General or local
    Abortificient drugs
    Instrumentation Mechanical violence:

General violence:
- Acts indirectly on the uterus by promoting contraction of pelvic organs and thus causing hemorrhage between the uterus and placental membrane.
- Application of severe pressure over the abdomen, violent exercise, cupping and application of very hot and cold water baths.

Local violence:
    Manual correction of uterus may leads to abortion.

Abortificient drugs:
i. **Ecbolics:** Act directly on the uterus and increase the uterine contractions.
ii. Example: Ergot, quinine, KMnO4 tablets, lead pills and strychnine.
iii. **Emmenagogues:** Increases the menstrual bloodflow. Act as abortificient in large doses. Example: Savin, borax, prostaglandins and estrogens.
iv. **Drugs which irritate the genitourinary tract** provide reflex uterine contraction.
v. Example, oil of turpentine, cantharides, KMnO4 application (through vaginal route).
vi. **Drugs which primarily irritate the gastrointestinal tract** reflexly stimulate the uterine contractions.
vii. Example, emetics (tartaric acid), purgatives (castor oil), croton oil, phenolphthalein and magnesium sulfate (MgSO4).
viii. **Drugs which are primarily toxic to other systems:** Inorganic metallic irritants (lead, copper, antimony, mercury and arsenic) and organic irritants (bark of plumbago rosea, juice of calotropis, unripe fruit of papaya and pineapple).

Instruments:
- **Those causing rupture of the membranes:** Uterine sound, catheter, pencil, hairpin, knitting needle, stick and fingers.
- **Those causing dilatation of the cervix:** Bark of slippery elm; it is hygroscopic which absorbs the cervical and vaginal secretions to swell resulting in dilation of the cervix.

Instrumentation by unskilled abortionists:
- Soft pieces of wood of different sizes with 3 mm thickness are passed into the cervical canal and are left in situ. It absorbs moisture and vaginal secretions, and swells up and thus dilates the cervical canal.finally it causes abortion
- **Disadvantages:** Unhygienic method and thus increase the chances of infection which leads to sepsis; it may also get lodged in bladder as a foreign body if improperly inserted and chances of perforation of the cervix or uterus is high.

Abortion stick:
Thin bamboo stick or stem of calotropis plant, 12 to 18 cm long; one end wrapped with cotton wool or rag, whose greater part is soaked with juice of marking nut, calotropis or a paste made of arsenic oxide, Sulfide or red lead, and is inserted into the uterus. This irritates the uterus and results in detachment of placenta from the uterus.

Air insufflations: Air is instilled into the vagina by means of syringes or pumps, which results in separation of the placenta from its attachments. Air embolism is a commonest complication.

Electricity: Positive pole is applied over the cervix and the negative pole over sacrum or lumbar vessels. Then current(110volts) is passed, which leads to uterine contraction and thus brings about abortion.

Pastes: Paste containing iodine, thymol or mercury is injected from a collapsible tube with uterine applicator into the uterus.

Cupping: It is a method in which a cup is placed over the lower abdomen and vaccum is created inside, which in turn produces detachment of the placenta leading to abortion.

Syringing: Enema syringe with a hard bulb is used to inject fluid into the uterus. **Higginson's** syringe is usually used; the suction valve is placed in a bowl of fluid and pressure is applied on the bulb. A mixture of air and fluid is forced into uterine cavity at high pressure; the fluid detaches parts of amniotic sac and placenta from the uterine walls. The uterus contracts causing hemorrhage and thus leads to abortion. It can be administered by patient herself or by an abortionist.

Signs of recent abortions:
Local examination:
- Undergarments show some staining with blood and occasionally with liquid abortificient agent which is used.
- Labia majora and minora appear congested and may show some injuries.
- Posterior commissure, fourchette and vaginal wall are congested with reduced rugosity.
- Vagina shows presence of blood clots.
- **Cervix:** Congested and os shows abrasion and tears; cervix remains dilated for a few days after abortion.
- The woman remains indisposed for 1 to 2 days with slight increase in body temperature.
- Serum and urine of the woman remain positive for HCG tests upto about 7 to 10 days.
- Evidence about the method used to procure abortion may be present.
- Discharge of milk or colostrum on squeezing the breast.

Postmortem findings:
External findings:
- Undergarments may be blood stained or show clots and stains.
- Body may look extremely pale and PMS not prominent due to loss of blood before death.
- Pigmentation of breast and abdomen may be present.
- Breasts: Enlarged with dark areola, Montgomery's tubercles and large raised nipples.
- Abdominal wall is lax with linea nigra and occasionally striae gravidarum.
- If cupping is done to induce abortion, then a circular mark may be noticed on the wall of lower abdomen.
- Labia majora appears laxed; labia minora is pigmented, injured and may be stained with blood. Injuries on fourchette and posterior commissure are commonly seen.

Internal examination:
- Uterus, ovary and vagina are dissected enmass for detailed examination.
- Injury to the intra-abdominal organs may be present.
- **Vagina:** Vaginal wall may show perforations near the fornix; the walls may be stained according to the chemical used with excoriation of epithelium.
- **Uterus:** Enlarged, soft and congested with prominent surface vessels; on cut section, the walls will be thickened; cavity may contain the products of conception in full or some remnants of products of consumption. There may be presence of blood clot, hairpin, nail or root of a plant inside the uterine cavity.
- Both the internal and external os are congested and distorted with injuries.
- **Ovaries:** Either of the ovaries will show presence of an active corpus luteum.
- **Lungs:** Evidence of air/fat embolism may be seen with marked congestion. If general anesthetic agents like ether were used, smell of ether will be present. In cases of death due to hemorrhage, the lungs will appear pale

Medicolegal importance of placenta:
- From the size and weight, the period of gestation can be made out.
- It is mere presence (even in pieces) along with blood clots, confirms abortion or delivery.
- Chemical examination of placenta can detect the type of systemic abortificient used.

Medical termination of pregnancy:
Medical termination of pregnancy is guided by MTP act 34 of 1971.

Indications for MTP:
I. Therapeutic: Where continuation of pregnancy has a threat to the life of the mother.
II. Eugenic: Where continuation of pregnancy may lead to the birth of congenitally defective children.
III. Social grounds: Where pregnancy is terminated to limit the size of the family in socially and economically underprivileged family.
IV. Humanitarian: When pregnancy is due to rape.

Persons authorized to perform MTP:
1. Registered medical practitioner who has conducted or assisted minimum 25 abortions in authorized centers.
2. RMP with diploma or master degree in obstetrics and gynecology.

MTP can be done during:
- MTP can be done only upto 12 weeks (3 months) of gestation.
- If any female goes to a doctor and tells that she doesn't want the child and if the gestation period is less than 3 months, then the doctor can very well go on with the induction of abortion (abortion on demand).
- If the period of pregnancy is more than 12 weeks (3 months) and less than 20 weeks (5 months) then opinion of two doctors is necessary for termination of such pregnancies. (it is because sex determination becomes possible after 12 to 16 weeks USG, and hence there is always a chance of sex selection in abortion after 3 months and hence the opinion of two doctors is taken to do MTP between 3 to 5 months).
- After 5 months of gestation, MTP should not be done and any doctor who indulges in such practice is said to have committed criminal abortion and is liable for the act.
- But during any period of gestation, if continuation of pregnancy has got an imminent threat to the life of the mother, then MTP can be done to save the life of the mother, even by the opinion of a single doctor alone.

Where termination should be performed:
Government, semi-government or private hospitals approved for this purpose.

Consent for MTP:
- Written informed consent is necessary and consent of the guardian is required when age of the female is less than 18 years of age.
- Consent of the husband is not necessary, even if the female is married.

Maintain records:
- Records containing all the details of the patient on whom MTP was conducted.
- All forms filled for the procedure of conduction of MTP must be kept confidential and are not to be kept open.
- The consent form filled up by the patient together with the certified opinion of the doctor along with the intimation of termination of pregnancy should be kept in a sealed envelope and marked "SECRET" and then sent to chief medical officer of the state or head of the hospital and kept safe in the medical records department.

Note:

Section 88 BNS:
Voluntarily causing criminal abortion with the consent of the woman. Both the woman and the abortionist are liable for imprisonment upto 3 years, with or without fine. If the woman is quick with the child, the imprisonment may extend upto 7 years.

Section 89 BNS:
- When abortion is caused without the consent of the woman, the punishment extends upto 10 years. Section 314 IPC:
- If a pregnant woman dies, from an act intended to cause miscarriage, the punishment shall not be less than 10 years and fine upto 2 lakhs.

Section 91 BNS:
Aperson doing an actintended to preventthe child from being born alive or to cause death of the child, is liable for imprisonment upto 10 years.

Section 92 BNS:
Causing death of a quick unborn child by any act, amounts to culpable homicide. The punishment may extend upto 10 years.

Section 93 BNS: (Abandoning an infant):
Abandoning a child of less than twelve years by the father, mother or caretaker, shall be punished with imprisonment upto 7 years.

Section 94 BNS: (Concealment of birth):
Whoever intentionally conceals the birth of a child; either dead born or still born and buries or disposes by other means, shall be punished with imprisonment upto 2 years.

CHAPTER - 19
SEXUAL OFFENCES

Classification

Natural Offences	Unnatural Offences	Sexual Paraphilias	Sex Linked Offences
i. Rape ii. Incest iii. Adultery	i. Sodomy ii. Tribadism iii. Bestiality iv. Buccal Coitus	i. Sadism ii. Masochism iii. Necrophilia iv. Fetichism v. Transvestism vi. Exhibitionism vii. Masturbation viii. Frotteurism ix. Undinism	i. Stalking ii. Voyeurism iii. Sexual Harassment iv. Trafficking v. Indecent Assault

Natural Offences Rape

Definition : Sec. 631 BNS -- A man is said to commit Rape if he
   a. Penetrates his Penis, to any extent, into the vagina, mouth, urethra, anus of women or makes her to do so with him or any other person
   b. Insert any object or part of the body, not being the penis, to any extent into the vagina.......
   c. Manipulates any part of the body of the women so as to cause penetration into vagina......
   d. Applies his mouth to the Vagina, ...
   Under the Circumstances falling under any of the seven description
   i. Against her Will
   ii. Without her Consent [Every act done against will is done without her consent but an act done without consent of person is not necessarily against her will]
   iii. With Invalid Consent i.e.,
      i. Consent obtained due to Fear of Death/Hurt
      ii. Consent due to Misrepresentation of facts/fraud/impersonation
      iii. Consent due to Unsoundness of mind/Intoxication/Stupefying subs.
   iv. Age <18yrs
   v. When she is unable to communicate consent.

Exception :
1. Medical Intervention / Procedure shall not constitute Rape
2. Sexual intercourse with one's own wife is not rape if the wife is not under the age of 15 years

Punishment for Rape

BNS	Definition	Minimum Imprisonment [in years]
64	Rape	10
64	For Special situation, incl. Custodial Rape, Rape on Pregnant, Repeatedly on same women, by Relative,...	10
65(1)	Rape on a Girl < 16yrs	20
66	Rape in case Victim is in coma / Persistent Vegetative State [Rape and Murder]	20
65(2)	Rape of girl < 12yrs	20
67	Forceful sexual intercourse by a husband with wife during Phase of Separation	2-7
68	Sex by a person in Authority [Seducing Women under his Custody to have sex]	5 - 10
70(1)	Gang / Group Rape (2 or more)	20
70(2)	Gang rape with a girl <12 years	Life time imprisonment
71	Rape by Repeated Offender	Life time imprisonment

Types of Rape

Statutory Rape	<18 yrs
Gang / Group Rape	Grp. Of ppl with single victim
Date Rape	Sexual intercourse with a women who is given a Sedative Drug like Flunitrazepam (Rohypnol), GHB (Gamma hydroxy butyrate), Ketamine. These Drugs are called Rape Drugs / Club Drugs
Marital Rape	Forceful sexual intercourse with wife who is living separately from him under a decree of separation, or any custom or usage without her Consent

Note :
- *Rape can be committed only by Man on a Women (Women cannot be charged for Rape)*
- *If a Women Forces an Unwilling Man to have Sexual intercourse, the women can be charged of Indecent Assault*
- *(max. Age)There is no age below which a man cannot be charged with the offence of Rape*
- *(min. Age)To bring a Rape against a Boy he should be >7years*
- *Rape = Children > Adult = Less Resistance and a False Belief that Venereal diseases are cured by sexual intercourse with a Virgin.*

Presumption and Proof of Consent
- Consent or its absence can be presumed from the accompanying circumstances of each case
- The Chief Evidence of Lack of Consent is a Sign of Resistance. The resistance offered depends upon the type of women, her age, Development and on the Social Status.
- The Women may Surrender from fear or Exhaustion which case it is regarded as Rape.
- In most cases of Rape involves Physical Injuries to the victim like: Hitting, Slapping, Pressing her neck, Knocking her to the Ground, or forcibly tearing her clothes.

What Constitutes a Rape ?

- Slightest Penetration of the penis within the Vulva or b/w Labia
- With or Without Emission of semen or Rupture of Hymen
- Completed act of Intercourse is not Necessary
- Rape can be committed even when there is Inability to produce a Penile Erection
- Rape can occur without causing any injury and such negative evidence does not exclude Rape. The doctor should mention Only Negative Facts, and give his Opinion that rape has not been committed.

Examination of the Victim

Objectives :
- To search for Physical Signs (Injuries) that will corroborate the History given by the victim
- Collect and Preserve all trace evidence for Lab Examination
- Treat the Victim for any injuries and against Venereal diseases Pregnancy.
- The police Should advice victim not to change Clothes, Bath or Douche prior to the Medical Examination

General Procedure
- The Victim should be Examined when there is requisition from investigating Police Officer or the Magistrate. The court has no power of forcing a women for medical ex. Against her will.
- Written, Witnessed Consent of the Women for Examination, Collection of Specimens, Taking of Photographs, treatment, and for the release of information to the Police. [If she is <12yrs / Unsound mind, get consent from parents]
- Girl <12 years should only be examined by a Female RMP in the presence of the person of trust.
- Male RMP can examine women in the presence of another Female.
- The Victim should be identified by the Escorting Police Constable, whose Name, No., Identification marks, should be noted
- Victim details are also noted
- Date and Time is important
- The Examination should be carried out without delay. Minor injuries may fade rapidly, Swelling and Tenderness of Vulva may disappear in few hours, Detection of Spermatozoa in the FGT also reduces with Time.
- Statement of the Victim and of Others are recorded separately.
- Previous History with regard to Sexual experience, Menses, Vaginal discharge, Venereal ds., Pregnancy, Pelvic Operation, etc. Should be recorded
- Age, Ht, Wt.
- Physical Development should be recorded to determine her capacity for struggle / Resistance.
- An attempt at Undressing the Women should not be made, but She should be asked to Undress Herself
- If the victim is in Menstrual Period, a 2nd Examination is made after stoppage
- Her General Demeanour, Emotional and Mental State Should be observed while she tell her story
- If she is under Alc. -- Collect Blood and Urine Sample
- Gait Observed. Pain --> Guarded Gait [Walking with legs apart and slow paces]
- Physical Development should be recorded to determine her capacity for struggle / Resistance.
- An attempt at Undressing the Women should not be made, but She should be asked to Undress Herself
- If the victim is in Menstrual Period, a 2nd Examination is made after stoppage
- Her General Demeanour, Emotional and Mental State Should be observed while she tell her story
- If she is under Alc. -- Collect Blood and Urine Sample
- Gait Observed. Pain --> Guarded Gait [Walking with legs apart and slow paces]

1. **Clothes**
    - Whether those clothes are worn at the time of Assault / changed
    - Ideally each item of Clothing should be removed by the patient in the presence of Doctor and by Standing on a Clean sheet of Paper, and Anything falls should be Preserved [Earth, Buttons, Hair, Fibres, Gravel, Leaves.
    - Each item of clothing should be examined for various stains (Blood, Seminal, Mud, Earth, Grease, Grass, etc.), Soiling, Tears and Loss of Buttons, The site and Type of Damage
    - Foreign Hair, Fibres, etc found on clothes or on the skin surface should be preserved.
    - Semen can be found in Clothes, Bedding, Carpet Sheets, etc.
    - Seminal fluid will be found on Underclothing due to drainage from the vagina
    - The Clothes should be Dried, Stored, in a clean Paper bag and sent to the Laboratory
    - Suspicious stains should be preserved for chemical analysis
    - Cloths are very important in Corroborating or Contradicting her Story.

2. **General Examination**
   - Victim should be completely undressed and examined using UV light to detect Seminal Stains.
   - Large and Closeup Photograph of injuries esp of sexual are should be taken.
   - Whole body must be Examined for Marks of Violence esp., Scratches, Bruises, Laceration, and area of Tenderness resulting from Struggles.[regarding Appearance, Extent, Site, and Probable Age of wound should be Noted]
   - Petechiae on face or Conjunctive indicate Partial Asphyxia caused during forcible restraint or with intent to make the victim unconscious or Silence her.
   - Fingernail clippings or Scrapings from beneath the fingernails should be pllaced in the envelopes marked right / left, Labelled and sent to laboratory
   - Absence of General injuries is due to
     i. A delay in reporting the incident during which minor injuries will fade or Heal. The age of Injuries should be noted
     ii. Bruises may not be noticed for 48 hrs following the assault
     iii. Submission of Victim due to fear of Injury or Death
     iv. The Force used / Resistant Offered is Insufficient to produce an injury

3. **Hair**
   - Pubic hair is combed out as non-matching male Pubic hair and Foreign material may be present
   - Diseased Victim --> Pull 15-20 Pubic hair for Root Characteristics
   - Living Victim --> Cut 15-20 Pubic hair (not pulled)
   - Hair Samples from head should be taken from Front, Top, Back, Lt, Rt.
   - All samples should be carefully retained, packed, Sealed and labelled and then sent to the laboratory
   - In Laboratory,
   * If Root is present = Tandem repeat analysis can be performed
   * If only Shaft Present = Mitochondrial DNA typing can be performed

4. **Seminal Stains**
   - If the Pubic Hair is matted, the entire matted hair should be cut away as close to the skin as possible
   - The pooling of Seminal Fluid in the vagina is a sign of Recent sexual intercourse, but this pooling rapidly disappears if an Upright Posture is adopted soon after ejaculation has taken place as semen will drain out of vagina [Underwear]
   - Swab must be taken from the area of introitus and perineum before hymen Examination
   - After Hymen examination, Low vaginal Swab should be taken by gently separating the labia minora, without touching the Labia or Perineum
   - Swabs to be taken before any digital examination
   - Give Anaesthesia -- Gross injury / Children before speculum is introduced
   - Collect Swab of
   1. Cervical Mucus [>48hrs] (or)
   2. Vaginal Swab with a Speculum (or)
   3. Contents are aspirated from the Post. Fornix [10mL of normal saline can be instilled in the Post. Fornix] by means of Blunt end Pipette and examined immediately for living Sperms
   - 1st swab -- Smears should be prepared immediately, and allowed to dry on the slide otherwise Sperms will disintegrate --> FIX [Heat / Absolute Alc. Or Ether] --> Label the slide.
   - 2nd Swab placed in Normal Saline -- To check for motility of Sperm
   - 3rd Swab is air-Dried and placed in clean dry test tube --> Test for Acid Phosphatase determination
   - UV light --> Fluorescence of area of Seminal Soiling [External genitals, Tops of thigh, Buttocks, Abdomen and Hands -->
   1. Cotton Swab --> Moistened with Saline --> Air-dried and placed in a sterile container.
   2. If Seminal stains are dried --> Scrape with a Blunt Knife --> Sealed in a Packet and sent to Chemical Examiner.

5. **Blood Stains**
    - Presence or Absence of Blood stains around the Vagina and legs should be noted.
    - Determine whether it is d/t Menstruation
6. **Venereal Diseases**
    - The degree of normal Cleanliness of women should be noted
    - oIn Unclean Women --> there may be Superficial areas of erythema, Irritation, and Sometimes abrasions.
    - Redness from chronic inflammation must be differentiated from Recent Injury
    - The presence of Discharge due to Gonorrhoea, Signs of Syphilis, Chlamydia, Trichomoniasis, HSV, HIV and HPV should be noted.
7. **Local Examination**
    - Women placed in good light
    - Lithotomy Position [If painful --Apply cocaine solution locally]
    - Genital injury are +nt in 1/5th cases
      Accused -- Only rubbing / touching the genitals
      Victim is Sexually Experienced
      Elasticity of Genitalia and Hymen in post-Pubertal female
      Use of Lubricants

Rape on Vergin
    - Pubic area -- Matted hair -- Fully cut
    - Entire area combed -- any loose hair
    - Inspect for injuries -- Top of Thighs, Labia, Perineum
    - Swab collected -- from the areas of Introitus and Perineum

a. **Hymen**
    - Inspect Labia before Retraction
    - Separate Labia -- Inspect Hymen
    - Collect Low Vaginal Swab at this stage
    - Rupture of Hymen occurs with the 1st intercourse [Main evidence of Rape in Virgin]

        During Intercourse
        - As the penis enter the Genitals, it tends to compress the Labia both ant. And laterally, Producing Bruising of both the Labia minora and Labia Majora.
        - The amt. Of bruising depends on Force Used.
        - Further penetration forces the penis backwards, because the Symphysis pubis prevents ant. Movement, and the Hymen is torn Post.

    - Hymen Tears
    - Penis -- Upto margin -- 5'00-7'00 clock position [Post. Tears]
    - Finger / Tampoons -- not reach margin
    - Full Fingerpenetration -- Can reach Margin
    - \> 2 tears are unusual
    - 1st intercourse = Several Laceration
    - Object > Hymenal Orifice = V shaped Tear
    - In prepubertal Children = U shaped Tear (may involve the Fourchette)

Time	Hymen Tear
Soon after	Margins are Sharp and Red which Bleed on Touch, The tissues around are Tender
8-24 hrs	Margins are Edematous swollen with Serosanguinous Oozing
2-3 days	Pain, Congestion & Oozing of blood
3-4 days	Pain, Congestion but no Oozing
7 Days	Completely Heal but not Unite

Note:
- *Ant. Concavities of Hymen --> Congenital and do not change with age*
- *Post. And Lat. Concavities --> attenuate with age*

Examination of Hymen
1. Glaiste-Keene Rods or Globes
   - Rods - Diameter 6mm
   - Globes - Diameter 1 to 2.5 cm
   - Warmed to body temperature
   - Passed through the Hymenal Orifice (Spherical head first)
   - Then passed round the post. Surface
   - Edges of Hymen slightly Everted
   - Slowly rotate the sphere around the edges
   - Natural Notches are easily differentiated from tears, recent or Old.
2. Foley's Catheter or Inflatable Balloon containing a small Electric light
   - Transilluminate the Hymen
3. Pass the Finger into the Rectum above the perineal body and push the Post. Wall of Vagina Forwards and Downwards
It pushes the Hymen forward
Hymen is Clearly seen entirely, lying against the Post. Vaginal wall
4. Hymenoscope
   - Excellent Transillumination of Hymen to detect Tears

Toluidine Blue Dye Test
- For Identification of Genital and Perianal Injuries, which are not revealed even by Colonoscopy
- After Ex. of Post. Fourchette apply 10% aqueous solution of Toluidine Blue dye to the Post. Fourchette and Fossa navicularis with a swab
- After 15 seconds, Remove Excess dye with Lubricant [K-Y jelly or 10% acetic acid and Gauze]
- Dye uptake is considered positive and affirms injury when there is residual blue colouring of the Lacerations or its border.
- Patient Experience Stinging at the site of application

b. **Labia**
  - Swelling and Congestion of the mucosa at Introitus, the Clitoris and Labia minora are caused by
  - Genital Stimulation
  - Digital Stimulation / Masturbation

Disappear by 1-2 hrs
  - Swelling and Tenderness in Labia Minora may indicate sexual activity
  - Redness may be d/t Uncleanliness
  - Bruising and laceration may also be present.

c. **Vagina**
  - High Vaginal swab should be taken using small Vaginal Speculum under direct Vision
  - With Speculum in site, the interior of vagina should be inspected for signs of Abrasions, Bruising and Laceration of Vaginal walls.
  - Bruising of Vagina is seen as a
  - <24 hr = Dark-red area against overall redness of the vaginal mucosa.
  - >24 hr = Deep-red or Purple
  - m/c in the Ant. Vaginal wall in the lower 1/3
  - Bruising = Penis >>> Digital penetration
  - Abrasions = Digital Penetration
  - Note : Rape -- Without consenting --> Preliminary stimulation has not taken place --> Lacks initial Lubrication --> More severe Local Bruising and Abrasion.
  - In children / Adult = Intercourse occur in Standing Erect Position --> Tears of Vaginal wall / Perineal body can occur

d. **Cervix**
  - Abrasion of cervix caused by
  - Digital Penetration >> Penile
  - Tampon
  - Abrasion are seen as Bright red areas on the overall redness of the cervix
  - m/c around the External OS with well defined margins which may bleed on contact
  - Colposcope (Binocular microscope) [gives 5 to 30 × Magnification] -- Directly Visualize the Cervix

e. **Injuries caused by Instruments**

  Tears in the deeper parts of vagina (Rt> Lt), and gross lacerating wounds of the Vault are not likely to occur during sexual intercourse, but are often caused by sexual Perverts using instruments.

Vaginal Examination
- In all cases where there are no fresh injuries, vaginal examination should be carried out to assess

i. Laxity of the vaginal orifice (indicating previous penetration)

ii. Length of the vagina into the post. fornix (elongation indicates Sexual intercourse on multiple times)

iii. The no. Of fingers that can be introduced through Hymenal Orifice

iv. Elasticity of the Hymen and to determine the degree of penetration which would be possible without rupture

v. The areas and the degree of tenderness complained by the Pt.

- Note : Two Finger test = If Vaginal opening is enough to admit 2 fingers easily, sexual intercourse is possible without rupture of Hymen.
  - This two finger test was BANNED in Supreme Court of India (d/t Privacy)
  - The circumference of the Hymen can be Measured by a Measuring Cone.
  - Circumference of 9-10cm is considered the least necessary for sexual intercourse

Rape on Deflorate Women
- Deflorate Women even without Child Birth
  - » Hymen is completely destroyed
  - » Vaginal Orifice dilated
  - » Mucous membrane Wrinkled and Thickened.
- Complete Penetration of Penis can occur in these women without any local signs or injuries
- If the women offers Resistance - Local injury may be seen in the Vulva like small Abrasions and Light Bruising
- Signs of Struggles may be evident like Bruising over Forearms, Shoulders, Buttocks, Nail marks, etc

Rape on Child
- Young Children - Few / no signs of general violence [Child has no idea of what is happening & also incapable of Resisting]
- Older child -- Typical grasping injuries and bruises from blows.
- Hymen -- Deeply situated
- Vagina -- Very small
- Impossible for Penetration of adult organ.
- Penis is placed b/w thighs -- Hymen intact, Redness and Tenderness of Vulva.
- It tends to compress the labia both anteriorly and laterally producing bruising of labia minora and majora.
- Note : The absence of marks of Violence on the Genitals of the child, when an early examination is made is strong evidence that rape has not been Committed.

Unnatural sexual offences:
  i. Sodomy.
  ii. Lesbianism.
  iii. Buccal coitus.
  iv. Bestiality.

Section 377 IPC
- Whoever voluntarily has carnal intercourse against the order of nature with any man, woman or animal shall be punished with imprisonment for life, or with imprisonment of either description for a term which may extend to 10 years, and shall also be liable for fine.

Sodomy:
- Sodomy denotes male homosexuality and involves penile-anal intercourse.
- Anal intercourse with a female is called buggery.
- The offender is the active agent; the other partner is the passive agent.
- If the passive agent is a child, the practice is known as pederasty.
- Habitual passive agents are called Catamites, (fairies, gays or queens)
- In India, Hijras (castrated males) and Zenanas (male transvestites) are the habitual passive agents of sodomy.

Local examination: The findings of examination are totally different on an individual who is not used to an act of sodomy and a habitual passive agent.

Victim not used to sodomy:
- Pain and tenderness are always present. Lubricant used and loose pubic hair in and around the anus.
- Perianal abrasions and bruising are always present; sometimes with anal laceration.
- Fresh/dried stains of semen and blood may be recoverable.
- Digital examination is painful and does not allow more than two fingers.

Habitual passive agent:
- Blood stains are usually not present.
- Lubricant and loose foreign pubic hair may or may not be present.
- Perianal hair is shaved and local hygiene scrupulously maintained.
- Thickening and keratinization of the perianal skin due to constant friction.
- No pain or tenderness during examination.
- Lateral buttock traction test is positive (funnel shaped depression of the anus)

Anus: Dilated, patulous and loss of rugosity of mucous membrane. Fresh and old fissures and/or sinuses (tunneling) is a common finding.

Rectum: Prolapsed mucosa, with thickening and disappearance of radial folds.
- Evidence of STD (Condylomata, chancre and gonorrheal discharge) may be evident.

Digital examination: Allows 3 to 4 fingers easily and pain is highly improbable.

LESBIANISM:

Lesbianism denotes female homosexuality; it is also called as tribadism or sapphism.
- Typically, it involves mutual masturbation and occasionally an active-passive relationship, by biclitoral/digital/lingual, vaginal stimulation, or the use of vibrators or artificial phalluses (dildoes).
- Active lesbian is known as Butch or Dyke, the usual passive agent is called Femme.
- Habitually active lesbians have a strong aversion to normal sexual behavior.
- Whereas the passive agent is not so, and infact, frequently bisexual.

Medicolegal aspects:
- Lesbianism is extremely difficult to prove:

Traces of fresh and dried saliva and/or mucosal cells can be detected on/around the external genitalia, or
- Injuries are present if there has been forcible introduction of a grossly disproportionate artificial phallus

SIN OF GOMORRAH:

Buccal coitus:
- Buccal-penile intercourse is called fellatio; the partner who performs the act is called the Fellator; and on whom it is performed is the Fellatee.
- Buccal-vaginal stimulation is referred to as cunnilingus.

Medicolegal aspects:

The only material evidence of commission of the offence would be:

i. Spermatozoa of the fellatee in the buccal cavity of the fellator, or

ii. Fresh or dried saliva and/or mucosal cells on the penis of the fellatee, or vulva of the subject of cunnilingus.

BESTIALITY:

Sexual intercourse with a lower animal is called as bestiality and it is a crime throughout the world.
- The animal usually selected are cows, bitches, female sheep/goat/donkey and large birds in males and bulls, horses, dogs, male sheep/goat/donkeys by the females.

Medicolegal aspects:
- Difficult to prove unless the accused is caught during the act.
- Young adult male, usually mentally challenged are the affected people.
- Injuries inflicted by the animal, hair/feathers and/or blood stains of the animal on the clothing or on the individual may be present

SEXUAL PARAPHILIAS:

All perversions:
- Achievement of sexual gratification by means other than sexual intercourse; they are called as sexual deviations, perversions or paraphilias.
- These form a group of psychosexual disorders, which involves involuntary, repetitive, unusual acts, on which sexual arousal and orgasm is dependent.

i. Fetishism
- Sexual focus is on relatively indestructible objects intimately associated with human body.
- Males are the affected ones; attraction is mainly on the clothes and articles which were in close intimation with the female body. For example, panties, petticoat, hand-kerchief, etc.
- Orgasm is obtained usually by masturbation.

ii. Transvestism
- Crossdressing or eonism; dressing in the opposite sex, for the purpose of arousal and as an adjunct in sexual intercourse or masturbation.

iii. Sadism
- Males are the affected; sexual arousal and orgasm linked to active infliction of injuries or torture of the sexual partner.

iv. Masochism
- Females are the usually affected; sexual excitement linked with passive experience of physical or emotional humiliation or torture.
- There arises no problem when a sadistic male and a masochist female go hand-in-hand.

v. Lust Murder
- Is an extreme form of sadism, where the sadistic male may pass a ligature around the neck of the female and strangle her (may also be a part of masochistic activity) during the act of sexual intercourse; at the moment of attainment of orgasm, he may tighten the ligature and hold it tight for some reasonable period of time and the woman may die due to ligature strangulation, this is called as lust murder.

There is no intension to kill, but death is due to accidental strangulation.

vi. Exhibitionism
- Exhibitionism involves repeated acts of exposing one's genitals to a female, who may even be a stranger or unsuspected person.

vii. Voyeurism
- Perversion with desire to observe the genitals or other private parts of the female, while they are bathing, or go still perverted and like to watch them urinating or defecating and orgasm is obtained by masturbation.

viii. Peeping Tom
- Watching people engaged in sexual activity without their knowledge.

ix. Troilism
- Extreme form of peeping tom, where the pervert gets sexual gratification by inducing his wife to sexual intercourse with another person and like to witness the same.

x. Frotteurism
- Practiced by a male pervert in a crowded place to drive sexual gratification by rubbing his private parts against a female's body.

xi. Necrophilia
- Sexual arousal and orgasm can be attained by intercourse with a corpse.
- Mortuary workers are the usual sufferers, as they have the access; people addicted to alcohol and who are impotent may involve in these types of activities.

xii. Necrophagia
- Is an extreme form of necrophilia where in sexual gratification is attained by tearing out the genitals or other part of body of a corpse and eating them.
- Necrophilia and necrophagia are punishable under section 297 IPC.

Section 297 IPC:
- Whoever with the intention of offering any indignity to any human corpse, shall be punished with imprisonment of either description for a term which may extend to one year, or with fine, or both.

xiii. Pedophilia
- Preferential sexual activity with children.
- Indulging the children in sexual activity by touching their private parts, kissing, hugging and make the children touch and fondle on their private parts; they make the children indulge in buccal coitus also.

xiv. Satyriasis
- Excessive sexual desire among males. These subjects are liable to commit sexual offences.

xv. Nymphomania
- Excessive sexual desire among woman; they may indulge in sex with multiple sex partners and when the access to sex is restricted, they may indulge in lesbianism.

INDECENT ASSAULT:

Indecent assault generally means sex-linked misbehavior towards a person of opposite sex or the same sex.
- Any offence committed towards a female with the intention or knowledge to outrage the modesty of the female.
- **Section 509 IPC:** Whoever, intending to insult the modesty of a woman, utters any word, makes any sound or gesture, or exhibits any object shall be punished with imprisonment which may extend to one year

CHAPTER - 20
INFANT DEATHS

INTRODUCTION
- Infanticide is defined as killing a child under the age of one year.
- Only the mother of the child can be charged of the offence of Infanticide, as she has the sole duty of protecting and taking care of the child.
- In India, there is no distinction between infanticide and murder of any individual, after delivering the child.

Foeticide:
The killing of the fetus at any time prior to birth.

Filicide:
The killing of a child by its parents.

Neonaticide:
The killing of a child within 24 hours of birth.

Legal Questions arised in Infanticide:
- Whether the fetus have attained maturity/ viability or not?
- Whether the child was dead born/still born/ live born?
- If live born, then how long did the child survive and what was the cause of death?

If the child born by dead within then it shows the following signs:
During birth the baby shows maceration and rigor mortis.

Note:

Rigor mortis only occurs in viable fetus, because myofi brilsgets developed only after 7 months of intrauterine life.

Maceration:
- This is aseptic autolysis and occurs when the child remains in the uterus for about 3 to 4 days immersed in liquor amni after death, but should be devoid of air.
- The earliest sign of maceration is slippage of skin, seen after 12 hours of death within uterus.
- Maceration is presented with purple skin, air blebs, flexible bones and abnormal mobility of joints, soft viscera.
- Rarely mummification may also occurs in maceration.

Spalding's sign:
As brain becomes shrunken after death of foetus, skull bones shows loss of alignment and overriding due to loss of intracranial tension and it is seen 48 hours after death

STILLBIRTH:
- If a child born after 28 weeks of gestation and didn't shows any signs of life after expelled from uterus then the child will be considered as stillborn.
- The child was alive inside uterus, but due to defects in birth process death occurs.

Indications Of Stillbith:
- Prolonged labor, indicated by presence of caput succedaneum and severe molding of head, and negative hydrostatic test are indicative of still birth.
- In these cases, the body is sterile and decomposition occurs only by aseptic autolysis.

Common causes of stillbirth:
- Prematurity.
- Anoxia and birth trauma.
- Placental abnormalities and toxemia of pregnancy.
- Erythroblastosisfetalis and congenital defects of the fetus.

Viability:
- Viability is the physical ability of a fetus to lead a separate existence of its own, outside the mother's womb, by virtue of a certain degree of development.
- A child is said to be viable after 210 days of intrauterine life. However, the minimum period of viability is 180 days (6 months).

Live birth:
- Live born child is one which is born alive and showed signs of life after it has been completely delivered out of the mother.
- The law presumes that every newborn child found dead was born dead, till the contrary is proved.

Signs of life after birth:
- Hearing of a cry
- movement of limbs or even feeble respiration after complete birth of the child is accepted as proof of live birth according to civil laws.

But in criminal cases, live birth has to be demonstrated by postmortem examination.

SIGNS OF LIVE BIRTH:

Autopsy findings in criminal cases:

Rule of Hasse:

Used to assess intrauterine age of the foetus.
- Crown-heal length of the fetus is measured and if the length is less than 25 cm,
- The square root of the crown heal length will give the approximate age of the fetus in months.
- If the length is more than 25 cm, then it is divided by 5, which will give the gestational age.
- For example, if the length is 16 cm, then the age of the fetus is 4 months and if the length is 35 cm, the age of the fetus is 7 months.

- **Shape of chest:** Before respiration, the chest is flat and its circumference is 1 to 2 cm less than the abdomen at the level of umbilicusstab wound on the chest may enter into the liver.
- Abdominal cavity is opened first to check the level of diaphragm. Position of diaphragm: Diaphragm is found at the level of 4th or 5th rib before respiration; after respiration, the diaphragm is pushed downwards to the level of 6th or 7th ribs.

Lungs:

Volume: Fully respired lungs fill the whole of the thoracic cavity and the margins of the lungs overlapping on the pericardium of the heart; whereas unrespired lung appears collapsed towards the hilum.

Margins: Margins are usually sharp before respiration, but becomes rounded after the first respiration, even if feeble respiration has taken place; presence of bullae suggests some form of obstruction and evidence of respiration.

Consistency: Lungs are dense, firm and non-crepitant like liver before respiration. It becomes soft, spongy, elastic and crepitant if respiration takes place.

Weight of lungs	
Static test or Fodere's test:	The average weight of the lungs before respiration is 30 to 40 g and it becomes 60 to 70 g after respiration due to increase in blood flow.
Ploquet's test:	After respiration, due to increased blood flow in the lung, their weight gets doubled from 1/70 of body weight to 1/35 of body weight.

Hydrostatic test or Raygat's test:
- Hydrostatic test is done to find out whether the lung has respired or not.
  Principle: Before respiration, the lungs are of same consistency as that of liver and do not float in water. After respiration, the specific gravity of lung is decreased which makes the lungs to float in water.
- **Procedure:** A ligature is applied to dissect the entire lung and is placed on water. If the entire lung floats, then each lung is cut into 12 to 20 pieces and then placed on water; a small piece of liver is kept as control. (if liver floats, it indicates decomposition has set in and the test is invalid).
- If the lung pieces still float, then they are squeezed under water to see if any bubbles escape. Then, the lung bits are wrapped in piece of cloth and squeezed to remove the residual air. The squeezed lung pieces are again put in water. If the pieces still float, it indicates that active respiration has taken place. If they sink, it indicates that respiration has not taken place
- If some pieces sinks and some floats, then it indicates feeble respiration has taken place.
- Important points:
  Respired lung may sink in cases of pneumonia, atelectasis and obstruction by alveolar duct membrane.
- Unrespired lung may float in cases of decomposition and artificial respiration.
- Hydrostatic test is not necessary in the cases of mummified and macerated foetus, foetus born before 180 days, if the foetus contains milk in its stomach, if umbilical cord got seperated and scar formed.

SIGNS OF STRUGGLE TO BREATHE:
1. Dark coloured blood as there is increased CO_2 level in blood.
2. Cyanosed and expanded lungs
3. Tardieu's spots on pleura, heart and thymus
4. Liver appears enlarged due to congestion
5. Large bowel filled with meconium and gets distended
6. Ascites and retroperitoneal oedema

Changes in stomach and intestine:

Breslau's second life test/ stomach- bowel test:
Following double ligature stomach and intestines are removed.
If respiration taken place then it will float otherwise it will sink.
If the stomach is dissected under water then both mucus and air bubbles with saliva will be present if breathing takes place or else only mucus will be present.

Changes in the middle ear:

Wreden's test:
Before birth, middle ear contains gelatinous embryonic connective tissue without air, but if respiration takes place then the tissues will be replaced with air in few hours to five weeks.
Opening the middle ear under water expels air bubbles indicates the test is positive.

Changes in child after birth:
1. Nucleated RBC's disappear after 24 hours
2. Meconium got completely excreted from large intestine in 24 to 48 hours after birth
3. Breech presentation and severe anoxia is common.
4. **Caput succedaneum:**
   The area of soft swelling in the scalp over the presenting part of head in vertex presentations which is associated with moulding is called as Caput succedaneum.
   In breech presentation swelling will be seen in buttocks and scrotum or labia.
   It diminishes or disappear within 2 to 4 days.
5. **Cephalohematoma:**
   It is the localized accumulation of blood deep to the scalp.
   Hematoma is limited to the periosteal sheath of single bone, commlonly the right parietal bone and it doesn't cross the sutural lines.
   Neonatal jaundice may be increased as extra load of blood pigment seen.

6. Physiological jaundice is seen by third day due to relative insufficiency of enzymes of bilirubin conjugation and excretion.
7. **Vernix caseosa:** It is a white cheesy substance of sebaceous secretion and epithelial cells. It protects foetal skin against maceration within the liquor amnii.
8. Umbilical cord attaches to the child got shrunken and dries after 12 to 24 hours. The cord falls off on the fifth or sixth day and leaves an ulcer, which heals and forms a scar in 10 to 12 days.
9. Contraction of umbilical arteries starts in 10 hours and complete cessation by 3rd day. Umbilical vein and ductusvenosus closed on the fourth day, ductusarteriosus closed by tenth day.

Medicolegal aspects of live birth:
- Death could be due to an act of omissions
  E.g: failure to give feeds, not protecting the baby with proper coverings, etc.,
- Death may also due to the act of commission like throttling, strangulation, foreign body in the larynx and trachea, poisoning or even injuries (usually concealed puncture wounds)
- A detailed postmortem examination will demonstrate the exact cause of death

BATTERED BABY SYNDROME:
Otherwise called as **Caffey's syndrome, child abuse or maltreatment syndrome.**
- There may be deprivation of nutrition, care and affection.
- The classical features are obvious discrepancy between the nature of injuries and the explanation offered by the parents. There will be unexplained delay between the time of sustaining such injuries and seeking medical attention.
- There is constant repetition of injuries, often progressive from minor to major injuries.
- The usual victims are childrenfrom low socioeconomic status, broken families, illegitimate and unwanted children
- It may also due to the psychiatric deviations of mother.

Findings in battered baby syndrome:
- Relatively more in male children and the age group is 2 to 5 years.
- Bruises around the wrist, forearm, thighs and ankles, which are due to rough handling and violent swinging of the child may occurs.
- Buttocks may show burns often with cigars and whip marks.
- Face and lips bruised and frenulum of tongue may be torn.
- Circular bruises of 1 to 2 cm in diameter, due to poking of adult fingers on the chest, abdomen and thighs. These are called as six penny bruises.
- Multiple rib fractures may be seen; limb fractures (fresh and old unhealed) occursmostly in regions of epiphysis of growing bones with periosteal separations.
- Crack fractures of skull associated with intracranial hemorrhages.
- Evidence of multiple external injuries of varying degrees under different stages of healing can be noticed
- Rarely these children may die of these injuries and brought for autopsy with fabricated history of sustaining these injuries accidentally. The autopsy surgeon must be aware of the probability of these conditions and help the investigation team as well as the court appropriately so that the culprits do not escape from the law.

SHAKEN BABY SYNDROME:
- Is a variant of battered baby syndrome and is serious form of child abuse.
- It results from extreme rotational movements, cranial acceleration and deceleration injuries produced by violent shaking.

Clinical features:
- They are popularly known as 'whiplash shaken baby syndrome'. It is characterized by retinal hemorrhage, subdural hematoma (SDH) and/or subarachnoid hemmorrhage (SAH). There may be little or no evidence of external injuries.
- Shaking itself may cause serious and fatal injuries; there may also be other forms of head trauma, including impact injuries by throwing the child on the walls

"Shaken slam syndrome" or "Shaken impact syndrome".
- The victims need not be babies alone, the age of the affected individuals may vary extensively.
- Intractable crying of the baby may lead to tension and frustration for the parents or guardians resulting in aversion towards the victim.
- The caretakers are of abusive behavior and have unrealistic expectation of their children. Many of them may expect their needs to be met with by the children.

Investigations:
- CT scan is the choice and may reveal SDH, mass effects and diffuse axonal injuries (DAI).
- The mortality rate is 15 to 30%
- Autopsy findings: External examination may show injuries which corresponds to violent shaking of the child. Internally, SDH, SAH, cerebral edema, intracranial or retinal hemorrhages, and multiple fractures of skull, long bones and ribs are seen.

CINDERELLA SYNDROME:
Sometimes in a family, a single child is chosen to receive the battering (commonly the youngest or the eldest) and repeatedly thrashed, while the other children are spared.

MUNCHAUSEN SYNDROME:
Also called as Hospital addiction syndrome.
- This is a type of child abuse, involving the mother.
- It consists of repeated pretentions of illness or repeated infliction of minor injuries.
- The child is brought to the hospital for induced signs and symptoms with fictitious injuries.
- The child is frequently admitted into the hospital for medical evaluation of any non-existent conditions.

Example:
- The mother may prick her fingers and add the blood drop to the urine of the child and take the sample to the doctor with complains of hematuria by the child;
- The child is repeatedly smothered to unconsciousness, then resuscitated and taken to the hospital.

SUDDEN INFANT DEATH SYNDROME: (SIDS, Crib deaths, Cot deaths)
- It is sudden death of an infant which cannot be explained and the cause of death in such cases remains a mystery, even after a complete autopsy and analysis of clinical history and death scene investigation.
- The incidence is 2 to 3 per 1,000 live births; with male preponderance.
- Most common age is 2 weeks to 2 years; maximum in between 3 to 7 months.
- Twins are at greater risk.
- Commonly occurs at nights and usually there is a history of running nose or coryza.

Autopsy findings:
- Blood stained froth in the mouth, evidence of laryngitis, trachea-bronchitis or congenital heart disease.
- Multiple petechial hemorrhages are often found on the heart, lungs and thymus.
- Etiology: The hypothesis of SIDS include:
- Prone sleeping position.
- Prolonged sleep apnea.
- Hypotonic babies, whose neck position reduces airway lumen due to obliteration of the air passages.
- Dust, mite and cow's milk allergy and anaphylaxis of unknown origin.
- Calcium and selenium deficiency andViremia.

CHAPTER 21
BLOOD STAINS

Introduction:
- Collection, preservation and examination of blood stains are the important areas to be focused by medicolegal experts in order to avoid misinterpretations.
- During collection and preservation of blood stains, care must be taken in order to avoid biological and mechanical damage to the specimen collected.

1. **Procedure to collect blood stains:**
   - It can be collect by soaking a piece of clean white filter paper, cloth, gauze (or) cotton into the blood stain.
   - After collection, it must be dried at room temperature because heating artificially may damage the properties of Blood Stain.
   - If the blood stain is on a porous material, the stained part along with non stained part must be collected as sample.
   - Blood can be collected by pipetting, if it is in fluid form.
   - After collection, solvents such as 10% solution of potassium cyanide (or) 10% solution of glycerine in distilled water or weak ammonia solution can be used as solvent.
   - Before collecting blood stains from the crime area, the experts must focus on other evidences in relation to Blood staining.

He must focus on:
1. Distribution of blood
2. Amount of blood at the crime scene
3. Direction of the fall of blood on to the surface.

Distribution of blood:
- Usually blood doesn't come out of a vessel immediately after injury. It may take a second or two after injury, as the vessel undergoes spasm.
- If small vessels alone are injured and much blood is present, it indicates serious injury before death, but if large vessels are injured, bleeding continues even after death.
- If the person fell unconscious and immobile after injury, then blood will be pooled near the person, if he is conscious, blood will be disturbed by his movement.
- Usually Sprayed appearance of blood at the crime scene is due to waving of weapon.
- But it may also be due to spraying directly from arteries, and if a carotid artery is injured, blood may spray upto a distance of half a metre.
- As veinous blood flow is steady, its injury doesn't sprays out the blood.

Direction of fall onto a surface:
- On falling vertically on a flat surface the drop is circular, if the height doesn't exceed a few centimetres.
- If the height is ≥ 30cm, the drop appears circular with irregular and prickly borders.
- If the height is too much greater then splashes from drop spreads out and can reach upto 15-20 cm.
- If the splashes of blood strikes a surface obliquely then it may appear as spears (or) exclamation marks, depending on the velocity and the angle of fall.

Points to remember:
1. Usually the site of blood staining and the site of injury are different, as the vessel undergoes spasm for a second or two immediately after injury.
2. A blood clot in a size of clenched fist is nearly of 500ml.
3. If blood spreads upto one square foot area, it roughly equals 100ml.
4. If blood spreads onto a wall by an upward sweep, the dots points upwards, and it points downward in case of a downward sweep.
5. Always photograph of blood stains at the crime scene must be taken. It will be useful in further investigations.
Finally, the collected stain must be sent to the State Forensic Science Laboratory (SFSL) for examination.

Preservation of Collected Blood stain:

1. Prevent from bacteria :
- It should be dried at room temperature in order to prevent the stain from bacterial infestation and putrefaction.
- If putrefaction sets in, it is difficult to find out whether the blood belongs to a human or animal.

2. Prevent from confusion:
- In order to avoid confusion, the collected stain must be initialized and dated otherwise a tag should be attached to it.

3. Prevent from misinterpretations:
- Each garment must be wrapped separately and should not come in contact with other clothing.
- Avoid contact between two stains by placing a clean paper in between them while folding the garment.
- Finally the collected stain must be sent to the State Forensic Science Laboratory (SFSL) for examination

Examination of blood stains:

General examination:
1. Examine the part of body from which the blood comes.

Source	Findings
Menstrual blood	1.Usually found in garments of female, diapers or pieces of clothes.
	2.Dark in colour.
	3.Fluid in nature because of fibrinolysins.
	4.Shows acid positive reaction.
	5. Epithelial cells from vaginaor endometrium seen.
	6. Bacterias such as Trichomonas vaginalis or Trichomonas monilia may be seen.
	7.Elevated levels of LDH4 & LDH5 seen
Hemetemesis	1) Dark and chocolaty in colour
	2) Shows acid positive reaction due to reaction with gastric juice.
Haemoptysis	1) Mucus and hair from nasal passage may be found.
	2) Frothy and bright red in appearance.
	3) Shows Alkaline (Base) positive reaction.

Estimation of age of Blood stains:
1. Based on appearance:
   - On light coloured clothes, fresh stains appear bright red in colour, moist and sticky.
   - Becomes reddish brown in 24 hours and turns brown within a few days.
   - After long time, the stain may becomes black.
   - Under normal environmental conditions, drops of blood dry in an hour or two but if blood is collected in pool then it takes 12 to 36 hours based on size and depth of pool.
   - Freshly shed blood from artery is bright red in colour and venous blood appears dark red.
2. Based on solubility:
   - Fresh blood is easily soluble in water and other liquids.
   - Solubility decreases with increase in age.

$$\text{Solubility of blood} \; \alpha \; \frac{1}{\text{age of blood}}$$

3. Based on fluorescence:
   - Fluorescence decreases with age of blood stain, due to formation of hematin.
   - Age of blood stain can be demonstrated only as shown below.

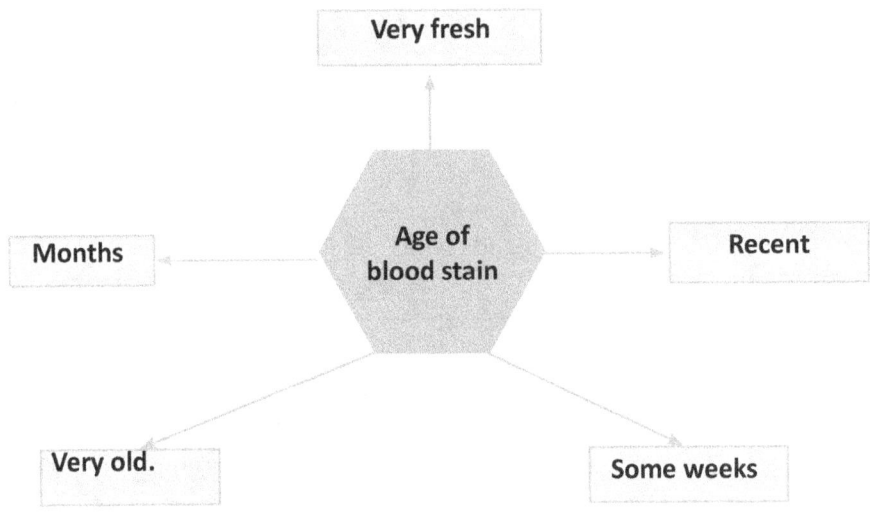

Important points.
- Sex of the person can be determined using sex chromatin in leucocytes.
- Presence of HbF (foetal hemoglobin) suggests that the blood belongs to a child.
- At birth, blood gives thinner and softer coagulum.
- If the blood comes out of body before death, then it can be removed in scales, on drying due to presence of fibrin.
- Blood effuses, and after death, it lacks fibrin and is reduced into powder on drying.

Chemical examination:
Principle:
Peroxidase present in blood oxidises active ingredients and produce characteristic colour in the presence of hydrogen peroxide (H_2O_2).

Name of test	Procedure	Result	Advantages	Disadvantages
1. Benzidine test:	1. Place the stained material on porcelain tile. 2. Add a drop of saturated solution of benzidine in glacial acetic acid. 3. Add a drop of 10 volume H_2O_2.	1. If blood is present, dark blue colour formed.	1. Reaction will positive for any age of blood and even if blood exposed to heat, cold or cleaning agents. 2. This is the best preliminary test for blood. 3. Can detect blood even at high dilution of one part of blood in three lakhs.	1. Positive reaction is not a proof of presence of blood. 2. Weakly it shows false positive reaction for pus, saliva, milk, rust. formalin, oxidising agents, bacteria etc...
2. Phenolphthalein test: -Also called as Kastle meyer test.	1. Add 10 to 20 drops of Phenolphthalein reagent, to the extracted solution of blood stain. 2. Then add a drop or two drops of 10 volumes H_2O_2.	1. Pink or purple colour forms immediately and it indicates precence of blood.	1. More specific test for blood than benzidine test.	1. Less sensitive. 2. Even traces of copper give positive reaction.

Points to remember:
1. Phenolphthalein reagent contains
    - 2 g phenolphthalein
    - 20g sodium hydroxide
    - Zinc and 100ml distilled water
2. Guaiacum (deep blue) and leucomalachite green are rarely used in medicolegal works.

Microscopic examination:
- As dried RBC's are unrecognisable the stain should be soaked in Viberts fluid (or) Normal saline for 30 minutes and then the teased solution must be observed under 40x (high power) microscope.
- Diluted ammonia solution or 2%. HCL can be used if the stain is not dissolved.

Observation:
- In all mammals except camel, RBC is biconcave, enucleated and circular.
- Camels have biconvex, nucleated and oval shaped RBCs like birds, fishes, amphibia and reptiles.

CHAPTER 22
FORENSIC SCIENCE LABORATORY

" **Every contact leaves a trace** " – Edmond locard

Forensic science : The study and application of scientific examination and evaluation of evidenc,for legal purposes.

Forensic sciences includes
1. Forensic medicine
    a. Forensic pathology
    b. Forensic psychiatry
2. Forensic toxicology
3. Forensic immunology
4. Forensic odontology (branch of dentistry - assesing the unique structures of the oral cavity)
5. Forensic anthropology
6. Forensic police sciences
    a. Criminalistics (involves evidence collection – such as blood stains , glass , soil, clothing and fire-arms)
    b. Questioned documents examination (involves examination of hand writing , type writing , printing ink , paper or other aspects of a document for determining various legal questions asked about documents.
7. Other forensic science specialists, (voice print examination , potygraph, fingerprinting etc.,)

Note : Forensic anthropology : The application of the science of physical anthropology of the legal process . forensic anthropology incules identification of skeletral , decomposed , or unidentified human remains.

Forensic science laboratory (FSLs):
- They are located in the state headquarters of each state . each districts also have FSLs.
- Most of the FSLs do examination of materials for commonly required investigations.
- Few FSLs do sophisticated and specialized investigations.

Function of FSLs:
1. To examine , compare and evaluate physical evidence .so as to link a suspect to the victim , or to the scene of a crime.
   (in most cases , the laboratory supplements the work of police investigator in order to convert suspicion into reasonable certainty of either guilty or innocence)
2. Protection of innocent (it determines facts, which are not subject to the bias and prejudice and other human failings of the eye witness.
3. Training of police investigators as to what constitutes physical evidence , how it is to be found , collected , preserved and delivered to the laboratory (sometimes , laboratory technicians and called to the scene of crime to collect specimens with which investigating officers are not qualified to the deal

---
Note :It is merely an aid in crime detection rather than a final judgement .

Principles of forensic science :
Law of individuality :
> Every object , natural or man made , has an individuality which is not duplicated in any other object

Principle of exchange (locard's principle):
> When 2 objects come & contact , there is always exchange of material

Law of progressive change :
> Everything changes with the passage of time

Principle of comparison :
> Only the likes can be compared

Principle of analysis:
> The analysis can be no better than the sample itself

Law of probability :
> All the identifications and identities are sometimes consciously and unconsciously correct based on circumstances .

Law of circumstantial facts :
> Facts never lie but men can lie . facts cannot be wrong , it cannot lie, it cannot be wholly absent.

The laboratory is divided into many areas of investigations :
1. Fingerprint laboratory
2. Trace evidence laboratory
3. Serology / DNA laboratory
4. Materials laboratory
5. Firearms laboratory
6. Photography laboratory
7. Chemistry laboratory
8. Other laboratories

Criminal investigation :
- All criminal investigation is concerned either with people or with material objects
- People commits crimes invariably through the medium of objects . it is these object that together constitute physical evidence
- The main objective of crime investigation is to recognize , collect , preserve , analyse , interpret and reconstruct all the physical evidence collected from the scene of crime
- **Physical evidence / trace evidence :** it includes any objects living or nonliving , solid, liquid or gas , and the relationship between all objects as they relate to the problem in question , **E.g** ., a crime .
  Physical evidence can be obtained from
1. Scene of crime
2. The victim
3. The suspect and his environment
   Physical evidence is usefull in two ways:
1. It is often the decisive factor in determining guilt or innocence.
2. It can be a material aid to link a suspect , a wepon or a scene to a crime.

Note : the evidence should be marked or Labelled with corresponding data so that it can be positively identified and it should be preserved in the same condition in which it was found.

Locard's exchange principle
- When any two objects come into contact , there is always a transfer of material from each object on the other , this is called locard's exchange principle.
- Traces from the scene of crime may be carried away on or by the person committing crime and at the same time traces may be left at the scene
- Whatever he touches , and whatever he leaves will serve as silent evidence against him

- **E.g** : fingerprint, footprints, hair, fibres from clothes, broken glass, tool marks, blood or seminal stains etc
- It is actual evidence, and its presence is absolute proof of crime. The evidence of eyewitness may be wrong as a result of their partisanship, faulty memory, or defective observation

---

Note : all laboratory findings are related to a probability, and a single piece of evidence is rarely sufficient in itself to establish proof of guilt or innocence.

Illustration on locard's principle of exchange :
In rape cases semen, blood, public hair etc., of the rapist can be found on the victim. vaginal epithelialcells, public hair, blood of the victim can be found on the rapist

Control sample :
- It means specimens of materials (eg . b;ood, hair, finger print etc.,) collected from the victim for comparision with any questioned material from the crime scene
- Blood stains found on garment, soil etc., will require unstained samples to rule out false positive test due to substrate interference.

Lie detection :
a. Polygraph:
- It is an instrument used to detect lie
- Keeler polygraph and stoelting deceptograph are used in common use.

Polygraph makes a continuous record of following parameters in response to stimuli in the form of questions
- » Blood pressure
- » Pulse rate
- » Respiration
- » Muscular movements
- » Electrodermal reaction

Principle: Mental excitation or stimulation causes alternation of the body functions due to sympathetic exciation
- Based on theory, that when the person tells a lie in answer to a question, and there is fear that lie will be detected, the emotion of fear results in stimulation of sympathetic nervous system. which results in certain physiological changes (psychosomatic reactions), some of which may be easily recorded.

Parameters that can be noticed during positive lie detection :
- » Relative rise in blood pressure and recovery
- » Increased pulse rate
- » Slowing down of breathing / fast breathing
- » Suppression of involuntary muscular movements
- » Lowering of galvanic skin resistance
- » Increased activity of sweet gland

Procedure :
- Consent of subject is essential
- A basic explanation of the attachments in the polygraph is given to the subject
- The questions will be suggestive in nature
- The person has to answer either yes or no
- Relevant (releted to the incident) and irrelevant (not related to incident) questions are asked loading questions are asked
- One question every 20 -25 sec , polygraph chart recorded in 3-4 minutes
- Repetition of same test to check error
- Experienced polygraph examiner can correctly detect truth /lie in 80-90%
- Offenders, suspects, complainants, witness & informants are examined

b. **Narcoanalysis or truth serum test:**

Principle :

At a point very close to unconsciousness, the subject will be mentally incapable of resistance to questioning, and incapable of inverting the falsehoods that he has used to conceal his guilt.

Drug used :
1. 0.5 mg scopolamine hydrobromide (s.c)
2. Sodium amytal or sodium pentothal (truth serum) 2.5 to 5% (iv)
3. 0.1 g sodium seconal + 15 mg morphine sulphate + 0.5 mg scopolamine hydrobromide (s.c)
- The subject goes to hypnotic or semicounscious state
- The answers are spontaneous, and the person is unable to manipulate the answers
- Subject is susceptible to suggestion & reveals repressed feelings / memories subject become talkative, looses inhibition.
- Depresses CNS,BP, heart rate.
- Wrong dose can cause coma or death of the person

Note : madras high court (in 2006) and Bombay high court (in 2004) ruled that subjecting of accused to narcoanalysis tests does not violate fundamental rights.

- In 2010, supreme court of india opined that narco – analysis cannot be forced on any subject for hypnosis.
- Helps in receiving memory of compressive subjects. It does not often enhances memory
- Many people cannot be hypnotized and many cannot be hypnotized to a deep level
- Hypnotized witnesses
1. Produce many fabricated recollections
2. More often influenced by interviewer's misleading Comments and questions
3. More confident in the accuracy of their recollection, than are non – hypnotized witnesses, even when their recollection are false

c. **Word association :**

Changes in reaction time of the subjects reply to word stimuli, either visual or auditory, or by stereotype of answers, or by exhibition of unconditional physical movements are observed to detect deception

d. **Brain mapping (brain finger printing)**
   » it is introduced by **Dr.Lawrence Farwell**.
   » it is a technique that measures recognition of familiar stimuli by measuring recognition of responses (p300) to words, phrases or pictures that are presented on a computer screen
   » It is based on the theory that the suspects reaction to the details of an event or activity will reflect if the suspect had prior knowledge of the event or activity. It detect evidence stored in the brain

Technique :
- Modern brain scanning technique consists of
  Electroencephalography (EEG)
  Magneto encephalography (MEG)
  Positron emission imaging (PET)
  Magnetic resonance imaging (MRI)
  Computed tomography (CT)
- The equipement called **"electrocap"** with 19 electronic sensors is fixed on the subjects shaven scalp for rewarding EEG
- The suspected person is questioned about the crime and also shown the visuals of the crime scene (victim, weapon, time, place and how he committed the crime etc along with irrelevant words photographs.

- Electrical brain responses of the suspect are measured non investively through "electro cap" equipped with sensors
- The specific wave response called MERMER is elicited when the brain processes the relevant information it recognizes.

  (**MERMER** – **M**emory and **E**ncoding **R**elated **M**ultifaceted **E**lectrocephalographic **R**esponse)

Types of stimuli:
  Probe stimuli – relevant to investigated situation, but the subject denies knowing
  Target stimuli - relevant to investigation situation and are known to subject
  Non – target stimuli – irrelevant and mostly does not elicit a MERMER.

- When the details of the crime perpetrator would know are presented, a MERMER is emilted by the brain of a perpetrator, but not by the brain of an innocent suspect
- Brain fingerprinting (said to be 99% accurate) is more accurate than polygraph test.

CHAPTER - 23
FORENSIC PSYCHIATRY

Definition:
- Psychiatry is a branch of medical science which deals with diagnosis, treatment and rehabilitation measure of the mentally ill people.
- Forensic psychiatry deals with application of psychiatry in the administration of justice.

Mental illness:
- Otherwise called as unsoundness of mind.
- It is defined as disease of mind or personality, in which there is derangement of mental or emotional processes.
- The term "insanity" is loosely used to refer any mental disorder or mental illness.

The Mental Health Act 1987:
- MHA is divided into 10 chapters consisting of 98 sections: Chapter 1 deals with definitions.
  i. **Psychiatric hospital or nursing home:**
     Is a hospital for the mentally ill maintained by the government or private authority with facilities of outpatient treatment and registeredwith appropriate licensing authority.
     Admitting a mentally ill person to a general nursing home is an offence.
  ii. **Psychiatrist:** A RMP with postgraduate or diploma
     degree in Psychiatry recognized by the MCI (MD in Psychiatry or DPM)
  iii. **Mentally ill person:** A person who is in need of treatment for any mental disorder other than mental retardation.

Reception order:
It is an order issued by the court for admission and detention of a mentally ill person in a psychiatric hospital or nursing home.

Cognition:
It refers to high mental faculties, such as memory, intelligence, concentration, orientation etc...

Delirium:
It is a disorders of consciousness.
- There is disturbance of consciousness an orientation is impaired.
- Thought content is irrelevant or inconsistent
- In the early stage, the patient is restless, uneasy and sleepless.
- Later, he loses self-control, becomes exited and talks furiously.
- Delusions and hallucinations may be present at this stage; and he becomes impulsive and may commit any crime, for which he is not liable.

Delusion
- **Delusion** is a disorder of thought.
- False belief in something which is not a fact; and continues to persists even after the falsity is clearly demonstrated.

Types of delusions:

Delusion of grandeur or exaltation	He is actually poor but thinks he rich.
Delusion of persecution	Usually co-exists with delusion of grandeur; the individual thinks that because he is rich and got lot of money, people closely associated with him (wife or children) are trying steal his money and also believes they are even trying to kill him or poison him to take away his imaginary property and money.
Delusion of reference	He feels that whatever he hears or comes across, he is being referred to.
Delusion of influence	He believes that all his actions are influenced by some external agency; he receives imaginary commands and obeys them (like telepathy).
Delusion of infidelity	The male is the sufferer; he suspects the fidelity of his wife, even though she is not like that in reality and is gem of a female; they are usually addicted to alcohol and may also be impotent.
Delusion of self reproach	He accuses himself for all the bad and mishaps in his life.
Nihilistic delusion	He does not believe in the worldly existence at all.
Hypochondriacal delusion	The individual is relatively healthy, but thinks that he suffers from a number of diseases, goes from doctor to doctor with cluster of imaginary complaints.
Erotomaniacal delusion	Females are the usual sufferers; usually people at a lower level develop some imaginary intimate affection towards one of a higher level and starts believing that they are also reciprocating.

Hallucination:
- Hallucination is a disorder of perception in which there is false sense perception without any external object or stimuli to produce it.
- This is purely imaginary and may affect any or all of the special senses.

Depending on the various special senses, hallucination divided into:

Visual hallucination	He sees something when actually nothing is present there.
Auditory hallucination	He hears some imaginary sounds, which do not exist.
Olfactory hallucination	He perceives some smell, when no such odor is present.
Gustatory hallucination	He feels some taste, when nothing is there in the mouth.

Tactile hallucination	He feels some insects are crawling over his body, which are actually not there. This type of hallucination is also called **"Magnan's symptom"** or **"Formication"**. It commonly occurs as withdrawal symptom of chronic cocaine poisoning and are referred to as **"cocaine bugs"**.
Psychomotor hallucination	He feels that some part of the body, usually the limbs are getting elongated, goes away from his body, performs some activity and comes back.

Illusion:
- Illusion is misinterpretation of a real existing stimulus or object.
- *Example:* Seeing a rope he may mistake it as a snake; the weight of the blanket may be mistaken as that of the weight of a collapsed building, etc.

Impulse:
- Impulse is defined as sudden irresistible desire/force compelling a person to the conscious performance of some act for which there is no motive or forethought.
- Every individual may have impulsive behavior at any one time due to emotional imbalance. But, a sane person is capable of controlling his impulse but an insane person cannot control the impulses.

Types of impulse

i. Kleptomania	Irresistible desire to steal articles of little value.
ii. Pyromania	Irresistible desire to set fire.
iii. Mutilomania	Irresistible desire to mutilate lower animals (pet animals).
iv. Dipsomania	Irresistible desire to drink alcohol in excess amount.
v. Sexual impulse	Irresistible desire to engage in some form of sexual activity.
vi. Suicidal impulse	Irresistible desire to commit suicide.
vi. Homicidal impulse	Irresistible desire to kill someone.

Obsession:
Obsession is a disorder of the content of thought.
- A single idea, thought or emotion is constantly entertained by a person which he himself recognizes as irrational, but persists in spite of all efforts to drive it from his mind.
- Any attempt to resist makes them appear more insistent, and yielding is the inevitable outcome.
- It is a borderline between sanity and insanity.
- Usually occurs in neurotic people, who are very well able to discharge their ordinary responsibilities of life.

Fugue state:
- It is a state of altered awareness during which an individual forgets part or whole of his life, leaves home and wanders away; he has a state of complete amnesia for the period.
- Occurs commonly in hysteria and also in depressive illness and schizophrenia.

Phobia:
An excessive or irrational fear of a particular object or situation.

> i. Claustrophobia: Fear of staying in a closed place.
> ii. Nyctophobia: Fear of darkness.
> iii. Agoraphobia: Fear of open space.
> iv. Acrophobia: Fear of height.
> v. Mysophobia: Fear of dirt.
> vi. Hydrophobia: Fear of water.
> vii. xenophobia: Fear of strangers.

Lucid interval:

This is a period occurs in insanity, during which all signs and symptoms of insanity disappears completely.

Causes of insanity

i. Hereditary	Huntington's chorea, family idiocy, etc.
ii. Environmental	Faulty parental attitude and lack of mental hygiene.
iii. Psychogenic	Unsuccessfully repressed mental conflict.
iv. Precipitating	Financial worries, frustrations and disappointment in sexual affairs, death of close relative, etc.
v. Organic causes:	Head injury, atherosclerosis, senile degeneration, myxedema, pernicious anemia, etc.

Classification of Insanity

Organic psychoses	Neuroses	Personality disorders (psychopath)	Sexual deviations	Drug dependence (drug induced)	Mental sub-normality (amentia)
Senile and pre-senile dementia, associated with disease, tumors, and endocrine, metabolic and nutritional disorders. **Functional:** Schizophrenia and affective disorders.	• Anxiety neurosis • Hysterical neurosis • Phobic neurosis • Obsessive compulsive neurosis • Depressive neurosis.				In mental subnormality (mental retardation), there is defective development of mental maturity and intelligent quotient of an individual is taken into consideration.

1. Idiocy: IQ 0 to 20 and Mental is 3 years.
2. Imbecility: IQ 20 to 50 and mental age is 7 years.
3. Moron or feeble mindedness: IQ 50 to 75 and mental age is 12years.

Diagnosis of insanity:
- Insanity is usually a slowly developing disease and the people close to the patient who are present around the individual can very well make out the difference if observed carefully. It may take two to ten years for the development of full blown psychosis.
- But in a less percentage of cases, it may be sudden in onset; especially in emotionally instable individuals who have sometraumatic episode of events in their life, like sudden loss of someone who were very close and on whom they were much dependent in life.
- In typical cases, the diagnosis is easy, but in early stages and inborderline cases, the correct diagnosis becomes very difficult.
- The objectives of clinical examination are to form an opinion about the patient's mind and the degree of responsibility.

Preliminary particulars:
- *Family history:* Psychosis, chorea, epilepsy, etc.
- *Personal history:* Previous mental illness and treatment,environmental factors, emotional conflict and anxiety, drugs, frustrations in life, love, etc.

Physical examination:
- Manner of dress and walk.
- Examine for deformities and organic diseases which may lead to psychosis.
- Pulse and temperature (may be increased).
- Tongue: Furred and coated.
- Skin: Dry and Wrinkled.

Mental condition:
- *Talk:* Mutism, distraction and irrelevant talk.
- *Speech:* Incoherent, slurred and stammering of speech.
- *Writing:* Flight of ideas, insulting language, meaningless and unintelligible.
- *Behavior:* Lazy, impulsive, stereotypy and echopraxia.
- *Mood:* Highly variable mood; emotion, euphoria, joy, anger, apathy, irritable, etc.
- *Memory:* Impaired and amnesia usually present.
- *Sleep:* Insomnia, hyposomnia, somnambulism, somnolentia.
- *Walk and gait:* Staggering gait.
- *Sex behaviour:* Abstinence or perverted.
- *Attention:* Focusing the attention to a particular object or incident is very difficult and concentration power is very much lowered or even absent.
- Thought process and thought content are irelevant and inconsistent.
- *Investigations:* Blood, urine, CSF, X-ray, EEG:

Observation and certification of insanity:
- No certificate of mental illness is to be issued by a singleexamination; minimum three examinations on different day and different times, before a certification of insanity is issued.
- The patient is admitted and kept under observation for 10 days in the first slot, if no clear opinion could be arrived in ten days, then it canbe extended to another 10 days to a maximum of 30 days.
- The patient is observed when he is unaware that he is beingobserved; nowadays, hidden cameras are used for continuous secret observation.
- No single feature is diagnostic, but many of the following findings are useful to arrive at a conclusion of insanity

Relationship between alcoholism and psycosis:

Alcohol is a CNS depressant and prolonged consumption of large quantities leads to psychiatric problems. Some of the important conditions related to alcohol are:

Alcoholic Blackouts: These are episodes of amnesia which occur after a sudden heavy alcoholic drink and the individual has a complete amnesia of the sequence of events which occur during this phase.

Delerium tremens:
- Delirium tremens is a withdrawal symptom of chronic alcoholism; occurs 2 to 3 days after the last drink and may persist for threeweeks; it is a consequence of sudden abstinence in a chronic drunkard.
- Injuries, infection and shock may be precipitating factors.
- The patient becomes sleepless, restless and irritable; then develops disorders of perception and coarse muscular tremors of the peripheries, mainly face, tongue and hand.
- He is prone to commit some offences during this phase, especially assault, sexual offences, suicide or murder.
- He is totally exempted from the law for any of the offences committed during this period, since delirium tremens is a psychotic condition.

Alcoholic hallucinosis:
The patient may suffer from different types of hallucinations and may also develop illusions due to chronic alcoholism.

Korsakov's psychosis:
Characterized by loss of memory for recent events both retrograde and anterograde amnesia; the individual remains responsive and alert despite the severe memory loss and learning impairment.

Wernicke's encephalopathy:
- The physical components of Korsakov's psychosis consists of opthalmoplegia, ataxia and peripheral neuritis and is known as Wernicke's encephalopathy.
- Delusions of infidelity and delusions of jealousy may develop due to the effects of chronic alcoholism

General paralysis of insane(GPI):
- Usually associated with menigovascular syphilis and tabes dorsalis.
- Chronic psycho-organic syndrome characterized by tempermental and personality changes, leading to paralysis and dementia.
- Memory is impaired and retarded thought are present.

Effects of epilepsy on psychosis:
Epilepsy is usually not associated with psychiatric symptoms; but 10% of patients suffering from epilepsy may have associated psychiatric problems; and may occur at any of the three phases:
i. *Pre-epileptic confusional state:* A state of confusion andirritability occurring just prior to the epileptic fits.
ii. *Post-epileptic automatism:* Occurs immediately after the epileptifits and the individual may commit any offence like assault or theft after the epileptic phase and usually same type of act is done repeatedly, after every attack of fits.
iii. *Epileptic equilent or masked epilepsy:* The epileptic fits phasemay be completely replaced by some criminal act; the individual may even commit murder. This is also called as psychomotor epilepsy or psychic epilepsy.

Psychosis in pregnancy:
- Psychosis may occur any time from the beginning of pregnancy to the end of lactation: Delusions are common and dislike or hatred towards the husband may occur and the patient may develop suicidal tendencies.
- Post-partum psychosis may take a great variety of forms: The commonest being Mania and the women may commit infanticide.

Lactational psychosis:
May occur after six weeks of confinement.
- Characterized by mental confusion, hallucinations and depression.
- Delusion of persecution may develop, which may lead to suicide and infanticide

Difference between True insanity and Feigned insanity

True Insanity	Feigned Insanity
Onset: Gradual	Usually sudden, after committing an offence
Motive: 100% no motive	Obvious motive (diagnostic)
Predisposing factors of insanity are present	No predisposing factors; absent
The symptoms are uniform and fall into any one of diagnosable psychiatric illness	The symptoms are varying and will not fall into any diagnosable psychiatric illness
Physical signs of insanity are present: Face will have the classical feature called vacant look (without any expression	Physical signs of insanity are absent: Changing facial expressions
Filthy behavior and worst hygiene	Hygiene and filthy behaviors are not to that extent as these cannot be mimicked
Can withstand hunger, insomnia and exertion for a very long period of time	Cannot withstand hunger, insomnia and exertion and hence becomes exhausted soon
Does not mind frequent examinations	Resists frequent examinations for fear of being detected.

I. **Immediate restraint:**
   Anyone who is present nearby can restrain a mentally ill person if:
   i. He is dangerous to himself or to others, or
   ii. He is likely to injure himself or others, or
   iii. He wastefully spends his money.
   iv. Persons suffering from delirium due to disease, and
   v. Delirium tremens.

II. **Methods of admission of a patient in psychiatric hospital:**
A. **Admission on voluntary basis:**
   - The patient himself or his relatives approaches the hospital for admission; such application has to be supported by medical certificate from two doctors (psychiatrists) and one of them should preferably be a government doctor.
   - If the hospital has enough facilities, even without such medical certificate admission can be made after examining by two psychiatrists from their hospital itself.
   - When he is admitted on voluntary basis, if request for discharge is made, then he has to be discharged within 24 hours of such request, even if he is not fully cured of the problem.
   - For a patient to get admitted into the hospital on voluntary basis, there has to be "Insight".
   - Insight is the ability of the individual to recognize that he is having some mental problem and because of that he is unable to adapt to the required standards of life; thus seeks the help of someone (usually psychiatrist) to get cured of his illness.

B. **Admission under special circumstances:**
i. **Reception order on application:**
   The relatives can make an application to the magistrate along with two medical certificates and get a reception order for admission; when such individual applies for discharge, then he will be discharged only after information to the magistrate and he has to wait for the period of time for completion of the process to get discharged.

ii. **Reception order on production of mentally ill person before the Magistrate:**
   A wandering psychiatric patient can be produced in front of the magistrate by the police of that jurisdiction and obtain a reception order for detention and admission of such patients.
   When some relative of such an individual comes forward after a period and requests for discharge, he cannot be discharged if he is not fully cured.

iii. Admission after judicial inquisition:
When a person accused of a crime, takes a defend on the grounds of insanity, then the magistrate issues a reception order for detention, Observation and certification of mental illness.

iv. Admission of mentally ill prisoner:
When a person, convicted of a crime, is found/proved to be insane, then he cannot be imprisoned; he has to be admitted and treated in a psychiatric hospital under the reception order of the magistrate; when such an individual is cured of his mental illness, then the doctor informs the magistrate and he may be discharged or imprisoned under the orders of the court.

v. Admission of an escaped mentally ill person:
When a mentally ill person escapes from the hospital, on production of the individual in the court, he can be admitted again on obtaining a reception order.

Civil responsibilities of insane:

i. Management of property and affairs:
The insanity is of such a degree as to make him incapable of managing his property and affairs; then the court may appoint a manager (when he is unable manage the property)

or a guardian (when he is unable manage the property and as well as his own affairs) depending on the condition of the patient, on opinion of two psychiatrists.

ii. Consent:
Consent given by an insane person is not a valid consent.

iii. Contract:
An insane person cannot sign a contract and is invalid; if any of the partner was proved to be insane at the time of signing a contract, then the contract goes invalid, but if he has signed in the period of lucid interval, then it becomes a valid contract.

iv. Marriage:
If anyone of the parties was proved to be insane at the time of marriage, the marriage is declared as null or void (invalid marriage).

But anyone of the parties became insane after marriage then it can be a ground for divorce by the other party, provided he/she has made enough efforts to treat the mental illness for a reasonable period of time.

v. Competency as witness:
An insane person is not competent to be a witness in the court of law, unless he is in the period of lucid interval.

vi. Testamentary capacity:
It is the mental ability of a person to make a valid will.

The requirements are:
- A written, properly signed and witnessed document.
- The testator must be a major and of sound disposing mind (compos mentis) and it should be certified by a doctor.
- Force, undue influence or dishonest representation of facts, should not have been applied by others.
- None of the witnesses should be beneficiaries of such a will.
- Bedridden and aphasic individuals are not prevented from making a will; provided they understand what the property they have got, to whom they are giving and why they are giving to them.

Holographic will:
- It is a will which is written by the testator in his/her own hand writing.
- Many a times, doctors are called upon to witness the execution of the will of a sick, and the doctor should check whether the individual is in compos mentis (sound disposing mind).

Somnambulism:
- Sleep walking.
- During sleep, the individual may leave the bed and walk out of the house; he is not asleep but in a state of dissociated consciousness, in a hallucinatory state.
- His mental faculties are partially active and are so concentrated towards one particular idea (that he may solve a difficult problem, which he was unable to do after working for hours on it to solve the issue).
- He may commit any crime or suicide, or meet with an accident, but rarely injures himself.
- There is no recollection of the events, but in some cases the events of one episode are remembered and consequently repeated in the next time.
- Such people are usually well-adjusted in life, socially well-behaved and are not aggressive.
- They are not criminally liable for any offence committed during this phase.

Effects of hypnotism and mesmerism in insane:
- Hypnotism is a sleep-like condition induced by artificial means.
- The individual during the hypnotic trance, may perform some act suggested by the hypnotist, but does not remember them afterwards.
- Medical hypnosis is safe and is used fortreatment of many psychiatric conditions.
- Usually the hypnotized individual cannot be made to do some immoral activities.
- An individual doing a crime underthis phaseis criminally liable, since even though he is under hypnotism, he will be able to regulate his conduct to the needs of the law and can prevent himself form doing such crimes.

www.ingramcontent.com/pod-product-compliance
Lightning Source LLC
LaVergne TN
LVHW061932070526
838199LV00060B/3820